CORY

Profile of a President

By
Isabelo T. Crisostomo

Library of Congress Cataloging-in-Publication Data

Crisostomo, Isabelo T.
  Cory—profile of a president.

  Bibliography: p.
  Includes index.
  1. Aquino, Corazon Cojuangco. 2. Philip-
pines—Presidents—Biography. I. Title.
DS686.616.A65C75 1987 959.9'046'0924 [B] 86-81561
ISBN 0-8283-1913-8

Branden Publishing Company
17 Station Street
PO Box 843 Brookline Village
Boston, MA 02147

Contents

Page

Foreword

THIS work is about the first woman to become President of the Philippines or of any other nation in the Asian region, Corazon Cojuangco Aquino. If only for her single feat, she has already earned a unique place in history. In a world dominated by men of action, she is a rarity by virtue of her sex. In a political world where men assume power through the traditional electoral process or through guile and violence, she became the nation's President through circumstances without any known precedent.

All this helps explain to a considerable extent why she is the focus of media and public attention customarily reserved only for world leaders like the Reagans, the Gorbachevs, the Thatchers. They command global attention and interest because of the impact and consequences of their policies and decisions; Cory Aquino invites intense curiosity because she has become a phenomenon.

Other women, but only a few of them, had been chosen to lead their people, often as Prime Ministers, the best known among them being the late Golda Meir of Israel and Indira Gandhi of India, and incumbent Prime Minister Margaret Thatcher of England. But even among them Cory stands apart, for as President she is both her nation's ceremonial Head of State, like a reigning Queen, and the Chief Executive who presides over the government, like a Prime Minister. In the Presidency are combined both ceremony and power, and as President she reigns and rules. As the nation's highest political authority she is responsible to no one else but the people, the real source of power in a democracy.

The fact of her being a woman utterly without any actual political experience, a pure novice in the game of power when she responded to a summons of destiny and became President, inevitably opens the question of compatibility between the office and its occupant. The Presidency of a country is historically, and traditionally, a man's job; for example, all Presidents of the United States, from Washington to Reagan, had been men. The main reason for this is the nature of the job itself.

The Presidency is the hardest job on earth. "My God!", exclaimed U.S. President James A. Garfield in reference to it. "What is there in this place that a man should ever want to get into it?" Upon the death of President Franklin D. Roosevelt, the Presidency fell on Harry S. Truman, his Vice President.

"Last night," the new President said, "the moon, the stars and all the planets fell on me. If you fellows (reporters) ever pray, pray for me." And as if to give final emphasis to the difficulty of the office, Truman put up a sign beside his desk in the White House proclaiming: "The buck stops here! "

That is the job history has entrusted to Cory Aquino.

I must hasten to say that this book is not a biography of its distinguished subject. Nor does it pretend to be a definitive compendium of her personal circumstances and experiences, dislikes and preferences, or an almanac of trivia accumulated from her childhood to maturity which altogether adds bulk and reader interest to works of that type. What I have attempted instead is an essay, in the politico-historical genre, which consequently concerns itself chiefly with her spectacular metamorphosis from an ordinary housewife to President of the Republic, a giant distance spanned. The time frame spreads across what I consider three historical stages: the killing of Ninoy Aquino, the descent and fall of Ferdinand E. Marcos, and the rise of Cory Aquino. The work extends up to the first hundred days of Cory Aquino the President, her first taste and exercise of presidential power, and includes observations, including unsolicited suggestions, on how that power should be used, based on the experiences of successful Presidents.

From a wealthy but unknown wife then widow of former Senator Benigno Aquino Jr., she became the leader of 54 million Filipinos distributed geographically in more than 7,000 islands comprising the Philippines, a nation conceived in the intellect and vision of Jose Rizal, Andres Bonifacio, Marcelo H. del Pilar and other founding fathers, and born in the crucible of the Philippine Revolution of 1896, the first successful armed uprising of its kind in Asia. She is the leader of 54 million Filipinos whose attitudes; persuasions and outlook are as diverse and heterogenous as the cultures of the powers that had ruled them in succession: colonial Spain and imperialist America and Japan. As a nation just emerging from the pale-blue fire of the Revolution, then a Commonwealth, and finally a Republic , this country had been led by a few giants that dominate its history: Emilio Aguinaldo, Manuel L. Quezon, Sergio Osmena Sr., Jose P. Laurel, Manuel A. Roxas, Elpidio Quirino, Ramon Magsaysay, Carlos P. Garcia, Diosdado Macapagal, and Ferdinand E. Marcos.

Cory Aquino, long locked in the womb of time, emerged from political anonymity and was suddenly thrust by history into the ranks of this exclusive group of men of power and now stands out conspicuously among them as the sole representative of the female sex.

It is an irony, even a historical oddity, that she occupies the Presidency though the idea never entered her mind before. The conquest of that office was the recurrent, undying dream and obsession of her husband. But Ninoy Aquino was not fated to become President. He died even before he could have an opportunity to challenge Marcos for the Presidency in a free and open election. With his death the Presidency continued to tantalize other dreamers from his own side of the political battleground, but the void his demise created seemed too big for any one of his heirs to fill. No single personality in the opposition loomed large enough to wrest the office from Marcos. Nevertheless, not a few pretenders exerted active efforts to assume the role Aquino had left.

There is something in the nature of historical events that twists the course of history in a direction that no man ever intended. The death of Ninoy Aquino is one such event. It pushed history to a direction it was not expected to take. The nation's most powerful ruler, Marcos, never entertained the thought of leaving the Presidency; that was precisely the problem that despaired the opposition. He was determined to be President for life and possibly bequeath that office to a chosen successor as in a monarchy. The event of Aquino's death, however, released the reined-in energy of the current of history which, moving imperceptibly but inexorably, and with so much power that no man could stop it, swept him off and ensconced his replacement.

"The individual man," Hegel writes, "is tossed aside if he tries to obstruct the path of history. He is powerless to change its course."

The former President was not tossed aside alone but with others who also stood as obstructions in history's ineluctable movement: former Senators Salvador Laurel, Jovito Salonga and Eva Estrada Kalaw, including former President Diosdado Macapagal. Laurel, for one, had long been preparing to run for the Presidency and had in fact filed his certificate of candidacy with the Commission on Elections as the candidate of his own party when Cory Aquino, greatly transformed after about two years as an active and highly visible leader of the opposition, quickly subdued him after a stunning blitzkrieg campaign. Against his will and to the dismay of his own family and followers, Laurel surrendered to the changed widow his right to run for President and agreed to run merely as her Vice President.

Cory Aquino actively pursued the Presidency only after overcoming her initial reluctance. Confronted with the prospect of running for President as her late husband's replacement or surrogate, she had passionately pleaded to be excused, admitting lack of actual experience in political affairs, especially the Presidency. She considered the idea a cruel joke, saying all that she knew about politics she had just picked up from Ninoy and that she knew her own limitations. But the pressure which events continued to apply increasingly upon her was unrelenting. Eventually she succumbed and decided, on her own free will, to challenge Marcos for the Presidency. Within such an incredibly brief period the metamorphosed "widow in yellow" succeeded in forcing two formidable leaders to accept her own terms: Salvador Laurel to swallow his towering regional, Batangueño pride and machismo and agree to be her running mate, and Ferdinand E. Marcos to abandon the Presidency and flee the country, thus ending his own quest for immortality.

As the President, Cory Aquino reminds one of a triumvirate of famous female leaders — Israel's Golda, India's Indira, and England's "Iron Lady," Mrs. Thatcher.

Although Golda, as the world called Mrs. Meir, was so steel-willed that Israel's first Prime Minister, David Ben-Gurion, had dubbed her "the only man in my Cabinet," she showed reluctance, as Cory Aquino was to do later, in accepting the leadership of her country. When she was elected, Mrs. Meir remembered in her autobiography:

"I know that tears rolled down my cheeks and that I had my head in my hands when the voting was over . . . I had never planned to be Prime Minister; I had never planned any position, in fact." The job intimidated her. "I honestly didn't want the responsibility, the stress and strain of being Prime Minister," she said. She cried because she knew that in that lofty office she would have to make decisions every day that would affect the lives of millions of people.

Installed in office, the lady Prime Minister realized that governmental power is not as limitless as it seems to be — she could only do so much. Knowing this she was unsympathetic to the idea of strikes especially in essential services like hospitals resulting from workers' impatience. The Israeli leader pre-echoed what Cory Aquino now must be realizing in these words:

"The government cannot do everything all at once. It can't wave a magic wand and meet everyone's demands simultaneously: eradicate poverty without imposing taxes, win wars, go on absorbing immigration, develop the economy and still give everyone their due. No government can do all this at one and the same time."

In at least one other important way, the similarity between

Britain's Thatcher and Aquino is equally striking. During the February 1986 presidential campaign, Cory was grossly underrated because of her lack of any political experience and the fact that she is a woman. She can take comfort, too, from the British Lady. This world-famous female leader was not taken seriously after her party had elected her. "She appeared naive," write her biographers, "badly advised, inexperienced and unlikely to appeal to enough voters to win elections." Familiar words. Both her partymates and rivals thought it was only a matter of time when her impulses would derail her and they had only to wait to resume their control of the party. They observed that, essentially insecure, her insecurity showed in her aggression; she appeared sometimes contemptuous and slightly afraid of most of her Cabinet colleagues, though some of them were also afraid of her. She talked a great deal during the Wednesday Cabinet meetings, although the stream of words abated later on. Her inexperience was painfully obvious to her senior colleagues.

But Prime Minister Thatcher proved them wrong. Instead of growing weak and falling from power as they had predicted, she became stronger. The Thatcher image was cultivated with a calculation which assessed the mood of the electorate more shrewdly than the men did; the issues which caused the greatest strains at the top of the party changed in her favor; and the party hierarchy was subtly moulded to reduce the influence of the old guard. She continues to prevail since her rise in 1974; moreover, she turned out to be strong, decisive and capable. "Iron entered my soul," she said of her own transformation.

These two examples alone — Golda and Mrs. Thatcher — should be enough to offset any built-in, chauvinistic prejudices against women wielding power. Indeed it can prove absolutely embarrassing to underrate them or belittle their capabilities.

But more so is the case of Indira Gandhi of India, the world's largest democracy, though it is different. Daughter of the illustrious Jawaharlal Nehru, India's first Prime Minister (and founder of a dynasty), Indira was deliberately prepared for leadership by her father. From him she learned statecraft, first as the mistress of the official household of the Prime Minister, who was a widower, and then his political confidante. When one night in January 1964 Nehru collapsed on the stage from a massive heart attack, his daughter caught him as he fell. The mantle of power, first over the party, then eventually over the government itself, also fell on Indira's hands. Nehru's sudden death was a historical event that saw Indira Gandhi picked up and borne by the moving current of history. A widow, like Cory Aquino, with two sons — Rajiv and Sanjay — she proved to the world that with will power and intelligence, a woman can match any male leader in the acquisition as well as the use of power.

Cory Aquino, like her three eminent predecessors, is a creation of history. She is an initiate in the office of the most sublime form of power. Learning from lessons of history, there is no reason to doubt that she will acquire the political subtlety and sophistication of Golda, Indira or Mrs. Thatcher. Time is the only element she needs.

She has already demonstrated that she has their capabilities. When she finally decided to challenge Marcos, she affirmed the truth of the Oriental proverb that nothing is difficult in the world for anyone who sets his mind on it: she became President. Now she is going through her baptism of fire, as the other female leaders did before her. She will find it difficult, but only in the beginning, for as that great founder of modern China, Mao Tse-tung, once said, "Initiation is not difficult and mastery is also possible so long as one sets one's mind on them and is good at learning."

Whether one likes Cory Aquino or not, one must admit that she is a fast learner. Her self-confidence is becoming evident as when in answer to a foreign journalist's question, she answered, "I was elected because I was the widow of Ninoy, and also because I am Cory Aquino."

Isabelo T. Crisostomo

Quezon City, Philippines
August 21, 1986

Introduction

I WELCOME with pride and humility this opportunity to introduce the latest book of Prof. Isabelo T. Crisostomo, *Cory: Profile of a President*. He has chosen to write about President Corazon C. Aquino, no less, but this is not surprising — he is used to writing about the Presidency, presidential power, and politics in general, as well as history. One cannot hope to do a whole book on Cory Aquino, however, without focusing on her famous husband, Ninoy, and the circumstances under which they lived. This Mr. Crisostomo, the writer, has done. What he has accomplished is a courageous and convincing dual portrait of Ninoy and Cory, the agony they shared under a despotic regime, and her own deep transformation after his assassination.

My introductory piece is an address I delivered for a testimonial dinner in honor of Cory Aquino at the Harvard Club in Boston on May 25, 1984, eight months after the assassination and nearly two years before her installation as President.

The poet, Cecilio Apostol, wrote that after Jose Rizal, our national hero and martyr, the Filipinos were never the same again. They forged the collective will to overthrow three hundred years of Spanish colonialism and proclaimed the first democratic republic in Asia. After Ninoy Aquino, our people will never be the same again. They marched in millions to mourn him and they began to assert their rights against the dictatorship. Almost overnight, the public indifference, cynicism and fear were broken — fear that had been cultivated over a decade with violence and repression of basic rights. They were not afraid anymore that the government would take away their jobs or that soldiers would come knocking at their doors at night. A great movement, peacefully but forcefully, had been set into motion, to win back our lost freedoms.

The people refused to accept a whitewash of the assassination and the Fernando Commission had to be replaced. They boycotted the government media and crony publications of Mr. Marcos while

enthusiastically supporting the alternative free press — and the freedom of the press was partly won. They marched with their yellow
banners and slogans taunting openly the regime and they reclaimed
their rights to free speech. They rallied, demonstrated in tens of
thousands, and in the business sector, they staged an on-going
"confetti revolution." They sported Ninoy Aquino T-shirts, the
young as well as the old, Ninoy Aquino buttons of all shapes and
sizes in everyday defiant, yet peaceful protest.

And in the election that followed, although some had boldly
called for a boycott as a twin approach to dismantle the dictatorship,
the people organized to confront a political machine that has made
an art of stealing elections. There were volunteer brigades, raising
funds, giving their time, campaigning and supporting the underdog
candidates of the democratic opposition. When the ballots had to
be counted, they manned the polls as watchdogs of the National
Movement of Citizens for a Free Election (NAMFREL). And in some
villages, where fraud would have been committed, people marched
with torches to make known their determination to protect their
ballots.

There were women's leagues, youth volunteers, workers' groups,
religious associations — all concerned and involved citizens sharing
their courage and determination for a free election.

Indeed, our people will never be the same again. They have
responded to Ninoy's supreme sacrifice. He was a great teacher.
Over the years as a democratic politician, from his jail cell, in exile,
and finally with his homecoming, he reached out to them, inspired
them, touched them in their consciousness — and, now, they have
mobilized their collective strength.

Over the last eight months since Ninoy's death, the dictatorship
that has wielded unrestrained power (even power of life and death
over people), has been grudgingly yielding some of those powers in
order to survive. An opportunity of moving Philippine politics away
from the repression and violence of the right towards a negotiated
democratic moderation of the center is emerging. That is the great
legacy of Ninoy, freedom through peace, transformation through
dialogue and grassroots power. Two months before his murder,
having made his decision to return, Ninoy posed a rhetorical question
before a U.S. Congressional Committee: "Must we destroy in order
to build? I refuse to believe that it is necessary to build the foundation of a nation from the bones of its young."

Can Ninoy's legacy of peace towards freedom and democracy
flourish? Or is this a Hungarian spring of freedom in the Philip-

pines? Mr. Marcos may choose to exercise his authoritarian powers using the same Constitution that ordained the recent election. He can rule by decree, as in the past, or arrest arbitrarily his opponents unprotected by the writ of habeas corpus. He could even dissolve the Assembly or rig a majority. Is it a fool's dream to attempt a democratic transformation within the framework of Marcos's so-called "constitutional authoritarianism"? That is a complex and a formidable political challenge. But a democratic opposition with an overwhelming support from a people aroused by the blood of their martyr will find the creative instruments to achieve that democratic transition.

The opposition, already cheated of a number of delegate seats, is probing for a course of action. It still does not have the answers. But the opposition can begin to consolidate — perhaps build coalitions or encourage defections to become a genuinely free assembly and gather power to check and balance Mr. Marcos. Or it can focus at strengthening the machinery of investigation of Ninoy's assassination, supporting and protecting with legislative measures, the investigating commission, empowering it to arrive at the crucial conclusions on the assassination. When the findings warrant it and political guilt is formally established, the Assembly could impeach Mr. Marcos or force his resignation, in cooperation with the other organized democratic forces at home and overseas. The nation and world opinion could be united behind these measures. The Watergate shame pales in the continuing cover-up of this amply documented crime. Philippine democracy then will need its friends. For over ten years, American policy towards the Philippines has worked at cross-purposes with our aspirations for democracy. Military aid and loans had grown by leaps and bounds progressively, encouraging and strengthening the repressive regime. Ninoy, in exile, was a voice in the wilderness. U.S. foreign policy was bound in the limited cold logic of global superpower politics. Stability has been the codeword: instant stability for U.S. bases, instant stability for American international investments, and the Philippine dictatorship has intimidated a succession of American executives to remain indifferent to the destruction of a seventy-five-year-old democratic tradition.

Today, an aroused public opinion has compelled President Reagan to cancel a reciprocal state visit to Manila. In Washington, a congressional resolution condemning the assassination and seeking for a thorough and impartial investigation while demanding the conduct of a free ballot and the restoration of basic human rights was overwhelmingly passed. The House has approved an amendment decreasing military assistance and shifting it to economic aid. All the Democratic Party presidential candidates have declared their commitment to a meaningful human rights policy with the Philippines. These are encouraging signals, but, certainly, not enough. American policy-makers should be reminded, in no uncertain terms, that Marcos had remained in power with American aid and American sponsored multi-billion loans; that America is losing the deep bonds of friendship of the Filipino people and that in Ninoy's words, "she damages her soul by going to bed with a dictator."

Is this narrow policy undergoing a reconsideration? I hope that the awakened sensitivity to the plight of freedom and truth in the Philippines will bring about this change or the message of Ninoy's death is lost to this country, the great citadel of democracy.

Seldom in the history of a nation is the life of one man of uncommon moral courage linked inextricably to his people's struggle for liberty. Like a Moses, destined to lead his people out of bondage, he relentlessly pursued the clear vision of his life's purpose, unselfishly offering his life, so that his people may live again in freedom. Truly, Ninoy is the greatest patriot of our times. He has indicated the vision and the path. The Ninoy Aquino Movement (NAM) was organized to advance his ideals and continue his search for answers to the difficult problems of development with freedom. In the name of the Ninoy Aquino Movement, I congratulate and wish to extend our support to the Benigno S. Aquino Memorial Foundation in its endeavor to honor Ninoy with scholarship awards and the acquisition of his home as a museum for his memorabilia. The preservation, as a physical monument of Ninoy's home, will remain a vivid reminder, far beyond our lifetime, of three peaceful years, following seven years and seven months in jail, that Ninoy had shared with Cory and their children; a haven that Ninoy chose to leave behind to reach out for his dreams and hopes of peace and freedom.

When martial law was declared, Ninoy, dubbed by the Philippine press as the "wonderboy of politics", the "superboy" of the opposition, had to be jailed for the regime to feel secure. He was too skillful a tactician, too brilliant and fearless a fiscalizer, too well-loved and respected by the masses, the intelligentsia and even the students that he would have been, in a free election, the President of the Philippines. In prison, Ninoy had become the incarnation of the hopes for the liberation of a people — twisted, cajoled and manipulated by an authoritarian government. And Cory, matching his own devotion and courage, never questioned to doubt the wisdom of his perilous journey.

At some point, he told me that with men who have committed themselves to a life of political struggle, the secret of their strength or failure could be their wives. In his typical, graphic language, he claimed that sixty percent of the success belongs to the wife and only forty percent comes from the husband.

What Ninoy meant becomes clear if one looks closely at his imprisonment as that of Cory's own jail term as she was subjected to the harrowing, dehumanizing experiences inflicted upon prisoners' wives. She went through the indignity of being searched, stripped and monitored in conjugal visits which, at times, were withheld. She was rejected, if not avoided, by friends, haunted by fear of a regime that spread public lies and false accusations about her husband in the government-controlled media.

But hers is an indomitable will. And she suffered everything with grace and dignity, often setting an example for other prisoners' wives, helping them in their needs, sharing with them her courage and compassion.

During those days of despair and grave uncertainties, Cory must have undergone a thousand deaths: when Ninoy was missing, removed by the Army from Camp Bonifacio to its secret prison; during his hunger strike for forty days, on the verge of death; facing a military tribunal programmed to sentence him to die; discovering a serious heart condition that needed an operation. In all those tribulations and dangers, Cory was constant in her strong support of his convictions. There was not a single moment of resentment nor even a slight complaint, but she bore the burden with love and encouraged him to pursue his vision.

I remember how he told me with quiet pride how he felt stronger and more secure, deep into his hunger strike and though, in fact, he was losing strength, as Cory, who had kept vigil over him, reassured him of her readiness to raise their children by herself. *"Dad, gawin mo lang ang kailangan mong gawin. Huwag kang magaalala. Kaya kong alagaan ang iyong mga anak."* (Do what you must do — don't worry. I can take care of the children myself).

During that historic LABAN campaign in 1978, she served as his very capable surrogate and his bright conduit to the world, delivering his messages, facing the press, plotting a campaign, negotiating with the generals while Ninoy remained isolated in prison.

In exile, she devoted herself to personally making a happy home with his children where Ninoy could retreat after endless conferences, travels, and his academic work. She was the guardian of his home and of his peace of mind. Yet, she freely allowed many impositions even as it means snatching away the privacy which had not been theirs for many years. When colleagues and friends like myself would come from different parts to converge in their home, no matter how ungodly the hour, she was always there, charming and pleasant, making everyone feel at home and welcome with a warm meal and even a warm bed.

When Ninoy was assassinated, all of us who had deeply felt the pain drew comfort in feeling her inner strength and witnessing her rare composure in bearing the sorrow and the tragedy of that great loss. After the shock of the murder (at the airport tarmac), she rose to fill the void left by Ninoy. Cory, with the entire Aquino family, became the embodiment of the anguish and the protest of a people abused and exploited. And in the recent elections, it was she who bravely made the decision, truly feeling the pulse of the people, to lead the democratic opposition to participate and confront Marcos in the polls.

Cory, who had lived a sheltered life, has re-oriented her private self to face one of the most painful and difficult challenges of a lifetime, rising to give as much as anyone can give to the crisis of a nation. In the passing away of her husband-hero, she has been a worthy custodian of his selfless commitment to freedom and peace.

If Ninoy, the martyr, is God's gift to our people, Cory has been God's gift to Ninoy, who whole-heartedly supported his work and is carrying on splendidly to fulfill his vision.

HEHERSON T. ALVAREZ

President
Ninoy Aquino Movement, U.S.A.
and
Minister of Agrarian Reform

Acknowledgments

I SINCERELY thank the scholars, journalists and authors whose contributions to the writing of this book are acknowledged in the footnotes or in the main text, notably but not limited to Renato Constantino, Luis R. Mauricio, Napoleon G. Rama, Luis D. Beltran, Maximo V. Soliven, Lorna Kalaw-Tirol, Nick Joaquin, Alice C. Villadolid, Belinda Olivares-Cunanan, Sheila S. Coronel, Amando Doronila, Teodoro Benigno, Teodoro F. Valencia, Neal H. Cruz, Vicente B. Foz, C. Valmoria Jr., Jose Burgos Sr., Willie Ng, Isidro M. Roman, Teodoro Locsin Jr., and others too many to mention here; the publishers and editors of the *Manila Bulletin, Daily Express, Times Journal* (now *News Herald*), *Malaya* and *Midday, Philippine Daily Inquirer, Philippines Free Press, The Manila Times, Veritas, Mr. & Ms.* the foreign news agencies — *United Press International, Associated Press, Agence France Presse, Reuter,* and the *Philippine News Agency;* as well as the authors and publishers of the books and other publications I consulted while preparing this work, who are otherwise identified in the footnotes.

Relly R. Yan, a youthful businessman-sportsman, deserves special mention for deciding to print and produce this book as soon as I let him know about my plan to do it as an expression of the faith and admiration we share for President Aquino. Other friends gave me encouragement and the benefit of their observations. Assistant Secretary Silvestre C. Afable, Jr. of the Ministry of National Defense lent some photographs for the illustrations and secured the clearance of Minister Juan Ponce Enrile for Chapter 13 and the general book idea. I am grateful, too, to Crispin G. Martinez, friend of long standing and now news editor of *The Manila Times.* Mr. Moises C. Canayon II extended valuable assistance during the book's production; Sonny F. Crisostomo typed the manuscript in final form.

My special thanks to the following personalities for taking time out to comment on this modest work: Vice President and Foreign Affairs Minister Salvador "Doy" Laurel, Justice Minister Neptali Gonzales, and Agrarian Reform Minister Heherson "Sonny" Alvarez, the boyish-looking president of the Ninoy Aquino Movement in America, who agreed not only to give his comment but to introduce the book with a brief scholarly essay on Ninoy and Cory.

Finally, I acknowledge with pleasure and gratitude the support and understanding extended to me by my wife, Norma; she never fails to make the toughest writing task pleasurable.

The Author

Books by Isabelo T. Crisostomo

Cory: Profile of a President

*Manalo: A Biography of Felix Y. Manalo
and History of the Iglesia ni Cristo.* (Pending publication).

The Challenge of Leadership

Marcos the Revolutionary

Heart of the Revolution

A Brief History of Quezon City

Modern Advertising for Filipinos

The Lonely Room and Other Stories

To my children and theirs:
  Sonny and Tessie
  Beth and Danny
  Norman and Elsa
  Jose Alejandro "Boyet"
      and
  Christine & Crystal
  Norman "Babi" & Maria Isabelle
  and Beverly,
with hope and affection.

ONE

Family Background

I am always very clear about my likes and dislikes.
I have never been neutral. I try to do it in a nice way but
I make it very clear that, for example, I'm sorry I can't
support you. Why bother pretending?

— Cory Aquino

TUESDAY morning, February 25, 1986, was fair, with some cloudy periods, and Manila Bay was slight as forecast by the Pagasa, the nation's Weather Bureau. But throughout the country the air was heavy with expectancy. This was the fourth day of the military revolt started by the Minister of National Defense and the Vice Chief of Staff of the Armed Forces of the Philippines, and two presidential inaugural ceremonies were scheduled, one at 8:30 in the morning, and the other at high noon.

The first inaugural would mark the oath-taking -- and first entry into the Presidency — of a new President who had been proclaimed by the minority members of the Batasang Pambansa or National Assembly, enthroned to that lofty office by the "power of the people" who had supported the military uprising spearheaded by the "Reformist" segment of the 250,000-man armed forces. The proclamation was to be held at the social hall of the Club Filipino, an old organization founded by members of the Propaganda Movement which helped precipitate the Philippine Revolution of 1896. Some leaders of the new uprising had called it the "Revolution of 1986" in an evident attempt to give it a historic identity. Among the illustrious names identified with the vanguard of the original Propaganda Movement were those of Jose Rizal, Marcelo H. del Pilar and Graciano Lopez Jaena. All young, idealistic men, their vision, courage and capabilities contributed to the formation of the nationalist underpinnings of the Filipino nation.

THE 1986 Revolution had claimed two lives on its third day —

those of two soldiers who were slain during the takeover by the rebel forces of the government-run television station, Channel 4, and its sister radio broadcasting stations, in a fortified compound in Quezon City, about 10 kilometers from Malacañang, the presidential palace. But on that Tuesday of the two inaugurals, 13 other persons were killed, increasing the fatalities to 15. The new fatalities included four soldiers loyal to the incumbent President and were labelled as "loyalists," who were slain by the rebellious "reformists" when they assaulted another television station, Channel 9, also in Quezon City, in a battle that began early in the morning and lasted for several hours. Another casualty in that gunfight was a young boy from neighboring Marikina town — he had been caught in the crossfire.

In the adjoining town of Makati, where the mayor, Nemesio Yabut, succumbed to a heart attack on the day after the revolt, eight persons were killed in a gunfight at the town's quadrangle. *The Manila Times* reported on February 26 that among the eight casualties was a policewoman who had been taken hostage by a police sergeant. The sergeant had led seven civilian companions to seize the police station in the name of the incoming President. By the 25th of February the total casualties of the revolt were 15 dead and 20 injured.

That same day the Vice Chief of Staff, one of the two leaders of the uprising, reported that 85 percent of the total Armed Forces of the country had joined the rebel forces. The claim was rather hard to confirm but it was made obviously to give the impression of victory and to convince the people that there was no more obstacle to the installation of the newly proclaimed President whom the "people's power"-reinforced military rebels had supported. They had withdrawn their support and loyalty from the incumbent Commander-in-Chief.

THE Club Filipino is a large, sprawling new building at the commercial center of the prosperous "village" of Greenhills, San Juan, Metro Manila. It is just four blocks away from the military camp where thousands of people had been keeping vigil, forming human barricades with their own bodies, and acting as patrol and sentinel troops to prevent loyalist soldiers from mounting an assault. In the bosom of the camp which had been named after a military hero, the Minister of National Defense and the Vice Chief of Staff, and their security forces, were holding fort. It had been their command post since the revolt began.

The social hall was not as huge and cavernous as one would expect the site of a presidential inaugural to be. Since early that morning it had been packed full of about 1,000 partisans, sympathizers and leaders of the soon-to-be-installed President. Another 3,000 supporters were outside. It featured a long presidential table at the front, occupied mostly by representatives of the old power elite — politicians, businessmen, professionals, religious leaders. Hundreds of middle and upper-middle class members teemed in the hall. Outside the building, on the spacious grounds and well-paved streets, milled thousands of "the people" who had provided the mass and number to the uprising, people from the lower brackets. Some journalists noted that they were not represented at the presidential table — or in the hall. "Blame it on the organizers," said one piqued observer. All wanted to share in the experience of witnessing the inauguration of a President.

The social hall burst into applause when the Minister of National Defense, wearing a pink, striped shirt with short sleeves over dark pants, appeared at 9:57 a.m. Like the Vice Chief of Staff he had taken a helicopter to attend the inaugural. He shook every hand extended to him and acknowledged their cheers. Then he took a seat at the presidential table, close to the incoming President. Both he and the Vice Chief of Staff were familiar national figures. They had been key men of the incumbent President for most of the years he had been in power. Their present popularity, however, stemmed from their role in the military revolt.

THE white van carrying the incoming President stopped in front of the Club Filipino at 10:10 in the morning amid a crescendo of hysterical applause. A smiling, light-skinned lady of normal Filipino height and build daintily stepped out of the vehicle and tentatively waved at the milling crowd which was chanting her name in unison, in sing-song — "Cory! Cory!" — then turned around toward the social hall. Hundreds of journalists, press photographers and television cameramen pressed and struggled against one another to record every moment of the event, their electronic flashbulbs and guns intermittently popping and flashing as the distinguished arrival, garbed in an embroidered yellow dress, made her way to the jampacked hall.

Corazon Cojuangco Aquino, "Cory" to the nation, entered the hall that was reverberating with unending applause and shouts of her nickname. She acknowledged their welcome with warmth and shyness, even with traces of awkwardness, as she smiled and waved.

After some time she took her seat at the presidential table, face all aglow. The widow of the slain Benigno S. Aquino Jr., "Ninoy" to all, looked much younger than her 53.

The program opened with an invocation led by a Catholic bishop, Federico Escaler. Apparently the program organizers were so excited and nervous that they called on Cory Aquino to speak even before she had been sworn in. The slight *faux pas* continued when she stood up and began to read her first official edict, Presidential Proclamation No. 1. She stopped upon realizing that she had not been inducted yet.

Before she took her oath, the new Vice President, Salvador H. Laurel, her running mate, was sworn into office by Supreme Court Justice Vicente Abad Santos. Then it was her turn.

Cory Aquino gently rested her left hand over a red-covered Bible held by her mother-in-law, Mrs. Aurora Aquino. If she was nervous, she tried to conceal her feeling. Before her stood the Honorable Claudio Teehankee, Senior Justice of the Supreme Court, who raised his right hand at the same time that she did hers, and administered the oath. Throughout the brief installation, the hall was in breathless silence.

It broke into thundering applause again as the new President and the Senior Supreme Court Justice shook hands.

Corazon C. Aquino had entered the threshold of history as the first woman President of the Philippines.

IN accordance with tradition, the new President delivered her inaugural address, perhaps the briefest of a Philippine President, which she read without the use of her eyeglasses. Her voice was small but clear and she pronounced and enunciated the words with a slight, clipped American accent — she had spent all her teenage years in the United States, returning to the land of her birth when she had become 21. Tinted with the dark mood of the past, the speech nevertheless sparked with hope, promise and compassion. She began by thanking her countrymen, her "brothers and sisters," who had given her the power to serve them. Then she said:

"It is fitting and proper that as the rights and liberties of our people were taken away at midnight 14 years ago, the people should formally recover those rights and liberties in the full light of day.

"Ninoy (Benigno Aquino) believed that the united strength of a people would suffice to overthrow a tyranny so evil and so well organized. It took the brutal murder of Ninoy to bring about that unity and strength in the phenomenon of people's power.

"That power, the people's power, has shattered the dictatorship, protected the honorable military, who had chosen freedom and today has established a government dedicated to the protection and meaningful fulfillment of the people's rights and liberties.

"We became exiles in our own land. We Filipinos, who are at home only in freedom when Marcos destroyed the republic 14 years ago, showed courage and unity. Through the power of the people we are home again.

"Now I would like to appeal to everybody to work for national reconciliation which is what Ninoy came back home for.

"I would like to repeat that I am very magnanimous in victory. So I call on all those countrymen of ours who are not yet with us to join us at the earliest possible time so that together we will rebuild our beautiful country.

"I would like to end with a plea that we continue praying so that God will help us, especially during these difficult times. And if you will all agree, I wish you to sing with me the Lord's prayer." (See also Appendix "A").

Having delivered her inaugural address, President Aquino signed and issued her first official edict, Proclamation No. 1 (see Appendix "B") dated February 25, 1986 which she prefaced with the statement that "Sovereignty resides in the people and all government authority emanates from them." Adding that on the basis of the people's mandate clearly manifested in the February 7, 1986 special presidential elections, she and Vice President Laurel "are taking power in the name and by the will of the Filipino people," she proceeded to reorganize the government and issued Executive Order No. 1 appointing key Cabinet ministers and task forces to help her run the government.

Among the first appointments in her Cabinet were Vice President Laurel as Prime Minister and Minister of Foreign Affairs; Minister of National Defense Juan Ponce Enrile as Minister of National Defense in her new government; and Lt. Gen. Fidel V. Ramos, former Vice Chief of Staff of the AFP, as General and Chief of Staff of the New Armed Forces of the Philippines. The last two were the leaders of the military revolt which succeeded with the support of people power.

AT high noon of that same day, the incumbent President, Ferdinand E. Marcos, took his oath of office as President of the Philippines. He had been proclaimed reelected President by the Batasang Pambansa on February 15 after the February 7 elections. The manner in which the elections were conducted and his proclamation by the Batasang Pambansa had been the object of nationwide protests which culminated in the February 22 revolt of the Reformist segment of the military. All this led to the worst political and social crisis ever to befall the Republic.

Chief Justice Ramon Aquino of the Supreme Court administered the oath of office to President Marcos at the ceremonial hall of Malacañang. Only a handful of people were present. Prime Minister Cesar Virata was nowhere, and Arturo M. Tolentino, Vice-President-elect, was similarly 'absent. As will be seen later in this book, a series of events took place immediately thereafter. That same night President Marcos was forced to vacate the Presidency and leave the country for an asylum in the United States. He was accompanied by the former First Lady, Imelda Romualdez Marcos, their children and grandchildren. The other notable personality in his party was Maj. Gen. Fabian C. Ver, Chief of Staff of the Armed Forces of the Philippines. He had joined President Marcos in exile, with his own family.

For the first time in Philippine history a woman, nationally known only as the widow of former Senator Benigno Aquino Jr. and an ordinary housewife with no political experience whatsoever, had deposed a President — not just a President but the most skillful political tactician and strongman ever to rule the Philippines. Cory Aquino had edged Ferdinand E. Marcos out of the apogee of power.

Who is Cory Aquino? What manner of a woman is she? How did she become President of the Philippines? What circumstances or forces were responsible for her rise to power?

The present writer will try to ascertain the answers to these questions in this modest volume in which he asserts that the rise of Corazon C. Aquino is the result of the fall of Ferdinand E. Marcos which, in turn, derived from the killing of Ninoy Aquino.

CORAZON Sumulong Cojuangco descended, on her father's side, from a wealthy, prominent family from the province of Tarlac in Central Luzon. They lived on a 15,000-acre sugar cane plantation. Her father, Jose Cojuangco, was also a banker aside from being a sugar magnate and hacendero, and had also served as an elected Congressman from Tarlac. Like other Filipinos with Chinese-sounding names, the Cojuangcos must have come from mainland China generations ago among the early waves of Chinese traders who plied their trade in the Philippines where they eventually established roots and founded their families through intermarriage.[1]

Jose Cojuangco married Demetria "Metring" Sumulong, daughter of the politically famous Sumulongs of Antipolo, province of Rizal. Metring's father was Juan Sumulong, a former Senator of the Philippines who was nationally known as a staunch oppositionist. When General Emilio Aguinaldo, President of the first Philippine Republic, fought Manuel L. Quezon for the Presidency of the Commonwealth in 1935, his candidate for Vice President was Juan Sumulong. Quezon and Sergio Osmeña Sr., his running mate, won the election and remained in power until Quezon's death in 1944 in Saranac Lake, New York, and Osmeña served as President in an interim capacity. On July 4, 1946 the Republic of the Philippines was inaugurated, with Manuel A. Roxas as President.

In his autobiography, *The Good Fight*,[2] Quezon reveals that Sumulong was very influential during the first years of the American regime. Together with Vicente Singson Encarnacion, he was appointed by the U.S. President a member of the Philippine Commission, a body which exercised exclusively both the executive and legislative powers of the Philippine government after the Civil Government had been established. It was composed of a majority of Americans and a Filipino minority that took part only in the legislative functions.

Two of Metring's brothers were also politicians and lawyers. Lorenzo Sumulong was a Senator who served four successive six-year terms after serving as Congressman or Representative of Rizal's second district. His younger brother, Francisco, was also a former Congressman, then member of the National Assembly. Like their eminent father, both were noted for their integrity, courage and intelligence.

As a Senator, Lorenzo "Enchong" Sumulong was the first Chairman of the Senate Blue Ribbon Committee, the bipartisan investigative body in the Senate dreaded by corrupt public officials. He was a member of the Philippine Economic Mission that negotiated and worked for the revision of the Philippine Trade Agreement with the United States in 1946, resulting in the signing by the United States and the Philippines of the Laurel-Langley revised trade agreement. Senator Sumulong also made international headlines in 1960 when, as a member of the Philippine delegation to the United Nations General Assembly, he engaged the bald-headed Russian Premier Nikita S. Khrushchev in a stormy debate on the proposal to seek solutions to end colonialism and to grant independence to all subject peoples. Sumulong accused Russia of depriving Hungary and other satellite countries in the Communist bloc of Eastern Europe of their independence. Raging, Khrushchev took off one shoe and raised it menacingly. Sumulong did not flinch. After some tense moments, Khrushchev brought the shoe down and apologized for his unparliamentary behavior. Sumulong was acting chairman of the Philippine delegation to the United Nations General Assembly in 1966 which worked for the election of former Chief Justice Cesar Bengzon to the World Court.[3]

Cory Aquino's other uncle, Francisco "Komong" Sumulong, was also a former Congressman. A practicing lawyer he was elected in 1971 as a delegate to the Constitutional Convention. He placed No. 9 in the bar examination and took a special post-graduate course at the Harvard Law School. In 1984 he was elected as a member of the Batasang Pambansa, and was a full-fledged active member (opposition) of that body until it was abolished in March 1986 by his niece, President Cory Aquino. As a lawyer, Komong was a legal counsel of the Cojuangco business interests, the first United Bank, and a law professor at the Far Eastern University. He is also a regular member of the Philippine Constitution Association (Philconsa).[4]

CORY's father, Jose Cojuangco, had a sister by the name of Isidra Cojuangco, considered one of the richest women in the Philippines in her time, from 1900-1950. She never got married, though it has been said that a revolutionary general at the turn of the century, during the revolution against the United States, only had eyes for her beauty and grace. With her money, Sidra founded a private commercial bank, the Philippine Bank of Commerce, in 1938. It is said that she was a benefactor of her three nephews Juan, Jose and Eduardo, who inherited her vast fortune.

A philantrophist, she contributed liberally and substantially to charitable institutions.

Doña Metring, as Mrs. Jose Cojuangco is endearingly called in Tarlac, is a bright and proper lady. Hers is the dominant role in raising Cory and her five other sisters and brothers.

The eldest daughter of Jose and Metring Cojuangco is Josephine, a talented, fashion-model type beauty who married the late Nicanor "Noring" Reyes Jr., a dashing sportsman-educator who served briefly with the British Royal Air Force during World War II. Son of the late Nicanor Reyes Sr., founder of the Far Eastern University, the younger Reyes eventually became the president of the university, a position he held up to his death. His widow, Josephine, is at present the president and prime moving spirit of the FEU.

Pedro or "Pete" comes after Josephine. He is a real estate businessman married to Sari Cacho, a cousin of the wife of Central Bank Governor Jose B. Fernandez.

After Pete comes Teresita or "Tessie," who is married to businessman Ricardo A. "Baby" Lopa, president of the Manila Auto Supply.

Cory is the fourth child in the family, followed by Jose "Peping" Cojuangco Jr.

The youngest daughter is Pacita or "Passy" Cojuangco, who is married to Ernesto "Esting" Teopaco, a successful sportsman and agribusinessman. The Teopacos of Tarlac are known to be an old-rich family but low-key. Esting helps run the family businesses from his office in Manila. He is very closely associated with his brother-in-law, Peping.[5]

JOSE "Peping" Cojuangco Jr., his late father's namesake, is the fifth child of Jose and Demetria Cojuangco. A natural politician like his forebears he served two four-year terms as Congressman of his native Tarlac, elected first in 1965 and again in 1969, beating his cousin Eduardo "Danding" Cojuangco Jr. Peping actually began his political career as an elected councilor of Paniqui, Tarlac in 1955.

He refers to his one-on-one with his cousin as a "crazy exercise." Actually, he says, they ran against each other in 1965 for a congressional seat, then again in 1969. "I won," says Peping, "but I don't think anybody won. It was a waste, a crazy bit of exercise, and when I look back, winning is no longer in my concept of public service. It's what you are in public service for."

Adds Cory's younger brother and currently top political adviser:

"People always say I'm a natural politician because I'm a product of the Sumulong and the Cojuangco families, but I'd rather be a private citizen."[6]

There were at least three national politicians on his maternal side—his illustrious grandfather Senator Juan Sumulong and uncles Lorenzo and Francisco. On his paternal side it was only his father, Jose Cojuangco Sr., who was an elected public official but who nevertheless started the Cojuangco dynasty in Tarlac.

The political background of Peping Cojuangco is relevant to this book because he would play an important role in the political life and career of his sister Cory.

Peping was a young graduate of economics from the Holy Cross College in Massachusetts when he was first elected councilor of Paniqui. As he puts it, "The people said politics was in my blood, so they filed my certificate of candidacy." After demonstrating that he could do something as a public official, he ran for mayor of his hometown — and won. He even became the president of the Tarlac Mayors League. When the people of his province spoke again, they urged him to run as their representative in Congress. He won and served them for two consecutive terms, then retired from politics to return to the life of a private citizen. He thought he had done his part.

A celebrated sportsman and business executive like his late father, he runs the family sugar central and administers the family's Hacienda Luisita in Tarlac, while at the same time attending to his stables of expensive race horses. His brother Pete takes charge of their Manila office. Both are low profile, preferring to go about their tasks quietly, beyond the glare of the public spotlight, in an obvious effort to avoid embroilment in needless controversies. On this aspect of his life Peping is the antithesis of his cousin and rival "Danding" Cojuangco who, during the fading years of the Marcos regime, began to be highly visible, thus enabling the curious nation to draw a picture of the extent of his wealth and influence.

The relatively obscure Peping Cojuangco maintains a running romance with horses. This is confirmed even by his wife, the lovely fashion model turned political activist, Margarita "Ting-Ting" de los Reyes Cojuangco, who reveals that he spends much time in the stables because "Peping really loves horses." He also has a weakness for fighting cocks and his name, like that of his brother-in-law Ernesto "Esting" Teopaco, is a byword among gamefowl enthusiasts and cockfighting fans across the nation. But he considers both horse-racing and cockfighting, not as gambling but sports worth his extra or idle time and expenses.

Peping Cojuangco and politics would not be apart for too long. When his famous *bayaw* or brother-in-law decided to run for a seat in the Interim Batasang Pambansa in 1978 at the head of a 21-man slate fielded by his newly founded party the *Laban ng Bayan* (People's Fight), *Laban* for short, Peping bounded out of his self-imposed temporary retirement from public life and joined the Laban to help in the campaign, particularly for Ninoy. He realized that other people were voluntarily and eagerly doing their bit for his incarcerated brother-in-law. By actively working for him and the slate he headed, Peping was aware he could do more because he knew Ninoy better than most other people did. Thus, once more the US-educated sportsman-businessman found himself neck-deep in active politics again.

The dreaded might of the Marcos political machine, long maintained at peak efficiency by the then President himself and his top political generals, crushed the Laban in Metro Manila. The whole ticket led by the magnetic Ninoy was defeated in what many observers considered the dirtiest election in the region. Bloc-voting was one crucial factor that did the Laban in, as well as sophisticated manipulation of voters and voters' registration lists. Unlimited money inundated the electorate. Few survived the KBL onslaught nationwide. But the whole exercise did wonders for the opposition. They knew that, in time, they could match the power of the ruling party if only they could get themselves organized and united, bound together by a firm and strong singleness of purpose and communion of interests. Organization, unity and logistical strength could, the opposition leaders knew, get them back on their feet again and eventually succeed in dismantling the Marcos regime by toppling him from power.

Cojuangco shared with other party leaders this hope which later evolved into a firm conviction. He could sense that in due time, with judicious planning and preparation, the then splintered and fractious opposition could succeed in deposing the seemingly invulnerable Marcos.

The Laban party of Ninoy and his opposition colleagues eventually merged in 1983 with another opposition group, the *Partido Demokratiko ng Pilipinas* (PDP) based in the south and headed by Mindanao's Aquilino "Nene" Pimentel Jr. The merger gave birth to a potent new party, the PDP-Laban, with Pimentel as national chairman and Peping Cojuangco as secretary-general. In the 1984 election for the regular Batasang Pambansa, the PDP-Laban actively participated.

The PDP-Laban was also the party of Cory Aquino. It was the organization responsible for finally drafting her as a presidential candidate. As will be seen later, however, she consented to run under the banner of the United Democratic Organization (UNIDO), former umbrella organization of the diverse opposition groups. Headed by former Senator Salvador Laurel, the Unido was acknowledged by the Commission on Elections as the dominant opposition party and was thus entitled to have its own poll inspectors and watchers. Cory acquiesced to run under the Unido with this built-in advantage in mind and as the only way to bring together all the important political opposition groups.

At this point it is well to take a casual glimpse into the nature.

philosophy and mechanisms of Cory's political party. It is apparent that its relationship with Laurel's Unido is at best tenuous and temporary, a marriage of convenience. As this book is being written, the perceived differences between the PDP-Laban and the Unido had surfaced and threatened to explode into a real war. Unido leaders headed by its secretary-general, former Senator Rene Espina, had been vehemently attacking Pimentel and his colleagues for "packing" local government offices with lacklustre discards and poll losers from the PDP-Laban ranks, leaving out in the process, from the Unido's viewpoint, the Laurel group from sharing in the spoils of victory.

As the secretary-general of the PDP-Laban, Cojuangco helps plot party strategies, implement party objectives, and develop grassroots politicos into leaders of national stature. Acknowledged to be politically sophisticated, it was Peping who is said to have plucked Pimentel from the political battlefields of Cagayan de Oro City in Mindanao, and supported, tutored and polished him until he was ready to do battle in the center of power. That Peping is a "kingmaker of the opposition" is an observation not remote from the truth.

He and Ting-Ting have five daughters — Lia, Josephine, Maikee, Mai Mai and Tsina, all pretty. No wonder: they have in Peping a youthful, dapper-looking father, and a mother who, in the late '60s, was called "one of the 20 most beautiful women in the world" by the popular American magazine *Harper's Bazaar.*

Asked about his mother, Peping replied: "She's fine, she's 83, her health is okay except that she can't hear very well. She is a Sumulong, and she's the politician in the family, not me, not Cory."

Doña Metring relished campaigning for votes and spending part of their wealth to advance the family's political fortunes. Cory herself has revealed to a journalist that when it came to politics the Cojuangcos were generous with their resources, something Peping would neither deny nor confirm. Nevertheless it must have been the political Sumulong in Doña Metring that made her egg and support her husband to start in politics in Tarlac, where he became a Congressman. Financially she went overboard providing logistics and funds for her husband's battles. As Cory puts it, speaking of her mother's love affair with politics:

"We always teased her because when it came to politics, *pwedeng todo-todo lahat* (there's no limit to expenses)."[7]

Indeed there were a number of things her children were usually forbidden to buy, but when election time came Metring Cojuangco would lift the prohibition and allow them to go to town on a buying spree, acquiring anything they wanted — a practice Cory herself adopted later as the wife of that rare political animal, Ninoy Aquino. When the only Aquino son, Noynoy, for instance, asked for a basketball, he would be told to make do with his old one, if any; yet when his father's constituents came with requests for basketballs and other sporting goods for their barrios, they were always accommodated with new ones.

No wonder then that when it was the turn of Metring's son Peping, who had been educated in the exclusive Valley Forge Military Academy for boys in Pennsylvania, USA, to seek political power, she extended to him her full and unconditional support and helped him all the way.

Peping Cojuangco, as we have seen, joined the PDP-Laban when the two opposition groups had already merged in 1983. He was a Laban (Ninoy's party) member in 1978 when Ninoy ran for the Batasan and got involved again in active politics since then. In addition to his formal duties as secretary-general, he also runs the day-to-day affairs of the party like scheduling national council meetings and implementing party resolutions. He also calls and conducts press conferences.

The PDP-Laban, according to Peping, is for "a federal system of government and for more local autonomy." As he explains the rationale for this party platform:

"There are conflicting laws among regions in the Philippines. To achieve democracy, we have to do away with the old system. The old system (under the 1935 Constitution) really centralized power in the hands of the President. From the time of Quezon, we have had some kind of virtual dictatorship — only Marcos formalized it."[8]

When he was in Congress he recalled there would be instances in which an administration bill would be passed but would not be suitable for his region, Central Luzon. But because it was proposed by the President, he could not do anything but follow. The culture of the various regions, in his view, should be considered in making laws. In Mindanao, for instance, the culture dictates that the men work and the women stay at home. In his home province of Tarlac, some guests of his from Mindanao were surprised to see women working in their hacienda. Asked where the men were, he replied that some of them were outside the hacienda while others had other things to do. He then asks: "Now, because of the differences in culture, how can you approve national laws regarding labor?"

If the PDP-Laban would have its way, they would centralize just the monetary system, foreign relations policy, and maybe the armed forces, according to Cory's politician-brother, as a way of adapting the laws to the conditions prevailing in a certain area.

Peping gives us a clearer insight into the thrust and workings of the PDP-Laban party, which he describes as "a very inexpensive party." According to him:

"We try to follow our ideology; our objectives are self-support-ing. The officers of the party are actually the servants of the mem-bers unlike in other political parties where they are the leaders. In our party, too, the officers can be replaced at any time if they are found to have violated party principles. There's no such thing as tenure of office."

The PDP-Laban, Peping claims, while still in the process of growing, has already established itself in certain regions. It does not need too much "fuel" to run because it practices "partici-patory democracy." Local leaders select their own leaders, he ela-borates. "Every member has to undergo a two-day seminar that will make him aware of his rights, privileges and obligations. Once we have established ourselves in a province, gasoline is no longer neces-sary. The chapter will run by itself."

He denies the common allegation that he is the kingmaker of the opposition, stressing that as Ninoy Aquino's brother-in-law he is just doing his bit. When things return to normal, he says, he will return to being a private citizen. "Politics is not my line, and being a kingmaker, that's very far removed. I don't have the resources to be one."[9]

ONLY the uninformed and naive would consider Corazon Cojuangco Aquino politically innocent, for the truth is that in her is a con-fluence of the political gifts and propensities of both sides of her family. Politics is in her blood. From an early age it was the unique, colorful idiom of politicians which she heard often spoken in their household in Paniqui; and whenever she was with the Sumulong side of her family in scenic Antipolo, Rizal, there never was any way she could escape and avoid the same earthy language and imageries streaming endlessly from the mouths of her elders and their political followers. Inherently brilliant and gifted with a precise and percep-tive mind, Cory must have absorbed during her formative years sufficient political lore and realism to bring her political innocence to an early end.

Born in Manila on January 25, 1933, the fourth of the six children of the landed and politically powerful Jose Cojuangco Sr. of Tarlac and Demetria Sumulong of Rizal, Cory Cojuangco, like her brothers and sisters, was ushered into this world with a silver spoon in her mouth. She had never known material want since birth nor found a need to work for a living. As children of the rich and powerful, the four Cojuangco sisters — Josephine, Tessie, Cory and Passy — were sent to exclusive convent schools for girls at that time, first at the St. Scholastica's College in Manila for grade school.

One of Cory's classmates who later became a journalist remembers her as "a petite, quiet, most unassuming wisp of a girl" in their grade school days at Sta. Scholastica's.[10] They were together in the fifth grade; it was 1942 and the Japanese occupation forces were in their first year in the Philippines and their class was made to chant songs in Nippongo. As young children they were neither bothered by nor concerned with what was happening about them; and doing calisthenics and other physical education exercises accompanied by chanting in Nippongo seemed to them a natural part of their way of life.

Cory (at the time she spelled and signed her nickname as *Core*, obviously sounding the second syllable like the musical note *re)* was popular in "warball," a kind of volleyball the pupils themselves improvised but played without using a net. She was one of the better players and a favorite of their newly formed team. But she was not the outgoing type; she was, rather, an introvert and often kept much to herself and immersed herself in books. Studious, she had no *barkada* or gangmates.

None, that is, except her own sisters. They were always together like bosom friends rather than sisters, held together by some strong bond, a distinct closeness that was the envy of some of their classmates. The four sisters were by themselves their own best friends, a relationship that kept them close together through the years.

The class to which Cory belonged finished the sixth grade (the seventh grade had by then been abolished by the Bureau of Education) under the tutelage of Sister Remigia, a large-framed, jolly-faced German nun who was reputed to be a disciplinarian in the good German tradition. The graduation ceremony was held in the spartan surroundings of St. Cecilia's Hall. About 60 young girls finished their intermediate grades, with Corazon Cojuangco as class valedictorian.[11] Even then Cory was already a prim and proper girl; based on extant photographs she was a delicate-looking, poised young girl.

The liberation of Manila from the Japanese came not long after Cory's graduation from Grade 6. Her alma mater, St. Scholastica's, was badly damaged and was unable to open classes immediately. Consequently a large group of St. Scholasticans transferred to another convent school, the Assumption Convent on Herran Street, Paco, Manila. Cory was with the group.

The Assumption method of teaching is entirely different from the rigid discipline St. Scholastica is noted for. Where the German nuns at St. Scholastica put great emphasis on religion and the textbooks, the Assumption, under French nuns, emphasizes social consciousness, the importance of being a lady, plus a curriculum that makes the girls enjoy school life rather than be a slave to the drudgery of homework and term papers.

All this could only have appealed strongly to young Cory Cojuangco, for when St. Scholastica's opened its doors again a year later, she decided to remain at the Assumption with a considerable number of her classmates. She took her first year of high school at the Assumption but not beyond that; she had to continue her studies in the United States when the whole family left in 1946.

Cory was always a top student at the convent schools she attended in Manila. According to a classmate, "She was always outstanding in math and all the 'heavy subjects' that made happy-go-lucky girls like myself groan." From thereon it was only logical that she would later decide to major in math or French as soon as she entered college.

After their freshman year a small group of Assumption girls left the Philippines to finish their studies in the United States. They all came from moneyed families; to study abroad was simply beyond the means of the ordinary Filipino family. Among them were Carmen Fabella (who became Mrs. Celso Bate) and her sister Virginia, Ana Marie Ledesma (Mrs. George Litton), and the Cojuangco sisters.

In the United States they entered Ravenhill Academy in Philadelphia, a sister school of the Assumption, where Cory studied and finished her sophomore year. For her junior and senior high school years she enrolled and graduated at the Notre Dame Convent School in New York.

It was in high school that Cory developed an interest in the French language. When she reached college, entering Mount St. Vincent College in New York, she chose to major in math and minor in French. However, to be "different" and to avoid taking physics, she shifted her major to French, with math as her minor. In 1953 she graduated with a bachelor's degree, major in French, minor in math.

A college classmate of Cory Aquino at the College of Mount St. Vincent, Sister Doris Smith, remembers Cory as "a serious young woman without any sign of political ambition." She told the *Associated Press* in New York that even as recently as 1984 when Mrs. Aquino returned to receive an honorary degree from her alma mater, "it didn't occur to any of us that she'd run for President." But she added that "I certainly thought at that time that she had the strength required to take on a bigger job." As an undergraduate, said Smith, who graduated in 1952, a year ahead of Cory, "she didn't show any evidence of wanting to take the world." The college was founded in 1847 by the Sisters of Charity and had a student body of about 1,000 in 1986. [12]

Being a rich girl Cory could afford to pursue non-utilitarian but high status-symbol college courses. Her father, the senior Cojuangco, was president of a bank besides having many other business interests back home in the Philippines. In New York he opened charge accounts for his family and allowed his children unlimited use of them. Cory remembers, however, that they never abused that privilege. In fact, according to her, "There was never too much. We were always comfortable but we were always taught to appreciate what we have and that it had taken my parents so much to be able to give this to us." They were expected to really do their best in their studies so that later on, no matter what befell the family fortune, they would be able to do it on their own.

AFTER her graduation from Mount St. Vincent College in 1953, Cory Cojuangco, then a 20-year-old beauty, returned to the Philippines to study law at the Far Eastern University in Manila, then the largest private institution of higher learning in the country controlled by the families of Nicanor Reyes Sr., the Roceses, the Palancas and the Cojuangcos. Eventually its president would be Nicanor Reyes Jr., who was married to Cory's eldest sister, Josephine. Cory was able to study law only for one semester for on October 11, 1954, at age 21, she married the ebullient, fast-rising journalist-politician Benigno "Ninoy" Aquino Jr. of Concepcion, Tarlac. Ninoy and Cory were married at the Our Lady of Sorrows Church in Pasay City.

The marriage of Ninoy Aquino and Cory Cojuangco brought together three prominent political families: the Sumulongs of Rizal and the Cojuangcos and Aquinos of Tarlac.

In a way her marriage would serve to complete the political

education — and enrich the experience — of Cory Aquino as an unintended preparation for her own political career. Moreover, as we shall see, the Aquino-Cojuangco marriage would also eventually change the course of recent Philippine history, cause the fall from absolute power of Ferdinand E. Marcos, the most formidable strongman ever to rule the Philippines, and precipitate the rise to the Presidency of the Republic of the most unlikely personality of them all, the all-too-feminine, seemingly apolitical wife and then widow of Ninoy — Cory Cojuangco Aquino.

TWO

Political Education

It would be almost 24 hours every Saturday where just he and I were together, locked up in his detention quarters. We had all the time in the world to open up to each other. It was the beginning of my political education.

— Cory Aquino quoted in
The New York Times Magazine,
April 27, 1986.

* * *

Some people tell me I did not have any formal education in politics. But I was living with one of the best teachers in politics.

— Cory Aquino

NOT many had heard of Cory Aquino during the lifetime of her husband, Ninoy. As was her wont even as a young student, she chose to stay in the background, beyond the limelight, as most serious, intelligent students do. But it did not mean she was as apolitical or disinterested in the dynamics of power as she has been pictured to be. For, as it is becoming evident at the present time, she used to extend, from her near-anonymity, quiet help and support to her husband, the ever-gregarious, colorful, rapid-talking politician from her own province of Tarlac. More importantly, based on just unfolding events, Ninoy Aquino was her political mentor. There is no reason to suggest, however, that she consciously, deliberately sought political education.

She knew early enough in her marriage to Benigno S. Aquino Jr. on October 11, 1954 that sooner or later politics would entice him and compete with her for his time and dedication. For she knew that like her, he came from a political family. She had hoped secretly, though, that his affair with politics would not come too soon. But she had hoped in vain: politics seduced Ninoy too early. Towards the second year of their marriage he decided to run for mayor of Concepcion, hometown of the Aquinos — and won. But two years after becoming the youngest mayor of Tarlac, and perhaps of the entire country, at age 22, he was unseated by a Supreme Court decision which sustained the Court of First Instance on an election protest filed against him by his opponent, Nicolas Feliciano. The issue: Ninoy's age. He was disqualified for being 19 days short of the required age at the time of his election.

Consequently, Aquino lost his seat as mayor of a small town. In return he gained tremendous publicity nationwide and people in all corners of the archipelago marveled at his genius and political savvy for having captured the mayorship at such an early age. He was, in fact, called by his townmates their "boy mayor," an appellation of endearment rather than pejoration. He raised high hopes in his people who dreamt of his eventually going places and winning higher, more powerful positions. His loss of the mayorship on account of age all the more endeared him to them. They were nevertheless embittered by the negative Supreme Court decision.

About the only person then who secretly — and genuinely — welcomed the decision disqualifying Ninoy was his own wife, though she never revealed her feelings to him or to anyone else. She rejoiced privately because it meant Ninoy's divorce from politics, however, temporary; to believe that the separation would last was to deceive herself.

For Cory Aquino knew that the mayorship of Concepcion was but the first kiss and embrace in Ninoy's life-long romance with politics. Though they were newly married, she knew her husband well. He was a restless but idealistic dreamer in a grand scale, and his vision of the future had dimensions of magnificence. And she knew he was armed with the dynamism, the patience and the audacity to pursue them. Ninoy was both methodical and patient, though he often gave the impression of being impulsive. He knew how to wait. He thus bided his time, waiting for himself to fully mature, to ripen, as he pursued his goal of capturing political power step by step: from the mayorship of his hometown to the governorship of his native Tarlac province, then the national arena where only the best, the wiliest and strongest could ever hope to prevail — Congress. From there the final giant step would lead to the rarefied summit of political power, the supreme dream of every politician: the Presidency.

It is reasonable to grant that many of Ninoy Aquino's followers were not privy to his grand vision. He was too intelligent, too shrewd, to strip himself naked even to his most avid idolaters. But it is reasonable to believe that Cory knew all about this, she being the votary of his confidence. In fact, by her own later admission, she helped him pave the way by willingly helping him in all his campaigns, whether for himself or the local officials whose support would be crucial in his quest for ultimate power.

There are other reasons to believe that though Cory outwardly maintained her enigmatic silence on matters of politics, her husband never withheld even the most sensitive political questions from her. For Cory has not only the capacity to keep secrets secret. She is gifted both with intelligence and independent-mindedness which Ninoy healthily respected. Her role, therefore, in their marriage was not merely ornamental. With their unique political backgrounds and healthy respect for each other, theirs could only be a give-and-take relationship.

She knew that her young husband had his eyes fixed on something big. Preparing to attain and capture it meant their giving up hope of accumulating great material wealth. For most of their resources, as a young couple, were going to election campaigns — for Ninoy and the other candidates. In 1971, for instance, they supported many of the candidates for town mayors and provincial governors as an insurance for his own campaign for the Presidency in 1973.

Ninoy Aquino, who was then a celebrated Senator, had all the reason to be optimistic about the 1973 presidential campaign. The main reason for his optimism was the fact that incumbent President Ferdinand E. Marcos was disqualified by the Constitution from running for another election — he was reelected in 1969 for the maximum second four-year term. It was the consensus of many political analysts in and out of media that it would be Ninoy's year even if Marcos, in his desire to hold on to power, should field his wife, Imelda, in the presidential contest.

In 1972, the year before the 1973 presidential election, Cory Aquino received her first great lesson in the use of presidential power. By one stroke of the President's pen, Marcos placed the entire nation under martial law, thus dismantling all the time-honored democratic institutions in the country. Congress was abolished, the Vice Presidency eliminated — and all elections were cancelled.

Consequently, Ninoy Aquino, as well as all the other politicians, was denied the opportunity of seeking public office as long as martial law lasted — which took all of 14 years — with Marcos at the helm of absolute power. Moreover, Marcos had him arrested and detained in military prisons for seven years and seven months, more or less, together with hundreds of others he considered as rivals or threats to his position. With all opposition eliminated, all agencies of government, business and industry and media of mass communications under his control, he continued to rule as the unchallenged leader of his people.

All this by the simple expedient of affixing the President's signature on a presidential proclamation.

It doubtless provided Cory Aquino with a lesson on the nature and extent of presidential power which, by some inscrutable twist of fate, she and not her husband who had desired it would have.

CORY Aquino's education as a politician's wife began with her transplantation from the big city of New York, where she spent all her teenage years and where she lived the life of a rich and sheltered girl, to the small town of Concepcion, Tarlac. At that time electricity was a rare commodity — it was rationed off to the households from 6 p.m. to 6 a.m. Beyond that period, everyone had to depend on other fuel for light and power — firewood, kerosene, charcoal. Under the circumstances, housekeeping was a chore, especially to one like Cory.

But what she found even more dreadful was the loss of her cherished privacy, a loss taken for granted by the families of Filipino politicians. For the first time in her life she experienced other people entering her bedroom, using utensils, furniture and other facilities in their house as though it were all theirs. They seemed to want to be accepted as part of their family, a part of the young couple's life, and acted it. At first she had found it galling, hard to accept, so unnatural. But then she told herself that nobody had forced her to marry Ninoy in the first place; she had no one else to blame for what she had gotten into — it was her own decision.

There was never a day when they did not have people in their house. Everybody knew everything Cory and the household did, including what items she ordered purchased in the market. Furthermore everybody wanted to teach her what Ninoy wanted — as though she didn't know. If anything, this last injunction by Ninoy's followers showed how much esteem they had for their idol, for their beloved *nino bonito,* and so little knowledge of how much Cory knew the preferences and dislikes of her own husband. They were even scandalized and worried that their baby then, Maria Elena or "Ballsy", their first-born, might catch pneumonia when during the summer Cory would dress her baby up in nothing but diapers. Then everybody would want to carry, hug and kiss the child.

To avoid displeasing them and thereby risking losing their votes, Cory would make up any excuse to be able to leave for Manila, claiming she would take Ballsy to her pediatrician — over Ninoy's protestation that there were enough competent doctors in Tarlac.

Boredom soon crept upon and overcame her — the rich girl who had majored in French with math as her minor in an expensive, exclusive convent college for girls in New York. As deepening ennui seized her, she fell into a vacuum of intellectual inactivity. With her mental faculty nearly frozen, she yearned helplessly for something challenging to do to stem her progressive deterioration — she became addicted to radio soap operas, and even stopped wearing a girdle and went about in plain step-ins. As a cinema freak she suffered every time she entered the solitary moviehouse in the town, for she had to bring a raincoat with which to protect herself from legions of fleas crawling on the wooden seats. Indeed it came to a point, at this stage in her married life, when she had to tell Ninoy she felt she had forgotten to speak English! What protected whatever was left of her sanity was the presence of her child Ballsy and the fact that she and Ninoy had some friends in nearby Clark Air Base whom they occasionally visited or invited to dinner.

NINOY the politician never demanded much from Cory but made it clear from the start of their marriage that her first priority would be their children. Her primary role as his wife would be that of a mother of their children — and a housewife. It was a radical departure from her former role as a very sheltered young girl who never knew any menial work or any material want. And she herself perceived her role to be that way. She was to be Ninoy's wife and mother of Ninoy's children, not his political partner.

Thus, throughout her husband's political career, she would stay in the background, never making any public utterance or political statement. She preferred to stay away from the limelight and deliberately tried to avoid close scrutiny by the public. At political rallies, whenever she had to be present, she would decline a seat on the stage. She would rather stay at the back of the audience, incognito, and listen to her husband talk non-stop far into the night, mesmerizing the people with bits of history and wisdom, dazzling them with his mastery of politics and economics, dreams of progress and equality, feats of heroic valor and conquests of poverty and want, solutions to the nation's seemingly endless problems, dreams of unity and peace among his divided people. Indeed, wherever Ninoy Aquino was, whether on an open public platform or in the august halls of the Senate, he spoke with the effectiveness and power of a master spellbinder. Eloquence was one of his gifts.

Cory feared the mere thought of delivering speeches in public — and never did when Ninoy was free and alive. It was only in 1978 when her husband, then still a political prisoner, ran for a seat in the Interim Batasang Pambansa or National Assembly, campaigning from his detention cell, that she was forced to speak publicly. She had to comply with much reluctance and with extra effort only because Ninoy had asked her to. In fact Ninoy virtually forced her to shed her shyness and stage fright and to speak for him and the opposition in public rallies. This was another aspect of her political education.

As delivering campaign speeches was extreme sacrifice, a terrifying ordeal, for Cory, she was therefore greatly relieved — and elated — when she discovered that there was another Ninoy Aquino in her family. This was her youngest child Kris, born Kristina Bernadette, who was then just seven years old. She found to her delight that the young, effervescent girl could speak in public — and speak clearly and effectively. Furthermore, she enjoyed doing it like her father. Moreover, showing no sign at all of stage fright however large the audience was, Kris seemed to relish the knowledge that the people enjoyed her presence and wanted listening to her talk. She seemed aware that she could do wonders with her presence and her soft little voice. She could stir the emotions of her audience, bring lumps to their throats and even cause them to shed a tear or two. In no time at all she became one of the big stars in the rallies of the opposition.

In addition, two other Aquino children — Ballsy, the first child, and Noynoy, the only boy — pitched in as speakers, and the three became surrogates of their father in the election campaign.

The fact that the Aquino children were speaking at the opposition rallies caught the attention of the Marcos camp. It must have made them apprehensive because the Ninoy Aquino children were preforming an effective job of speaking for him.

The Kilusang Bagong Lipunan (KBL) party of President Marcos was said to be "running scared" in that campaign for 21 Batasan seats for Metropolitan Manila or the National Capital Region. Their ticket was headed by no less than the First Lady, Imelda Romualdez Marcos, who was concurrently Governor of Metro Manila and Minister of Human Settlements. Other illustrious names were in the ticket: Carlos P. Romulo, Emilio Abello and several other notables, some of whom were too old to campaign actively. The KBL advantage was overwhelming: a political machine operating at peak efficiency; unlimited funding and logistics; KBL mayors in control of the region's four cities and thirteen municipalities; control of mass communications media.

But the ruling party had reason to quake in its boots. It was going to be the first real elections since Marcos imposed martial law in 1972 and the people were impatient to assert their right to vote. All those years they had been governed by decrees, proclamations, letters of instruction and general or executive orders issued by Malacanang. It was the first time that they would elect their representatives in the lawmaking body; naturally, they would want to vote for those who would be their real spokesmen, their representatives, in the Batasang Pambansa. For so long had they been without a voice.

Pitted against the KBL was the Laban headed by Ninoy Aquino himself. Through the lapse of considerable time, the name of Ninoy had lost much of its lustre. Nevertheless it still had a magic power because the people knew that Ninoy had not gone down on his knees to beg for his freedom. He continued to be a figure of dauntless courage, a leader capable of heroic sacrifice and even martyrdom and who could die in defense of his principles.

Consenting to run for election despite his detention, he was looked up to as the supreme symbol of the opposition. He was the most famous victim of the tyranny of the Marcos government which was evidently not democratic but an absolute dictatorship. For, were not both executive and legislative powers vested in the President and that the Supreme Court was composed of justices handpicked and appointed by him? Ninoy Aquino was the rallying symbol of all the oppressed whose rights had been violated. For fear of their lives they would wage their campaign cautiously; they would give Ninoy and his ticket their unconditional support quietly. They would use word-of-mouth, gestures, signs, wordless sounds — everything — to help the opposition win in the country's premier region, the urban heartland of the Republic and seat of the national government.

It would be sheer insensitivity, of course, to suppose that the ruling KBL was unaware of all this. On the contrary, as the campaign went on, the party in power took all known precautions to ensure KBL victory. For the stakes were too high to take for granted. Opposition victory in Metro Manila would unforgivably embarrass Marcos, the First Lady, and the entire KBL. Worse, from the viewpoint of the administration, it could spell the end of the Marcos regime.

The KBL thus left nothing to chance. All local officials and leaders were encouraged — and compelled — to guarantee KBL victory. Post-election reports indicated that "safehouses" were established in many parts of the megapolis where specialists in electoral frauds were ordered to conduct pre-election "operations." Such operations included stuffing ballot boxes with prepared ballots, manipulation and tampering of voters' registrations, listing of fictitious or non-existent voters, including those who had long been dead, multiple registration of reputed "flying voters" in as many voting places as possible, and training and instruction of teams of specialists in election terrorism and violence. It was reported afterwards, too, that in the commission of these frauds, certain criminals were temporarily freed from jail, police, military and paramilitary units like the Civilian Home Defense Forces were likewise utilized to ensure victory. As for vote-buying, money was no problem.

All of these practices were, of course, not new in Philippine politics. They had been part of the election process since its introduction in the country by the Americans who, since the time of George Washington, had already been practicing electoral frauds including the use of money and goods, deception and even violence. Being avid students and admirers of the Americans, Filipinos copied and adopted the techniques of their masters with great facility and zeal — they have not been far behind.

To minimize Ninoy Aquino's exposure to the public, use of mass media was withheld from the opposition. During the campaign, Marcos yielded to pressure and allowed Aquino to appear once on television. It turned out to be a great TV event. Thousands of Metro Manilans, many of them skipping work, particularly drivers, housewives, students and factory workers, flocked before television sets to see and hear Aquino. When he appeared on the TV screen, Ninoy had shed his baby fat and his reduced weight became him. He was sporting a modern "iper" haircut which gave him an intensely masculine but youthful *macho* image. He spoke and answered questions with the usual rapid, staccato pace associated with his speech. In all, he came across very well. That was the last time during the campaign that he would be seen speaking on the TV screen.

Meanwhile, informed that the Marcoses where chiding them for allowing their children to speak at the public rallies, Cory Aquino bristled with annoyance. The insinuation was that they were exploiting their own children for political ends. Her anger was roused by their temerity to point an accusing finger at Ninoy and her, and she replied by addressing a message to Imelda that it would be easy to make their children stop campaigning if Marcos would release Ninoy at least for the duration of the campaign.

The Marcoses knew what was good for them. Quietly, they ignored Cory Aquino's challenge.

So efficiently did the Marcos Machine function during that election that after the votes in Metro Manila were counted, the whole KBL slate headed by Mrs. Imelda R. Marcos swept all the 21 positions, wiping out the entire Laban slate led by Ninoy Aquino. From that debacle, Cory Aquino must have learned the urgency and validity of the slogan that in politics, as in war and love, "there is no substitute for victory."

CORY AQUINO was aware that her husband knew that beneath the shy, introverted veneer of her persona was a strong-willed, gifted woman with a mind of her own — the real Cory. He respected her for what she was and let her know about it. He proved this by refusing to reshape or change her personality into something else in the manner that, for instance, the mythical Pygmalion did of his Galatea, or even Ferdinand Marcos of Imelda. He allowed her to retain her own unique individuality. For her part, she never forgot her primary role in their marriage, that of a mother to their children, a housewife in charge of their household.

Ninoy was careful not to impose his will upon her. He knew that, like him, there were certain things Cory did not want to do, and he never forced her to do it. Cocktail parties, for one, were shunned by Cory — with their insincerity, hypocrisy, pretense and all.

And she did not make demands on him, either. There were certain musts, but since they respected each other, they did things without compulsion. Cory told a journalist, for instance, that every Friday they had a reunion in her mother's house. If he wanted to go, well and good. If he did not feel like going, he did not have to. The same thing was true when her father was alive: Ninoy would just drop by the house on his own volition. As Cory puts it: "He hated being pressured into a certain schedule. He wanted to do things because he liked doing them."[1]

Not only did Ninoy hate to be pushed or pressured into doing things. It seems that his decision to relegate Cory to the background, to give her a quiet, unobtrusive role, was impelled by a syndrome common to leaders: a matinee idol or superstar complex. A person with such a complex hates to be upstaged by another; he wants to be bathed in the full glow of the limelight on center stage, performing alone like some Shakespearean actor, with all eyes focused upon him and his gestures, all ears keyed to every syllable that streams from his mouth. Egotism? Definitely, yes. In the case of Ninoy, the widow uses, good-humoredly, an appropriate phrase: "a first-class male chauvinist."[2]

Be it egotism, chauvinism or superstar complex, the fact is that leaders as a rule hate to be "outshone" by others, including the wife. This is the reason why one seldom finds a chattering smart aleck around a leader, in politics or elsewhere. He wants the undiluted attention of all those around him. He resents and rejects unsolicited advice or suggestions and refuses to concede anything as superior to his own. Again, in the case of Ninoy, Cory reveals that he would not concede anything to her, especially when there were other people around. She thought the fact that he was a Pampango (Pampangos are known for their towering pride and ego) had something to do with it. "I learned soon enough that I wasn't supposed to come out the victor in front of other people," says Cory.[3]

Ninoy Aquino shared this propensity with numerous other leaders. Manuel L. Quezon, for instance, would rather that his wife, Aurora, stay out of the Palace and tend to their household and farm. President Ramon Magsaysay encouraged his wife, Luz, to be a retiring First Lady. So did President Jose P. Laurel in his time. Of all Philippine Presidents, it was only Ferdinand E. Marcos who deliberately encouraged his wife, Imelda, to be his partner and share the limelight — and power — with him. He patiently coached and tutored her until she developed a disposition for it.[4]

There were no major conflicts between Ninoy and Cory on the matter of their respective roles. They had earlier agreed on their respective areas of authority and responsibility. The demarcation was clear on what should be or what should not be done. Criticizing each other in public, to be sure, was taboo. The arrangement was clear that when it concerned politics, Ninoy's field, he was the master and she the novice, a teacher-student relationship reminiscent of U.S. President Woodrow and Edith Wilson, and President Franklin Delano and Eleanor Roosevelt.[5] But on other matters which were nonpolitical, Cory was unchallenged. Ninoy, for instance, never strayed into any of their children's school activities, believing that those were Cory's domain. He respected the exercise of her authority over them.

As his wife she was entirely supportive, though sometimes dissenting. She always made it a point, by mutual agreement, to help him conscientiously. When he was still the mayor of Concepcion, Cory went to the extent of converting the family car into an ambulance that rushed patients — Ninoy's leaders or their kin — from Concepcion to Manila. As further proof of her support, she backed him up completely in every political campaign. She gave much of herself smiling, giving small talk and shaking hands with hundreds and, later, thousands of anonymous, idolatrous people no matter if their hands, bodies and clothes were soiled. She was doing it for her husband to help him with the people's support and vote. It was, in fact, out of her desire to support and back Ninoy up that she had been tolerating, and suffering, all the intrusions into her treasured privacy.

Cory confesses to having very strong likes and dislikes and to being a very frank person. This last trait is perhaps the result of her immersion in American culture, according to which frankness is a desirable value. She tries to let people know how she feels about them, though in a nice way, but does not bother to pretend she is not feeling the way she does. It is said that when Cory dislikes someone, she punishes him or her with silent treatment. By her own admission, she has never been neutral.

In this respect, she differs radically from Ninoy — and this is another lesson she had learned from him. For Ninoy would talk with people whether he cared for them or not, even those who had hurt him. As a politician's son he had known defeat and from that experience he himself had drawn a lesson which he imparted to Cory: "When you lose an election it is as if somebody close to you died, as if part of you died. So you must go out of your way if you are the victor, to make amends."[6]

Ninoy lived by this nobility. He always went out of his way after every election victory to see the loser and probably even comfort him. Cory herself not only absorbed this lesson but began to apply it as when, in the course of her inaugural speech on February 25, 1986 she appealed to everybody to work for national reconciliation "which is what Ninoy came back home for" and emphasized:

"I would like to repeat that I am very magnanimous in victory. So I call on all those countrymen of ours who are not yet with us to join us at the earliest possible time so that together we will rebuild our beautiful country."[7]

Much earlier, when Ninoy Aquino was elected vice governor

of Tarlac as a Nacionalista, he invited Jose Yap, the Liberal candidate who had lost the gubernatorial fight, and his wife, to join him and Cory on a trip to Tokyo. Since then the Aquinos and the Yaps became close friends. When "Aping" Yap ran for a seat in the Batasang Pambansa in the 1984 elections, he narrowly missed winning. One of his most indefatigable campaigners, it is reported, was Cory Aquino. She had learned well.

Cory knew that Ninoy could be stubborn when he was right or had made a decision. Once he had set his mind on something, it would be hopeless to change it, particularly if it concerned politics. In 1978, she recalls, he accepted the invitation of his colleagues in the Laban party to lead their ticket for the interim Batasang Pambansa in Metro Manila. Cory objected — Ninoy was a detainee, a political prisoner, since 1972. He had been isolated from the people for a long time and this could be an obstacle in the campaign. Besides, how could he wage an election campaign from his detention cell? Surely, Marcos would not release him to work for his election.

Ninoy listened to her but decided to go ahead nevertheless. He could not let such an exciting challenge pass him by. He overruled Cory.

The wife understood. She knew that like a caged animal Ninoy was waiting for a chance to be free even briefly and respond to the challenge of the wild: politics, election. She knew that she must not stop him as soon as he had made up his mind — it would be too unfair, even cruel, to Ninoy. She thus accepted his decision and assured him that she would do everything to help, she and their children and relatives. But in return she exacted a promise from him: he would not run for public office again, however that campaign turned out, as long as he was still in detention.

CORY remembers that while Ninoy had a volatile temper, it would cool off as fast as it had exploded. He was compassionate and forgiving. Once, he lost his temper at a family driver who figured in an accident while driving one of the Aquinos' cars. Ninoy told him to go on vacation; he actually fired the erring driver. But after three months, taking pity on the man, Ninoy rehired him. At another time, just after Cory had given birth to their child Viel at the FEU Hospital in Manila, Ninoy, who had gone to visit her, slept inside the car on the way home to Pasay City where they then lived. Soon he was startled to find out that the driver had turned off the engine and left the car — and Ninoy. He naturally fired the driver. Not long afterwards, the driver's wife begged his forgiveness, saying that her husband's strange behavior was a case of hunger getting the better of him. Cory remembers that Ninoy relented. He forgave the man and rehired him, even promoting him later to the security force of the Cojuangcos' Hacienda Luisita in Tarlac.

Ninoy was a most forgiving man, according to Cory — forgiving even of his enemies who had done him harm, as well as of errant and thoughtless friends.

Cory remembers one episode during her husband's incarceration. In 1979, the year after the Batasang Pambansa election, he asked her to approach the other former Senators, his Liberal and Nacionalista colleagues in the defunct Senate, with a simple request for their signatures on a petition for his release. He considered the matter urgent and wanted a categorical yes or no for an answer.

To her astonishment, one Senator reportedly told Cory he could not sign the petition just then; he was hedging. But Cory informed him that Ninoy had clearly stated: "If you sign this, we will always be grateful. If not, then at least we know." The Senator pleaded to Cory not to get him wrong — they were friends anyway. But Cory would not take his excuse. Ninoy had been in jail for a long time and it was time that they knew who their friends were, she said, evidently piqued. The Senator did not sign, says Cory, thinking perhaps that to continue to be friends with Ninoy did not matter anymore since Ninoy was down and out anyway.

If Ninoy had lived to become President, he would have been different from Marcos as far as the President's wife was concerned. When he was still obsessed with the Presidency, Ninoy confided to Cory his own concept of what her role would be as First Lady. He would make her different from and be the opposite of Imelda Marcos, who was a highly visible presidential wife and who unofficially shared the reins of presidential power with her husband. If he became President, Ninoy would want his First Lady in the background, concealed as much as possible from public view. He would not allow her to interfere with affairs of state or with his governance of the country, much less to undertake, as Imelda was inclined to do, monumental showcase projects financed by government and private sources. She would not have any powers to exercise, not being an elected official in her own right, a fact to which he gave extra emphasis. And he did not want the people to think the First Lady could influence the President, one way or the other. But more important, he emphasized, the First Lady must be an example to the whole country: she must not indulge in luxuries and extravagance.

Cory realized and admitted the fact that she had learned much from Ninoy, particularly during those years of his confinement. As she told *The New York Times Magazine*[8] her "central ideas of politics and government" date back to what the magazine terms as "a sad, intimate, now-cherished time when she made weekly conjugal visits to her husband." During those hours she listened intently to him, almost 24 hours every Saturday, while they were locked up in his detention quarters. Said Cory in recollection:

"Ninoy would outline certain questions and then he'd say, 'Well, this is how you would answer that.' He did, as a matter of fact, coach me from his prison cell."

In the prison room, while in solitary confinement, says Cory, Ninoy "forced" her to shed her shyness to become his spokesman and to keep the opposition alive. She recalls that the first time she spoke alone in public, she was so nervous. "But then," she adds, "like everything else, once you get the hang of it, then it's really no big deal."[9]

It was also while in detention that Ninoy went through a profound and unexpected political metamorphosis, according to Cory. His obsession with the Presidency began to cool off, and in place of his intense and consuming ambition to become President someday, he began to see a more magnanimous role for himself: as a kingmaker for the opposition, as a peacemaker for his people.

Cory welcomed this transformation, thinking that they were through with politics at last, that peace would finally engulf their life. But she was wrong. In 1980, when former Senator Salvador Laurel wanted to challenge Marcos for the Presidency, he and former Senator Lorenzo M. Tañada went to see Ninoy in Boston and asked him to return to the Philippines to manage Laurel's campaign. This upset Cory who told Laurel on his face that she would never talk to him again if he insisted on running for President with Ninoy as his campaign manager. To her relief and rejoicing later, Laurel changed his mind after a meeting of the oppositionists in Tokyo.

But though politically inactive while in Boston, Massachusetts for three years, they were continuously pursued by politics. People constantly dropped by their house, according to Cory, at Ninoy's invitation either as visitors or as house guests. Unaided even by a solitary househelp, she asked Ninoy to stop inviting people as she needed to rest. Furthermore, she told him, there were certain people she did not care to see, much less have in the house as guests. Ninoy, says Cory, would not complain. All he could say was that if Cory did not want anybody, her feeling was very transparent. It was his way of telling her that in dealing with certain people, even those whom one disliked, one must learn how to mask his feelings.

As time continues to reveal more of Cory Aquino, it is becoming evident that she is not the politically naive ordinary housewife she had been pictured to be. She was an amateur, yes, but only in so far as lack of actual work in a political office was concerned. She could not be any more correct in stating that in Ninoy she had one of the best teachers in politics. Her education under his expert tutelage was brief but intensive, and it began sooner than most of those who knew them could have expected — from the beginning of their marriage. In fact her political education could have really begun at the period of their courtship, before his actual baptism in politics, when they were just beginning to know each other, exploring their respective traits, experiences and capabilities, looking into the future and putting their dreams together. That period of tentative exploration and preadjustment is an ideal time for young lovers like Ninoy and Cory to know each other to a reasonable degree of frankness and intimacy.

Cory was not unprepared for her future historical task.

At this point the revelation of Ninoy Aquino's sister, Lupita Aquino Kashiwahara, about Cory could be very instructive. There can be no doubt about her credentials: Lupita had long been a respected name in Philippine television and one of the acknowledged confidantes of her elder brother and sister-in-law Cory. In fact she was in charge of the public relations aspect of Cory's campaign for the February elections.

Mrs. Kashiwahara believes that Cory came as an answer to a need. A political vacuum was created with the killing of Ninoy, the only hope of the political opposition — and of the country at large — of removing Marcos peacefully; he was the only recognized leader who could unite a fragmented opposition. But with Ninoy's death, all that was gone. Marcos and the opposition thought so. And then Cory Aquino came along.

For 28 years of her marriage to Ninoy, Cory, according to Lupita, was a housewife who remained in the background, in his political shadow, supporting him as she stayed behind the scenes.

"Cory fit that role very nicely," relates Ninoy's sister. "She was and is a very private person who had no desire to step out into the public world. But she didn't live with a man for nearly three decades without sharing his ideals, his goal for a free Philippines. During the nearly eight years Ninoy was a political prisoner, Cory was forced to step out of her traditional role and act as Ninoy's surrogate, making the family and political decisions."[10]

When Ninoy died Cory had two choices. She could adopt the

role of a grieving widow and stay at home, or carry on the mantle
of her martyred husband and fill the political void. But even the
Aquinos did not know what course Cory would choose until she
returned to Manila for the funeral. Then something unexpected
took place. As Mrs. Kashiwahara relates it:

"All of us in the family — along with several hundred thousand others — were marching in procession, accompanying Ninoy's
body to the church. When suddenly, out of the blue, Cory quietly
beckoned to my husband Ken. She consulted him and said Marcos
was hinting at condolence thru the media but that she would refuse
to accept them unless he released all political prisoners as proof
of his sincerity.

"She wanted to make a political statement. Her first. And
from that moment on, we all knew that Cory would remain in the
background no longer. We knew she was serious about the promise
she made when she kissed Ninoy's bloodied body: to carry on his
struggle for freedom and democracy."[11]

She confirms that for the next two years Cory became the
symbol of the anti-Marcos sentiment in the Philippines and continued to speak out, to demonstrate, to fan the flames of protest.
She shares the belief of other perceptive observers that Cory stood
out prominently among the opposition leaders because she possesses what no other leaders could claim: a highly moral character,
deep religious convictions, and an obsessive honesty. "In short,"
says Mrs. Kashiwahara, "she was everything Marcos was not. That's
what made her attractive and a clear alternative during the election.
That's what made it clear from the beginning that only she could
defeat Marcos."

Nevertheless, when Marcos called the special elections, Ninoy's
widow hesitated. She really had no desire to leap into a political
arena she knew would be dirtied with mudslinging and political
wheeling and dealing. Of this she had been only too familiar. However, the people would not take no for an answer and pressed her
on, with more than one million signing a petition urging her to run.
Political and even religious leaders across the country told her they
were ready to challenge Marcos but that they had to have someone
to rally behind — Cory. Now she realized, after urging the people
for the past two years to continue Ninoy's struggle, that it was her
turn to do something, that she had to run.

"So she ran, not only as Ninoy's widow, but as a person in her
own right," Lupita Kashiwahara stressed. "She became the hope
of the future, the clear alternative for change. And the fact that
she was a woman was incidental."[12]

THREE

Faith and Courage

*Mom has always been cool under pressure. When my
Dad was arrested in 1972, she was upset, yes, but she was
in perfect control. We could always look up to her as a
source of strength.*

— Benigno C. "Noynoy" Aquino III

AN ordinary woman especially of Cory Cojuangco Aquino's class
origin could not have endured or survived with grace the long nightmare and ordeal she went through. From birth she had always had
a sheltered life typical of a girl born with a silver spoon in her mouth,
which she was, together with her other sisters and brothers. Her
formal education began and ended in convent schools — in Manila
for grade school, in the United States for high school and college —
with all their snobbishness and aristocratic values. All throughout
her student years Cory was a pure *colegiala*, a status in Philippine
society reserved for children of the wealthy and powerful. Unlike
most Filipino girls she had never known want.

From childhood she had been known to be religious, deeply
spiritual, a result evidently of the fact that from the beginning
Catholic nuns, among them French and Germans, had presided over
her formal education and adventures of the mind. It was to be
expected that such characteristics as a French flair and *joie de vivre*
and German fortitude and stoicism should influence the development of her personality. A blending of these characteristics shows
in her college course: a bachelor's degree with French as major and
mathematics as minor. This blending shows too in her possession
of the gifts of stoicism and inner courage, and the ability to bear
pressure with grace.

But more than these external influences exerted by the Catholic nuns, Cory was the product of her own cultural matrix.
Their parents never spoiled or pampered them. They grew up in
a home environment which was disciplined without being too rigid.

They lived by the old value of family togetherness, one of the reasons why Cory and her sisters were always very close to each other and why they were not spoiled by gangs or barkadas. Even in the United States, Cory was said to live a convent girl's reclusive life, beyond the reach of the profane and secular influences dominant in public schools. Ever the proper, religious young lady, she moved within a limited circle of friends which included her own sisters. According to *Newsweek Magazine*[1] she had the strength of a deep religious faith and a fiercely independent will. Her strong faith became evident early when she joined the Sodality of Mount Sinai Vincent, a club for especially religious students, to study Roman Catholic liturgy.

She could have been more outgoing as a student in the United States, considering the liberality of the milieu and the modern outlook of her American classmates. But she seemed held back by her built-in constraints, aside from the religious discipline that governed her personal life and reined in her impulses. Her own parents always made sure their children would never stray from the right path; with their old-fashioned Filipino values they wanted their children, particularly the girls, to become paragons of the most desirable Christian traits and virtues: honesty, uprightness, respectfulness, willingness to help others, understanding and compassion.

Because of their economic status, Cory and the other Cojuangco siblings needed no training for a job, for employment; otherwise, instead of pursuing a non-utilitarian discipline like an A.B. in French and math, she would have taken such courses as law, engineering, medicine or accounting, or some other more pragmatic course. She simply did not have any need for such a course; she did not have to work for a living. They never ran short of money for their needs--their father had opened bank accounts for them which they could use freely. But they learned and practiced frugality because the parents always reminded them of how hard they themselves had worked and perspired to accumulate what they had. Cory remembered this thought well and carried it through her adult life. She is not reputed to be a spender or a conspicuous consumer.

And neither is Cory a habitual worrier, or one who is inclined to lose sleep or to tremble quietly with fear and anxiety about things beyond her control. She is a fatalist in her own way, as her husband was; she still shares with Ninoy his *bahala na* or "so be it" attitude, a strong strain of oriental belief in predeterminism. According to Cory, Ninoy believed that "you only have one time and we all have to go," and it was not important to him when he would die. What was really important, in his belief, was to be able to accomplish as much as possible during the time allotted to him. So if he could do something today, he would not put it off for the morrow. In fact, says Cory, "he'd like to have finished it yesterday — he was that kind of a man."[2] In this sense, Ninoy differed from many of his countrymen who have the *mañana* habit or the tendency of putting off for tomorrow things that could be done today.

Such fatalism on the part of Cory Aquino could have its disadvantages. But one singular advantage it held for her was that it helped her withstand or bear even severe shocks, the most emotionally powerful and exhausting of which was the death of Ninoy. That he had to die on a particular day and under those circumstances was to Cory all a part of God's plan or design. She believes that everything happens as God has intended it to be.

"I am a fatalist," Cory declared once, "and I know that when my sign is up, there's nothing I can do about it." Referring to a reported assassination attempt on her life, she said: "I don't worry about it so much, otherwise I wouldn't perform my function well. No amount of security could protect me in the face of a determined assassin. If President Kennedy who had the best security possible could be shot, then it could also happen to me."[3] True believers in God, who entrust everything to him and believe that nothing happens unless it is part of God's designs, are often people of marked courage. Their deep faith strengthens them and makes them feel secure in the belief that since God is love, all His plans are beneficial to them. Even tragedies like deaths in the family, while hard to accept at first, are taken in stride--every loss has its own compensation.

It is evident that being a deep believer in God, Cory is not any different from other people of profound religious faith. She believes that in the complicated scheme of things no problem is too big and insurmountable that prayer cannot conquer. Throughout her life it is said she has never doubted the power of prayer and therefore resorts to prayer whenever she is faced by serious problems. Prayer fortifies and strengthens her— and helps clarify her thoughts. Thus, Cory often says that before making an important decision, she turns to prayer.

This fervent faith in God was what gave her the strength and the indomitability to withstand with grace and overcome with humility an ordeal of no less than eleven dark and anguished years. That ordeal began with the arrest of Ninoy upon the imposition of martial law by President Marcos in 1972 and his imprisonment for seven years and seven months. Granted personal freedom in 1980 by force of necessity, he went through an extremely dangerous triple heart bypass operation in the United States, where he stayed for approximately three years. Ninoy survived that operation and later decided to return to his native land not to challenge Marcos for the Presidency but to perform a new self-imposed role — as peacemaker and conciliator. But before he could even begin his new mission, he was killed by an assassin's bullet while alighting from an airplane at the Manila International Airport.

Any of those problems — Ninoy's arrest and detention from 1972 to 1980, triple bypass heart operation in 1980, and his assassination at the airport — could have been enough to break a woman's spirit and batter her heart and soul. But not Cory Aquino. Though she looks delicate, particularly during those early years of trial and privations — "as delicate as a silk thread," in the words of a magazine writer — she proved agile and tough and never wavered. She remained undaunted. As her only son, Benigno "Noynoy" III, puts it, she was upset when Ninoy was arrested in 1972, but "she was in perfect control. We could always look to her as a source of strength."[4]

A woman with less strength and courage than Cory Aquino could not have withstood the impact of the airport tragedy that saw the gruesome death of her husband. She received the news with coolness and equanimity in their house in Boston, Massachusetts, where she was busy packing, expecting to follow Ninoy to Manila within two weeks. Throughout, she successfully concealed her emotions. When the children had more or less confirmed the news that their father had been killed, they began to cry. Then Cory asked them to just pray because at that point there was nothing they could do.[5] Later, upon the suggestion of Ballsy, the eldest daughter, Cory and the children went to church to attend mass. Again, at that hour of tragedy, Cory led her children in turning to God for support.

Up to that point she succeeded in maintaining her calm, refusing to betray her emotions, maintaining a posture of bravery and courage. If she had impending tears she held them back.

From Boston Cory and her children flew to Manila.

There was a big crowd outside their house on Times street, Quezon City, when they arrived. She had arranged that she and the children were to have a few minutes alone with their dead upon their arrival. Her sisters, on the other hand, had warned her that the corpse had not been retouched in any way. The warning was intended to protect her from shock: the sight could be too unsettling and gruesome.

With her first sight of her assassinated husband, his face deformed by a powerful bullet and unmade up, his light-colored bush jacket soiled and bloodied, the new widow was unable to control her emotions. She finally broke down under the severe strain and the tears she had been holding back began to stream down her face as she wept quietly and gave way to her long pent-up grief.

Much later on, reminiscing on that episode in her life, Cory refused to talk about the wake and the funeral for her husband. Instead, she preferred to recall the activities that occupied her during the first year of her mourning: the successive rallies, the political campaign which she used to dread, the 1984 elections for the Batasang Pambansa in which she campaigned and which resulted in a respectable number of opposition candidates waving the banner of the slain Ninoy and chanting his name as battlecry getting elected to the regular (no longer interim) Batasan. She chose to remember all this rather than the pain and sadness that enveloped her life upon Ninoy's assassination.

That 1984 election campaign was to mark her own baptism in politics, no longer as Ninoy's wife consigned to the background but as Ninoy's widow — Cory the politician. For the first time since her marriage to the colorful journalist-politician in 1954, she was finally on her own. She had virtually risen on the very spot where her husband had fallen. And now, more than ever before, deprived of Ninoy's steadying hand and expert counsel, she must prove to all, particularly Ninoy's admirers and followers, that she had the talent, skill and capability to carry on where her husband had left off, that she could be her assassinated husband's worthy surrogate.

WITH her husband gone Cory swiftly went through another transformation. Circumstances compelled her to slip out of her chrysalis and venture into the world of political reality. She had ceased to be, beginning on that first year of mourning for the slain Ninoy, the quiet, retiring housewife and mother of five that she used to be but a new full-blown political personality in her own right, bearing in her hand the torch that had been passed to her by Ninoy. Ninoy's death had triggered a massive social upheaval that rocked the nation to its very roots. It also pushed the hardly known Cory Aquino to the surface and gave her a new, expanded role; the replacement (some say reincarnation and karma) of her husband, the rallying symbol of the diverse, often warring factions of the anti-Marcos political opposition.

Now in the thick of things, she found herself marching arm-in-arm with leaders of various groups opposed to the Marcos government and bitterly protesting the assassination of Ninoy who, in death, had regained much of his diminished stature and began to tower anew like a man ten feet tall in the consciousness of his people.

For in reality, as Luis R. Mauricio has correctly pointed out, Ninoy's name before his murder was in danger of being forgotten by the youth of the land, most of whom were pre-martial law babies, to whom he was just one of the Filipino emigres to the United States. To the radical nationalists and activists, he was in fact being labelled as an "Amboy" — an American boy — if not a CIA operative. Some considered him an "egg held in reserve in the U.S. basket" to be used once the Marcos egg could no longer serve American interests.

Mauricio is right in saying that, on the other hand, the liberal intelligentsia considered Ninoy, at that time, irrelevant, for other than he was against martial law and Marcos he could not be pinned down on where he exactly stood on the gut issues of ideology and nationalism. Even his stand on American bases was ambivalent, Mauricio, a nationalist editor and political analyst, observes. Among his fellow politicians in the opposition ranks, Ninoy was just one Liberal party leader whose every stand on public issues was believed to be consciously taken with an ear cocked to and an eye focused on the Presidency.

"This appraisal of Ninoy by those who were later to become his ardent idolaters is not strange," writes Mauricio. "Even in his younger days, his personality invited hatred as deep and criticism as vehement as the love and admiration he inspired."[6]

Cory found herself joining and even leading rallies or parliaments of the streets. She delivered speeches before organizations like the Rotary Clubs, schools and various societies. Her popularity grew with every day that passed; she was fast becoming a phenomenon. During huge rallies, people from all walks of life would line up streets. sit on top of walls, perch precariously on the windows and ledges of tall buildings to wait for her to pass by, to get a glimpse of this petite, curly-haired, youngish-looking widow of Ninoy whom they had by then acclaimed as a hero-martyr, showering her with yellow confetti fashioned out of shredded yellow pad paper and yellow pages torn out of telephone directories.

Before that campaign in 1984, Cory had returned to the United States for the memorial services for her husband in Harvard University where he had served a fellowship. She stayed abroad for three weeks, gathering up the things they had left behind in their old Boston house. Then she came back to Manila, not knowing that in doing so, she would begin her date with destiny, her appointment with history.

UPON her return to Manila she found herself fully engaged in the campaign for the Batasan. Ninoy's Laban party had coalesced with the Partido Demokratiko ng Pilipinas (PDP) headed by Aquilino Pimentel Jr., as chairman and Cory Aquino's younger brother, former Congressman Jose Cojuangco Jr., as secretary-general, and was fielding its own candidates. The merged parties, the PDP-Laban, became the umbrella organization of the so-called "cause-oriented" groups, that is, non-traditional political parties with their own causes or ideologies. On the other hand, another opposition umbrella organization, the United Nationalists Democratic Organization (Unido) headed by former Senator Salvador Laurel, was also in the fight, with more candidates than the PDP-Laban. The Unido was better organized, too, and reputed to have more funds and logistics. In addition there were other unaffiliated groups with their own candidates. But they were all bound together by one overriding common goal: to topple Marcos and dismantle the monolithic power structure he had established.

Cory's courage would come to the surface again this time. A number of anti-Marcos forces were opting to boycott rather than participate in the elections. Cory's brother-in-law himself, Agapito "Butz" Aquino, a well-known organizer and leader of the parliament of the streets, was against participation. So were notable opposition figures like former Senator Lorenzo M. Tanada, lawyer Joker Arroyo, and former *Manila Times* publisher Joaquin "Chino" Roces. Their rationale for boycotting the elections was that to participate was to extend legitimacy to the Marcos government which the opposition had been insisting as illegal.

Cory chose participation, not boycott. It was a bold, even unpopular, decision, considering the number and caliber of the boycott advocates. But she had a strong, valid reason for her decision: Ninoy himself had participated in the 1978 elections although it was Marcos who called for the exercise; Ninoy had urged that the nation should try to save itself through the use of the ballot rather than through a boycott.

"Even in 1978 when we did not have any kind of public support," Cory stated, "Ninoy said to participate in the polls, because this was the only system available whereby we could have a peaceful change of government. Until somebody comes up with a better system, we'll just have to make do with this one. And my feeling was that we should give it one more try. If we're not able to make any headway with that try, then I'll be convinced once and for all that Filipinos don't want a return to that kind of system. But I was determined to give it just one last try."[7]

She agonized over the choice between participation and boycott. She had hoped she would dream about Ninoy and that he would tell her in a dream whether this was the right thing to do or not. She admits that there were times when she doubted having made the right decision because the arguments for either side were equally convincing, but that she had the feeling that she just had to participate. She believed that Filipinos should be given a chance to participate, a chance they would have lost if she and the rest had chosen to boycott. In Cory's belief, by choosing participation, boycott was still possible for those who wanted it.

Her participation stand had been justified. The results of the elections showed that a number of the opposition candidates made a good showing at the polls. The opposition as a whole succeeded, in fact, in having about 60 candidates elected, roughly 30 percent of the total Batasan membership. Cory had been vindicated.

If the opposition candidates' showing had been bad, Cory would have left the country and probably returned to the United States for good. For then she would have been embarrassed, her decision would have been proved wrong.

After the elections she received several letters, some praising her to high heaven, others condemning her and claiming that Ninoy would not have acted the way she did. "But how could they have known Ninoy better than I did? ", she asked, visibly annoyed. "Where were they when Ninoy was in jail for seven years and seven months? And all of a sudden they're claiming to know him better than I did. Many people had told me they wanted to take part in the elections. Why prevent them from doing so? At least give them the option of being able to choose, instead of just boycotting. Anyway, I'm happy that things turned out the way they did."[8]

She began telling everybody, boycotters and participants alike, that she hoped they could all get together again, she told the writer Nick Joaquin. They might have different ideas as to the tactics employed but were all united in the aim to dismantle the Marcos dictatorship, she argued. They should not veer away from that goal. Some people could not understand how her brother-in-law Butz and she could have such different ideas when they belonged to one family, but her answer was that the Aquinos were very independent-minded and believed in democracy.

THAT 1984 election campaign proved to be a dress rehearsal as far as Cory was concerned in preparation for another election two years later, with no less than the Presidency itself as the prize. She went on the road urging the people to participate in the polls, not to boycott them, and to campaign for and endorse opposition candidates. The campaign gave her an opportunity to test herself, to determine whether she could overcome her fear of speaking before mammoth rallies, to find whether she had the ability to cast a spell, to magnetize, to move large audiences, and whether, like Ninoy, she could elicit desired responses from them. She campaigned all over the country, in places where there were opposition candidates, and soon seemed to enjoy, even relish, the experience. She surprised herself when she realized she had been speaking in public during those political tours. Said Cory:

"I didn't know what I was in for. When Ninoy was a candidate, the most I ever did was to go to markets and factories to shake hands, but I never went up on stage to speak. This was completely not my line."[9]

But she had to address people, not really to discuss issues but to talk about Ninoy. Most of her listeners, especially the young ones, had not really known Ninoy: so she would narrate to them the story behind Ninoy's incarceration, what their lives had been and why Ninoy wanted to come home. She would tell them how Ninoy was determined to suffer all because he did not want to surrender to the dictatorship. Then she would say she hoped they too would be willing to fight for freedom, adding: "This is what's demanded of all of us: that each of us do our share in restoring democracy in this country." Then she would point out that whereas, before, she stayed home and just took care of the children, now she felt it was her duty to work hard to bring back justice and freedom and democracy.

In the past, she would stay at the farthest end of a rally audience, there to listen to Ninoy speak his piece in that staccato, breathless pace of his that never failed to mesmerize his listeners. She avoided having a seat on the stage, fearful that she might be called upon to speak. But during the 1984 campaign, she was even willing to climb a platform and speak albeit briefly. At first she would limit her talk to about five minutes. But she sensed that this was not enough to satisfy the people who had walked kilometers, long distances, just to see and listen to her, and it would not be fair to talk to them so briefly. Besides, the leaders would urge her to talk longer. She had to yield and say more.

To their great surprise she found herself speaking as long as thirty minutes — a half-hour! — and was surprised because she did not think she had that much to say. Once at a rally her daughter Ballsy timed her then exclaimed: "Oh, Mom, you really went all the way! Thirty minutes!"

That campaign, a preview of what was to come later on, provided her with interesting experiences. Joaquin notes that in one town in Zambales, she tried to cut short her speech because it had begun to drizzle. She told the crowd she did not want them to get wet; they might get sick and be unable to vote. But the crowd ignored the drizzle and begged her to continue. The drizzle turned into a downpour, but still the crowd remained.

Cory, the opposition candidates and the leaders often held their public meetings out in the fields since the mayors, mostly belonging to the administration's Kilusang Bagong Lipunan party, would not allow them the use of many plazas. They often used a basketball court, a ricefield or a churchyard. In the town of Iba, Zambales, the only illumination in one of their meetings was provided by three electric bulbs and Cory could not tell what kind of place it was. Someone told her it was a ricefield. The rain fell and she got soaked as she ran with others for shelter — the field was far from the highway. Reaching a house, someone gave her an electric fan with which to dry her dress. This was the first time she was experiencing what a politician had to go through. Because of the driving rain she supposed the next meeting, in Olongapo, had been cancelled, but, no, a big crowd was waiting for Cory in that city.

In Las Piñas, Rizal, the site of the meeting was so deep in mud Cory had to ride a tricycle to get to the stage, and the tricycle carried the streamers of a KBL candidate. After the meeting she found the same tricycle waiting for her. She must have charmed and converted the driver, who proudly announced he had removed the streamers. Then in Caloocan City Cory had to ride an open truck in a motorcade of the candidates, though it was raining throughout. Afterwards she rushed home and changed into dry clothes. This experience taught her a lesson: in political sorties, she must always have reserve clothes and other personal necessities in case of any eventuality.

Cory Aquino also astonished herself by realizing she could be so fluent in Tagalog, the language she used mostly in addressing rallies even in such non-Tagalog-speaking places as Cebu, Cagayan de Oro, Bukidnon and the Bicol provinces. She found to her pleasant surprise that she could be understood in Tagalog. But the biggest surprise of all was that a girl who, while married to a politician, had such a sheltered life, should now be campaigning in any kind of weather all over the country — and savor it, knowing that Ninoy would have enjoyed every moment of it. He would have greatly enjoyed seeing her savoring her new experience.

FOUR

Cory and the Wonder Boy

Cory became a familiar public figure only after the assassination of her husband Ninoy. Before then she had been content to remain his silent partner. Politically discussions were confined to Ninoy's cell at Fort Bonifacio and to the dinner table at their Boston house during his exile. Obviously, Cory could not have had a better mentor.

— *Panorama* Magazine, Feb. 2, 1986

"THE only time I had ever been active politically was when Ninoy was campaigning to be governor or Senator. I went the usual rounds of shaking hands with people in markets, farms and factories asking them to vote for Ninoy. But beyond that I was simply a politician's wife. I was completely in the background. I took care of the home and the children and Ninoy took care of the rest."[1]

That was the relationship between the then youthful couple, Ninoy and Cory Aquino, as defined by Cory herself: Ninoy, the political star performer on center stage, bathed in a flood of light, acting his role alone while his wife patiently waited in the background, on the wings, simply watching him perform, ready to extend any support he would need.

They had agreed on the definition of their respective roles as soon as Ninoy decided to enter politics by running for mayor of his hometown, Concepcion, when he was not yet 22 years old, and she had never departed from her role. She was ever the self-abnegating, supportive wife of Ninoy, the political wonder boy, who had burst upon the political scene like a flaming meteor, leaving a swath of brilliant but evanescent light in its wake.

It was the popular President Ramon Magsaysay who cut Ninoy's teeth in politics. Although Ninoy was then just a little past voting age he was commissioned by the populist President as a Special Assistant on Political Affairs in recognition of his role as one of the original "rah-rah" boys who helped plan Magsaysay's presidential campaign, determining the issues and shaping the strategy that propelled Magsaysay to power.[2]

As Special Presidential Assistant, Ninoy scored the famous coup that older, more experienced journalists had failed to get; he negotiated the surrender of Luis Taruc, the Huk supremo, who had eluded the best efforts of the Armed Forces of the Philippines to bring him to heel.[3] At age 22 he was elected mayor of Concepcion but after seven months of running the town, the Supreme Court sustained the lower court which had disqualified him from the mayorship because he was underaged at the time of his election. Known as the "boy mayor," he bided his time while campaigning for other candidates until he was ready to run for governor of Tarlac, his province.

That early, Ninoy Aquino already had an eye fixed on the Presidency of the Philippines. He believed he was preordained for the office.

From boy mayor, the rising politico — rotund, pink-cheeked, with an infectious grin and full of raw vitality—captured the governorship of Tarlac, the sugar granary of Central Luzon, thus proving once again that he was an important political figure on the ascendant. He could not escape the appellation once again; and to all, particularly his admiring provincemates, Ninoy was their "boy governor." To them he was the man to watch. Young, charismatic, nationally famous and concededly brilliant, Ninoy was looked up to as a future President who could conceivably dislodge Ferdinand E. Marcos, who was first elected President in 1965, from the Presidency.

The parents of Ninoy Aquino were Benigno Aquino Sr., a former Senator, and his wife Aurora. The elder Aquino was a widower when he married Aurora in 1930; she was then an education student at the University of the Philippines. Aquino Sr. brought into the marriage two sons and two daughters from his first marriage, and he and Aurora had seven children together in this order: Maur, Benigno "Ninoy" Jr., Ditas, Lupita, Agapito "Butz", Paul and Teresa. Servillano Aquino, his paternal grandfather, was a well-known insurgent who fought against the Spaniards and then the Americans; he gave Benigno Jr. his nickname of "Ninoy." A Senator, Speaker of the National Assembly, and a Cabinet Minister, Aquino Sr. died in 1947 when Ninoy was barely 13. From that time on Ninoy, too proud to ask for an allowance, worked with his half-brother Billy.

Born on November 27, 1933, Ninoy married Corazon Cojuangco from his hometown of Concepcion when they were both 21.

Only 22 when he was elected mayor of Concepcion, Tarlac province, he was elected governor of Tarlac at age 28, the youngest in the history of the province. In the 1967 elections he became, at

34, the youngest Senator in the Philippines.

The next stop for the young Senator was the Presidency of the Republic which Ferdinand E. Marcos had captured for the second time in 1969. The Constitution barred Marcos from running for a third term, in 1973, a presidential election year. Ninoy was believed far and wide as the most logical presidential candidate in that election under the Liberal party banner, and the odds were overwhelming in favor of his victory. But events, natural or man-made, intervened and deprived him of the highest and most sublime form of power in the nation.

IN 1967, when he was only 34 years old, Ninoy Aquino took what some observers and sympathizers considered an ill-advised gamble: he decided to run for the Senate. He had been governor of Tarlac for six years. Marcos had just been installed in Malacañang as the nation's sixth President and his popularity had yet to peak. Marcos had been swept into office, toppling incumbent President Diosdado Macapagal, on ringing promises of eliminating graft and corruption, stopping the spiralling of prices and all those tested vote-getting slogans, and the people were willing to give him a chance. Marcos had, after all, a brilliant record—a war hero, outstanding law student, No. 1 bar topnotcher, famed Lothario (a reputation that never fails to titillate female voters), and husband of the lovely Imelda Romualdez, then the "secret weapon" dreaded by his political opponents. Did Ninoy miss his timing?

In contrast Ninoy Aquino, the boy governor of Tarlac, more than ten years Marcos's junior, did not have much going for him. He was running as a candidate of the Liberal party which Marcos had systematically and methodically pulverized in 1965. He laid claim, in his campaign posters, to having experience, but his opponents in the ruling Nacionalista party ticket scoffed at his claim. For what experience, indeed, could he talk about, considering his youth and how limited his public service had been? They branded him as immature, inexperienced, still wet behind the ears.

But Ninoy responded that youth should not be equated with inexperience. After all he had served under crisis situations: in Korea where, as a war correspondent, he had to work on and file his newspaper dispatches against a backdrop of relentless machinegun fire; in Concepcion, heart of the Huk territory in Central Luzon, where he demonstrated his ability to handle people with conflicting interests; and in the Tarlac provincial capitol where, as governor of the province, he had to deal with crisis after crisis of alarming proportions. The Huks, for one, precursors of the New People's Army, were on the rampage, and the boy governor had to face them squarely.

Youth, experience—hope. Yes, Ninoy held out hope to the people. He charged that the nation, contrary to the claim of Marcos and the Nacionalista party administration, was not headed for greatness but for greater failure. He attacked Marcos for making too many broken promises, for forgetting too many campaign pledges, for failing to stabilize and bring down the prices of commodities, for the escalating venalities in government, and for "cronyism" which was then fast becoming an incipient evil threatening to choke the economy.

Ninoy then presented himself—and the Liberal party senatorial ticket—as the alternative to the nation's inevitable descent into chaos. He offered himself as someone who could open some windows and allow the fresh winds of reform and hope to cleanse and revitalize the body politic. Ninoy had held himself up as a promise of hope, of change, of reform. And the people believed him.

The people believed him and accepted his promise. In one splendid show of political power and nationwide grassroots strength, Ninoy Aquino won the No. 2 spot in the eight-man Senate slate, the only Liberal party survivor in the Nacionalista sweep that year. The once boy mayor and boy governor had been entrusted by the people with a higher national office, Senator of the Philippines.

Notwithstanding the loftiness of his new elective position, people who loved and admired Ninoy continued to address him with intimate fondness, this time as boy Senator, an expression of affection and endearment rather than derision.

THE wonder boy of Philippine politics whom his widow Cory Aquino calls her best teacher in politics, was no less a wonder boy in the field that first made him a household word—journalism. He was a crew-cut, chubby, cherubic-faced teener astir with boundless energy when he began covering political beats for *The Manila Times*, the largest English-language daily in the Philippines at the time. At 16 he was a "cub reporter" and at 17 he graduated as a full-fledged war correspondent in Korea, attached to the Philippine Expeditionary Forces (PEFTOK); he was the favorite of *Times* editors Dave Boguslav and Jose Bautista. In fact, Boguslav chose Ninoy, over others, to send out to every choice journalistic assignments.[4]

Ninoy Aquino once recalled his newpapering stint in this manner:[5]

"I was the youngest and the lowest in rank among the *Times*

reporters when the military authorities sent a call for a correspondent to cover the Korean war. There was a lot of dickering among the
veteran reporters for bonuses and allowances. I knew it was a short-
cut to the 'big time.' I didn't bother about extra pay. So I saw the
editor, Dave Boguslav, and told him that I was ready to volunteer
to go to Korea. He thought I was kidding. But when I insisted, he
told me to see Chino (Joaquin P. Roces, publisher), the big boss—
perhaps just to humor me.

"I went to Chino and told him the same thing. Chino was
bemused. 'What will your mother say?' That was all he told me, but
he didn't say no to my idea. The next day, without informing
anybody in the office, I was off in an army plane with my typewriter.

"Before my bosses knew it, I was already filing my dispatches
from Korea.

"They couldn't do anything about it. I was filing may stories
day and night. Of course, Dave Boguslav had to rewrite my copy.
I was the newest, greenest reporter on the *Times* and in Korea. I was
in the company of some of the world's best war correspondents.
When they saw may first lousy copy, they told me, 'Just as we
suspected, you have been sent here because you are the son of the
publisher.'

"But I was their pet. To them I was The Kid. They taught me
the techniques of journalism, how to file dispatches, how to interview. A top camera man from *Life* taught me how to shoot pictures.
I was training on the job. I seized on every opportunity to learn.
I was studying journalism with the best correspondents in the world
as teachers. I learn fast, you know.

"When I came home, medals and all, I was already nationally
known. No longer the obscure cub reporter of the *Times*."

THE political writer Napoleon G. Rama of the *Philippines Free Press*
coined an apt description of Ninoy Aquino: "the go-go-go Senator
from Tarlac." He maintains that the colorful Tarlaqueño had daring
and determination and was afire with ambition, impatient with the
humdrum, in a hurry to grow up, always on the lookout for the
quickest way to get where he wanted to go, never letting any opportunity pass unexploited, always competing with his elders and
cashing in on his youth.

Ninoy had always pursued that rule in politics and in other
fields, and the formula has paid off: "He is now, at 35 (as of 1968)
the youngest Senator in our history," says Rama: "He is married to
Cory Cojuangco, a very charming and very rich girl—which is not

the least of his instant successes."[6]

Aided, in his 1967 campaign for the Senate, by a huge army of followers, including Cory who had to frequent public markets and factories to shake hands with and court the votes of the teeming masses, the youthful neophyte Senator immediately assumed his role as a fiscalizer of the administration with seriousness. Although he was not a lawyer and had had no experience in legislation, it only took him a few weeks to master the legislative mechanics and to size up and confront the Senate heavyweights as their equal in their own domain. Their reputations as grizzled debaters and veteran power brokers did not faze him.

On the other hand, he enjoyed one distinct advantage over many of his peers in the Senate—his youth, glamor and celebrity status. Reporters and press photographers competed with one another seeking him out, shooting his pictures, getting statements — often witty, frank and irreverent—from him on any current issues. As the darling of the mass media, he was also the cynosure of the eyes of people who filled the corridors and galleries of the Senate, watching his every gesture, hanging to every word he uttered, anxiously waiting for some devastating statement or witticism to issue from his lips. He was a past master of inventing quotable quotes.

Unlike the ordinary run of politicians Ninoy carefully and assiduously prepared for each performance. Having chosen a particular subject matter for a privileged speech, for instance, he would thoroughly bone up on it, gathering as much research and background materials on the subject to strengthen and reinforce his arguments. Consequently his listeners, including his peers, would be amazed not only by the novelty and sensitiveness of his subject matter but also by his encylopedic knowledge and scholarship that went with it.

Thus, when Ninoy delivered his maiden privileged speech, he provoked unprecedented editorial comment. Notable for the research, investigation and courage that went into it, his inaugural speech in the Senate was a well-documented expose of the "Garrison State" into which the Marcos administration, according to Ninoy, wanted to convert the country.

The boy Senator from Tarlac drew the nation's attention to the sinister plot of setting up armed forces civic action centers in every province. As he described it, all barrio leaders would be invited to attend seminars in those centers, there to be fed not only food for the body but also for the mind and the spirit, and told of the greatness of Marcos as the "Great Provider." To complete the picture, all those civic action centers would be connected by ribbons of communication and controlled by an operation center in, say, Camp Aguinaldo. Thus would start, said Ninoy, the beginning of massive thought control, all done in the name of democracy.

Then he produced, in that same expose, a roster of overstaying generals. Of the 17 regular generals then, 11 had overstayed, President Marcos having extended their tour of duty beyond their compulsory retirement dates. Why were those officers allowed to overstay? he asked. Then, answering his own question, Senator Aquino stressed: "What it all means is that it is easier to extract blind obedience and loyalty from the overstaying generals, a President can exact his bidding—faster."[7]

Next, Ninoy called attention to the escalating budget of the armed forces, with 90 percent going to personnel salaries, traveling expenses, housing allowances, retirement premiums, and only something like 10 percent going to equipment and capital outlay. He also deplored the AFP's over-dependence on U.S. aid when it came to hardware as a result of the lopsided budget, concluding that this was the reason the defense establishment had to toe the Pentagon line.

THE neophyte Senator followed up his "Garrison State" expose with other dramatic, headline-hugging revelations, among which was the mismanagement of the Philippine Charity Sweepstakes Office. But, it is said, it was at the hearings of the Philippine Civic Action Group (Philcag) bill that he showed his genius as a potentially outstanding legislator. He astounded his older colleagues with his ability to detect flaws in the testimony at the hearings, to ask penetrating questions, and discourse on history.

In one of the hearings, Philippine Ambassador to the United Nations Salvador P. Lopez, the best witness that the foreign office could field, cited the Battle of Tours as an argument in favor of fighting Communism in Vietnam. The erudite Lopez drew a parallel between the Vietnam war and the Battle of Tours in which Charles Martel stopped the rampaging Saracen army and saved Europe from Moorish conquest. The Christians made a determined stand at Tours, said Lopez, and turned the tide of the battle.

Rising, Ninoy Aquino cross-examined Lopez on the battle between Moors and Christians that took place in the year 732. When Lopez failed to state details, the young Senator recounted to him the incidents, the names of combatants and their respective strategies. He disputed Lopez's contention that the rout of the Moors was brought about by the Christian forces, reminding the ambassador, a respected writer and intellectual, that the Moors' defeat was precipitated not so much by the generalship of Charles Martel or the valiant stand of his forces as by the rebellion of the Berbers (Moslems from Northern Africa) in the ranks to Abdul Rahman's army. Lopez was impelled to compliment Ninoy on his scholarship and retentive memory.

IN just two months of session since his election to the Senate, Senator Aquino, along with Senators Jovito R. Salonga and Juan R. Liwag, surfaced as one of the most effective and resourceful leaders of the "Doves" in the Senate and was in the thick of the fight to get some of the "Hawks" to sign the substitute Vietnam measure which would call for a civilian medical corps instead of a combat engineering battalion like Philcag.

Ninoy was also the first to be tipped off about some "strange happenings" on Corregidor island in connection with the secret training of some special forces tasked with invading North Borneo. For reasons of national security, President Marcos prevailed upon him not to deliver his speech on the special forces training program. Nevertheless he spent sleepless nights shuttling from Manila to Corregidor and then to Cavite and back to Manila and several other places interviewing all those who knew something about the Corregidor incident. Then he sent word later from Jolo in Mindanao that he had met with all the 24 allegedly missing or massacred recruits in the port of Jolo and was coming back to Manila to make a report to the Senate, in a privileged speech, on how special forces officers bungled their project code-named "Jabidah."

Jabidah was the code-name of a secret operation involving a special force organized by the Philippine Constabulary, the members of which were mostly Muslims and a few graduates of the Philippine Military Academy. Their assignment was to disguise themselves as Malaysian soldiers, infiltrate Sabah and commit atrocities against the civilian population. The idea was to discredit the Malaysian government and thus facilitate the Philippine claim to Sabah. The whole secret operation would mean the massacre of whole villages and was extremely risky by any standards.

The whole nation was shocked upon learning that one of the young officers, a certain Lt. Nepomuceno, said to be a PMA graduate, Class '65 and a member of the Jabidah secret force, mysteriously vanished along with several Muslim soldiers. It was then that the government ordered an investigation but nothing ever came out of it. The entire project, including the training of the special forces, was to have been the subject of Ninoy's aborted privileged speech.

As a Senator, Ninoy Aquino hardly stayed put in one place. When not working in the Senate, he was on a fact-finding mission, or on a speaking engagement in the provinces, being very much in demand as a guest speaker of all kinds of organizations. Ever on the go, he seemed to be "always two steps ahead of his colleagues in the Senate." Why was he in so much of a hurry trying to do so many things at the same time? he was asked.

The reason, according to Ninoy himself, was that the administration was determined to remove him from the Senate, again on the question of age qualification. In fact a petition questioning his age qualification had been filed with the Senate Electoral Tribunal. Ninoy believed that if the administration scheme was pushed through, he would be out of the Senate in six months; hence, he was working double-time as a Senator. But before that happened he would like to show all the people whose votes had made him the Liberal topnotcher in the 1967 Senate elections that he was capable of doing his job in the Senate with singular competence and honor, regardless of what any tribunal might say about his qualifications. Actually he was being disqualified for being 13 days short of 35 years old on November 14, 1967, and was certainly 35 years of age on the date of his proclamation. The question would be decided by the Senate Electoral Tribunal composed of three Justices of the Supreme Court (J.B.L. Reyes, chairman of the tribunal, Fred Ruiz Castro and Conrado Sanchez, members); three Nacionalista Senators (Dominador Aytona, Rodolfo Ganzon and Wenceslao Lagumbay), and three Liberal Senators (Ambrosio Padilla, Gerardo Roxas and Juan R. Liwag). They decided in his favor.

IT was obvious that Senator Benigno Aquino Jr. had to be, if possible, removed from the Senate because he posed a real threat to the continued supremacy of President Ferdinand E. Marcos. The Senate was just one step away from the Presidency and Aquino, as a Senator, could use the influence of his office in projecting himself nationally as a potential presidential candidate. By continuously fiscalizing and attacking the administration, exposing its secret and sinister schemes such as the institution of a garrison state in the country, venalities in offices such as the Philippine Charity Sweepstakes and secret training programs for special forces on the Armed Forces of the Philippines for some undisclosed purposes—all through the privileged speech—Ninoy would continue to dominate newspaper headlines and magazine articles including the all-important (to the provinces, particularly) newscasts and commentaries on radio and television. And for a media expert like the celebrated former war correspondent, access to a public forum like the Senate and to mass media facilities like the press, radio and television could be infinitely devastating to a political power-holder like President Marcos.

To the administration, Ninoy Aquino could continue to rave and rant, disclose and expose, as long as he was a mere provincial governor; but to continue doing so as a member of the Senate was quite another matter that could be tolerated only at much risk to the permanence and stability of the government. For in political reckoning the Senate was but a short distance to Malacañang. The frontrunners in a senatorial election were, by popular acclaim if not party decree, potential candidates for President. Even their less spectacular colleagues could find themselves vying for the supreme nomination, for they were all elected from the nation at large and could lay claim to a broad-based strength to justify their aspirations. As the *Philippines Free Press*, formerly the nation's most respected and most influential weekly magazine, once observed:

"Apart from this proximity to the Presidency, the office of Senator carries with it power and prestige enough. Senators occupy the highest posts of the party which no House legislator, no matter how exceptional, may usurp, and in such lofty council fashion policy affecting the entire nation." Measures involving national honor, dignity and survival, the self-respect and the very existence of the nation, went through trial and judgment in the Senate, elevated there from the lower chamber or submitted by the President himself. No bill, no amendment, could approach the binding force of law without the Senate's stamp of approval. The august assembly had produced or made possible all the legislation that had proved beneficial to the nation or brought it infamy and disaster, in foreign affairs, trade and finance; in the conduct of politics, and the pursuit of peace, justice and order. Thus the Senate had been called, hopefully if not in fact, the soul and conscience of the people.

Such power and influence, adds the *Free Press*, must be accompanied by the utmost sobriety and the noblest sense of responsibility, for the stakes were more than partisan and regional. More than their colleagues in the House, Senators were expected to champion the public good, the people's interests. They were in a position to do just that, for the whole country, not just a district with its limited needs, was their constituency. Senators, unlike Congressmen, need not be bothered by such petty considerations as pork barrel. Unlike Congressmen, they were expected to be less vulnerable to presidential pressure and unscrupulous lobbies. Intelligence, honor, courage, integrity—Senators must have these.

MEANWHILE, aside from gaining considerable publicity mileage from his daring and resourcefulness as a young Senator, Ninoy was continuing to reap honors. Within just one year since his election as Senator he was voted one of the five "Most Outstanding Senators" by the *Free Press*, the others being such heavyweight advocates of freedom and integrity as Senators Jose W. Diokno, Jovito R. Salonga, Tecla San Andres Ziga, and Juan R. Liwag, whom the magazine cited for honorable mention.[9]

The *Free Press* cited Ninoy for his role as an opposition Senator, a role he himself had defined as early as 1962, when he was still governor of Tarlac, in these words:

"The opposition must remain ever alert, ever awake in the face of those vast powers ranged against the people it purports to defend, lest those powers reach out and engulf us all. There are, for instance, the vast powers vested in the President of the Republic, powers which can make or unmake any man or citizen. A ruthless President . . . blinded by partisan considerations, bludgeoned by compromises, indifferent to constructive criticism, obstinate, opinionated, dema- gogic, hypocritical, demands in our time an opposition that needs to be alert as well as brave, conscientious as well as sober, sincere as well as honest."[10]

Knowing that his days in the Senate were numbered, expecting to be given his walking papers soon if the administration moved to wind up the case of his age disqualification, Ninoy had been going double-time in pursuit of that opposition ideal. No solon had ever subjected a general appropriations act to a more thorough and devastating analysis than he did in his scrutiny of the P275 million "unitemized outlays" the President had included in the administra- tion budget. With incisive logic and hard statistics he attacked the sheer waste and inherent defects of various budget items beginning with the P100 million "Presidential Barrio Barrel" and outlined how the funds could be put to better use: strengthening the educational system, for instance, or increasing agricultural production. He deplored the administration's excessive funding of the Armed Forces and measly appropriation for education. More funds should be given to the Filipino youth, he cried, and teachers should be given better pay.

He was also cited by the magazine for his first privileged speech on the garrison state; his expose of mismanagement at the Philippine

Charity Sweepstakes; his performance at the Philcag bill hearings; his sleuthing in the Tawi-Tawi island group to get at the facts of the Corregidor incident, and his special report, delivered on the Senate floor, on how the AFP special forces had bungled the Jabidah project.

Simultaneously the publication underscored the range and depth of his concerns as indicated by the nature of legislation he had proposed: a bill seeking to amend the Revised Election Code by transferring the power to postpone an election for serious causes from the Office of the President to the Commission on Elections; a bill providing for special retirement privileges to public school teachers similar to those enjoyed by the military; an act to make education available to the greatest number through the creation of a Student Loan Fund Authority; and a measure calling for a "permanent freedom park" where any person could express himself with the utmost freedom on any subject under the sun, without government permit or molestation.

Summing up its impression of Ninoy Aquino as Senator, the *Free Press* describes him thus:

"Daring, determined, tireless, he is for all his boyish looks as sharp and unrelenting a fiscalizer, and as shrewd and mature a politician, as the most grizzled veterans in the opposition camp."

DESPITE the threat of removal from the Senate because of the question of being underaged at the time of his election, Senator Benigno Aquino Jr. remained in office and the Senate continued to be his principal platform. Ferdinand E. Marcos had won reelection in 1969, the first President of the country to be so reelected, against Senator Sergio Osmeña Jr. of the Liberal party. But by mandate of the 1935 Constitution Marcos was banned from running for a third time; the next presidential elections would be in 1973.

By that time, 1969-1970, the voice of revolution was reverberating across the country. The new Communist Party of the Philippines whose chairman was Jose Ma. Sison (*nom de guerre*: Amado Guerrero) and whose political tract, *Philippine Society and Revolution*, was a favorite reading fare of student activists in the campuses, and the New People's Army headed by Bernabe Buscayno, alias "Commander Dante," were gaining a rapidly increasing number of adherents not only among the students but the workers, employes, academics and writers, and even the social dregs known as *lumpen*. Though he had beaten Osmeña Jr., handily, but at great expense of the people's money and, as Ninoy Aquino had predicted, with the eager backing of the military, the newly reelected President was unpopular with the insurgents and anti-government forces. In fact, less than one month after his second inaugural, after delivering his traditional State-of-the-Nation message to Congress on January 26, 1970, President Marcos personally felt the explosive convulsion of a real revolution right at the Congress site.

A mammoth rally that day had been organized and called by the moderate National Union of Students of the Philippines (NUSP) headed by Edgar Jopson of the Ateneo de Manila. The huge multitude of some 20,000-50,000 consisted of students, teachers, priests, nuns, seminarians, workers, peasants, curious onlookers and assorted sympathizers of activism, who had been pouring into the large area in front of Congress since early that Monday morning. As in all such gatherings, the moderates were later joined by the radicals belonging to such organizations as the *Kabataang Makabayan* (KM) and the *Samahang Demokratiko ng Kabataan* (SDK). Government security and law officers were in full force, including anti-riot contingents. Many militant labor organizations were also represented in the rally. They, together with the radical students, were chanting *Dante, Dante, Dante*, the underground name of Buscayno who at that time was hailed by the militants as a folk-hero *a la* Che Guevara or Fidel Castro.

When the President arrived at 4:45 p.m. taking the south side of the Congress building, booing exploded from the ranks of demonstrators and stopped only after he had disappeared into the building. But the rally speakers continued reporting to the people the "true state of the nation" as they saw it. Shortly before the NUSP permit would expire, Jopson announced that the last speaker would be an SDK leader, after whose speech Jopson declared the rally formally closed and urged NUSP members to disperse and return to their buses. This angered the radicals, some of whom grabbed the microphone from Jopson and attacked the NUSP for being counter-revolutionaries. By the time the speaker was through the audience had begun chanting: *"Rebolusyon! Rebolusyon! Rebolusyon!."*

At this moment the President and the First Lady emerged from the Congress building surrounded by security agents, Metrocom troopers and other law enforcement units led by then Colonel Fabian C. Ver, chief of the Presidential Security Force, and Colonel James Barbers, deputy chief of the Manila Police Department. The President waved smiling at the large crowd. A moment later people in the crowd began to boo the President. To silence the crowd someone started to sing the national anthem, *Bayang Magiliw*, over the public address system and was joined in by the audience. But before the anthem was through another big group in the forefront began to sing the Tagalog version of the Communist Internationale, *Bangon!*

Then it happened. After the singing, while the President and the First Lady were being escorted by security aides to their waiting limousine, people began to throw stones, empty soft drinks bottles, sticks, placards and other improvised projectiles at their direction. Security men formed a human cover to protect them. Perhaps fearing an assassination, Colonel Ver pushed them into the car while his men covered the limousine. Then a black mock coffin and a *papier-mache* crocodile passed from hand to hand and were hurled at the presidential car — but fell short of the target.

Upon reaching Malacañang the President heard that students and the police were battling on the streets. Everybody had been caught by surprise–intelligence had told him nobody had expected violence. Immediately he sent word to the PC and the other law enforcers to leave the area and not to hurt any of the students except in self-defense, and to protect the people inside the Congress.

With the President and the First Lady out of the area, the soldiers and police attended to the demonstrators. Armed with truncheons they gave chase to the young rebels. As in all confrontations between trained men with arms and unarmed citizens, the outcome was predictable. Before that long night of January 26 ended, at least five persons had been killed and scores wounded, a senseless carnage that provoked intense outrage among the population. Responsible citizens condemned police brutality or the excessive use of police power. Others raised the hypothetical question of whether it was still possible to transform society by peaceful means.

THE revolt of January 26 was followed on January 30 by what may appropriately by called the "Siege of Malacañang," an incident called an "insurrection" by a police officer and "a revolt by local Maoist Communists" by President Marcos.

The day after the 26th, about 120 student leaders assembled at the Far Eastern University and met for three hours. They passed a resolution demanding the resignation of some police officers and set January 30 as the starting date of a series of rallies. On the eve of the 30th, four groups held simultaneous but separate rallies–some in front of Congress, others at the Manila City Hall, still others at Malacañang. The police brutality of January 26 had united all the activist groups; the first blood of the revolution had radicalized even the moderates, most of whom came from wealthy families, and who now found common cause with the militants.

On Friday, the 30th, they demonstrated simultaneously. Some groups proceeded to Malacañang for a meeting with the President. Before the meeting was over, those who demonstrated in front of Congress marched from Congress to Malacañang, arriving at the gates of the Palace at about 6 p.m. The first sign of trouble revealed itself during that march when the young revolutionaries, angered by the sight of a police traffic stand, destroyed and burned it at the corner of Ayala and Marquez de Comillas streets, at the southern foot of Ayala bridge. Getting unruly now they proceeded on foot, their fists clenched, chanting and singing revolutionary songs, and crying *Rebolusyon*! Dusk had set in as they reached Malacañang, and someone shouted, *"Sindihan ang ilaw! Sindihan ang ilaw!"* (Turn the lights on! Turn the lights on!) and the lamps at the Palace gates were lit.

Then someone hurled a rock at one of the vapor lamps, smashing it. Others followed suit, blasting the Palace lamps with rocks and pieces of wood until the front of the Palace was plunged in darkness. Meanwhile, at the Mendiola street entrance to Malacañang, the young rebels were trying to storm the gate. Palace security positioned a firetruck on the gate and trained its firehoses on the rebels. Later at about 7 p.m., a Manila Fire Department truck arrived and also trained its hoses at the demonstrators. But the water pressure was too weak. The students charged at the truck, commandeered it from the firemen whom they beat up, drove it toward the gate and used it as a battering ram until the lock gave way, the chains broke and the gate clanked open. The students then lobbed Molotov cocktails and pillboxes into the Palace grounds as they surged inside. They stoned the buildings and set fire to the fire truck and to a government car parked nearby. Then the Presidential Guard Battalion came in force.

Before they were forced to retreat, the demonstrators had lobbed so many rocks, pillboxes and Molotovs and caused considerable damage to the buildings. Windows and glasses of the new Budget Commission building were smashed, as well as the clinic building beside it. The infirmary was set on fire. At the gate the rebels burned a waiting shed, dragged a guardhouse up to adjoining Arlegui street and burned it there. At the main Palace gate they destroyed the telephone booth beside the Presidential Guard Battalion outpost with Molotov bombs.

To those outside of the center of action the situation seemed desperate, with radio and television announcers flooding the airlanes with panicky, emotion-charged reportage. The panic and hysteria that seized their voices contaminated their listeners, many of whom felt Malacañang was in real and immediate danger of falling to the rebels.

When reinforcements from the PC, the Army, Navy and the Metrocom arrived that night, the pattern of the January 26 battled was repeated: the military would attack, the students would retreat; the students would counterattack, the military would draw back. The soldiers gained control of Mendiola and J.P. Laurel streets at about 9 p.m. The students were holding Tuberias, Legarda and Claro M. Recto streets. Some had retreated down to Arlegui and into Quiapo, where looters broke display windows and grabbed jewelry and shoes.

The "invasion" by the rebels was later repulsed, and some PC and police officers were hurt but did not fire a single shot. When the Palace grounds had been finally cleared of demonstrators Metrocom troops rushed out in pursuit of the fleeing rebels, while other state troopers secured the presidential Palace against any counterattack.

BUT the rebels would not leave. Instead they converged in the center of the cross formed by Recto, Mendiola and Legarda streets, flinging rocks and insults at the government men nearby. On the left side of Legarda other rebels were screaming. There were other demonstrators in that area and the soldiers had to guard the bridge against two armies of students, one attacking from the front, the other from the side.

Then the troopers started firing into the ground, and dust and tiny pebbles exploded from the cement. The firing was preceded by the advance of two firetrucks from the Mendiola side, with the soldiers trotting behind. What followed was a prolonged battle of nerves.

Finally the demonstrators were pushed back to Mendiola bridge. Several students turned right on Legarda street, others toward Recto. They lit bonfires in the middle of Lepanto and Recto streets near the University of the East and the Philippine College of Commerce. Other groups filled bottles with gasoline at a gas station across the street from the UE to make Molotov bombs. A few meters away from the station smouldered an army truck and a private car which had been set on fire by the rebels.

This so-called "Battle of Mendiola" ended around midnight of January 30 when government forces took complete control of

Mendiola bridge.

The following night President Marcos appeared on television to inform the nation of the "premeditated attack on the government, an act of rebellion and subversion." He said the mob that attempted to burn Malacañang was not a mob of students or of arsonists but men dedicated to an evil purpose: to destroy or take over Malacañang. This plan, he said, was conceived by two groups, one Communist-inspired and the other not Communist-inspired. Both were under surveillance, said the President, then assured the nation that the situation was under control. Malacañang, the country and the government were well-guarded, he stressed, and there was no takeover by any group of the military or of the civilian government. He added:

"In the matter of preparation of the plans of reaction against any attempt to take over this government, the action that will be taken will be well-studied, deliberate, cautious, and legal, and there will be no attempt to curtail constitutional freedom."

To the rebels he gave the warning that any attempt at the forcible overthrow of the government would be put down immediately. "I will not," Marcos emphasized, "tolerate nor will I allow Communists to take over."

At the time he was announcing this hard line against the Communists, the entire Armed Forces of the Philippines had been put on red alert.[12]

THE following year, 1971, the leadership of Ferdinand E. Marcos was put to a severe test again. Since his election as President in 1965 he had successfully consolidated power and his gains. The midterm or off-year senatorial elections of 1967 saw his handpicked team sweeping the senatorial race with only former Tarlac Governor Benigno Aquino Jr. surviving the Marcos onslaught and in fact winning the No. 2 slot in the 8-berth contest, proof of Ninoy's nationwide popularity and the efficiency of his own personal organization. Then in 1969, running for reelection, Marcos easily defeated Senator Osmeña Jr., 5,017,343 to 3,043,122, for a commanding margin of almost 2,000,000, thus earning a place in history as the first President of the Republic to be reelected and reinforcing his reputation as a myth-breaker.

The victory of Ninoy Aquino in that 1967 election, on the other hand, further improved the young politico's stock as a potential candidate for the Presidency, the only man in the opposition Liberal party who could perhaps match Marcos "blow for blow and gun for gun." Moreover he had youth and exuberant dynamism on his side, plus the other qualities often associated with the incumbent Ilocano President: intelligence and perception, gift of gab and vision, audacity and daring. In fact it was widely talked about during that time that of all the possible rivals of Marcos, only Ninoy Aquino had the brazenness, toughness and resourcefulness to fight and possibly depose Marcos. As men in the streets would say, *"Kung bandido si Marcos, bandido rin si Aquino."* (If Marcos is a tough bandit, so is Aquino.")

Ninoy was, indeed, despite his baby fat and cherubic face, a tough nut to crack. He was not a soft Manila politician without access to hard-bitten peasants. Ninoy was a Central Luzon political figure who got his baptism of political fire in his native Tarlac, hotbed of agrarian unrest, cradle of peasant-led insurrections, and spawning ground and choice battlefield of the Huks, notably those insurgents led by Supremo Luis Taruc. As mayor of Concepcion however briefly (until he was disqualified for lack of the mandatory age), he admitted having co-existed with the Huks without turning Communist himself. He never denied that he had had dealings with them even when he was six years governor of Tarlac. As he once explained:

"What can I do about that? I have lived in Tarlac where the Huks operate most. The point I'm driving at with my frequent mention of Huks is that as governor of Tarlac I tried to arrive at a condition of peace that was not reached through bloodshed. In my six years of governorship, I don't think there were more than 21 Huk killings. It was not until Mr. Marcos arrived on the scene that these things began to escalate. From 1960 up to the present (1972) about 1,500 have been killed. My policy as governor had been to let everyone come to my office and talk things over: Huk and non-Huk, Nacionalista and Liberal. I believed that was the only way I could maintain peace in the province. I told the Huks. 'This is a free country. So long as you don't kill anyone this is a free country for you. You can speak against me, attack me in the barrios. Go ahead. I believe in our democracy. You have the right to air your views. If the people should ultimately prefer your system to the one I espouse, who am I to oppose the people?'

"The Army calls this co-existence.

"I call it survival. Moreover I have extreme faith in our democratic way of life. I firmly believe that exposed to both the democratic and Communist ideologies, the people will opt for democracy."[13]

Regarding his frequent meetings with the Huks, Ninoy said he had arranged those meetings not to solicit Huk support for his candidates but, on the contrary, to ask the Huks not to interfere in Tarlac politics. One such meeting had been at the request of Eduardo Cojuangco Jr., right-hand man of President Marcos and Ninoy's cousin-in-law, who was then running for governor.

Ninoy believed that the Marcos administration was continuing to smear him and implying that he was a Huk or a Huk coddler to deprive the Liberals of support from any sector. For one, the charge of Communism dangling over his head kept the Chinese from giving him any aid. Moreover, to deny the Liberals American support, Marcos invited a *New York Times* correspondent to interview him; he repeated his charges against Ninoy and said that if the Communists entered a candidate in 1973—meaning Ninoy Aquino—he would be compelled to field his wife Imelda as his party's presidential candidate. In answer, Ninoy said eight years of Marcos was enough and to inflict six more years of Imelda on the country would be unthinkable. Then addressing the President, he said:

"If Mr. Marcos is fielding his wife in '73 just to stop Ninoy Aquino, I'm telling him now, I'm not running. Keep your wife home, Mr. Marcos, do not tire her out with a gruelling campaign. I would like to spare her the hardship. I will not run in 1973, so long as Imelda doesn't run either. Let Imelda and I make a blood compact, vowing not to run in 1973 as presidential candidates."[14]

Ninoy recognized and acknowledged the role played by the Huks in Philippine society. When he was younger, a war correspondent in Korea and Vietnam, he had no commitments, according to Ninoy. Then in 1954 he negotiated the surrender of Luis Taruc and it was Taruc who opened his eyes to social ills.

"During those three months in the mountains with Taruc," said Ninoy, "this man opened my eyes to the *takipan*, the *talindua*, the usury in our place. And he challenged me: 'You are a writer, your father was a national leader; why do you shirk your duty? You could be a tremendous influence.' That was why, at age 22, I decided to go back to my hometown and run for mayor. And that's why I always say that the Huks are a necessary evil: they bring about a social conscience. Without the pressure they exert, our society would not change."[15]

THE principal problem of President Marcos in 1971 was not the election of eight Senators but the presidential election in 1973. He was, as we have seen, barred by the Constitution from running for President again, and it seemed that there was no one else in his Nacionalista party who had his full trust and confidence to run in his place. Talk was rife that he might indeed field Imelda as the presidential candidate of his party, as, in fact, the First Lady's brain-trusts and propagandists had already been reported to be preparing to launch her bid. But Marcos might really be having second thoughts for it seemed the Liberals would put up no less than the charismatic, courageous and politically sophisticated Ninoy Aquino.

The Liberal party at that time was dominated by at least three big names—Liberal party President Gerardo Roxas, Senator Jovito R. Salonga, and Senator Ninoy Aquino. Each of them was the fair hope of the party. According to many political observers, however, Ninoy had the edge over either Roxas or Salonga. He was perceived as the candidate who could confront Marcos in a bruising, no-holds barred presidential encounter. At the same time he seemed to be the overwhelming favorite of the youth and the workers; they could identify easily with him because of his Central Luzon background, his activism and oratorical prowess—and courage. He was *macho, matapang* (brave), beyond intimidation or fear.

The Marcos administration apparently shared this public impression of Ninoy Aquino as evidenced by the fact that more than either Senator Salonga or Senator Roxas, Marcos often made Ninoy the object of propaganda attacks, desperately trying to pin on him the label of Communist.

The Marcos people, moreover, tried to label him with such epithets as opportunist, ruthless, deceitful and over-ambitious. But however hard the administration tried, the labels would not stick. In fact, the more they attacked him the faster the legend and the mystique grew about his persona—of boldness, strength, potential invincibility.

MEANWHILE the Liberal party finally completed its senatorial lineup for the November 8, 1971 elections. The slate included Senator Salonga, John Osmeña, Eddie Ilarde, Ramon Mitra, Eva Estrada Kalaw, Salipada Pendatun, Genaro Magsaysay and Melanio Singson. They were chosen by the party at a time when student acitivism was at its height, revolutionary graffiti, posters and red-lettered streamers with the Communist hammer and sickle plastered over fences and walls of buildings, private or public, and when department stores, movie houses and other public places were often rocked by exploding bombs, resulting in massive destruction of private properties and the loss of lives and limbs; and when the Constitutional Convention, tasked with drafting a new Constitution, was agonizing over the question of banning President Marcos from running for a third term or allowing him to run again. It was also a time when Marcos kept on repeating his threat of utilizing his emergency powers under the Constitution to protect the people and the government from anarchy and communication.

Then it happened.

On the night of Saturday, August 21, 1971, during the proclamation rally of the Liberal party at Plaza Miranda, two fragmentation grenades were hurled onto the stage, killing nine persons instantly and wounding 95 others. The leadership of the Liberal party could have been entirely wiped out. Though not one politician was killed many of those who stood on the stage were hurt. One (Mayor Ramon Bagatsing of Manila) lost a foot and, for more than one week, Osmeña Jr. and Salonga fought for their lives on separate operating tables. Others suffered from terrible, ugly wounds that took a long time to heal.

The Plaza Miranda carnage proved to be a good excuse for the Nacionalistas to smear Ninoy Aquino. He was not present when it happened. The rumor swiftly spread that he had masterminded the bombing to eliminate his rivals for his party's nomination for presidential candidate in 1973. The press discredited that rumor; the opposition was bombed and the opposition was to be blamed! It simply did not seem logical.

On Monday, August 23, President Marcos announced on nationwide radio and television that he had as of midnight, Saturday, August 21, suspended the privilege of the writ of *habeas corpus*. His justification for this was that, according to him, there was a Maoist rebellion in progress. Consequently twenty persons were arrested and were being detained in Camp Crame. The nation was stunned, not knowing what the President would do next.

Ghastly silence followed the President's announcement.

Suddenly, the deathly calm was broken: Ninoy Aquino, ever voluble and tireless, began his counter-offensive. Wherever he appeared he bore a submachine gun—at a time when no one outside the administration would have dared be seen with a gun. At the Manila Medical Center the milling crowd gave way to his large frame when he arrived to check on the condition of his wounded partymates. He did not even glance at the government troops in the place as he passed them by, tight-lipped, confident. The President learned of Aquino's "insolence" later.

The following day, Tuesday, President Marcos went on television and laid the blame for the bombing on the Communists who were planning, according to him, to stage a revolution, of which the opening act was the Plaza Miranda blitz. In the same breath he charged Senator Aquino with lending support to the Communist movement, saying he had reliable information that Ninoy had frequently met with such Huk field commanders as Dante, Mallari, Alibasbas, Freddie and Ligaya. Then he produced a carbine with telescopic sight and a nickel-plated grease-gun which, he said, had been given by Ninoy to Huk commanders. He then presented two men—Max Llorente and Hernan Ilagan—who, according to him, had been close friends of Ninoy until they realized what he was up to. Neither of the two spoke a word; they just stood before the TV cameras with blank expressions until the President motioned them to go away.

Later that same night, Ninoy Aquino appeared on Channel 13. He looked dead serious, while opposite him Secretary of National Defense Juan Ponce Enrile sat grinning. When Ninoy spoke the television audience knew here was a man who had the nerve, the courage, to challenge the powerful President to prove his charges.

He denied all the President's charges and dared him to prove them for the sake of truth and justice.

He explained later that he had not been able to join his colleagues on the stage because he was attending his god-daughter's *despedida de soltera*, a pre-nuptial party. His absence, he knew, had lent some credibility to the speculation that he had a hand in the bombing. He felt that Marcos was really determined to send him to jail, but he was prepared to spend one or two years in a stockade. He had no plans of escaping into the hills and would join his jailers if they came to get him. As for the two silent witnesses, Ninoy said that if one added up all the time he had seen Hernan Ilagan, it would amount to no more than three hours. As for Max Llorente, Ninoy saved the man's life once and "his skin several times over"—and this was how the man repaid him. "Classic Filipino," he exclaimed. On the affidavits made by other witnesses implicating him in the crime of subversion, he said all the witnesses of the President were dead.

Still, every day from then on, the Marcos government hurled a new charge or threat at Ninoy. But he exposed every charge as a lie and met each threat with smiling nonchalance. Yet the threats were real. One night the PC ringed his house to frighten his family. At another time members of the medical staff of the Central Azucarrera de Tarlac were picked up and questioned by the PC, who tried to force them into signing affidavits implicating Ninoy with the Huks; houseboys and cooks were also arrested. His brother-in-law, Antolin Oreta Jr., was "invited" by the military and then detained in the military camp.

Was all this a preview of things to come?

The victims of the Plaza Miranda bombing were unable to take to the hustings by reason of their wounds. Ninoy and some of his party colleagues had to perform much of the work for them. There was a tremendous outpouring of sentiments and sympathy for the Liberal candidates — and vehement hatred for the Marcos candidates who were at the receiving end of the campaign slogan,"*Ibagsak ang mga tuta ni Marcos*! (Down with the dogs of Marcos!)".

The *Free Press* put Ninoy Aquino on its cover on January 8, 1972 as the magazine's "Man of the Year," with this encomium:

"Ninoy Aquino's audacity and defiance bore fruit on November 8. The Liberal senatorial candidates swept the elections. In Ilocos Sur, (Luis) Singson won as governor and in Isabela, despite the presence of Task Force Lawin, (Faustino) Dy won as well. Ninoy's cause had, indeed, been vindicated. Even the poorest and most downtrodden emulated the example he had set. In Tarlac, the barrio folk themselves went out to protect the ballots they had cast, forming long processions to escort the ballot boxes to the municipalities. The Senator had given a new lease on life to the democratic idea, which cynics had dismissed as an empty catchphrase incapable of firing anyone's imagination, let alone convincing anyone to risk his life for it. The 'people's victory,' as Ninoy called it, of November 8 proved them wrong.

"Because he stood for the people's will to resist tyranny, drawing upon himself all the fury of its wrath without flinching, Senator Benigno Aquino, Jr., did more than anybody else to make that victory possible and is, therefore, the Man of the Year 1971 in the Philippines."[16]

To Ferdinand E. Marcos, Benigno Aquino Jr., was indeed a real, gigantic problem. The President had all the reason to worry about his and his family's future. There seemed to be no way to stop the contry's fastest-rising wonder boy.

FIVE

Arrest and Detention

The worst of my life is over,
I hope,
And may the best things, please,
come soon. '

— Cory C. Aquino, a haiku.

ON January 11, 1972, President Marcos restored the privilege of the writ of *habeas corpus* which he had suspended on August 21, 1971 on the night of the bombing of the Plaza Miranda proclamation rally of the Liberal party. The restoration was followed by renewed and intensified activities by the insurgents and other unknown elements. A new series of bombings ensued, causing great damage to private and public property and injuries to a number of innocent persons.

The decadent, sick society further deteriorated. As a result of the escalating anarchy, violence and terrorism the economy drastically slumped: the productive sectors were virtually immobilized because the frequent bombings, picketing, violent strikes and boycotts prevented people from working and numerous business establishments were compelled to close shop. The people were paralyzed by insecurity and fear.

The people had more than enough reason to be fear-stricken: the government itself, to which they had looked for protection, had seemingly been reduced to absolute impotence. National and local government functions could hardly be carried out. The judiciary, itself ridden with corrupt elements, could not administer justice. Local police and civilian authorities could not regulate, much less control, the raging tide of criminality and lawlessness, largely because their own ranks were infested with criminal elements and proteges of warlords and corrupt politicians. Crimes like kidnaping, blackmail, armed robbery, hold up, swindling, profiteering and hoarding of commodities were rampant.

Moreover, there was total decay of moral values among the

people themselves as evidenced by the widespread lack of discipline, respect for authority, and regard for even the most elementary rudiments of ethical human conduct.

Because of the corrupt system of politics and the pervasive social malaise Philippine society descended rapidly into the maelstrom of chaos, anarchy and immorality. It became a society seemingly without a soul or conscience—a sick society, an afflicted society whose condition was so advanced it was on the brink of death. That condition had been caused by a myriad factors, others manipulated and induced, and recovery seemed utterly hopeless.

Marcos knew, more than anyone else because he was on top of things, that while the national condition was critical it was not beyond redemption. He knew that the lawless elements had grown in strength and that the people were beginning to yield to the seduction of Communist ideologues and the clerico-fascists precisely because of the uncertainty of their future but he also knew that in reality the government had not lost its power to check and dismantle the incipient rebellion, lead the people along the democratic course, and inspire them to channel their talents and energies toward the improvement of their own lives.

He must have known, too, with certitude that if he acted fast and decisively, he would succeed not only in arresting the rapid deterioration of the country but, using his emergency powers granted by the Constitution, also ensure his continued stay in power. For with the use of his emergency powers, which he earlier experimented on when he suspended the privilege of the writ of *habeas corpus,* no election would be held in 1973 or even years afterwards. It would all depend on how effectively and successfully his use of emergency powers—the power to declare martial law—would turn out.

To Marcos, at that point in history, there was sufficient justification for the imposition of martial law, among which was to nip the rebellion and rebuild Philippine society. These two objectives alone would justify, in his mind, putting the entire country under martial law and his assuming absolute executive and legislative powers in accordance with the provisions of the 1935 Constitution. Such assumption of absolute powers would be drastic, but it would be legal and constitutional.

ON September 21, 1972 Ferdinand E. Marcos made the most profound and audacious decision he ever made as President of the Philippines. He issued Proclamation No. 1081 placing the entire country under martial law. According to him it was the last alternative open to him under the Constitution and he resorted to it because it was a historical necessity. He needed extraordinary powers, Marcos stressed, the full authority vested in the Presidency by the Constitution, to quell and dismantle the rebellion and thus save the Republic from the lawless elements. Simultaneously, said Marcos, he would use his full powers to revolutionize—modernize—the sick society and build a new one, a New Society.

Although he signed the proclamation on September 21 Marcos formally announced his decision only in the evening of September 23, a Saturday, in a nationwide radio-television address. As with the suspension of the writ of *habeas corpus* he delayed the announcement to enable the military to make arrests with the least obstruction. His statement that preceded the proclamation was designed to allay the fears of many that he would use martial law to install himself as a totalitarian dictator for life and that his martial regime, as in other countries, would be characterized by violence and terror. Utilizing his TV charm to the fullest, though it was obvious that the weight of his problem had etched lines on his face and forehead and gave him a haggard appearance, Marcos assured the people that martial law did not mean a military takeover of government, and that the civilian government would continue to function under him as civilian Chief Executive. He emphasized that he proclaimed martial law pursuant to the powers vested in the President by the Constitution. Marcos could not be faulted for insisting on having a legal or constitutional basis for his actions and decisions. He stressed that as the duly elected President of the Republic he was using his power to proclaim martial law to protect the Republic and democracy, adding:

"A republican and democratic form of government is not a helpless government. When it is imperilled by the danger of a violent overthrow, insurrection and rebellion, it has inherent and built-in powers wisely provided for under the Constitution. Such a danger confronts the Republic."[1]

Then he set the general demands of his martial regime. He said every form of corruption, culpable negligence or arrogance of public officials and employees would be dealt with immediately. The armed forces would be cleaned up; military offenders would be swiftly punished. No one, whether friend, relative or ally would be allowed to offend the New Society, his label for the reformed sick society. Persons who did not actively participate in the rebellion, he added, could move about and perform their daily activities without any fear from the government. But those who had actively participated in the conspiracy and operations to overthrow the duly constituted government by violence would be adversely affected, he pointed out. He then set a high moral tone for the bureaucracy, calling on all public officials and employees, whether of the national or local governments, to conduct themselves in the manner of a new and reformed society.

Moving fast and decisively he simultaneously issued general orders for the government to control media and other means of dissemination of information, as well as all public utilities. He ordered all schools closed for at least one week. He made illegal carrying of firearms punishable with death and established curfew from midnight to four o'clock in the morning. He temporarily suspended the departure of Filipinos abroad with the exception of those on official mission. In the meantime, he said, rallies, demonstrations and labor strikes were prohibited.

President Marcos then announced that he had ordered the arrest—and detention—of those directly involved in the conspiracy to overthrow the government.

Admitting that while he had used the other two alternatives under the Constitution—call the troops to quell the rebellion and suspend the privilege of the writ of *habeas corpus*—the rebellion worsened rather than stopped. He stressed that his objective in proclaming martial law was two-fold: to save the Republic and reform society. This, he said, would require eliminating the threat of a violent overthrow of the Republic and reforming the social, economic and political institutions in the country.

NINOY Aquino, regarded as a major presidential candidate, No. 1 critic of President Marcos, and secretary-general of the opposition Liberal Party, was among the first to be arrested by the martial law troopers. He was arrested at the Manila Hilton by a team led by then Colonel Romeo Gatan while in the midst of a conference with other party leaders, then placed under maximum security at Fort Bonifacio in Makati, Rizal. No formal charges were made against him at the time of his arrest although the government alleged that the young firebrand had "generally" been involved with subversive activities.

Nearly a year later, on August 27, 1973, Aquino was formally arraigned on charges of murder, illegal possession of firearms, and subversion by a military tribunal. In an unexpected move Ninoy refused to participate in the trial, calling it "an unconscionable mockery." In his statement before the tribunal, Ninoy, according to former Senator Jovito R. Salonga, was very pleased with his own performance. He had been ordered to plead guilty or not guilty to the charges of murder, subversion, and illegal possession of fire-arms. Instead of pleading not guilty, he delivered a speech announcing his decision to boycott the proceedings as an act of protest against the injustice of it all. Salonga had advised him to confine himself to the prepared text — something which was difficult for him to do as he was given to improvisations — and to deliver his lines at a slower pace so the foreign newsmen, whom they expected to report the proceedings faithfully, could keep up with him. His pacing was just perfect as he came to the high point of his speech, which contained a paraphrase of *La Pasionaria* (Dolores Ibarruri of Spain):

"Sirs: I know you to be honorable men. But the one unalterable fact is that you are the subordinates of the President. You may decide to preserve my life, but he can choose to send me to death. Some people suggest that I beg for mercy. But this I cannot in conscience do. I would rather die on my feet with honor, than live on bended knees in shame."[2]

Because of the unexpected impact of that speech, Salonga said, the proceedings before the military tribunal had to be suspended indefinitely. The foreign press was obviously impressed and the limited audience in the courtroom was spellbound. A few hours after the session, at Fort Bonifacio, Ninoy told Salonga: *"Prof, pwede na akong mamatay* (I can die after that speech). They can shoot me now for all I care."[3]

The following day President Marcos announced he would create a five-man committee to reinvestigate the charges against Ninoy. The committee was meant to demonstrate that everything was being done to ensure utmost fairness, impartiality and objectivity. But the prominent former jurists requested by the President to sit in the investigative body refused to participate. Even former Senator Lorenzo M. Tañada, Ninoy's lawyer, also declined to participate, claiming that the new agency did not conform with the requirements of due process because of existing agencies, specifically civilian courts, which could reverse cases such as the Aquino case.

Ninoy Aquino then filed a petition with the Supreme Court requesting an injunction against the military trial on grounds that he was being deprived of his constitutional right to a hearing in a civilian court. He claimed that in the absence of a state of war the military courts had no jurisdiction over civilians. He also claimed he did not have a "ghost of a chance" in a trial by a military court created by President Marcos who, according to him, had already prejudged his guilt.

In his book, *The Conjugal Dictatorship*,[4] Primitivo Mijares says that as of April 1975 Ninoy Aquino had spent 30 months in detention under maximum security, of which 24 months was solitary confinement. In the first eleven months of detention, he became 45 pounds lighter than his 190-pound weight. When he appeared before the military tribunal, he could hardly be recognized by the newspapermen who had long known him because he appeared pitifully underweight, weak and pallid.

Together with former Senator Jose W. Diokno, Ninoy was at one time subjected to physical and mental torture at a dungeon-like structure in Fort Magsaysay, Nueva Ecija, in Central Luzon, where they were earlier detained separately. He had at various times been denied visitation rights by his family and access to counsel.

CORY Aquino recalls that Ninoy's incarceration gave him "a chance to see himself, to really find out for himself what he should do, what are the good things he has done — in other words, a complete examination of self, which very few of us do." She believes imprisonment of the nemesis of the Marcoses brought about a mellowing. As Cory recalls to Lorna Kalaw-Tirol:

"When he was in Bonifacio he was so caring. I guess he was always like that except he didn't have time. And there was a change of priorities. Before that he was so busy trying to be popular we just had to be relegated to the background. Now he felt he owed each of us something. He really tried his best to make up to us for whatever he lacked before. He always told me, 'I guess this is one way of punishing me. Before I was so busy with political life and I had no time for you people. And now I miss all of you so much and I cannot be with you."[5]

She lived in constant uncertainty about Ninoy's fate during the more than seven years of his imprisonment. She considers the first few months of martial rule real torture for her. She could not read, and when she did even the simplest thing would not go into her head. She could not understand anything, perhaps because she was too nervous.

"I would go to Mass every day but really and truly maybe my body was here but my mind was elsewhere," she says. "I couldn't watch TV because I couldn't bear to see the face of Marcos or Ponce Enrile or anybody." Then she would pray that Ninoy and the other detainees be released. She would change her mind, thinking she was not praying the right way and maybe she should pray for Marcos and Enrile and the generals so they would change and treat Ninoy better. So she and the children would say the rosary together, say three rosaries together at one time, asking God to enlighten Marcos, Enrile, Ramas and the other generals. Going farther, she told her children to make sacrifices and to offer these up for their father's release. She even forbade them to attend parties — she herself had stopped visiting the beauty parlor and ordering new clothes — until a priest advised her to allow herself and her children to live as normally as possible.

Cory remembers that when Ninoy was in prison she never failed him. No matter what he asked her to do she had always been loyal and supportive. This was confirmed by one of Ninoy's sisters, Ditas Aquino Ebner. "The prison years were when we started really admiring her," she said. "She never failed to be there and she lived for her family."[6]

She worried about Ninoy's health when he was in detention, especially when he staged a hunger strike during his trial. She served as the principal link Ninoy had to the outside world, his eyes and ears. She could hardly wait for her visitation days to come — Wednesday, Saturday and Sunday — during which she brought him news about relatives and friends and the political climate outside Fort Bonifacio. Cory smuggled out Ninoy's thoughts and letters which were later reproduced through the xerox machine or mimeographed and distributed through the underground grapevine at a time when there was no "alternative press" to speak of.[7]

ON April 4, 1975, when he was undergoing trial, Ninoy Aquino began a hunger strike in protest against the martial law government after the military court had ruled that he could not absent himself from the court proceedings.

On April 8 the Supreme Court issued an order temporarily restraining the military commission from proceeding with the case. This was the first time since the proclamation of martial law that a civilian court had restrained a military commission.

It was Cory who announced Ninoy's plan to stage a hunger strike in protest of the government's charges against him and the manner the trial was being conducted. In a press conference at their residence on Times street, Quezon City, Cory Aquino said her husband specifically wanted to take up with Marcos four issues, namely:

1.   The trial of civilians before military tribunals for alleged

offenses committed prior to the proclamation of martial law;

2.   The lack of judicial independence;
3.   The absence of a genuine free press; and
4.   The repression and further continuation of martial law.

Ninoy then announced, through his wife, that he would go on with his hunger strike "not only for myself but also for the many other victims of today's oppression and injustices."

The prosecution in the Aquino case filed a petition to "perpetuate the testimony" of their witnesses, justifying the petition with the claim that the lives of the witnesses were allegedly in danger. The military court granted the petition without (1) Aquino knowing of its existence, and (2) without any opportunity to contest the petition. Moreover, the defendant Aquino was not given any opportunity to contest the testimony of the witnesses.

In effect, the military commission had in its possession testimony and evidence the validity of which could not be questioned by Aquino in the proceedings or in a civilian court. Once the military commission had perpetuated the testimony of the witnesses, they would no longer be subject to recall in a civilian court.[8]

During the last days of his hunger strike in 1975 (it lasted 40 days), former Senator Salonga, one of Ninoy's closest friends and confidantes, was allowed by the military authorities to see him and talk to him from day to day inside his detention room. Upon seeing Ninoy, Salonga felt as if something died within him. His recollection of Ninoy goes this way:

"He was shrunken, very weak and pale — he had lost so much weight he could hardly stand up and his breath had a different smell. He was in tears — something unusual — as he talked to me about his death wish, now that it was clear to him that Marcos, his fraternity brother, would not even care to send for him and talk to him. He showed me his typewritten letters of farewell, addressed to each one of the lawyers who had volunteered to assist in his defense. Each letter showed the kind of person he was — eternally grateful, generous in spirit, and so forgiving despite what Marcos and his associates had done to him. It was perhaps this aspect of Ninoy's character that Marcos could never, never understand. Ninoy Aquino was so big-hearted and charitable he was willing to understand and forgive those who had tried so hard to malign, persecute and humiliate him."[9]

WHILE languishing in prison at Fort Bonifacio, headquarters of the Philippine Army, Armed Forces of the Philippines, Ninoy

Aquino refuted the claim of President Marcos that he imposed martial law as a means of saving the Republic from its enemies. Marcos, according to Ninoy, did not really establish a New Society, but "the oldest society recorded by history — a society of absolute rule by one man who in various epochs was called a *pharaoh*, a *shah*, an emperor, a king, a *duce*, a *caudillo*, a *fuehrer*, a chairman or a President."

He attacked Marcos for claiming that a new Constitution had been overwhelmingly ratified by the Filipino people in January 1973, a Constitution that ordained a drastic change from a presidential to a parliamentary form of government. The truth, said Aquino, was that "what we have today is a worse centralized Presidency, a totalitarian regime where both legislative and executive powers have been merged under one man. We have a parliamentary government without a parliament. Instead of moving forward to parliamentary democracy, we moved backwards to the very extremes of presidential authoritarianism."

Of the President's claim that he had checked the privileges and the rule of an entrenched oligarchy, Aquino said, "Yes, the rule of the few has been eliminated. It has been reduced to the rule of one."

Pointing out that Marcos never missed a stroke in his incessant flogging of the old society as if he were a complete stranger to that society, Ninoy called the nation's attention to the following:

1. It was during the incumbency of Marcos, as early as 1966, when "documented rake offs from public works contracts reached into the millions," when he encouraged the proliferation of private armies and the smuggling by his political henchmen of high-powered weapons with impunity, when 26 Muslim "Jabidah" volunteers were murdered in cold blood in Corregidor, when the Republic nearly got embroiled in a foreign adventure with a neighboring state to secure a "power of attorney" granted by the heirs of the Sultan of Sulu to Marcos.

2. It was during his incumbency when the currency was "debauched and devalued" by an unprecedented 58% as a result of wanton election spending "overkill" in 1969. Marcos, said Ninoy, squandered almost P900 million to reelect himself as per findings of the Senate committee on finance.

3. It was during Marcos's incumbency when despairing youth took to the streets to denounce his abuses and misrule, when several idealistic young demonstrators were mowed down in cold blood while some others were picked up during the night by agents

of the law and disappeared forever.

4.   It was during his incumbency when the prestige of the House of Representatives hit rock bottom with the revelation of scandalous fund transfers from Malacañang to finance and rig the elections of handpicked Marcos-type Constitutional Convention delegates.

5.   It was during his incumbency that a Constitutional Convention was openly, flagrantly and shamelessly subverted with fat "payola" envelopes, triggering a massive expose of lurid pay-offs in the very precinct of Malacañang. And when his Con-Con manipulations began to falter, Marcos, according to Ninoy, declared martial rule, jailed the independent and opposition leaders who opposed his wishes in the Convention, and rammed through a Marcos Constitution in record time.

6.   It was during his incumbency, Ninoy said, when a few favored presidential cronies cornered billions of loanable funds of government financing institutions while the rest of the business community starved for capital, when the national economy teetered on the brink of near-total collapse as a result of massive graft and gross mismanagement and when, finally, the Filipino lost his freedoms and the flame of liberty was snuffed.[10]

PRESIDENT Marcos and the government prosecutors threw the book at Ninoy and found him guilty of every conceivable crime from illegal possession of firearms, through murder and arson to subversion. In the end, to cap his trial which no one seriously believed had factual basis, Ninoy Aquino was finally sentenced to death.

But nobody really believed that the sentence would be implemented, that Ninoy would be executed for having been found guilty of innumerable "crimes." Meanwhile his case had been brought to the Supreme Court for review.

While waiting for the Supreme Court decision, Ninoy was stricken with *angina pectoris* or severe chest pains at his Fort Bonifacio detention quarters on March 19, 1980. He was brought to the Philippine Heart Center for Asia, a project of Mrs. Imelda R. Marcos. He requested President Marcos for authority to seek treatment in the United States when it was discovered that he needed a heart bypass operation. The President approved his request for travel, subject to the approval of the Supreme Court. His request was sent May 7 and the President approved it at 10'oclock that night.

In the morning of May 8, his departure date, Ninoy was visited at his Heart Center suite by Mrs. Marcos to convey to him the President's approval of his request. She was accompanied by Maj. Gen. Fabian C. Ver, Chief of Staff of the Armed Forces of the Philippines, and Vice Governor Ismael A. Mathay Jr. of Metro Manila. Mrs. Marcos stayed with Aquino for about one and a half hours. During that period she telephoned Deputy Foreign Minister Jose Ingles to expedite the travel papers of Ninoy and his family. She requested U.S. Ambassador Richard Murphy to grant visas to the Aquino party to enable them to take the 6 p.m. flight of the Philippine Air Lines to the United States. Then she called Philippine Air Lines President Roman Cruz Jr. to facilitate the tickets and insure their accommodations. Having done her part, the President's wife wished Ninoy and his family well.[11]

Before Mrs. Marcos left, the former Senator removed from his neck a golden chain with a crucifix and handed it to her, asking her to give it to the President, saying it was his own *anting-anting* or amulet for the past seven years.

On the appointed date of departure Ninoy Aquino, accompanied by his wife Cory and three of their five children, took the PAL flight for the United States where he would enter Baylor Medical Center in Dallas, Texas, for his coronary bypass operation. To Dr. Avelino Aventura, director of the Heart Center, he left a note thanking him for his concern and the efficiency of his staff and complimenting Mrs. Marcos, of whom he had been most critical, for giving the people such an institution as the Heart Center.

Then he took off on his flight to the United States, a flight that would take him closer to his rendezvous with history — and immortality.[12]

THE Aquinos settled in Boston, Massachusetts after Ninoy had undergone a triple heart bypass in Dallas, Texas. They stayed in their house in Newton, a well-to-do suburb which they made their main residence during their three-year stay in the United States. Ninoy and Cory also owned a 17-acre (7-hectare) country estate in Brookfield, Massachusetts which they purchased in 1981, about a year after going to the United States. The property, part of a family trust, was being sold (as of April 1986) for $50,000.[13]

The house in Boston where Ninoy and his family lived together during the last three years of his life had been taken over by the Aquino Foundation, a group of Filipinos in Boston, mostly doctors, who pay the monthly amortization on the house and hope to own it eventually and to maintain it as a typical Filipino home, in Ninoy's honor, possibly with students admitted as lodgers. It was a nice house, says Cory, looking back with fondness to their life in Boston.

"We chose that house because of its ideal location," she says, "just across from Boston College, the biggest Catholic University in the United States, run by Jesuits, where my third daughter was studying, and also very near my youngest daughter's school. So that was the prime consideration. And Ninoy could drive to Harvard. After Camp Bonifacio it was such a beautiful change for him. We were living like a regular family again. All of us were there. The first year, no, because our son Noynoy had to finish his fourth year college in Manila. But afterwards all of us were there and it was the first time in a long time that we were all together."[14]

In fact, Ninoy had been putting on weight, says Cory, though he had been shockingly thin when released from Fort Bonifacio. He was determined, however, not to return to his old stoutness.

In Boston Cory went back happily to being a housewife. She played the role of companion to her husband. An Aquino friend from those years, Dov Ronen of the Harvard Center for International Affairs, recalled that: "She was in the background all the time. I never heard her express her own political view. When I talked politics with Ninoy, Cory was sitting on the side, smiling."

But Cory was not as meek as she might once had been. A professor who knew the Aquinos then, Scott Thompson, remembers one dinner party he gave for the couple. After dinner Thompson's wife suggested that the ladies leave the men to their cigars, as was the custom of Americans. Cory made it clear that she wanted to stay where she was. Says Thompson: "It was not done with any bravado and she wasn't making a statement. She was involved in the conversation and she didn't want to leave. And she knew, as the guest of honor's wife and a woman of wealth and breeding, that she could get away with it."[15]

Cory loved to cook, for Ninoy, especially, and she had a separate oven to use for her specialty — Peking duck. She usually prepared that dish for Ninoy's birthday. And she served it to him the night before he flew back to the Philippines in August 1983.

Cory and the Aquino children had pleasant memories of Boston; she had likened her family's three-year residency in Boston to life in legendary Camelot. Even Ninoy himself was fully adapted to the place, where he enjoyed teaching fellowships at Harvard and at the Massachusetts Institute of Technology. A Filipino journalist who had waited for him at the Harvard campus grounds was pleasantly surprised to see him for the first time since Manila; when Ninoy emerged, he looked neat and formal as a diplomat, in a dark suit and tie. "He was thinner and I remembered him to be in Manila, and seemed more reserved. The brash politician of old had mellowed into a smoother, suaver, more cosmopolitan Ninoy. When he spoke, there were traces of a Yankee drawl, but it was natural and unobtrusive, pleasant to listen to as he identified buildings and people passing, recounted the highlights of the lecture he had just delivered, how accommodating the university had been to extend his fellowship for another year."[16]

Ninoy's house in the Harvard campus grounds was described as one of the cottages outlying the university which had no fences, with lawns spilling into one another, heavy with flowers and scented with the smell of pine. It was a cozy rustic cottage set on the slight incline that was called Chestnut Hill. The living and dining rooms were spacious but modestly furnished, with a minimum of personal touches, as though they were sitting rooms for the public. The kitchen was more the hub of the household where Cory, two Filipino doctor friends and the Aquino children were lounging about at the time of the journalist's visit (May 1981, when Boston was as chilly as Baguio City on a December night), watching a football game on TV.

The next day, after a brief tour of Boston, the visitors saw Ninoy again; he could have passed for a campus "preppie." Ninoy looked trim, eager and boyish in a pair of sneakers, levis and a polo shirt that fit snugly round his flat tummy. There was "a freshness and confidence about him, a bounce to his walk and an air of immediacy about everything he did that was infectious. This was the unsinkable youthfulness that had survived Fort Bonifacio, and I looked and looked again, trying to figure how seven years in captivity had vanished from his mien without a trace."[17]

CORY remembers their life in Boston with nostalgia and fondness, which is perhaps why she likens it to life in legendary Camelot. They were very close together then, a continuation of their life when he was still incarcerated at Fort Bonifacio, and Wednesdays, Saturdays and Sundays were visitation days she always looked forward to. In Boston the chilling possibility of something terrible happening to them later on seemed to bring them closer together. Discussing possible scenarios for his homecoming, for instance, Cory and Ninoy were both certain he would be taken straight to Fort Bonifacio upon arrival in Manila and resume his life as a detainee. This thought

frightened Cory for it brought her bitter memories of 1972-1980.
So unsettled and scared would she be that she had to seek the help
of their psychiatrist-friends for assurance that this second time would
not be as bad and terrible as the first.

She remembers Ninoy speaking with dread about the possibility
of Imelda Marcos meeting him at the airport in Manila. "*Lagot na*
(That's the end)," Ninoy told her once. "I'll never be able to regain
my credibility."[18]

His apprehension had a basis. When Marcos allowed them to
leave the country in 1980 they were aware of speculations that
Ninoy did not really have heart trouble but that he had in fact
entered into a "deal" with Marcos and his wife. And now that Ninoy
was coming home there was ugly talk again of a deal; otherwise, why
would Ninoy, brilliant and perceptive that he was, insist on coming
home? Cory thinks this is the sad part about Filipinos. "We always
want to think the worst of other people. This thing was so dismaying
to me when I heard it. *Sabi ko*, 'Wow, Ninoy had to die,' if only to
prove that he really meant to bring about peace."[19]

Having gone through at least three crises in their life Cory had
thought they had already passed the worst possible thing — "until
something really bad happens and you think, *naku, meron pa pala.*
(God, there's something else!)" Ninoy had been encouraging her then
to write but she could not find time to do so. Later she turned to
writing haikus in English, and remembers this one very well:

> The worst of my life is over, I
>   hope,
> And may the best things, please,
>   come soon.[20]

She said that when she read the haiku to Ninoy he said he was
sorry but he thought she was in for more things. Cory could not
understand what he meant and she asked, what could be worse than
this? She felt they had already gone through his incarceration, his
40-day hunger strike that almost cost him his life, his heart attack
that led to a triple bypass surgery. Was she not entitled to better
things? But Ninoy, said Cory, was so convinced that when they went
home they had to continue, that they would never be away from
excitement.

And they all knew they would have to return to the Philippines
someday. Thus, during those last few weeks in Boston they tried to
crowd everything into every moment, savoring each meal shared,
enjoying each outing no matter how simple, "wringing out of every

second they were together the joy that had been denied them during the seven years Ninoy was in prison." Cory herself was counting on spending at least two more weeks in Boston to wind up her packing; for his part, Ninoy had had the foresight to ship his books home, saying he would need them when he re-entered Fort Bonifacio.

The Aquino children refer to the days in Boston as "the three years of togetherness." Ballsy, the eldest, speaks of rummaging through warehouse sales with Ninoy, an adventure they both loved, and consulting with him on plans for her December (1983) wedding. She misses her father when thoughts turn to Boston. The Aquino family had never been as complete as it was then, Ballsy states, as even in the past year "we were hardly complete in the evenings for dinner. Mom was never this busy. Kris lived with my lola because she was studying and Pinky; is in the States." Ballsy herself had gotten married in 1983 and now lives with her husband, Eldon Cruz, in a little house built for them at a corner of the Aquino compound on Times street.

According to Ballsy they had decided to push through with the wedding because they felt it would have made her father happy and, besides, he had already known of the plans. She recalls that Ninoy would even make her wedding his last reason, when all others had failed to convince his friends, that he was doing the right thing in coming back. "He would tell them, jokingly of course, 'no, I really have to go back because Ballsy wants to get married there,'" she recalls with a smile.[21]

Viel, the fourth child, had always been very sure of what she personally wanted for her father. "If he just got out of politics and maybe just became a professor in Harvard, that would have been fine. Look, my Dad's great — I know he is, and it's an honor. But given a choice, I'd rather have an ordinary father — to have him still at home, to have him still alive."

She cherishes most the years in Boston, and this is always her reference point in the moments when she misses Ninoy. Coming home to their Quezon City residence has not been too painful for Viel although the head of the house is missing because, in her own words, "more or less, I don't know what it is like to come home to Times and see him there so there's nothing really I can say I miss. He'd been in Bonifacio all that time and before that he was so busy in the Senate."[22]

NINOY Aquino in Boston was a many-faceted genius unmarked by the trauma of his incarceration at Fort Bonifacio for seven long years

and seven months. The military had tried to break him in Fort Magsaysay, Laur, Nueva Ecija by putting him in solitary, keeping his
glasses away from him, his clothes and books, and locking him up in
a four-by-five-meter cell where there was nothing to do but stare at
the blank wall as the days passed without a perceptible break into
nights, and the nights into an interminable month. He had coped by
thinking back, as far back into his life, down to his earliest remembered boyhood, reconstructing, in his alert and agile mind, the
passage of events in chronology, forcing himself to remember names
and places, and conversations and events — things he had worn,
things his teachers had said at school, names of classmates and play-
mates, the littlest and the most significant events — anything to
occupy himself and keep his mind off the sordid, sorry chapter of his
life as a solitary prisoner who was not sure if death would come to
him on the morrow. They failed to break Ninoy in body or in
spirit.[23]

And so in Boston he was as good as new, as if he had not gone
through hell, as if his long, horrible ordeal had left neither wound nor
scar on his person. He was sprightly, bouncy, full of youthful vitality, pulsing with boyish elan, a philosopher-politician whose genius
included an ability to make a difficult feat look easy and natural,
a rapport with all breeds of people, a quiet blending into the ivy-
covered walls of academe.

One close associate of Ninoy in his years of exile in Boston, Professor
Benjamin Houston Brown, Director Fellows Program of the Center for
International Affairs at Harvard University, saw through the surface
veneer of the Filipino political thinker and intellectual — and saw three
Ninoys in one single person. "None of us who knew Ninoy Aquino at
Harvard can ever forget him," Brown described his colleague in his
speech eulogizing him at the Holy Family church on August 26, 1983 in
New York City. "The brisk walk — the clear, precise gestures — the
lightning-quick mind — the electric enthusiasm. With Ninoy, everything was 'up front' as they say. He seemed to hold nothing back. Seldom
have I known anyone who revealed himself so fully and defined himself
so clearly — who seemed so much of one piece."

"Yet there was a paradox. With this evident simplicity, he was
also very complex. If often seemed to me that there were many
Ninoys, not always compatible on the face of it — and the harmon-
ious blend of them that we knew was a kind of miracle.

"There was, first of all, the public man, the political leader,
with the sensitive antennae — the alert eye and ear — the quivering
nostril — registering every nuance of the movement of opinion and

events — committed to action, engaged in the fullest degree.

"Second, there was Ninoy the thinker, detached in analyses, hungry for knowledge and ideas — the Ninoy who read everything, forgot nothing, and always had what was germane to the discussion right at his fingertips. If I am not mistaken, he was the most comprehensively informed public figure I have ever known. But reserved, skeptical.

"Henri Bergson enjoined the young men of his generation to think like men of action and act like men of thought. Ninoy seemed to embody that form of excellence in the fullest measure.

"What made this possible was the third Ninoy, a kind of presiding officer, who kept order in the house, and guided all the conflicting tendencies of this complex personality to a high purpose. I am speaking now of Ninoy, the man of conscience — profoundly concerned about issues of right and wrong — about the compatibility of means and ends — and especially, as his final statement suggests, about the need for a program of non-violent political and social change that could be effective in the Philippine context.

"I think it was this Ninoy — the man of conscience — and I should add, of faith — who made the important decisions, including of course, the fateful decision to return, which he made against the advice of many of his friends, including myself."[24]

Ninoy Aquino had, after three years of exile in Boston, decided to return to the Philippines against the advice of his closest friends, even against the advice of Imelda R. Marcos who had informed him of the dangers to his life awaiting him in Manila. The Harvard faculty, including Professor Brown of the prestigious Fellows Program at the Harvard Center for International Affairs, a conference room of which had been dedicated to Ninoy's name to ensure he would not be forgotten, had unanimously rejected as suicidal and preposterous Ninoy's growing obsession to return to Manila. [25]

Ninoy's purpose in returning to his native land, according to one version, was to help the opposition rather than himself. For while in detention he had begun to shed all personal ambition and to see a larger, more magnanimous role for himself — to be a kingmaker for the opposition, a peacemaker for his people, to manage, if necessary, the campaign of any candidate of the opposition for the Presidency against Marcos.

Another version would indicate that he had another reason for wanting to come home. When he was being interviewed by Teodoro Benigno, Manila bureau chief of the *Agence France Presse* on August 1, 1983 in Boston, their conversation veered to the topic of "macho mystique." Ninoy, according to Benigno, asked him which the Filipinos preferred — courage or intelligence? The journalist answered, "Both." Ninoy said, "Choose one." Benigno replied, " Courage." "Right you are!" exclaimed Ninoy, adding that Filipinos as a rule went for fighters who slugged their way through,like Dommy Ursua, Speed Cabanela and even Pancho Villa, fighters who always took the offensive, not the counterpunchers. They preferred go-for-broke fighters who kept on wading in and throwing punches, come what may. Then Ninoy, the journalist said, told him:

"That's why I'm coming home. I want to prove to the Filipinos that I am not afraid. Because I know they respect courage above anything else!"[26]

But America's most widely syndicated columnist, Jack Anderson, saw a different reason for Ninoy Aquino's decision to return to the Philippines. Citing reports of the United States Central Intelligence Agency (CIA), he writes in his column — *The Washington Post*, August 10, 1986 — that politics came to a boil inside Malacanang as Ferdinand Marcos's health deteriorated. According to the CIA, Imelda intensified her political activities and struck a secret alliance with the army's chief of staff, Gen. Fabian Ver.

"In 1983," Anderson writes, "whispers reached Ninoy Aquino that his ailing rival might not survive much longer. The time had come, he decided, for him to return to the Philippines and make his bid for the Presidency. He had no plan to overthrow Marcos but wanted to be available to succeed him."

From the defense intelligence agency came word that Imelda Marcos arranged a secret meeting with Ninoy in May 1983. She reportedly warned him that assassins might await him if he returned.

"He disregarded the warning and, shortly thereafter, flew back to the Philippines," says Anderson. "He was gunned down as he stepped off the plane. Secret intelligence reports suggested cautiously that he may have been murdered on orders from Imelda."

Apparently Marcos had no advance knowledge of the assassination plot. Anderson quotes Filipino columnist Teodoro F. Valencia as saying that he was present in Malacañang when Marcos learned Aquino had been shot, and that Marcos realized the gun that killed Aquino would backfire against himself. In fact Marcos was so furious he began throwing objects at his aides, according to the celebrated American columnist.

ARRIVAL STATEMENT OF SENATOR BENIGNO AQUINO, JR., AT THE MANILA INTERNATIONAL AIRPORT TO BE DELIVERED BEFORE HIS WELCOMERS ON AUGUST 21, 1983

I have returned on my free will to join the ranks of those struggling to restore our rights and freedoms through non-violence.

I seek no confrontation. I only pray and will strive for a genuine national reconciliation founded on justice.

I am prepared for the worst, and have decided against the advice of my mother, my spiritual adviser, many of my tested friends and a few of my most valued political mentors.

A death sentence awaits me. Two more subversion charges, both calling for death penalties, have been filed since I left three years ago and are now pending with the courts.

I could have opted to seek political asylum in America, but I feel it is my duty, as it is the duty of every Filipino, to suffer with his people especially in time of crisis.

I never sought nor have I been given any assurance or promise of leniency by the regime. I return voluntarily armed only with a clear conscience and fortified in the faith that in the end justice will emerge triumphant.

According to Gandhi, the willing sacrifice of the innocent is the most powerful answer to insolent tyranny that has yet been conceived by God and man.

Three years ago, when I left for an emergency heart bypass operation, I hoped and prayed that the rights and freedoms of our people would soon be restored, that living conditions would improve and that bloodletting would stop.

Rather than move forward, we have moved backward. The killings have increased, the economy has taken a turn for the worse and the human-rights situation has deteriorated.

During the martial-law period, the Supreme Court heard petitions for habeas corpus. It is most ironic after martial law has allegedly been lifted, that the Supreme Court last April ruled it can no longer entertain petitions for habeas corpus for persons detained under a Presidential Commitment Order, which covers all so-called national security cases and which under present circumstances can cover almost anything.

The country is far advanced in her times of trouble. Economic, social and political problems bedevil the Filipino. These problems may be surmounted if we are united. But we can be united only if all the rights and freedoms enjoyed before September 21, 1972 are fully restored.

The Filipino asked for nothing more, but will surely accept nothing less, than all the rights and freedoms guaranteed by the 1935 Constitution — the most sacred legacies from the founding fathers.

Yes, the Filipino is patient, but there is a limit to his patience. Must we wait until that patience snaps?

The nationwide rebellion is escalating and threatens to explode into a bloody revolution. There is a growing cadre of young Filipinos who have finally come to realize that freedom is never granted, it is taken. Must we relive the agonies and the bloodletting of the past that brought forth our republic or can we sit down as brothers and sisters and discuss our differences with reason and goodwill?

I have often wondered how many disputes could have been settled easily had the disputants only dared to define their terms.

So as to leave no room for misunderstanding, I shall define my terms:

1.   Six years ago, I was sentenced to die before a firing squad by a military tribunal whose jurisdiction I steadfastly refused to recognize. It is now time for the regime to decide. Order my immediate execution or set me free.

I was sentenced to die for allegedly being the leading Communist leader. I am not a Communist, never was and never will be.

2.   National reconciliation and unity can be achieved but only with justice, including justice for our Moslem and Ifugao brothers. There can be no deal with a dictator. No compromise with dictatorship.

3.   In a revolution there can really be no victors, only victims. We do not have to destroy in order to build.

4.   Subversion stems from economic, social and political causes and will not be solved by purely military solutions; it can be curbed not with ever increasing repression but with a more equitable distribution of wealth, more democracy and more freedom.

5.   For the economy to get going once again, the working man must be given his just and rightful share of his labor, and to the owners and managers must be restored the hope where there is so much uncertainty if not despair.

On one of the long corridors of Harvard University are carved in granite the words of Archibald MacLeish: "How shall freedom be defended? By arms when it is attacked by arms; by truth when it is attacked by lies; be democratic faith when it is attacked by authoritarian dogma. Always, and in the final act, by determination and faith."

I return from exile and to an uncertain future with only determination and faith to offer — faith in our people and faith in God.

(Reprinted from *The New York Times*,
August 22, 1983)

More seriously, Aquino believed that Marcos was the key to a peaceful resolution to the unrest, lack of democracy, brutal killings, corruption and the restoration of basic human rights and a sound economy to the Filipino people. From reports of the deterioration of the Philippine economy as well as Marcos's health, Aquino believed that time was of the essence, and that he must make an attempt to convince Marcos of the importance of a peaceful national reconciliation. This was, in Ninoy's own view, the fundamental reason for his decision to return to the Philippines.

Whatever his motivation was, Ninoy Aquino did take the risk and decided to return to the Philippines from the safety and comfort of America. The prizefighter, the peacemaker, the potential kingmaker, dared to return home — only to be shot to death at the airport in Manila.

That shot ended the mortal life of Benigno Aquino Jr. but inaugurated a myth, a legend. It also signalled the beginning of the fall of Ferdinand E. Marcos from the pinnacle of power.

SIX

Appointment with Death

I have returned on my free will to join the ranks of those struggling to restore our rights and freedoms through nonviolence.

I seek no confrontation. I only pray and will strive for a genuine national reconciliation founded on justice.

I return from exile and to an uncertain future with only determination and faith to offer — faith in our people and faith in God.

— Ninoy Aquino, August 21, 1983.

SENATOR Benigno Aquino Jr. decided to return to the Philippines against the advice of those closest to him — his mother, his spiritual adviser, many of his tested friends and a few of his most valued political mentors. Even his friends in academe — Harvard University and Massachusetts Institute of Technology — were, cautiously, against his homecoming after three years of exile in the United States. He knew that a death sentence, by firing squad or musketry, awaited him in Manila and two more subversion charges, both calling for death penalties, had been filed since he left three years ago and were pending in the courts.

Ninoy could have taken the easy way out to escape the real and imminent danger to his life simply by opting to seek political asylum in America. But he chose to meet his fate head-on because he felt it was his duty, as it is the duty of every Filipino, to suffer with his people especially in time of crisis. According to Ninoy he never sought nor had been given any assurance or promise of leniency by the Marcos regime. He was returning voluntarily, armed only with a clear conscience and fortified in the faith that in the end justice would emerge triumphant. He believed, with the great Gandhi, that the willing sacrifice of the innocent was the most powerful answer to insolent tyranny that had yet been conceived by God and man.

He was returning to help the people win back their lost rights and freedoms through nonviolence and strive for a genuine national reconciliation founded on justice. He knew that returning from exile he was facing an uncertain future, equipped only with determination and faith — faith in the Filipino and faith in God.

AFTER his successful heart bypass surgery at Baylor University Medical Center in Texas, Ninoy accepted prestigious fellowships at Harvard University and the Massachusetts Institute of Technology. While one of the conditions for his release from prison was that he should not speak out while in the United States, he decided three months later that his duty to his people was paramount to his "pact with the devil." He lectured, studied and wrote about historic and current peaceful transitions from dictatorships to democracies. He travelled to several countries to discuss and discover possible solutions for the return of democracy in the Philippines. He served as a peacemaker among exiled representatives of warring factions within the Philippines and tried to inform the world about what life was really like in his country.[1]

During this period of exile Ninoy was said to have reached a fuller political maturity. He had "grown" and made the journey from charismatic politician to statesman of the world. He became a Gandhi believer, having studied Gandhi's works during his seven years and seven months imprisonment and watched the movie on the great Indian exponent of civil disobedience and nonviolence. He found Gandhi the embodiment of all he believed in: peace, human concern and moral leadership.

Martial law had been lifted technically by President Marcos in January 1981 but he continued to rule by decree, aided by a rubber-stamp parliament or Batasang Pambansa and a subservient Supreme Court which never ruled against him on any issue brought before it.

Ninoy Aquino watched with concern as the military under Marcos continued to grow in size and influence. At the same time the increasing number of radical, revolutionary guerrillas in the hinterlands from north to south of the nation bothered him; he became increasingly concerned that democracy would not be restored. He could no longer stay on the sidelines.

The Senator met with Imelda Marcos in New York in December 16, 1980. Mrs. Marcos showed him, during that meeting, a film of a dinner she had hosted in honor of former President Richard M. Nixon and pointed out several prominent people among the guests, stating that Nixon was back in the Reagan camp. In the videotape, Nixon has grand praises for Imelda and refers to her as "The Angel from Asia."

Ninoy related later to Steve Psinakis that in his December

meeting with Imelda Marcos, "She told me that you and I have sent assassination teams to Manila to knock off some of her people. She said if we do, they'll do the same to us and no one will come out ahead. She told me we should put a stop to that . . . She sounded confident that the Reagan administration will go after us here, especially you."[2]

Thus, it is reported, Mrs. Marcos was not only threatening Senator Aquino but was also claiming influence with two American Presidents to bring about harm to an American citizen, Psinakis. Three days later she reiterated the threat to Psinakis.

Sometime in May 1983, Ninoy made a firm decision to return home, which was the third of the conditions demanded by Marcos upon his release from solitary confinement.

NINOY Aquino was determined to organize the Philippine opposition for the parliamentary elections scheduled for May 1984 should his peacemaking efforts fail to convince Marcos that democratic reforms were essential for the future of the Philippines.

During the wake for former Senator Gerardo Roxas in New York, Ninoy and Imelda saw each other again. During a breakfast meeting after the wake (Roxas was eventually buried in the Philippines) Aquino mentioned to Imelda that his passport was expiring and Mrs. Marcos said she would take care of it. Aquino gave her his passport, but it was never renewed or returned to him.

They met again at the Philippine Center in New York on May 21, 1983. Mrs. Marcos was said to have made several statements and offers to Ninoy, who mentioned to her that he might go home since his fellowships were completed and he wanted to return to his homeland rather than have them renewed for another year. One of the offers allegedly made by Mrs. Marcos was the position of Prime Minister if Ninoy would join the Marcos government. Another offer she reportedly made was for Aquino to set up a business if he continued to stay in the United States.

The truth was that he was hoping to come home to attempt a peaceful reconciliation and improvement of life in a democracy in the Philippines. He also saw the possibility of organizing a legitimate opposition political party and then campaigning for four months before the parliamentary elections in May 1984.

The final attempt of Mrs. Marcos to dissuade Ninoy from returning to his country was to tell him not to come home because, according to her, there were plots to kill him.

Even before that May meeting, President Marcos had urged Aquino to remain in the United States. As part of the apparent lifting of martial law in January 1981, presidential elections were set for June that year. Marcos, still ruling by decree, could not lose under the situation. He publicly challenged Ninoy to run against him but privately sent former Senator Lorenzo M. Tañada to the United States in February 1981 to tell Aquino that he would be rearrested if he came back.

Ninoy applied for travel papers in June 1981 despite Imelda's veiled threat. But the Philippine consulate in New York refused to issue him the papers because the military intelligence had allegedly uncovered an assassination plot. In July Deputy Foreign Minister Pacifico Castro warned all international air carriers not to allow Aquino to board their planes without proper documentation at the risk of losing their landing rights to the Philippines. Japan Air Lines, for instance, was told it could lose its flight privileges to the Philippines if it carried Aquino.

On August 2 Defense Minister Juan Ponce Enrile joined in. He cabled Aquino to delay his return for "at least a month, because I have been directed to inform you that we are convinced beyond reasonable doubt that there are plots against your life upon your arrival in the Philippines."[3] Ninoy responded publicly that he would meet them half way and delay his return two weeks to August 21. He said that should give the government time to catch any plotters and at the same time give his friends and relatives in the Philippines time to prepare a public welcome; on a Sunday his supporters would not be working and could meet him at the airport.

On Saturday, August 13, Ninoy Aquino flew from Boston to Los Angeles. He was armed with a counterfeit passport he had obtained in "a Muslim country" which bore the name of "Marcial Bonifacio." Ninoy took great delight in that name, said his brother-in-law, Ken Kashiwahara, an American ABC newsman on vacation and husband of his sister Lupita, for it stood for martial law and his old prison, Fort Bonifacio.

Ninoy hoped to keep the Philippine government, which had apparently been monitoring his movements, in the dark. He moved from Singapore to Malaysia, back to Singapore and finally to Taipei, capital of Taiwan, on Friday, August 19. There he was met by Kashiwahara whose wife Lupita and another of Ninoy's sisters, Tessie, had preceded him to Manila to help organize a homecoming reception.

Taipei had been chosen as the final embarkation point because it did not have diplomatic relations with the Philippines, a fact that reduced the chance of discovery by Philippine officials.

From his hotel in Taipei Ninoy Aquino telephoned friends in the Philippines. In one of the calls he was told he might be shot at the airport. Apprehensive that the call could alert the Nationalist Chinese government which might not allow him to board the plane, an intermediary for Ninoy, alias Marcial Bonifacio, checked with the government and was told that they had never heard of Aquino and did not know that he was in Taiwan.

PERHAPS from experience as a former newspaperman, Aquino believed that being accompanied by journalists was advisable from two standpoints: it would insure that his story would get maximum publicity even if he were kept on the plane or jailed on his return, and the media's presence would reduce the possibility of an attempt on his life. Consequently, by Saturday about 10 journalists had congregated in Taipei to accompany him on the final leg of his journey home. And later in the afternoon of August 20, the group was joined by two television crews from Japan.

Cory explains why Ninoy chose to come back in the month of August. According to Cory:[4]

"The first scheduled date was August 7 and the reason for that was Senator Tañada's 85th birthday on August 10. Also, August 7 was a Sunday. I think they had decided that a Sunday would be the best day for coming back because then people would, well, be free to go to the airport to meet him, to welcome him. And there would be five or six flights coming in that Sunday afternoon; you would have a crowd there. So Doy Laurel felt it would be the best time, the most opportune time for Ninoy to arrive. But when Ninoy got the telegram from Johnny Ponce Enrile saying it would be best to delay his arrival, Ninoy said, well, why should he be unreasonable?"

Moreover, he had no travel documents yet. Says Cory:

"Ninoy did not have a valid passport. When he applied at the Philippine consulate he had indicated that he needed his papers right away because he was leaving on such and such a date and intended to be in Manila on August 7. But they told Ninoy they had to wait for the directive from Manila on whether to issue him his travel papers or not."

She confirmed that Imelda Marcos took Ninoy's passport and did not renew or return it: "When Ninoy saw Imelda on the occasion of Gerry Roxas's death — this was in April 1983 — he told her of his plans to return home and how therefore he would have his passport renewed. And she said: 'Give it to me and I'll take care of it.' And that was the last he saw of the passport.''

But Ninoy, as we have seen, did get a passport under the name of Marcial Bonifacio, and Cory saw it was useless to stop him from leaving.

"I knew we couldn't stay permanently in the United States and that Ninoy was longing to come home," Cory relates to Nick Joaquin. "He felt that three years was long enough to be away. Besides, what he had gone there for, he had already accomplished. He had survived a triple bypass operation and was feeling very good, in very good health. Also, he had already done two years at Harvard and one year at MIT. Whatever learning there was to do, he had maybe done it already during those years."[5]

On August 13, 1983, the former Senator left Boston.

Cory recalls that the night before, both of them could not sleep. "I felt rather chilly," she recalls, "which was unusual since it was August and supposed to be summer, and though the night was cool it wasn't cold enough to make one feel chilly. However, I decided to get up and put on socks. And I said to Ninoy: 'You know, this is exactly how I felt after you were arrested, the day of martial law.' And he said, 'Oh, let's not talk about it; I told you long ago this is what we have to do.' And I said: 'Yeah. I just wanted to let you know how I felt.' So that was that."

They heard mass the next morning with the children, Ninoy's flight was at noon. People had come to the house to say goodbye. At the airport, before Ninoy disappeared into the embarkation area, Cory said: "Just call me up at every stop."

His first stop, says Cory, was in Los Angeles. He called up from there and Cory told him he was in the papers: "You remember that reporter who was with us yesterday? Apparently you didn't tell him not to write about your leaving and so it's in the *Boston Globe*. And people know you're in Los Angeles now, on your way back to the Philippines."

During the stopover in Tokyo Ninoy came upon an Indonesian friend. He asked the Indonesian to spread the word around that he was going to Indonesia. He was obviously doing everything to cover his tracks. When Cory next heard from him, Ninoy was in Hongkong. He did not actually say so, but Ninoy and Cory had devised a code whereby she could guess where he was without his having to say so. He had arranged to fly to Manila from Taipei to avoid getting any officials in trouble over his flight since there are no diplomatic relations between Taipei and Manila.

In Boston Cory was busy packing their things up. She had told

Ninoy that within two weeks she would be through with the packing and would be able to follow him to Manila. Ninoy had asked if she would not prefer to stay in Boston with the children and she had replied that the idea was for them to be together, and what would they do in Boston without him? It was settled that they would join him in Manila as soon as possible. One plan was, in fact, for Ninoy to leave with two of the children, Noynoy and Kris, but this became impossible when none of them could get travel documents.[6]

In another call from Manila on Saturday, Ninoy was told that opposition leaders would not be allowed to meet him at the plane. He told Kashiwahara it was a "bad sign," since it could mean the plane might be turned around upon landing without letting him out, or that he might be whisked off to prison incommunicado. He told his brother-in-law when they were alone that he felt assassination was only a "remote possibility" but nevertheless showed him he had a bullet-proof vest.

"But if they hit me on the head," Ninoy said, "I'm a goner."[7]

After midnight Ninoy drifted off to sleep, still fingering his rosary. Then, four hours later, he phoned Cory and his children in Boston. Cory read a Bible passage to Ninoy, and he spoke briefly with each child. As he was talking to them his emotion got the better of him and he began to cry softly. After hanging up he wrote a letter to each of his children.

By the time Ninoy reached the Chiang Kai-shek International Airport at 10:10 a.m. his spirits had revived. His car circled the airport so he could arrive at the last minute while Kashiwahara and a friend checked through the luggage of "Marcial Bonifacio." He got through immigration without much difficulty and was then pulled aside by two Chinese officials. He later told Kashiwahara that it was the Taiwan garrison commander who wanted "to make sure I got through OK." But, Ninoy added, the commander said something very curious. "He said he was called that morning by Philippine Air Lines and was told to take good care of me."

China Airlines Flight 811 bearing Aquino for Manila was a Boeing 767, a jumbo jet carrying over a hundred passengers. It cleared Taipei at 11:15 a.m.

IN Manila a huge number of opposition supporters, by the busloads, had begun arriving at the Manila International Airport. Yellow ribbons and strips of yellow cloth were draped over the buses and jeeps and trunks of trees. The numerous friends and admirers of Ninoy Aquino were identified by yellow ribbons and even yellow shirts and blouses, a symbol from the song about a returning freed prisoner, "Tie a Yellow Ribbon Round the Old Oak Tree." Some of the most revered names of the opposition were on hand, including the Senator's 73-year-old mother, Aurora Aquino, and Ninoy's sisters, brothers and in-laws. Family and close friends of Ninoy were packed into the V.I.P. Lounge of the airport while thousands filled the parking lot. The welcoming party easily numbered more than 20,000.

At 11:30 a.m. TV cameramen and other reporters on hand were ordered to congregate at the entrance to the tunnel of the jetway at Gate 8 and further instructed not to leave that location. Later it was reported that some 2,000 military people had been assigned by the government to secure the area and protect the returning Senator.

As recounted in the book, *Aquino Assassination*, Ninoy Aquino wore a white safari suit, the same suit he had worn during his trip to Texas three years before. As expected of him, the voluble Ninoy spent much time talking to the press. He was alert, lively and, as usual, sharp and witty. At one point two Filipino women, both young and pretty, walked along the aisle and kissed him on the cheek, laughing as they wiped away the lipstick smudge on his face. The gesture apparently pleased Ninoy who laughed along, too, and began shaking their hands and wishing them well. No one could have known that Ninoy Aquino, at that moment in time, was about to keep a secret appointment with death.

As the plane entered Philippine territory over the island of Luzon, Senator Aquino, occupying Seat 14C on the aisle, prayed silently, his fingers sliding along the beads of his rosary. Now the plane began its descent over rice fields and sprawling villages near the airport. Ninoy then walked briskly toward the rest room, where he put on his bullet-proof vest and covered it with his white shirt and safari jacket. Then he handed his gold watch to his brother-in-law, saying: "I just want you to have it." As an afterthought, Ninoy added: "Don't forget to go to my house as soon as we land and have someone take my belongings to me in prison." He thought he would be taken directly to prison. He told Kashiwahara that in his bag were four days of clothes for the first few days in prison.

The China Airlines plane touched down. "Ninoy," said his brother-in-law, "we're home." Ninoy looked up at him and smiled.

As the giant plane swung smoothly around toward the jetway to Gate 8, a crowd could be seen beyond the main terminal. Alongside the plane a blue mobile van of the Aviation Security Command (AVSECOM) tasked with providing security for the airport pulled

up. Instantly the van's door opened and soldiers, wearing Constabulary or AVSECOM uniforms, spilled from the bowels of the van and
rushed to their respective positions to surround the plane, all facing
out away from the aircraft, their high-powered rifles at the ready.
The soldiers were members of teams codenamed "Alfa," "Bravo"
and "Charlie."

The plane's motors were shut off, and three men swiftly entered
the passenger compartment — one in the uniform of the Philippine
Constabulary and two with AVSECOM patches on their khaki uniforms. The Constabulary man passed Ninoy, but an AVSECOM
soldier recognized him and leaned forward and shook Ninoy's hand,
mumbling something in Tagalog. The word "boss" formed by his
mouth was distinguishable. It was 1:14 p.m.

The television crews of the ABC and TBS pushed forward to
catch and record the scene. As Ninoy rose from his seat, one of the
AVSECOM men took his small bag and the other took a firm grip on
his arm and started to lead him down the aisle. Kashiwahara got up
and began to follow saying: "I'm coming with him. I'm his brother-
in-law." But an AVSECOM man with sunglasses told him to sit
down, then turned to follow Ninoy.[8]

The Senator had been smiling, but suddenly his face took on a
stoney, melancholy expression and his mouth became a taut, grim
line.

The television crews and reporters Wakamiya and Matsumoto
then pressed after them with cameras rolling. Kashiwahara and other
reporters followed. A plainclothes security man stood facing the in-
terior of the plane. Two more uniformed men stood guard inside the
mouth of the tunnel to the main terminal — one a Constabulary man
and one from AVSECOM. Four to six more plainclothesmen dressed
in white *polo barongs* were standing guard inside the plane.

Now a side door on the left of the tunnel was opened, leading
to a stairway to the ground. The AVSECOM man who had told
Kashiwahara to sit down was at Ninoy's elbow, and the soldier grip-
ping his wrist was at his right. Suddenly the two military men swung
Ninoy out onto the platform and were followed by two of the uniformed men and a plainclothesman in a white shirt. A second security man, also in white *polo barong* shirt, stepped out onto the platform with his back to the reporters.

Ninoy quickly disappeared from view, and the remaining
uniformed soldier and several plainclothesmen immediately blocked
the doorway to the stairs with their bodies.[9]

At that moment the TBS television crewmen tried to lift their camera over their heads. The hands of a plainclothesman came forward to cover the camera lens while audio booms from both television crews swung high in the air aimed toward the open doorway. The media men pushed, shoved, and jockeyed for position. Then,

"Bang!" A single gunshot, ear-shattering, ominous.

A piercing scream burst from a woman's throat.

Pandemonium broke loose among the people around the stairway door. Reporter Wakamiya heard the shot and saw Senator Aquino pitch forward and fall like a heavy log. Trapped inside the plane, on the aisle, reporter Ueda looked out the window after the sound of the shot. He saw Ninoy Aquino sprawled on the ground, face down, blood spouting from his neck.

Between Ninoy's rising from Seat 14C and the sound of the single gunshot was an incredible period of 50 seconds, it was determined later. The man who would be President had come home from exile — for the last time.

CORY, who was in Boston with the children, sensed the tragedy before she got word about it. As she recalls it:

"I couldn't sleep, I was waiting for his call. It was past midnight. Then Ballsy our eldest came into my room and I asked why. "Aie, Mom,' she said, 'I can't sleep either.' So we talked and then she asked what time it was. It was just then one o'clock. I went to the bathroom, then I decided to pray the rosary. Later, taking account of the 12-hour difference between Boston and Manila, I realized that it was then, between one-ten and one-fifteen, that he was shot. Ballsy and I were awake, and Noynoy was also awake, watching TV. Because we have cable TV he was getting the news, which they have every hour on the hour."[10]

The first call came at around 2:30, says Cory.

"It was a reporter from *Kyodo News Agency* in New York. Ballsy answered the telephone. From the sound of her voice I knew something had happened. I asked her what it was all about and she said: 'Mom, they say somebody has been shot at the airport in Manila and they think it's Dad and they want to know if we've heard.' So I took the phone. 'What's this?' I asked. And the reporter said: 'We have heard from Tokyo that your husband has been shot.' And I said: 'Are you sure?' And he said yes and he wanted to know if I had heard anything and I said no."

By 3 a.m. Cory had put in a lot of calls trying to confirm the report.

Finally she got a call from Tokyo, from Congressman Ishihara, a very good friend of the Aquinos. He said: "Cory, I'm very sorry but I think Ninoy is dead." He had been told by a Japanese correspondent who was with Ninoy (Wakamiya, a freelance journalist) and Wakamiya said Ninoy had been shot in the head. Wakamiya had seen blood spurting from Ninoy's head.

Then Cory told her children the news but added she hoped it was just a rumor. They were crying so she asked them to join her in prayer. Noynoy had caught the report on TV. Then people started calling up one after the other and friends started coming in at around three-thirty. They decided to go to church at six then came back to see more people dropping in to condole with them. She was worried about not getting a call from her family in Manila, and explained it thus:

"They didn't know now to tell me, they didn't know how to break it to me, and anyway they weren't sure themselves until my mother-in-law had seen Ninoy's body. They were still hoping it was a false rumor and that Ninoy was still alive. So I didn't get a call from Manila until much later, after they had called up other friends and had found out I already knew."[11]

On Monday Cory started making arrangements to leave for Manila.

SEVEN

Prelude to the Fall

I have died, I told you. This is a second life I can give up. Besides, if they shoot me, they'll make me a hero.

— Ninoy Aquino, on the eve of his
return to the Philippines.

IT is sometimes difficult to comprehend how a single act of man can transform another man. The execution of Jose Rizal by musketry in 1896 made him a hero whom his countrymen invested with nearly divine qualities. His death stirred and catalyzed his people. It gave them courage and liberated them from fear. It inspired them to band together and resist the Spanish government, the fascistic clergy and their native minions. They knew how risky their resistance would be. But no matter: the death of Rizal had taught them to overcome fear.

The single gunshot that killed Ninoy Aquino as he was alighting from a plane at the Manila airport on August 21, 1983 transformed him into a hero-martyr. Like Rizal, he was accorded near-superhuman qualities and attributes by his countrymen. As in the execution of Rizal, they found courage in his death. It opened their eyes to the need to unite and protest the abuses of the government. Ninoy's death ended their indifference.

Ninoy could have continued staying in the United States and enjoyed life as an academic and scholar and as a political godfather to other opposition leaders. He had found his place and earned the respect of his peers in such important institutions as Harvard University and the Massachusetts Institute of Technology. He was much in demand as a lecturer and resource person especially in his specialized field — politics and government. His own family, from his wife Cory to their children, were having the finest days of their life in their Boston home. That was the only time they were really enjoying his company.

Life in Boston was so unlike his life in the Philippines, where he had been a prisoner since Marcos imposed martial law in 1972. It had been one long hell for him and his family. He knew that his country was gripped by a reign of terror, but there was nothing he could do about it. In fact he himself was a victim of severe injustice and repression. Aside from being condemned to prison he was also facing a death penalty because he had been convicted of subversion and other crimes.

In protest over the injustice he was suffering, he went on a hunger strike and fasted for 40 days. He practically died as a result. When he emerged from the fast, he was emaciated, his dehydrated skin barely clung to his bones, and he was too weak to stand unaided. The few who visited him, like former Senator Jovito Salonga, claimed that Ninoy's breath smelled of death. In 1980 severe attacks of *angina pectoris* almost killed him, and President Marcos was forced to release him temporarily to undergo treatment and surgery in the United States.

Ninoy himself confirmed that the fasting almost killed him. In his own words.

"On the 38th day of my hunger strike, I thought I was as good as dead. A dead man. I have regarded the years that followed as a second life that I should be able to give up. I have already lived and died and I am ready to go."[1]

Aquino said this on the eve of his departure from Boston, according to the newly reopened *Free Press*. He had decided to return to the Philippines. His overriding reasons were to "join the ranks of those struggling to restore our rights and freedoms through nonviolence" and to "strive for a genuine national reconciliation founded on justice."[2]

He knew that dangers awaited him. To be sure, as he himself had told his wife, Cory, he would perhaps be sent back to the military detention center upon his arrival. He could also be the target of assassination as implied by those who had tried to convince him to postpone his return, including First Lady Imelda R. Marcos and Minister Juan Ponce Enrile. No member of his family agreed with his decision. Even his political friends and advisers, including his academic colleagues, were against his coming home. But, as his wife knew very well, Ninoy could be very stubborn once he had made up his mind.

He was said to insist that he believed there was something good in the President, that Marcos would not want to appear in history as the man who took away the liberties of the people and gave them only suffering in return. He wanted to talk to that "good side" of Marcos, Ninoy said. He would propose a caretaker government composed of independent and respected men so that free and honest elections could be held and democracy finally restored. "I think he will agree to that," he said. "Then, first, he must step down, resign. He has had so many years of power! Now, he can resign, he can retire from public office to the thanks of a grateful people that will forget what it had suffered in its joy at being free again."[3]

Reminded that anything could happen to him, that it was not only his freedom that he could lose, Ninoy replied: "This is a second life I can give up. Besides, if they shoot me, they'll make me a hero. What would Rizal have been if the Spaniards had not brought him back and shot him? Just another exile like me to the end of his life."

Before boarding the plane from Taipei for Manila, Ninoy told a television crew accompanying him on that fateful day to be ready with his hand camera because "this action can come very fast. In a matter of three, four minutes it could be all over and I may not be able to talk to you again. Now I am taking precautions. I have my bullet-proof vest. But if they hit me in the head there's nothing we can do."[4]

They did hit him in the head and killed him with just one single shot. And they made him a hero.

In effect, those responsible for his death saved him from a fate worse than death itself: oblivion. His long absence from the public eye had robbed Ninoy of much of his glamor. Worse, it had opened him to suspicions of selling out to the Marcoses in exchange for his freedom. The unexcelled tactician that he was, Marcos denied Ninoy the chance to be immortalized as a martyr. Although Ninoy had been meted a death penalty, Marcos refused to execute him. He even allowed his lawyers to go to the Supreme Court to have the case reviewed. In addition he granted Ninoy some liberal concessions under the circumstances: regular visitations by his wife and children, access to books and other publications, a television set in his prison cell. Finally he allowed the prisoner to leave for the United States for heart surgery. Much earlier, in fact, he allowed Ninoy to run for the Batasang Pambansa in 1978 and even granted him an opportunity to appear on television to campaign.

Those who knew the mind of Marcos must have known that he was not doing all this to Ninoy, his nemesis, without a purpose.

The murder of Ninoy Aquino at the airport changed everything. It saved him from sliding off into obscurity. In the eyes of a great number of Filipinos he immediately assumed an aura of greatness.

Whatever suspicions the people had about his integrity and patriotism were erased including his share of virtue and sin.[5]

Alive, he was an ordinary mortal like anybody else. In death, he was transformed into a mythic figure. His admirers, who were suddenly in the legions, began to invest everything he had written, uttered or done with wisdom or even genius. As object of their admiration and worship, they started to cleanse him of any taint of weakness or imperfection. The object of their adoration must be pure, immaculate and strong.

Even Ninoy's death was providential. It came at a time when the people deeply needed a champion. Writing in *Veritas*, the Catholic weekly magazine, Salvador P. Lopez froze this point in focus with this comment:

"At the airport a year ago there occurred a rare conjunction of need and opportunity — a people's deep need for a champion and a manifest resolve to eliminate him. Ninoy filled that need and was therefore eliminated. But in death he became a deathless hero."[6]

The people enshrined Ninoy Aquino in the pantheon of Filipino heroes, among the greatest of them, in a niche assigned to him by a grateful nation. He had become a symbol and hero of the Filipino people, Lopez adds, a hero by the will of the people, not by legislative fiat or edict of a President or commission.

In an election, therefore, where the opposition would challenge the Presidency, Marcos would be up against not a mere person like him but a national hero, Ninoy, or, in his absence, his representative or surrogate. The President would have a hard time trying to hold on to his office.

And Ninoy's death was dramatic. It did not come after a long period of idle and disconsolate vegetation in a prison cell or from lack of food, care and medicine. Nor did death come to him senselessly in Boston in the hands of a drunken taxi driver as he had feared and told his wife Cory. Rather, he died almost at noon of Saturday, August 21, 1983 while stepping down a plane that had flown him back to his country. One single gunshot, fired at close range while he was descending on the aircraft's stairway in the arms of his military escorts, snuffed his life.

The fact that Ninoy was killed while under protection by the military made the tragedy even more shocking. About 1,199 officers and men had been assigned to provide him with security, all presumably highly trained specialists in their chosen lines under the overall direction of the Chief of Staff himself, Maj. Gen. Fabian C. Ver. The people found it hard to believe that one single person, as claimed by the military, could penetrate such a tight security cordon, confront Aquino at the plane's stairway and kill him with one bullet fired from a sidearm. All the while Aquino was held on both arms by soldiers, protected on the plane's sides by other soldiers, while still other soldiers were ahead of him and behind him.

The people considered as too fantastic the story that a lone gunman, Rolando Galman, had indeed penetrated the security cordon and killed Ninoy. It taxed their credulity.

LIKE the deaths of the three activist priests — Fathers Gomez, Burgos and Zamora — and the execution of Rizal, the death of Ninoy Aquino awakened a great number of Filipinos. They learned to overcome their fear. Angered by the murder they began to slide out of their paralysis of fear and march on the streets, hands clasped together, to express their rage over government injustices and abuses. Assuming yellow as their battle color, the color of protest, they marched arm-in-arm down the streets of the financial district of Makati, in Metro Manila, their fists clenched and raised. Their voices rose in unison as they chanted "Ninoy! . . . . Ninoy! . . . . Ninoy!" like a battlecry and *"Ibagsak si Marcos! Ibagsak ang diktadurang Marcos-Estados Unidos!"* (Down with Marcos! Down with the Marcos-US dictatorship!).

The marchers were from all walks of life — businessmen and employees, students and workers, clerics and peasants, teachers and street vendors, society personalities and professionals. Their leaders were of the Makati bourgeosie but much of the number and mass came from the urban poor. Still it had been an unusual spectacle until then: rich, well-dressed mestizos and mestizas marching in the rallies, condemning the Marcos government, protesting the death of Ninoy Aquino, military abuses and economic crisis. It was strange indeed that the people from the middle and upper middle classes, traditional targets of revolution, were now crying revolution themselves.

The color yellow came not only in the form of T-shirts and headbands, kerchiefs and wristbands, but also in showers of confetti. For the first time in the history of the protest movement in the country, people showered street rallyists and demonstrators with floods of yellow confetti. Shredding any yellow paper or light material into thin strips, executives and employees of the large business establishments in Makati would wait at windows and ledges of their offices, often at the top stories of towering concrete buildings, then unleash cascades of confetti upon the marchers as they passed by. All this gave the demonstrations a festive, carnival air, and somehow relieved the tension of the protest actions.

If the color of protest was yellow, the battle sign was "L", formed by an extended thumb and forefinger. It was originally the sign of the Laban party of Ninoy that became more prominent and popular after his death. Even when Cory Aquino was a candidate for President under Laurel's Unido party, she continued to use the "L" sign in the campaign.

ALTHOUGH President Marcos had preempted any investigative body by claiming that, based on reliable military intelligence reports, Ninoy Aquino was killed by a lone Communist gunman, he was compelled to order a formal investigation of the crime. He formed a commission and designated Supreme Court Chief Justice Enrique Fernando as its head. The public vehemently objected to Fernando's designation and he was forced to give up the position. The President next offered it to former Senator Arturo M. Tolentino, a member of the National Assembly, but Tolentino declined for reasons of his own. Finally the post was given to a retired lady justice, Corazon Juliano Agrava.

Named by Marcos to assist in the investigation as members of the Agrava board were Dante Santos, a businessman and industrialist; Amado Dizon, lawyer-educator who was a leader in the movement for reforms in private education; Luciano Salazar, a respected practicing lawyer; and Ernesto Herrera, a relatively young but well-known labor leader.

For legal assistance the Board had a panel of lawyers composed of the following: Mario Ongkiko, Bienvenido Tan Jr., Francisco Villa, Albino Arriero, Alhambra Alfafara, and Proceso Fernandez. For general counsel, the President appointed Dean Andres Narvasa of the College of Law, University of Santo Tomas. Narvasa turned out to be a dramatic Board personality and earned the sobriquet "Grey Dean" because of the sandy color of his cropped hair.[7]

Meanwhile, the U.S. government, worried that the problem of Communist insurgency was deteriorating and thereby aggravating the risks to their security interests in the Philippines, applied stronger pressure on President Marcos to institute reforms in the military, starting with the removal of Maj. Gen. Ver as Chief of Staff and his replacement by Lt. Gen. Fidel V. Ramos, his deputy who is an alumnus of the United States Military Academy in West Point. Marcos yielded substantially by allowing Ver to go on leave while the investigation was in progress, and named Ramos acting Chief of Staff, at least nominally. In reality, Gen. Ver continued to hold power over the military. He was said to maintain office in Malaca- nang Palace and continued to command the Presidential Security Command and the National Intelligence Security Agency of the government. Under the circumstances, Ramos could not institute any meaningful changes in the defense establishment.

Significantly, even before the beginning of the investigation into the Aquino case, Cory had steadfastly refused to have herself or any member of her family participate in any manner. She insisted that she believed justice would not be done as long as Ferdinand Marcos was in power.

The investigation was a long and tedious process. It was con- ducted daily in a large hall at the Social Security System building in Quezon City which had been specially prepared for the purpose. Local and foreign media caught and reported the highlights of each day. No other investigation of any murder could even approximate the fanfare and public interest it generated. The Board Chairman, the members of the Board and the panel of lawyers became more prominent with every passing day, and soon began known in the collective as the "Agravatars." For personal courtroom flair and histrionics, the "Grey Dean" was incomparable. He and the Board Chairman later shared the limelight almost equally. Media recorded with gusto the clothes they wore, hairdo and haircut, courtroom mannerisms, speech and gestures, as well as points they raised or challenged. Everything was good copy. Meanwhile, in various parts of the country, politicians and their leaders were busy storming the barrios and towns in preparation for the May 1984 elections for the National Assembly or Batasang Pambansa. The political opposition — former Senator Laurel's Unido, the PDP-Laban of Aquilino Pimentel Jr. and Jose Cojuangco Jr., the two irreconcilable factions of the Liberal Party headed by former Senator Jovito R. Salonga and former Senator Eva Estrada Kalaw, and the groupings consisting of independent regional parties and cause-oriented political organiza- tions — were all bearing the Ninoy Aquino banner and united in the common objective of toppling Marcos from power.

The oppositionists had their own unique ways of fighting Marcos and his KBL machine. Some, like the cause-oriented groups, opted for boycott — not to participate in the elections which they denounced as illegal. They insisted that to participate was to legi- timize the illegitimate government of Marcos. But there were those who chose to participate, among the most celebrated being the widow of Ninoy Aquino, Cory, who had just emerged from her cocoon of anonymity. Among those who cast their fate with her was Pimentel Jr.[8]   Her reason for participating in the elections, although she herself was not a candidate, was to give the people a chance to express themselves freely. Ninoy himself, she pointed out, participated in the 1978 election for the Batasan by consenting to head the opposition slate in Metro Manila.

Cory Aquino, we have earlier noted, worked very hard in that campaign, harder than she had ever worked in any political campaign before. To her surprise she discovered that she could even enjoy the work in spite of the hardships. She also discovered that she could deliver public speeches much longer than she ever did before — that she even relished it. Without her saying it, she began to accept and enjoy the attention and care the "little people" in the poor areas showered on her — happily taking her in their tricycles to their meeting or rally places, offering her bits of food and drinks, protecting her from the rain or sun with anything that they had at the moment, returning to pick her up in tricycles after meetings, offering her an electric fan to dry her rain-soaked dress, touching and holding her hands and clothes and calling her name with endearment: all of these had become part of her political experience during that period of campaign. These little episodes in the non-candidate's life would occur again not long afterwards when it was she herself that Cory would offer to the voters.

Cory felt vindicated after the results of that May 1984 elections were known. A number of opposition candidates had won, and all together they captured approximately 60 seats in the Batasan. There were rumors that the oppositionists won because President Marcos allowed them to, in obedience to an imposition by the U.S. government. Anyone who knew the nature and complexities of Philippine politics would wonder how even a President could manipulate an election to such an extent and with such mastery: the opposition victors came from various regions of the country, in areas where Marcos was concededly weak, as in the Bicol region and Mindanao. Even in Metro Manila, which became "Marcos country" since 1969, the opposition candidates shouting Ninoy Aquino's name as battle-cry swept all but a mere handful of positions in the Batasan.

The KBL of President Marcos was able to maintain the majority. But they had to contend, for the first time, with a responsible opposition graced by such political personalities as Jose B. Laurel Jr., Edmundo Cea, Francisco Sumulong, Neptali Gonzales, Rogaciano Mercado, Ramon Mitra and Rafael Lazatin and women leaders such as Eva Estrada Kalaw and former Supreme Court Justice Cecilia

Munoz-Palma. Nevertheless, when it came to voting on important issues partisan in character, there was no way in which the opposition could win. Two such issues were the opposition motions to (1) impeach President Marcos on charges on stashing billions of the nation's wealth in foreign countries and (2) defer his proclamation as duly reelected President in the February 7, 1986 elections. Both motions were killed by the ruling KBL majority in the Batasan.

THE 1984 Batasang Pambansa election took place during the investigations of the Aquino assassination.

The investigation by the Agrava Commission started on November 3, 1983 and was formally closed nearly one year later, on August 20, 1984. It was a thorough, exhaustive inquiry that cost the government millions of pesos. The crime itself had been described as "the ugliest and most public crime in Philippine history."[9]

In a large sense, that crime — the killing or murder of Ninoy Aquino — was to mark the beginning of a historical development in the Philippines: the descent and fall of Ferdinand E. Marcos from power. Simultaneously, it would trigger the rise and ascendancy of Corazon C. Aquino to power.

When the Board formally ended its investigation on August 20, 1984, it had gathered and examined 1,294 documents, 1,472 photographs, 14 videotapes, and 91 pieces of physical evidence. It had conducted 125 public hearings involving 193 witnesses with 20,377 pages of transcripts.

On October 23 Justice Agrava submitted her official report to President Marcos. She appeared on television while in Malacanang, unaccompanied by the Board members, being received by the President in his study. Both were obviously happy that the task had been completed after so much hurt had been inflicted on the national psyche.

It turned out that the lady chairman was alone in submitting the report because it was not the Board report but hers. It was different from the majority report but only "in form and manner" and "the level of liability," she claimed. It bore only her signature. In the report she named Gen. Luther Custodio, former AVSECOM chief, and six of his men as the plotters of the Aquino assassination.

The following day, October 24, the Fact-Finding Board members submitted their official report to the President. On television it was obvious that Marcos received them coldly, unlike the way he received Justice Agrava. There was not even the hint of a smile on his face. He simply received the report and said something unintelligible to the TV listeners. He briskly thumbed through the thick report then stood up to shake hands with the Board members, who quietly passed out of the room. The President was evidently disappointed.[11]

In their majority report the Board members unmasked the conspiracy involving several generals, colonels, captains and lesser officers of the Armed Forces of the Philippines. On them they lay the blame for the murder of Ninoy Aquino and that of Rolando Galman, a hired gunman from Nueva Ecija whom they had made a fall guy for Aquino's death and whom the soldiers had riddled with bullets on the tarmac.

The following highlights of the investigation of the Aquino assassination would be instructive to the reader:

After a detailed analysis of physical and testimonial evidence gathered over 11 months, the Fact-Finding Board confirmed in essence the conclusion of its lawyers' panel that contrary to publicized claims, "military authorities knew beforehand the details of Aquino's arrival in Manila International Airport on August 21, 1983 . . . and the elaborate plans ostensibly geared to protect the life of Aquino were in fact designed to camouflage the taking of that life." Finding that the existence of a military conspiracy rests not only on circumstantial but also on direct evidence, the Board invoked the Philippine penal provisions that in crimes of conspiracy "the act of one is the act of all" and that those who actively participated in the shootings must be punished along with their superiors and those who lent moral assistance. Following this the Board pinpointed a hierarchy of powerful men for prosecution, starting with Gen. Ver, the Chief of Staff of the Armed Forces.

Taking into account the testimony of Saturnina Galman, mother of Rolando Galman, and other Galman kin that Rolando could not have had the motive nor the means to kill Aquino (Rolando, they claimed, had left his house in San Miguel, Bulacan on August 17 in the company of his friend, Col. Arthur Custodio and some military looking types), and the testimony of his 10-year-old son Reynaldo and his stepdaughter Roberta that some of the men who fetched their father also came to get their mother, Lina, in January, the Board saw its way clear to ruling out the single assassin theory: Aquino could not have been killed by Galman.

That there was "an ugly conspiracy" became clear to the Board as they followed a crooked line and unearthed two coverups. As Alice C. Villadolid saw it:

"Lighting the way was the judicial experience of the chairman herself as she ruled on motions, kept track of exhibits and weighed evidence. Amado Dizon's years of wisdom as an educator were called forth, as was Luciano Salazar's evenhandedness as a corporate lawyer. Daring and persistence were obvious in Dante Santos, the businessman, and Ernesto Herrera, the labor leader. Ex-Police Chief Francisco Villa pursued witnesses, recalcitrant though they were. Kind-looking Benny Tan gained public trust. Mario Ongkiko kept his sharp, scholarly eye on the evidence, spotting fakes as they came along. Andres Narvasa steered the inquiry through with caution and cunning."[10]

The Board said that it was President Marcos who first noted a conspiracy theory when he told a news conference on August 22, 1983 that one of the theories was that the killing "might have received the blessing of the NPA or the Communist hierarchy. They would eliminate Aquino," he added, "who was responsible for some killings . . . and they would embarrass the government." General Prospero Olivas, one of the generals suspected to be involved in the conspiracy, had earlier (on August 20) also referred to a "conspiracy" in his memorandum prescribing riot control measures in connection with Ninoy's arrival.

Chief of Staff Gen. Fabian C. Ver later testified that he had activated the intelligence project because a "penetration agent" had reported that Commander Bilog of the Communist New People's Army had ordered Aquino's assassination. The military also presented Rosendo Cawigan as witness to the alleged Communist plot which would utilize the services of Galman and Cawigan. The latter eventually died of an alleged heart attack.

The Board decided that the Communist conspiracy theory was absurd after finding that Cawigan had been an agent of the National Bureau of Investigation and later the National Food Authority and were unable to reconcile Ninoy's conciliatory posture toward the Communists with a Communist plot against him.

As far as Brig. Gen. Luther Custodio was concerned, the Board's lawyers concluded that an "incredible series of coincidences" would have been necessary to make Galman an agent of a Communist conspiracy. For instance, the Board's lawyers observed, the Communists would have had to know Ninoy's unpublicized arrival by China Airlines, and they would have read the mind of Gen. Custodio who claimed he decided to take Aquino down to the tarmac only ten minutes before he planed in.

Moreover Galman, who took a full lunch as shown by the autopsy, would have known that he must return to the tarmac at exactly 1:04 p.m. when Ninoy began his descent from the aircraft. Also, for an experienced gunman, he had no getaway vehicle and was found with only P2.10 in his pocket, not even enough for fare to San Miguel, Bulacan. Far more credible, said the lawyers, was the supposition that Galman was brought to the tarmac by superior clearance.

The Board became increasingly suspicious as Gen. Custodio and his men in the AVSECOM testified by turns. Salazar, for instance, asked why of so many monitoring cameras, none was focused on Gate 8 as Ninoy Aquino disembarked. The lawyer got such answer as: the man assigned happened to be new, or the electrical circuits were overloaded.

More questions were asked but left unanswered. Justice Agrava repeatedly asked Sgt. Prospero Bona why he refused to identify himself as the man shown taking several pictures in front of Ninoy. Where, she wanted to know, were the pictures?

Dizon wondered why the escorts claimed they were all unarmed, for how would they protect Ninoy? He also asked why a sergeant of the Presidential Security Command was trailing the escorts inside the plane and what happened to the clutch bag he was carrying? Did he pass on a gun? Why was AVSECOM Sgt. Armando de la Cruz standing at the top of the stairway as Ninoy passed and why did he claim not to have seen how Aquino was shot?

Labor Leader Herrera could not understand why Lt. Jesus Castro, if he was indeed the head of the escort party, did not wear his uniform and did not go down with Aquino. Nor could he understand, Herrera said, why Capt. Felipe Valerio, who was supposed to receive Aquino for transport in the van, did not alight from the van. If Valerio remained seated in the front seat, where would he ask the former Senator to sit? The answer was that Ninoy would sit with the enlisted men in the back of the van.

The lawyers could not understand why the escorts, who were trained and able-bodied, ran away with the first shot, according to their own testimonies. Moreover, why were some of them instructed to go target-firing the day before Aquino's arrival? Was it to have a convenient excuse for proving positive in the paraffin tests?

The Board had received official copies of diplomatic communications from Singapore and Taipei about Ninoy's travel itinerary. The government knew he would come from Taipei, using a passport in the name of Marcial Bonifacio. Nevertheless, why did the military claim they did not know he was coming via China Airlines? Why did they plan to meet nine planes? And why was there an order to check Ninoy's papers when they knew these were fake?

The Board studied for months the video and audio tapes of three well-known foreign news companies: Tokyo Broadcasting System, American Broadcasting Corporation, and *Time* magazine. They found that all contained dialect words suggesting a conspiracy to shoot Aquino at the service stairs of Gate 9. The tapes also carried the pattern of gunshots — five shots in the beginning, followed by a 17-second gap, then a volley of about 20 shots.

What was shown in the networks' films were later confirmed by the chronology of still shots: Galman was already felled by gunshots before the men emerged from the SWAT van and fired the last volley on him. Asked the Board: Why did the military witnesses insist it was the SWAT men who killed Galman? Who were the other soldiers who must have fired the fatal second to fifth shots that killed the fall guy?

Justice Agrava asked why Capt. Romeo Bautista did not admit he was on the platform of the service stairs until he was shown a videotape of himself there. And why did he have a blue jacket over his polo barong when it was a warm noontime?

Moreover, Gen. Custodio and his subordinate officers claimed they assigned 1,199 men to protect Aquino, yet they did not check Galman and other civilians as they entered the tarmac. They claimed they searched nine planes, but did not actually board them. They claimed they did not plan on taking Aquino down the stairs till ten minutes before they did, yet more than eight men were tasked beforehand to guard the door from newsmen who would follow. And why, the Board wanted to know, were the local airport reporters told to assemble where they could not photograph Aquino as he went down?

When the Agrava Board went into semi-seclusion in July 1984 to fend off the media and the curious public as they pieced together what Mrs. Agrava had called "the puzzle," they agreed that what had been presented to them was "a gigantic hoax." They realized that the whole incident had two coverups, one before and another afterwards. Using military jargon, one Board member said there was an overt security plan to cover up for the covert plan. They agreed that Ninoy Aquino was killed as he descended the service stairs by one of his escorts, while Galman was shot immediately after by other soldiers.

CORY Aquino, as we pointed out earlier, rejected any participation in the investigation. She had her own reasons.

After the release of the two Agrava reports, one by the Chairman and the other by the majority members, Mrs. Aquino issued a statement stressing that the reports confirmed "what we knew all along — that it was not Galman who shot and killed Ninoy but that it was a military conspiracy."

But, the statement added, "the report does not answer the question which has troubled me since August 21, 1983 — 'Why was Ninoy assassinated by the military?'"

Reproduced below are excerpts from Cory Aquino's statement: [12]

Wasn't Ninoy's assassination a political decision of the gravest import so that no military man, no matter how high in authority, would think of making that decision on his own?

Can Mr. Marcos, in Ninoy's words, "wash his hands of my blood?"

Or that Mr. Marcos was kept in complete ignorance of what was going to be done to Ninoy?

The Agrava report confirms what we knew all along — that it was not Galman who shot and killed Ninoy   but that it was a military conspiracy. But the report does not answer the question which has troubled me since August 21, 1983 — "Why was Ninoy assassinated by the military? "

In trying to answer this question, I find one overriding fact very relevant:

Throughout Ninoy's incarceration, it was clear to us that everything that concerned Ninoy had to be cleared with Mr. Marcos. As a matter of fact, when Mr. Marcos proclaimed martial law, Ninoy headed the list of persons to be detained. The records will show that Ninoy was the first to be booked in Camp Crame on the early morning of September 23, 1972. Ninoy was arrested while discharging his duties as Senator of the Republic, in palpable violation of the Constitution. Mr. Marcos exercised and insisted on complete control of everything that affected Ninoy. Nothing could be done regarding Ninoy without Marcos' approval. Let me illustrate this with incidents which speak for themselves:

I.   The Military Tribunal that tried Ninoy was under the control of Mr. Marcos.

II.   Minister Juan Ponce Enrile and the entire military establishment charged with Ninoy's detention were under the control of Mr. Marcos

    a)   On August 17, 1974 Ninoy was granted a home pass

by Secretary Juan Ponce Enrile in connection with my eldest daughter's birthday. Then on the very day itself, the pass was suddenly cancelled. When I inquired from the officers at Fort Bonifacio, I was informed that higher authorities had cancelled the pass given by the Secretary of Defense. Who else could possibly be higher than the Secretary of Defense?

III. The conditions of his release and his travel papers after release were under the control of Mr. Marcos:

a) On June 9, 1978, Secretary Juan Ponce Enrile, Secretary Vicente Abad Santos and Solicitor General Estelito Mendoza came to Fort Bonifacio. Senator Lorenzo Tanada and the LABAN group were also allowed to come. A meeting was held at the Campos Hall of Fort Bonifacio. Secretary Enrile told Ninoy that Mr. Marcos had agreed to release him by amnesty grant but that Ninoy should leave the country and go into exile. Ninoy was also asked to write a letter to Mr. Marcos promising that he will not engage in any activity that will tarnish the image of the government. I myself asked Secretary Enrile when we would be allowed to leave the country and he answered: "By the end of the month." I still remember how excited and happy we all were and Ninoy started sending home his books and other personal belongings. Our excitement soon died down when we saw Ninoy still a prisoner in Fort Bonifacio not only until the end of June but for many, many more months thereafter. As most of you know, it was only on May 8, 1980 that Mr. Marcos finally allowed us to leave.

b) At the time of Gerry Roxas' death in April 1982 in New York City, Ninoy met and talked with Imelda Marcos. Ninoy requested her to help him secure an extension of his passport and that was the last Ninoy ever saw of it.

The following year, on May 21, 1983 Ninoy again met with Imelda Marcos and he informed her of his plans to return home. Again, he reminded her of his passport. In spite of his repeated requests for travel documents from the Philippine Consulate General in New York through his lawyer Ernie Maceda, the only reply he got was a telegram from Minister Juan Ponce Enrile asking him to delay his return.

In the light of all these, are we now to believe that Mr. Marcos is innocent of the death of Ninoy in the hands of the military under his control? Are we now going to believe that the assassination of Ninoy was planned and executed without Mr. Marcos' foreknowledge or expressed approval?

LATER, after ruling out the possibility of seeing justice done under the regime of President Marcos, Cory Aquino expressed the hope that in some future time she would see an atmosphere where one could speak freely and without fear of being detained or even eliminated which, she said, was what happened to witnesses when Ninoy was on trial under the military commission. When asked if she would be satisfied with a death sentence for those found guilty of killing her husband, she answered evasively: "If you don't punish the guilty how can you at least discourage or frighten people from committing the same crime?"

But she was not in a hurry to see that justice was done for the death of her husband. In fact she emphasized that it was not only justice for him that she wanted but justice for all the victims of the Marcos regime. She could wait. "After all," she said, "whether we have what I consider a real court of justice now or later, that will not bring Ninoy back to me." Like her husband she had learned to be patient, to appreciate patience as a virtue.

At the time she was saying all this, it was 1984, two years before people and the forces of history would set up their own conspiracy to catapult Ninoy's widow to the zenith of power.

EIGHT

Sophistication and Resolve

> *For the past two years I have been telling the people to be involved. But I have never told them to be involved in Cory. I cannot tell them to stop now. I will never be able to forgive myself with the knowledge that I could have done something but I didn't.*

> — Cory Aquino, at a rally in
> Tarlac, Tarlac.

NEITHER Cory Aquino nor President Ferdinand E. Marcos could have foreseen the unexpected twist of history that would bring them to a direct confrontation and collision. Marcos knew that there were pretenders to his throne from the ranks of the opposition, and among those most prominently mentioned as potential presidential candidates were the veteran politicians Salvador Laurel and Aquilino Pimentel Jr., the former being the President of the Unido, an umbrella organization of a number of opposition groups, and the latter the national chairman of the merged PDP-Laban both of which had succeeded in making some of their candidates win seats in the Batasang Pambansa during the May 1984 parliamentary elections.

There were other names mentioned as probables: former Senator Jovito R. Salonga, one of Ninoy's closest advisers whom he deferentially addressed as "Prof" and who had returned to the Philippines after years of exile in the United States, and former Senator Eva Estrada Kalaw, who had been elected as one of Manila's members of Parliament in 1984.

It must be in recognition of Ninoy Aquino's great drawing power and wide popularity that all these presidential potentials sought to impress upon the public mind their close affinity with him. Doy Laurel called attention to his close relationship with the slain Senator by recounting their common sacrifices and frequent consultations on vital political matters. Pimentel harked on a reported statement of Ninoy that he believed Pimentel would be the next President of the Philippines (after

Marcos). Salonga spoke of his playing the role of confidante and consultant to the young Senator even when they were in the Senate together (a mentor-student relationship). And Eva Kalaw emphasized her role as a "genuine oppositionist" whose name had never been linked with Marcos or his government, plus her blood kinship with Ninoy. It was transparent that their common objective in invoking Ninoy's name was to win the support of his admirers and the party leaders who had benefited from his well-known generosity.

At that time the name of Cory Aquino was not even remotely mentioned as a presidential possibility.

The problem that had been plaguing the opposition was lack of unity. There were scores of small opposition groups from north to south, especially in the Visayas and Mindanao, which were nearly equally divided between the Unido and the PDP-Laban. The rest, refusing membership in either group, chose to stay independent. Between the Unido and the PDP-Laban yawned an apparently unbridgeable chasm: where the Unido was a traditional political party, the PDP-Laban claimed to be ideological and cause-oriented; its members had first to go through an intensive two-day seminar. To get Laurel and Pimentel together was a nearly impossible task for both had been eyeing the Presidency. Indeed their active participation in the 1984 elections was seen by political observers as a preparation for the presidential contest in 1987. Laurel, for his part, had in fact visited the entire archipelago three times since 1984 evidently with an eye on 1987.

Both groups were determined to bring down Marcos, to put an end to his regime which began with his first election as President in 1965. But both groups also knew that their goal would remain a pipe dream, a wishful thought, unless they united.

They certainly needed a dominant, overpowering personality larger than themselves to resolve that problem, to bring them together and forge a strong united front against Marcos. Finally the leaders thought of forming a National Unification Committee chaired by former Supreme Court Justice Cecilia Munoz-Palma, a member of the Batasan. Mrs. Cory C. Aquino was the other dominant personality. Their task was to come up with a united opposition presidential ticket.

Meanwhile, Laurel, as President of the Unido, had ensured his nomination as Unido's candidate for President.

Throughout that period of indecision Mrs. Aquino was being courted by her supporters to be the candidate of the Laban ng Bayan. She eventually yielded to the pressure but imposed two conditions: first, that she be drafted by at least one million Filipino voters who would sign a resolution for the purpose; and, second, that President Marcos sign Cabinet Bill No. 7 calling for sudden or "snap" presidential elections on February 7, 1986.

The first condition did not seem forbidding to the Cory Aquino for President Movement spearheaded by white-maned Joaquin "Chino" Roces, publisher of the pre-martial law *Manila Times* chain of newspapers. In just 41 days, 35 days ahead of its self-imposed deadline, the CAPM was able to complete its task of collecting a million signatures — it had launched the signature-gathering project on October 15, 1985 and hoped to gather the million signatures by December 31. The effort had been lukewarm at first because Marcos had not yet officially announced the holding of the snap elections, but when he announced that he intended to call elections in January 1986 the CAPM shifted its efforts to high gear. Volunteers poured in and started to solicit signatures in churches, offices, department stores, public markets and even in front of bus stations. The volunteers, coming in droves, usually arrived in the morning to pick up some forms from the CAPM offices and return later in the afternoon with 300 to 500 signatures.

"We don't simply list down every name that is given to us at the office," said Jesus Marcos Roces, head of the CAPM ways and means committee. "We screen them first and then run them through a computer to check for duplications."[1]

When the one-millionth signature arrived, the venerable street parliamentarian Chino Roces, tough veteran of many a firehosing by Metro Manila firemen at several rallies and protest demonstrations, was immediately swept upon the shoulders of the volunteers and given a victory ride, much like the one given to a winning basketball coach. Everyone at the CAPM office along Teodoro M. Kalaw street in Ermita, Manila, was hysterical with joy. Roces, clad in a pair of old jeans, a Cory Aquino T-shirt and rubber shoes, was paraded around the room before being put down. He himself was all smiles. Then on the wall just above the tally board they posted a hastily made poster proudly proclaiming that Cory Aquino, "is the first Filipino presidential candidate nominated and drafted by the people." And indeed she was.

Not all signatures had been turned in, however, up to that time. Later, when all the signatures had been counted, those who endorsed

Cory Aquino's candidacy for President totalled more than 1,200,000.

THE two leading presidential aspirants of the political opposition as of November 1985 were Laurel and Aquino. Laurel was backed by the Unido, the umbrella grouping of the Nacionalista Party (Laurel wing) and the Liberal Party (Kalaw faction). It was acknowledged to have control over the National Unification Committee, "the giant coalition of all opposition political parties and groups." It was the Unido which proposed the holding of a political convention on December 8. A crisis confronted it when the NUC chairman, Justice Palma, resigned after a "shouting match" with Laurel. Former Senator Francisco "Soc" Rodrigo took over the chairmanship.

Cory Aquino, on the other hand, had the support of the Laban ng Bayan coalition composed of a major political party, the PDP-Laban, a faction of the Liberal Party (Salonga wing), the Convenor Group, and cause-oriented groups such as BAYAN and BANDILA. Also backing up the coalition were nine regional parties: Pinaghiusa of Cebu, Timek ti Umili of Cagayan Valley, Concerned Citizens Aggrupation of Zamboanga, the Mindanao Alliance, the National Union of Liberation of Bulacan, Bicol Saro, the Laban ni Ninoy sa Sentral Luzon, the Christian Social Democratic Party, and the Muslim Federal Party.

Both Aquino and Laurel had been holding meetings to thresh out the problem of unity. Both were convinced they could win against Marcos though their chances would be vastly improved if they had a common slate for President and Vice President. As of December 1, 1985 Cory had not announced her acceptance of the draft but her supporters had announced that she would make her acceptance soon. [2]

To direct and manage Cory's campaign the coalition supporting her formed a governing council. Former Senator Salonga was elected President of the new coalition. Its other officers were former Senator Lorenzo Tanada and Justice Palma, chairmen; former Senator John Osmena, national vice president; Emanuel Soriano, vice president for internal affairs; Teopisto Guingona, vice president for external affairs; Agapito "Butz" Aquino, secretary-general; and Mary Concepcion Bautista, treasurer. The governing council was composed of opposition leaders representing various political areas in the country.

The coalition said its leaders would not participate in a convention called by the National Unification Committee on December 9 to choose a presidential and vice presidential candidate, stressing that Cory Aquino should run on a popular draft and not on the basis of a convention. They believed the convention of the NUC was called to favor other aspirants, to the detriment of Mrs. Aquino. As Osmena charged, "The original selection rules of the NUC were changed to favor other aspirants."[3]

More than anything else, the struggle of Laurel and Aquino for nomination as the common opposition candidate for President revealed that Cory was, after all, not the politically innocent, wide-eyed novice in politics and in the nitty-gritty of power play that she had been pictured to be. She proved she was no stranger to the traditionally men's game of political maneuvering and backdoor infighting. Not only did she demonstrate that she had learned well from her late husband, and had inherited the political genes of her grandfather and parents, but also displayed for all political leaders to see a strength of will, resoluteness of purpose — and the determination to pursue it.

To be sure, during her first two meetings with Laurel, the Batangas politician had preferred that advisers attended their meetings. But Cory had rejected the idea and insisted that one-on-one talks between them be continued for the moment to resolve the quandary. Backers of both sides felt that this procedure was not achieving much and that precious time was running out on the opposition, and some of them even suggested calling in mediators, mentioning such names as Judy Araneta Roxas, widow of the late Senator Roxas, and Jaime Cardinal Sin. A group of impatient assemblymen even took it upon themselves, reports Belinda Olivares-Cunanan, to impose some kind of deadline on the two or face the prospect of having a third opposition candidate fielded in the person of one of the Batasan members.[4]

On the other hand Rodrigo was optimistic that light was visible at the proverbial end of the tunnel; he arrived at this conclusion after talking individually with the four aspirants: Aquino, Laurel, Kalaw and Salonga. Rodrigo reported to the NUC executive committee, after his talks with the aspirants, that Laurel was noncommittal about a solution to the problem of whom to field but expressed a desire to continue dialoguing with Cory. Rodrigo quoted Kalaw as saying she would conform with what Cory and Laurel would agree upon. Salonga, on the other hand, told Rodrigo he was backing up Cory but would himself run if she were to drop out of the race.

Cory's statements were significant. She told Rodrigo that she felt "events had so contrived" that she must perform a role for the country. Cory felt, according to Rodrigo, that running for the Presidency "is a cross on my shoulder" which she had to bear.[5]

It was quite obviously a Laurel-Aquino or Aquino-Laurel battle for nomination. Cory's supporters were trying to whip up a bandwagon for her while simultaneously organizing at the grassroots level. On the other hand, the Laurel camp, which had been badly shaken by Laurel's fierce confrontation with the venerable Cecilia Munoz-Palma, was trying to hang on to more than 30 Batasang Pambansa members who were said to be supporting him. In contrast Cory could count on some 20 MPs, a number they expected to grow as her sympathizers continued wooing the Laurel supporters. The timid housewife had indeed revealed herself as an aggressive, shrewd politician.

Aside from their respective strengths, Cory Aquino and Doy Laurel had to contend with two vital questions: funding and dominant opposition party (DOP) status. Observers believed Cory had the advantage over funds the Laban coalition could count on the support of many businessmen, while Laurel's fund sources were said to be drying up. On the DOP status, the Unido, if accredited, would strengthen its bargaining position. It had the edge on this issue over Laban. President Marcos, the real power behind the granting of DOP status, was not likely to grant it to his strongest potential rival, in this case Cory Aquino. In all likelihood Laurel's Unido would get the DOP status which would entitle it to have its accredited inspectors — and watchers — in the voting precincts.

So tight was the fight between Aquino and Laurel for the opposition's nomination that within the opposition itself Cory became the object of suspicions and speculations. Some became mortally afraid of her now perceptible strength. A number of Laurel sympathizers began to suspect that all along she had been feigning political innocence, when in fact she had a master plan prepared and managed by certain business and professional leaders behind her. They felt that even her reluctance to be drafted and her imposition of two conditions prior to announcing an acceptance was one grand show and part of an integrated strategy to wrest the nomination from Laurel. Furthermore it was bruited about, at that stage of the power play, that the withdrawal of former Justice Palma from the NUC chairmanship was part of the Aquino master plan, a tactic designed to discredit Laurel in order to boost her chances.

In accusing Cory Aquino of adopting these manipulative techniques it was apparent that they intended to discredit her by destroying what concededly was her strongest and unique selling point — her unassailable moral impeccability.

TIME was fast running out on the still disunited opposition. On the KBL side, President Marcos had convened the party leaders at the Manila Hotel Fiesta Pavilion and proclaimed Arturo M. Tolentino, a former Senator, member of the Batasang Pambansa and for a brief spell Minister of Foreign Affairs whom Marcos had fired for uttering certain recalcitrant statements against the President and his policies, as his vice presidential running mate. To many Marcos had chosen Tolentino over such aspirants as Minister Juan Ponce Enrile of National Defense, Minister Blas F. Ople of Labor and Employment, and Deputy Prime Minister Jose Rono to win a slice of the independent votes, Tolentino being reputed to be an independent-minded party man, a political maverick. Besides, some observers pointed out, Tolentino was 75 years of age, too old to pose a serious threat to the monolithic Marcos leadership (and to be feared by Imelda Marcos and her private faction), aside from having no solid power base of his own. Unlike Enrile, Ople or Rono, Tolentino had no bloc to speak of, being an old politician from intractable Manila.

But Tolentino, as shown by past elections, had a nationwide popularity which could help Marcos, and this fact made the opposition exert one last brave effort to bring Cory Aquino and Doy Laurel together in a make-or-break final meeting. To temporize further could be fatal to either of them and to the opposition: it could mean the election of the powerful Marcos-Tolentino team.

Meanwhile, the deadline for the filing of certificates of candidacy was at hand. They had to beat that deadline.

Thus, four hours before the deadline, Aquino and Laurel agreed to unite in a joint ticket under Unido, Laurel's party, with Cory Aquino as presidential bet and Doy Laurel as her running mate.

The question, therefore, of what party to run under was resolved. New relationships and arrangements among the once-contending but now apparently united parties would be worked out and certain demands Laurel had earlier made would also be discussed and negotiated in the coming days.

For all intents and purposes this agreement was Cory's first significant political victory. Though described as an amateur, an upstart absolutely without any actual political experience, she had subdued and overcome the experienced, shrewd and fighting Doy Laurel who had been a political gladiator all his adult life and had in fact been a close associate of her murdered husband for several years. To the surprise of many and the apparent consternation of Laurel's backers who could not understand the twist of events, the

shy, retiring housewife of Ninoy who had always stayed in the background and waited in the wings, as it were, now found herself on
center stage to perform the demanding role of principal actor and
star.

THIS final union between Cory Aquino and Doy Laurel meant,
in a deeper and larger sense, giving up much of themselves for the
sake of the entire political opposition and patriotism. For Laurel it
meant surrendering his lifelong ambition — temporarily at least — to
be President of the country. He had worked so long and so hard to
realize that ambition; like Ninoy and Marcos long ago he had kept
an eye on the Presidency, and the past campaigns which saw him
traversing the archipelago and campaigning for Unido candidates
nationwide was just a preparation for his assault on the nation's
No. 1 position. And now, with Cory Aquino thrust into the picture,
he had to give up all his sacrifices and investment of time, energy
and funds to ensure that his own personal machinery, the Unido,
was positioned well enough and efficient enough to carry him
through a presidential campaign. No wonder his closest supporters
and ardent backers were vehemently opposed to his surrendering
his bid in favor of Ninoy's hitherto nonpolitical widow.

For Cory Aquino, consenting to run for President under the
banner of the Unido instead of her Laban ng Bayan party was likewise a sacrifice as well as a gamble since her consenting to be a
Unido candidate could be considered by the political purists in her
party as a capitulation, a surrender to the expediency of compromise, thus making her no different from ordinary politicians. She
knew her credibility would be eroded to a certain extent. It could
also mean the end of the illusion of political innocence that had been
carefully cultivated about her, thus opening her to charges of being
cut in the same mold as all traditional politicians whose ability to
survive and prevail was measured by their ability to wheel and deal,
to enter into dirty and even sinister backroom pacts and unholy
arrangements. Furthermore she knew she would have to contend
with the considerable resistance of her partymates against Doy
Laurel on whom they, particularly the elder statesmen, looked with
distrust and suspicion because of his background as a long-time
Marcos associate who severed his relationship with the President
only lately.

But all this notwithstanding their unity had to be forged if
their larger interest of deposing Ferdinand Marcos from the Presidency were to be attained. To the two, no sacrifice was big enough

to divert them from their common goal. Personal ambitions could be, as they were, temporarily shelved or set aside in the meantime; they could be attended to later.

Politics makes for strange bedfellows, and Cory Aquino and Doy Laurel were distinctive prototypes. Until this unity was forged Cory was a nonpolitician alien to the almost exclusively man's world of politics and the often incomprehensible, ruthless and compunctionless bargainings and horsetrading that characterize it. As we have seen, however, she did not prove entirely naive, insensitive and undiscerning, for certainly a lady who could achieve what she had in dealing with a Doy Laurel could not entirely be a political novice. Surely, to succeed as she did in forcing the Batangas leader practically to his knees and getting him to suspend, however temporarily, pursuing his ambition to become President is no mean feat that only a woman of some superior gifts or traits could accomplish.

Where Doy Laurel had been deliberately and consciously working hard to become President, Cory Aquino, at that time, regarded the Presidency as "a heavy cross to be borne" and the attempt to win it was a "crusade" rather than the pursuit of an overpowering ambition. A crusade implies a moral approach to a problem, a sincere dedication to an ideal and fighting in a clean and honest way for something a person believes in. In contrast, fulfilling or pursuing an ambition connotes the end justifying the means — whether fair or foul — lack of humanity and compassion in attaining a goal, a rationalized use of ruthlessness. A crusade is often identified with moral or spiritual leaders, ambition with politicians.

Such differences also seep down on the followers of the leaders. Thus, those supporting Laurel were by and large veteran politicians and professional ward leaders, while many of those lending support to Cory were nonpolitical personalities identified with cause-oriented and even ideological mass organizations, together with some senior but idealistic political elements personified by former Senators Lorenzo Tanada and Ambrosio Padilla.

The two also differed in their speaking styles. Where Cory appealed and exhorted in her plain and simple manner, Doy the veteran politico hurled challenges like thunderbolts, hypnotizing people with the fire, color and power of his oratory.

Nonetheless, their differences notwithstanding, Cory and Doy had to work in harmony to harness their strongest assets: the unarguable charisma and popularity of Cory Aquino, as a writer puts it, as the "quintessential nonpolitician," and the efficient machinery put together by Doy Laurel, the "quintessential politician."[6]

The persistence of certain leaders from both sides who worked all day on the day of filing of certificates of candidacy to bring Cory and Doy together finally paid off. Present at that final meeting, aside from the aspirants, were Doy Laurel's brother Sotero, president of the Lyceum of the Philippines, banker Vicente Puyat and Cory's eldest daughter Ballsy. Sotero Laurel reportedly advocated unity and agreed, for the sake of opposition unity, to have Doy run for Vice President. Doy's wife, Celia Diaz-Laurel, was said to be against the idea but soon relented like her husband who had turned hardliner until that final day of decision.

Among the very few personalities who were said to have played a vital role in forging the political marriage of Cory and Doy was Jaime Cardinal Sin of the local Roman Catholic Church.

AFTER the unity had been verbally sealed Cory Aquino, now assured of running against President Marcos with the backing of the coalesced political opposition, acted with dispatch and decision. She filed her certificate of candidacy for President at the Commission on Elections office in Intramuros, Manila. The excited, glowing widow of Ninoy Aquino was fetched from their residence on Times street, Quezon City, by a motorcade organized by the Quezon City chapter of the Laban headed by former Justice Cecilia Munoz Palma, and escorted to a rousing, euphoric reception at the Comelec offices.

The unprecedented reception for a candidate at the Comelec was a clear gauge of Cory's popularity. Reports a journalist on the scene:

"There was a stampede among the employees of both Comelec and the nearby Ministry of Education and Culture, as well as Cory's fans; the crowds had all lined up in the streets and the Comelec corridors. This was swelled by the participants of the Cory motorcade."[7]

Then she filed her certificate partyless; not all the kinks had been ironed out yet.

The pressure for her to agree to run under the Unido standard had reached unbelievable proportions. She wanted to be sure she would be doing the right thing. Consequently Cory requested Justice Palma to discuss the matter with Laban President Salonga, who posed several questions. For instance, Salonga wanted to know, what would happen to her credibility after having denied previously that she had accepted Laurel's original demand that she run under the Unido? Furthermore, what about the moral aspect of it all?

Salonga foresaw trouble within the Laban itself and from various other parties in the coalition if Cory ran under the Unido.

Justice Palma left Salonga's residence and immediately reported to Cory Salonga's observations and objections. But Cory and Doy had agreed on unity and it was paramount to all other considerations; Salonga's objections had therefore become moot and academic. They agreed that they would sign the unity agreement at about 10 p.m., after which Doy would proceed to the Comelec and change his certificate of candidacy, having filed one earlier as a candidate for President.

After this verbal agreement Cory rushed to the residence of Senator Tanada to inform him of the development. The grand old man of the opposition, a close adviser and lawyer of the late Ninoy Aquino, was against the idea but pledged to abide by their decision for the sake of unity — and opposition victory over Marcos. Cory thanked the statesman profusely for all the help and encouragement he had been extending to her.

Bidding Tanada goodbye, Cory next motored to Salonga's home in Pasig, accompanied this time by Justice Palma who had followed her in the house of Senator Tanada. She would inform Salonga, too, about their unity decision. Salonga, who had objected to the idea of Cory's running under the Unido from the beginning, re-stressed his reservations but, like Tanada, also relented and pledged his support to Cory.

Parenthetically Cory and Doy, before the unity agreement, had to tackle the problem of selecting their own vice presidential candidates. Cory reportedly had in mind either Aquilino Pimentel or Senator Salonga, though Salonga weighed heavier after Marcos had chosen former Senator Tolentino as his running mate. The reason for Cory's preferring Salonga was that in the old Senate, Salonga's record as a brilliant and honest legislator, as well as his having been a bar topnotcher and legal luminary, could match that of Tolentino. Besides, Salonga had been a Senate election topnotcher and therefore, like Tolentino, had a broad nationwide following. On Cory's suggestion Salonga was put on standby until 5 p.m., Cory's "cut-off hour," after which she was to call him to file his certificate of candidacy. At 5 p.m., since the Cory-Doy talks were not yet concluded, the former Senator from Rizal received word to file his candidacy anyway. Meanwhile, at the Laurel camp, Minnie Osmena-Stuart, daughter of the late Senator Sergio Osmena Jr., was also put on standby just in case the talks would collapse. At 4:30 p.m. she showed up at the Comelec and filed her certificate of candidacy for Vice President.

THE snap presidential election, the holding of which had been one of the conditions required by Cory Aquino before agreeing to run as the opposition candidate for President, had been the talk of the town since early 1985. As early as May a foreign newsmagazine reported that William Casey, chief of the CIA who had visited Manila, had pressed President Marcos to call an early election reportedly to rebuild confidence in the government and to stem the tide of insurgency. The following month, June, Undersecretary of State for Political Affairs Michael Armacost, former American ambassador to the Philippines, was told by Marcos there would be no snap polls and that the local and presidential elections would be held as scheduled in 1986 and 1987, respectively.

But the talk of a snap election persisted. On June 12 former Senator Salvador Laurel, president of the Unido, was proclaimed Unido candidate for President during a convention at the Araneta Coliseum in Quezon City. It was a master stroke that put Laurel and his party at the forefront of the race to carry the banner of the fragmented opposition in case of a snap election.

In August, despite earlier denials, President Marcos again spoke of the possibility of a sudden election. Political analysts saw the presidential announcement as a smokescreen to divert attention from impeachment motions which had been filed against him in the Batasang Pambansa following exposes of "hidden wealth" made by a California newspaper, the *San Jose Mercury News*. That same month, a KBL caucus decided against the holding of early polls, a decision which the ruling party reaffirmed during another caucus on September 11, just after the Supreme Court upheld the quashing of the impeachment resolution in the Batasan.

In October, U.S. President Ronald Reagan's personal envoy, Republican Senator Paul Laxalt, visited President Marcos. The President reportedly brought up the possibility of an early election, allegedly in response to increased pressures for a more open political system, and Laxalt was said to have welcomed the idea. The polls, which would shorten the term of Marcos by one year, were supposed to be held in February 1986, months before the local elections. Among other things the February snap elections would leave the badly fragmented opposition little time to organize and campaign, an idea that must have been foremost in the mind of Marcos. For an organized, unified opposition, given much time to campaign, could seriously threaten his hold on the government and power.

In retrospect it was in 1985 that the various opposition groups restudied plans made in late 1984 to get together and select a common presidential candidate should snap polls be called. They formed a Convenor Group, headed by former Senator Tanada, Cory Aquino and businessman Jaime Ongpin, which by then had devised a "fast-track" system of choosing the opposition presidential candidate from a pool of nine potential presidential standard bearers. But the proposal was severely attacked by both the cause-oriented groups and some traditional political parties from the ranks of the opposition like the Unido. In fact the latter groups decided to try out their own unity formula through a National Unification Committee (NUC) led by the Unido. The NUC was formally launched on March 10, 1985 though it failed to get all the opposition groups under its wing.

By the second half of 1985, still unable to resolve the problem of unification, the opposition groups placed the problem in the hands of two women, Cory Aquino, who represented the Convenors, and former Supreme Court Justice Cecilia Palma.

In October the Cory Aquino for President Movement was launched. It propelled Ninoy's widow to the frontline of the presidential contest. Other opposition presidential hopefuls bowed out of the race, with the sole exception of Doy Laurel. As rivals for nomination as common presidential candidate of the diverse opposition groups, Cory and Doy engaged each other in a bruising, emotionally charged power play which, as we have seen, saw Mrs. Aquino emerge as the victor but running for President under the banner of Laurel's Unido party.

The KBL and the newly united opposition began their campaigns even before the question of whether the snap elections would be held or not remained unresolved. No less than 11 petitions had been filed in the Supreme Court questioning the constitutionality of the polls. On December 19, by a split vote of 7-5, the high tribunal dismissed all 11 petitions and ruled that the election was constitutional, thus pushing Marcos into the most difficult political battle he had ever encountered throughout his life as a politician.

It was the first time in Philippine history that a woman would seek the Presidency of the country as an official candidate, and the first time the grizzled Marcos would face a female rival for the nation's highest office — a woman known only as a housewife who had no previous political experience and who had never held a job, except that of being a housewife, all her life.

It seemed clear, except for the incurably naive, that in calling for snap elections President Marcos had indeed yielded to American pressure. As one analyst has observed, at no other time perhaps in the 20-year alliance between Marcos and the Americans had there been "so much enmity on either side." The world media focused on the American foreign policy dilemma in the Philippines more than ever before: "how to deal with Mr. Marcos without laying the groundwork for a Communist takeover that would spell the end of U.S. bases in the country." Indeed it was apparent throughout the year 1985 that the U.S. government was haunted by images of Vietnam, Iran and Nicaragua which, they feared, could be repeated in the Philippines.

Then in March a document containing an outline of American policy toward the Philippines was "leaked" to Filipino oppositionists in the United States. That document read partly:

"The U.S. does not want to remove Marcos from power or to destabilize the government of the Philippines. Rather, we are urging revitalization of democratic institutions, dismantling 'crony' monopoly capitalism and allowing the economy to respond to free market forces, and restoring professional, apolitical leadership to the Philippine military to deal with the Communist insurgency. These efforts are meant to stabilize while strengthening institutions which will eventually provide for a peaceful transition." [8]

After President Marcos had announced the snap elections, American pressure centered on ensuring free and credible polls.

The United States tightened its squeeze on Marcos in terms of diminished or withheld aid and loans, diplomatic pressure applied both privately and publicly through statements and resolutions from a vocal and critical U.S. Congress, and an obviously orchestrated media blitz on the Philippines which included exposes on "hidden wealth" and top-level official corruption. Soon the media assault would include exposes on the supposed fake war medals and falsified war exploits of President Marcos, which certainly brought him untold embarrassment and humiliation before the world.

In addition the U.S. government publicly "distanced" itself and tried to disentangle its fate from that of an increasingly unpopular ally.

Yet contrary to U.S. expectations, Marcos did not immediately respond to pressure. In fact, it was pointed out, the President actually set the timing, terms and conditions of the snap election in such a manner that these would weigh heavily in his favor. For instance, the polls would be held, as he announced, in February, months before the local elections — a period when more than 90% of local government posts would still be controlled by his party, the KBL. It was thought, too, that with the passing months, the President's health and the national economy would further deteriorate; an early election would thus be in his favor. Moreover, early elections meant only a few months' notice and a short campaign period, to the disadvantage of the opposition. It seemed that the old political warrior had outfoxed the Americans. While giving the impression that he was succumbing to their pressure, he was actually determining and dictating things to his advantage.

AS the snap election neared, the problem of insurgency strongly called attention to itself. The year 1985, for a fact, saw spectacular raids by the New People's Army on military camps, town halls, plantations, logging concessions and private armories. The insurgents also took major political offensives by forming National Democratic Front regional councils in the islands of Mindanao, Panay, Negros and the Bicol region in Southern Luzon, and announcing this in daring press conferences in the hills to which selected local and foreign media representatives were invited.

In June 1985 acting Chief of Staff Fidel Ramos estimated that there were 10 to 11 insurgency-related incidents of violence daily, and an average of three soldiers or militiamen killed every day, including three civilians and four NPA guerrillas. The military answered with an iron hand and initiated encounters, food blockades to drive the insurgents out of their lairs, and mass evacuations of people to deprive the guerrillas of mass support.

All these insurgency-related incidents generated apprehension and anxiety among U.S. policymakers, who pressed the panic button on the insurgency situation and went so far as to predict civil war in the country on a massive scale within three to five years. They believed that the answer to the growing insurgency was wider economic, political and military reforms. The problem of Philippine insurgency was magnified worldwide by the media, making it one of the world's top ten news stories of the year.

The mass protests triggered by the Aquino assassination in 1983 continued unabated through 1985, though the large-scale protest rallies and demonstrations shifted venues from Metro Manila to the provinces. General strikes or *welga ng bayan*, for instance, erupted in Mindanao, paralyzing entire towns and cities for days. By May no less than 16 such general strikes had been held in Mindanao alone. In the months of May, June, August and September, many other places throughout the country were forced to a standstill by the giant strikes. One such strike was held in Escalante, Negros Occidental on September 20, during which militiamen fired at striking farm workers, killing 21 persons in that biggest massacre of protesters.

That year, 1985, eve of the snap presidential elections that would change the course of Philippine history, was a banner year for increased militance by the people and repression by the forces of government. By the middle of the year the forces of citizen protest were dichotomized with the formation of two centers of protest: the bigger and left-leaning *Bagong Alyansang Makabayan* (New Nationalist Alliance) which spearheaded the *welga ng bayan* and the *Bayang Nagkakaisa sa Diwa at Layunin (Bandila)* or Nation United in Thought and Objectives. The latter is identified with the Social Democrats. Both were vehemently anti-Marcos.

STILL another factor that would have much bearing on the February 7 snap elections was the so-called "Trial of the Century" logged in the dockets of the Sandiganbayan court as Criminal Case No. 10010 (for the murder of Benigno Aquino Jr.) and Criminal Case No. 10011 (for the murder of Rolando Galman). The two cases were combined and tried as one case by the court with 25 military officers and one civilian indicted for the crimes. At the top of the list of accused was Maj. Gen. Fabian C. Ver, Chief of Staff of the Armed Forces of the Philippines. Although accused only as an accessory, Ver and the others were virtually condemned by the Agrava Board reports. They had demanded a speedy trial in order to be able to clear their names.

It was this case of Ninoy Aquino which precipitated the massive protest rallies and demonstrations that shook the nation and the Marcos government to their very roots immediately after August 21, 1983 when Aquino was gunned down at the airport upon returning from the United States. The assassination unleashed a massive economic crisis which in turn aggravated the poverty of the masses, which inevitably resulted in an escalation of insurgency not only in the countryside but in towns and cities and fanned the flames of the people's anger against the national leadership which by 1985 had almost totally lost its credibility.

The trial started on February 22, with Presiding Justice Manuel R. Pamaran of the First Division of the Sandiganbayan promising a brisk, no-delay procedure that would take no more than three to four months. Hearings were scheduled on Mondays to Fridays from 8:30 a.m. to 12 noon, and then from 2:30 to 5 p.m. But the inevitable delays and postponements made the trial drag on to seven months. Prosecution was the responsibility of Tanodbayan Bernardo Fernandez and his deputy, Manuel Herrera. The accused were represented by several lawyers. Some of them, including Antonio Coronel and Rodolfo Jimenez, became national celebrities. Of the accused, Brig. Gen. Prospero Olivas dispensed with the services of a lawyer and instead opted to defend himself.

Before the trial began, on January 23, Pamaran made the first of several decisions that had a direct bearing on the case and which did not in any way help the government improve its credibility. He ordered that the accused military men, except one civilian, be turned over to the custody of their commanding officers after earlier ordering their detention in a civilian jail. For the entire period of the anticlimactic trial, the accused remained "confined to barracks." On February 1 they all pleaded "not guilty" during their arraignment.

Presenting its witnesses, the prosecution had by March run through the testimonies of Ramon Balang, Ramon Layoso and Olivia Reyes confirming that Aquino was shot on the last few steps of the stairway rather than on the tarmac. Another witness, journalist Sandra Burton of *Time Magazine*, seemed to corroborate this with her tape-recording of the last seconds before the first gunshot was heard. Highlighting the prosecution's argument was an eyewitness account by Rebecca Quijano, who failed to testify before the Agrava Board but now agreed to report in court what she saw: a Metrocom soldier shooting Ninoy Aquino on the emergency stairway.

The defense sought to minimize the prosecution's evidence. Although they at first decided not to cross-examine Quijano, dubbed by the press as "The Crying Lady" for having allegedly wept upon witnessing Ninoy's killing, they demanded her recall. The next time around the defense lawyers exposed Quijano's troubled past in an attempt to destroy her credibility. Then they presented their own witnesses who claimed to be eyewitnesses themselves but flatly contradicted Quijano's version.

Meanwhile, another legal issue arose. Two weeks after Balang's testimony, lawyer Antonio Coronel, counsel for Ver, announced he would seek the general's exoneration with an appeal to the immunity supposedly granted his client by a provision in the presidential decree creating the Fact-Finding Board. He claimed the provision protected all those who testified before the Board from the use of their testimonies for any crime other than perjury. Pamaran and the two other justices found this acceptable, but the prosecution, encouraged by intense public clamor, raised the issue to the Supreme Court.

Voting 10-3, the high court upheld the Sandiganbayan ruling.

Trouble also started brewing for the defense when foreign news sources revealed that Philippine Air Force jets had been "scrambled" on August 21, 1983 to intercept the plane bearing Aquino. The U.S. State Department sent affidavits by U.S. servicemen that they had been asked to leave their radar stations, and threatened to blow the case wide open with new angles to the incident. This time the prosecution itself chose to inhibit the evidence. Tanodbayan Fernandez, chief of the prosecution, justified his action by saying that he thought the new evidence was irrelevant to the prosecution theory, besides not being properly authenticated and based on hearsay.

But later, when Fernandez overruled his own deputy, Herrera, from presenting 14 rebuttal witnesses, the ground was prepared for a petition for mistrial. The petition reached the Supreme Court late in November, after the trial had been declared formally ended on September 26 and both sides had submitted their memoranda summing up their arguments. The justices then reserved for themselves a period of 120 days to resolve the case.

The Supreme Court dismissed the final petition.

Then on December 2, much earlier than anybody had expected, the Sandiganbayan gave its final, unappealable verdict, overthrowing all the conclusions arrived at by the Agrava Board one year earlier. The decision: not a single one of the 26 accused was guilty.

"The Pamaran court found many inconsistencies in the argument of the prosecution while it noted the seamless logicality in the argument of the defense," writes a magazine reporter. "It decided to resolve all doubts in favor of the defense. The final picture was an exact verification of the theory proposed by President Marcos days after the killing: a lone Communist-hired gun had killed Aquino just as he was about to board a van full of protecting soldiers."[9]

As President Marcos had promised, Gen. Ver was reinstated as AFP Chief of Staff upon his acquittal.

The acquittal of all the accused in the Aquino assassination trial further exacerbated the public disenchantment over President Marcos and the government and generated several new protest actions. It was the final action that stripped the entire government machinery of credibility and completely eroded public faith in the administration of the President. It also lent credibility to Cory Aquino's statement, in refusing to participate in the investigation — and trial — of her husband's death that she could not expect justice as long as President Marcos was in power.

The fact that the court verdict acquitting Ver and company and Ver's reinstatement as Chief of Staff by President Marcos took place just two months before the snap elections further aggravated the people's anger. The February 7 election became, to them, the propitious time to vent their anger, frustration and hatred.

Such was the situation when Cory Cojuangco Aquino, the aggrieved widow of the assassinated Ninoy, found herself thrust in the center of the political arena to face the shrewdest and most accomplished politician of this country in the bitterest contest ever in its history.

NINE

A Contest of Giants

*If Cory has come out of a chrysalis in this election, it
isn't as a butterfly in a yellow dress but as someone with
a great deal more guts and nerve than you might have
expected.*

— Reuter, British News Agency

VIEWED with objectivity and without passion, the February 7, 1986
"snap" or presidential election was actually the much-delayed final
showdown in the extended power struggle between two great political giants: President Ferdinand E. Marcos, the reigning champion,
and the late former Senator Benigno S. Aquino Jr., challenger. At
stake was the highest and most powerful office in the Philippines.

This final battle should have taken place as early as November
1973, a presidential election year, but for the intervention of events,
natural and spontaneous, or man-conceived and manipulated. Marcos
would then have served the last few days of his second term as
President; he was reelected overwhelmingly against Sergio Osmena
Jr., in 1969 and was prohibited by the Constitution from seeking
another reelection. But before his second term was over, on September 21, 1972 Marcos declared martial law under the now infamous
Presidential Proclamation No. 1081. Using his emergency powers
provided by the Constitution he abolished Congress — both the
Lower House and the Senate — arrested and jailed his political rivals,
the first and most famous of whom was then Senator Ninoy Aquino,
cracked down on what he called the "oligarchy" and "economic
royalists" and closed down and "sequestered" their powerful press,
radio and television media in an attempt to build a new Philippines,
a "new society."

Aquino, boyish in looks but tough, resourceful and charismatic, was serving his first term as Senator of the Philippines, the
youngest and most colorful in that body, having been elected in
1967 after serving as the youngest municipal mayor (Concepcion)

and the youngest Governor of Tarlac province in Central Luzon. He was then widely talked about as the most probable opposition presidential candidate in 1973. But with the imposition of martial law, Marcos had him arrested together with many other important political leaders, and was kept in detention, first at Fort Magsaysay in Laur, Nueva Ecija, then at Fort Bonifacio in Makati, Rizal, for approximately seven years and seven months. Aquino was given freedom by Marcos only in May 1980, when he was allowed to fly to the United States to undergo a triple bypass heart surgery. Then, returning to the Philippines on August 21, 1983 he was killed by a single gunshot on the head as he descended the stairway of China Airlines Flight 811 at the Manila International Airport. Aquino, escorted from his seat and down the aircraft by selected military officers, was then under the protective custody of the Armed Forces of the Philippines.

Since his proclamation of martial law, President Marcos had ruled the nation by decree. Both executive and legislative powers were concentrated in him. He had also abolished the office of Vice President, thus consigning his long-time partner Fernando Lopez to inutility and oblivion. Behind him, providing the guns and the muscles, was an incredibly large military organization — approximately 250,000-strong — which he had lovingly nurtured and built up since he first assumed the Presidency, ensuring that its top and most important officers were Ilocanos loyal to him. The "pampering" of the military establishment by Marcos was denounced by Ninoy Aquino during his first year in the Senate when he delivered on the floor a privileged speech attacking and exposing Marcos's nearly imperceptible transformation of the country into a "garrison state."

As the martial-law ruler secured by the military, aided by a new media empire controlled and owned directly by him, his relatives or "cronies," and served by a small army of presidential and special assistants and a loyal — if toothless — Cabinet, Marcos issued in rapid succession numerous presidential decrees, general orders, proclamations and letters of instruction which became parts of the laws of the land. As an adjunct of his political reorganization he put an end to customary political activities and abolished elections which he replaced with plebiscites and referenda. With the abolition of Congress and the feeble presence of an apprehensive judiciary, the old systems of checks and balances and of advise and consent were cast aside to give way to a new concept of governance euphemistically called "constitutional authoritarianism." His critics and rivals more aptly called it dictatorship.

Ferdinand E. Marcos, first elected as President of the Philippines in 1965 and then reelected in 1969, became since September 21, 1972 a dictator with near-absolute powers by the audacious but simple expedient of putting the entire country under martial law. In the process he abruptly put an end to the democratic political system in the country by abolishing the institution of free elections.

IT was only on June 16, 1981 that the next presidential polls were held. Marcos decided to run for the office for the third time, not against Ninoy Aquino whom he had jailed since 1972 and who was then in the United States recuperating from a heart surgery, but against Alejo B. Santos whom the Nacionalista party (Jose J. Roy Wing) had plucked from the obscurity of the directorship of the Bureau of Prisons just to give Marcos a "passable" opponent, a token one. As expected, perhaps even by Santos himself, Marcos pulverized the prisons director with a score of 18,309,360 as against 1,716,449 for Santos.[1]

That 1981 victory gave President Marcos a new six-year tenure and came five months after he had lifted the nine-year-old martial-law regime. In the interregnum before the elections, the Interim Batasang Pambansa or provisional parliament provided in the Constitution of 1973 had been organized and its members elected in 1978. The Batasan replaced the abolished Congress. With martial law theoretically and apparently lifted, he would rule again as a duly elected President. His election and the existence of the Batasan gave the world an indication that democracy in the Philippines had been restored. According to the new rules of the game, Marcos would be due for another reelection only in 1987. That would be the time when the political opposition headed by such leaders as Ninoy Aquino, the late Senator Gerardo Roxas and former Senator Jovito R. Salonga could engage Marcos in a struggle for the Presidency and when Aquino could perhaps finally face Marcos in their often-postponed, much-delayed final showdown.

But it was not to be for as in the past, events intervened again. Aquino, as we have seen, was gunned down while alighting from a plane at the Manila International Airport while in the protective custody of military officers.

News of the Aquino assassination reverberated 'round the world, which television had shrunk into what Marshall McLuhan has called a "global village." Domestically the tragedy proved cathartic and polarized the forces of Aquino as against the forces of Marcos.

But while emotionally catalyzed by Aquino's death the anti-Marcos forces could not in reality get together and harmonize. They could not "get their act together," to use a common expression. One of their top leaders, Gerry Roxas, was dead; he died in 1982 in the United States. Salonga, on the other hand, had been in self-exile in the United States, and the Liberals at home, behaving like they were in power, were busy tearing each other apart. The forces of the opposition were considerable in number but utterly fractious, a big army without an able commanding general.

Clearly what the opposition forces needed was one leader who could inspire, unite and put them together into one single fighting machine. It was the role that had long been waiting for the likes of Ninoy Aquino and which he himself had been wishing to perform. Unfortunately for the opposition, when he did come home to play that vital role, death intervened.

Many other opposition leaders desired and coveted his part. But great roles in history are reserved for great actors. It seemed that not one of the aspirants, those waiting quietly in the wings, was big and capable enough to creditably perform Ninoy Aquino's part.

And time was fast running out on the leaderless, fragmented opposition forces. The date President Marcos had chosen for the snap elections, February 7, 1986, was fast approaching and the deadline for filing certificates of candidacy for President and Vice President was almost at hand. Former Senator Salvador Laurel had preempted other opposition aspirants by filing his certificate ahead of the rest. But he did so only as a candidate of one opposition party, the Unido, to the exclusion of the other opposition groups. It was the prevailing consensus at the time that Laurel and his Unido would be putty in the hands of Marcos and his powerful machine, the KBL, which had at least 90% of all local officials under its control. Without the support and active help of the rest of the opposition groupings, Laurel was considered to have little chance to topple Marcos from power. This could be the reason why at that moment in history the Marcoses, in Malacanang, were said to be delirious with joy — they felt that with Doy Laurel as their rival in the snap elections, Marcos was as good as reelected.

But as fate would have it, an upheaval within the opposition ranks in particular and the national political situation in general took place. Through a conspiracy of forces, personalities and events, the soft-spoken, politically inexperienced widow of the slain Ninoy

Aquino was prevailed upon to accept a draft for her to run for President, with Laurel as her running mate. This was the first time in the history of the Philippines that a candidate for President received a direct draft by the people — 1,200,000 of them in the case of Cory Aquino. Not even the popular Ramon Magsaysay was so drafted by the people by signed endorsements when he wrested the Presidency from incumbent President Elpidio Quirino. And, it might be stressed again, this was the first time in the nation's history that a woman was seeking the Presidency as an official candidate of a major political party or coalition of parties.

Such was Corazon Cojuangco Aquino.

BY herself alone Cory Aquino was a simple, hitherto obscure widow and mother or five. Though born with a silver spoon in her mouth into a family of politicians on both her maternal and paternal sides, she herself had no previous political experience and had publicly admitted that she knew nothing about the Presidency. She was a political novice. a rank amateur in a game her husband had delighted in playing with finesse, subtlety and sophistication. As the Marcos sloganeers put it in one of their leaflets, Cory was *walang alam* (knew nothing) in politics especially in the position she was seeking, the Presidency. Marcos himself had described her as "an inexperienced pilot" to whom passengers were not likely to entrust their lives and a person without any management experience at all and should not be appointed president even of a small private firm.

Moreover, as the propagandists of Marcos frequently emphasized in their political advertising, Cory Aquino was "only a woman" and therefore could not be expected to be equal to the Presidency which is properly "a man's job."

But in reality Cory Aquino was more than a housewife, a widow, a mother of five with no political experience whatsoever. She was Mrs. Ninoy Aquino. To the people she was Ninoy's replacement or substitute — some say his *karma* or resurrection. This was the only plausible reason why the Marcoses — the President and his wife Imelda —reportedly became sleepless upon knowing that Cory had consented to be the united opposition's candidate for President, and Laurel merely her running mate. They knew how formidable an opponent they had in her.

Thus, though death had eliminated her husband bodily from the climax of his epic struggle with Marcos, she had stepped into his shoes, as it were — she had taken his place bearing the magic of his name, the mystique and charisma of his persona.

A jubilant Cory Cojuangco Aquino raises both hands in a double *Laban* (fight) sign as she acknowledges cheers of adoring multitudes at one of massive popular rallies in support of her presidential bid. The pose has become her personal symbol.

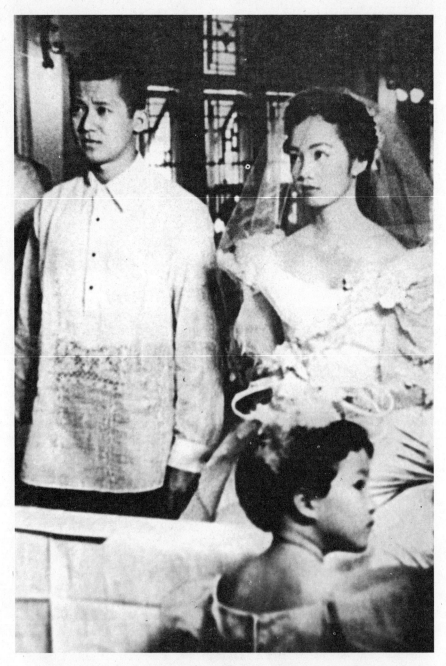

Ninoy and Cory are married at a Manila Catholic church. She had to give up her law studies at Far Eastern University, Manila, to assume role of Ninoy's wife — until destiny enshrined her in the nation's Presidency on February 25, 1986.

Cory's parents, Jose Cojuangco and Demetria Sumulong Cojuangco, with other Cojuangco siblings. She is partly hidden by her father symbolic of her eventual emergence from the background to occupy and perform her role at center stage. Others in photo are, from left: Terry C. Lopa, Passy C. Teopaco, Pete and Jose "Peping" Jr. Young girl in grandfather's arms is Marisse C. Reyes, daughter of Josephine C. Reyes.

Ninoy with author at a students' con-vocation-rally in Manila, one of last youth assemblies he addressed before Marcos declared martial law and kept him in detention.

Ninoy and Cory receive one of numerous awards and testimonials from apprecia-tive organizations.

Former President Diosdado Macapagal (in dark coat) is assisted by Cory and Ninoy (partly hidden, center) in opening a project. Macapagal, a peasants' son from Central Luzon, served as President from 1961-1965.

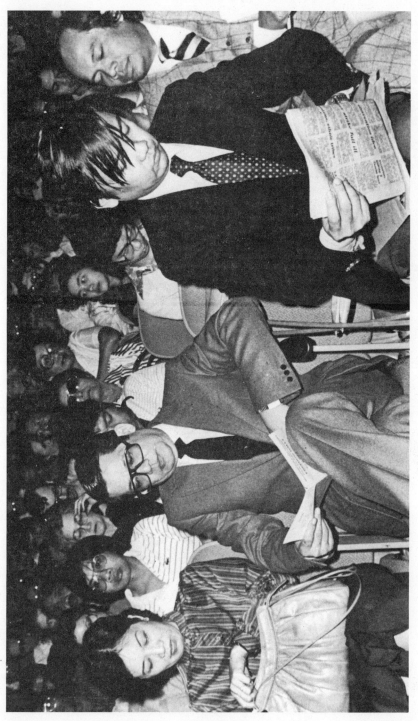

Ninoy (center) and Cory at an opposition symposium in Los Angeles, California, under auspices of the Ninoy Aquino Movement headed by Heherson T. Alvarez, president (right). Cory has appointed Alvarez new Minister of Agrarian Reform.

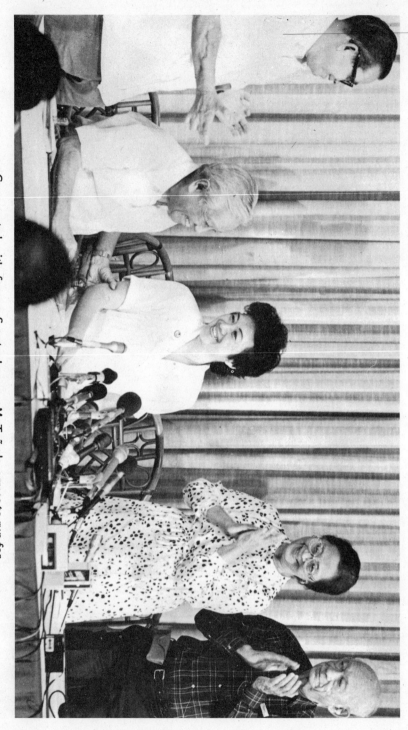

Cory seated with former Senator Lorenzo M. Tañada, agrees to run for President after much pressure and delay. Standing from left: ex-Senator Jovito Salonga, ex-Justice Cecilia Munoz-Palma of the Supreme Court, and Joaquin P. Roces, head of the Cory Aquino for President Movement.

Former Senator Francisco "Soc" Rodrigo raises hands of Cory Aquino and Doy Laurel as grand coalition candidates for President and Vice President. Laurel withdrew from presidential race to give way to Cory.

Cory and youngest daughter Kris hitting campaign trail at Dinalupihan, Bataan.

Part of huge crowd that attended Cory and Doy's *miting de avance* or election eve rally at Luneta Park, Manila, on February 4, 1986.

Cory the Candidate (left) and Celia Diaz Laurel, wife of Doy Laurel, perform an Igorot ethnic dance at Lagawe, Ifugao, Mountain Province, to court cultural minority votes in Marcos country.

Enrile (center) and Ramos trek back to Camp Aguinaldo from Camp Crame. The rebels had seized both camps as the first step in the revolt.

Two makers of history, Defense Minister Juan Ponce Enrile (right) and General Fidel V. Ramos, then Vice Chief of Staff of the Armed Forces, announce on Saturday night, February 22, 1986, their fateful decision to withdraw support from President Marcos and shift loyalty to Cory Aquino whom they perceived to be the winner of the people's mandate in the February 7, 1986 "snap" elections.

Cory (at table) addresses first press conference on election night, February 7, 1986 during which she claimed victory over Marcos.

Soldiers rush firearms and ammunition to Camp Aguinaldo in anticipation of assaults by Marcos-Ver troops on first day of uprising, while Enrile (uppermost photo, left) flashes Laban sign.

Enrile (hand raised) and Ramos (right) thank volunteer supporters morning of February 24, the day before Marcos fled the country. At left is Lt. Col. Gregorio "Gringo" Honasan, a RAM leader.

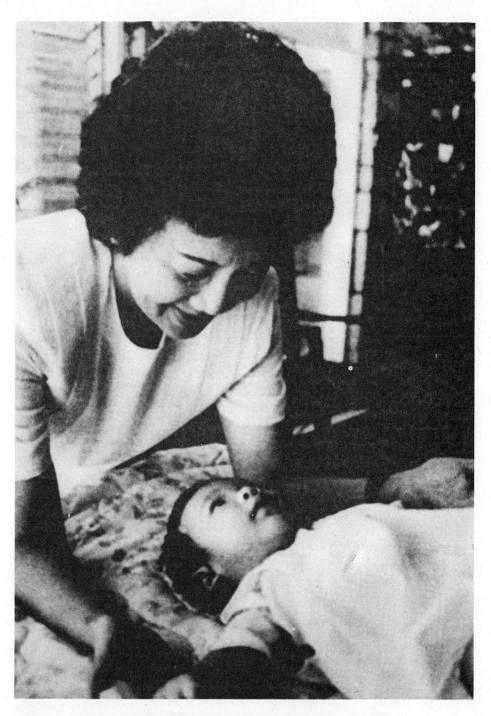

Cory the President and Grandmother dotes on first granddaughter.

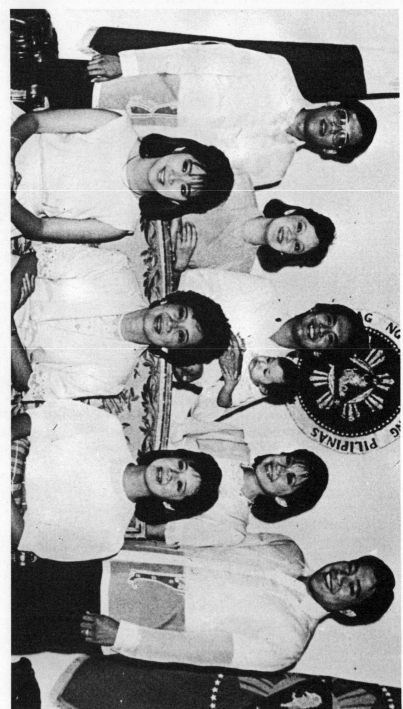

The First Family of the Philippines. President Cory Aquino is flanked by daughters Kris (left, seated) and Viel. Standing from left are Benigno "Noynoy" C. Aquino III, the only son, Maria Elena ("Ballsy") and husband Eldon Cruz, with first grandchild. At right: Pinky and Manolo Abellada.

It was because Cory was in effect Ninoy reincarnate that she succeeded in uniting the various opposition forces — the partisans, the ideologues and the cause-oriented, the clerics, the moneyed elite, the disenchanted. They all rallied to her flag chanting her name — "Cory! Cory!" with the same beat and intensity as "Ninoy! Ninoy!" — and inspired and buoyed her up with their collective hopes and enthusiasm, because they could see in her the embodiment of all that was to them desirable in their beloved Ninoy Aquino. They looked up to Cory as their savior, as they had done to Ninoy.

Marcos, therefore, had all the reason to be apprehensive, to consider this Marcos-Aquino encounter as the toughest battle of his long political career. He knew his opponent was not Cory alone but Cory *and* Ninoy, and that concealed within that extremely feminine body of Cory was the distillation of the people's long pent-up passions, dreams, frustrations, suspended ambitions — and the surging tidal waves of sympathy and outrage generated by Ninoy's brutal assassination at the airport. Gifted not only with the courage of a lion but also the cunning of a fox, Ferdinand Marcos most certainly perceived — and appreciated — this political reality. In fact he eventually admitted that it was indeed his toughest political fight and then was said to have remarked with unconcealed regret that calling the snap elections had been his biggest and fatal mistake.

BE that as it may, Cory Aquino, although armed with a most formidable name and enigma and buoyed up by the adulation of millions across the country, was not facing a political nonentity. She was in reality pitted against a Goliath, a giant in politics who had never known defeat in an election. Gifted with eloquence, courage, imagination and dash, Ferdinand E. Marcos emerged after World War II from the once-forlorn province of Ilocos Norte, in Northern Luzon, and strode with confidence into the storied halls of Congress representing his congressional district. Having made his mark in Congress and marrying, after just 11 days of courtship, House Speaker Daniel Romualdez's niece, Imelda Romualdez, he soon aspired and ran for the Senate — and won at the head of a pack of eight winners, even as an opposition candidate. As a young Senator with an eye fixed on the Presidency, he waged a blitzkrieg campaign to seize the Senate presidency from the venerable Senate President Eulogio "Amang" Rodriguez Sr. — and successfully bearded the old king lion right in his own den.

From there, Marcos was just one step away from Malacanang. As Senate president he kept his eye focused on the Presidency while keeping his feet — and a growing army of followers — on the ground. The Presidency was then held by a fellow Liberal, Diosdado Macapagal, who reached the summit of power and glory after campaigning as "the poor boy from Lubao," his hometown in the province of Pampanga, Central Luzon. Marcos yearned to get his party's nomination as candidate for President but Macapagal would not allow him for he himself was determined to seek a second four-year term. Impatient to become President and claiming that President Macapagal had reneged on a promise not to seek reelection, Marcos bolted the Liberal party and got himself sworn in as a member of the Nacionalista party, with then Speaker Jose B. Laurel Jr., administering his oath.

As a new Nacionalista Marcos fought the party kingpins for the nomination. As another proof of his political skill and prowess as a strategist and fighter nonpareil, he captured the nomination after vanquishing some of the most illustrious men of power in the party: Senator Gil J. Puyat, Senator Arturo M. Tolentino, former Vice President Fernando Lopez and former Vice President and Senator Emmanuel Pelaez. Now, as NP presidential standard-bearer, the young lion was prepared to fight Macapagal on even ground.

The wounds inflicted during those struggles, from the Senate presidency to the NP presidential nomination, were deep and many. But Marcos, with the assistance of his then "secret weapon," Imelda Romualdez Marcos, bound and healed the wounds. Moreover he succeeded in winning the leaders to his side. He then proceeded to transform the Nacionalista party into a reconditioned machine and primed it for peak efficiency. At the same time he continued developing his own personal organization, the soon-to-be dreaded Marcos Machine, consisting largely of the "Solid North" or the Ilocano Bloc. This was his own power base, entirely personal and distinct from the party organization.

Along the way on his rise to power, some friends had to be discarded by Marcos and alliances swept away and replaced with others. He was criticized by his enemies as ruthless, with a heart of stone — that he would not stop at anything to get what he wanted. The criticism was not without basis: ruthlessness is a fact of political life. U.S. President Richard M. Nixon, one of its most celebrated exponents, has written that:

"Those who reach the top, particularly in the political world, have to develop a certain tough realism as far as friendships and loyalties are concerned."[2]

As the NP presidential candidate he challenged his former colleague in the Liberal party, President Macapagal, and waged a fierce, relentless campaign to oust him. As in past elections official graft and corruption was one of the key issues. He continued harping on this alongside with the administration's "inefficiency." Backed by the big party leaders, although reluctantly — and suspiciously — by some, he stormed the ramparts of Malacanang from whose portals he was determined to flush out Macapagal, crying to the incumbent President endlessly: *"Alis d'yan!"* (Get out of there!), implying that although Macapagal was merely serving his first four-year term, he had already been overstaying in the Palace.

Again, as proof of his superb political skill, Marcos succeeded in wresting the crown from the reigning champion. Through creative and sophisticated marshalling of his forces, which were admittedly inferior in number and resources to those of Macapagal at the start, he waged his campaign so successfully that on November 9, 1965 he obtained a total vote of 3,554,840 against President Macapagal's 3,187,752 or a difference of 673,572 votes in favor of Marcos.[3]

The new reign of Ferdinand — and Imelda — Marcos had begun. It would continue without interruption for a total of 20 years, up to 1986.

IN 1969, another presidential election year, Ferdinand E. Marcos was uncontested in his party in his quest for what he called a "second mandate." His running without any competition from within his party proved conclusively that he was the Nacionalistas' unchallenged head. It meant that he had succeeded not only in subduing the great party leaders but in transforming them into vital instruments for the attainment of his personal purposes. The party convention, to select the presidential nominee, was held nevertheless but merely to confirm his renomination by wild acclamation.

Marcos's unchallenged renomination as NP presidential candidate demonstrated to the Liberals and the people at large that the entire Nacionalista leadership and forces had accepted him as their leader and were solidly united behind him. It gained added impact for it marked also the sudden shift of other vital forces from the Liberal side to the Nacionalistas. Among the new Marcos partisans were the Ramon Magsaysay forces, the Cornelio Villareal forces, and some forces of former President Macapagal headed by Pampanga Governor Francisco Nepomuceno.

These forces were added to his own legion of leaders and followers, his personal machine.

Meanwhile the NP officialdom which he had captured earlier

proved their loyalty to him when Senate President Puyat himself, who was expected to be his principal rival, personally nominated Marcos. Nobody else challenged him.

In his classic book, *The Art of War*, Sun Tzu writes:

"Generally in war the best policy is to take a state intact; to ruin it is inferior to this.

"To capture the enemy's [state] is better than to destroy it . . . to win one hundred victories in one hundred battles is not the acme of skill. To subdue the enemy without fighting is the acme of skill."[4]

This was exactly what Marcos did with the Nacionalista party.

Marcos insisted on holding the 1969 convention, even if he had no opponent for the nomination, as a tactical move. He saw it as an occasion not for fighting but for all his leaders to get together and reconcile so they could work together again as one big, efficient fighting team.

This was the same reason why in December 1985 he insisted on holding a grand proclamation rally of the Kilusang Bagong Lipunan at the Manila Hotel. He used that occasion to announce to the party leaders — and to the nation at large, since the event was fully covered by media — his choice of Arturo M. Tolentino as his candidate for Vice President. With characteristic political wisdom he also used that occasion, as he did the NP convention in 1969, to give public recognition to all the delegates who had come from all parts of the country, acknowledge their support and assistance to the party through the years past, and extend patronage to them as an expression of gratitude. And like the past master of political leadership that he had always been, he utilized that largely social event to whip the party leaders into line after boosting their morale with recognition and patronage, applying the necessary pressure on the regional, district, provincial, city and municipal party bosses for the purpose of securing maximum votes for him and his running mate.

As a political strategist par excellence, Marcos believes deeply in maintaining an organization, a machine, whether his or the party's, at highest efficiency. He believes that an organization is "the basic factor in a political fight." For an efficient organization will enable a candidate to cover those parts of the country which he could never hope to reach and penetrate unaided, alone. An organization is also the candidate's instrument in implementing his campaign plan.

A MARCOS campaign plan is prepared by several groups and think tanks. But Marcos himself prepares the master schedule because, as he puts it, it affects him and because it is he who knows what he could do. He studies everything that goes into his plan, including the details — how to handle disputes between factions, appointment of inspectors, distribution of patronage, handling of media. He is, as already pointed out, extra particular about the condition of the party machine as well as that of his own — he would not rely solely on the party organization. Where other leaders would shirk from fights among local officials to avoid getting enmeshed in inter-party struggles, Marcos relished swinging into them.

As always he is a severe and strict party leader and allows no "free zones" where his candidates fought one another. Whenever feasible he would pick his own candidates. In his hands the party is run and maintained as a single disciplined fighting machine, ever perfectly tuned up, functioning with minimum waste of power and energy. It was observed, for instance, that not since President Magsaysay had the Nacionalista party machine been so powerful and effective.

Obviously, as late as 1985, the same strict and severe party leadership was brought to bear on the KBL by Marcos.

Like all effective campaign plans, a Marcos war plan is always abundantly funded, and funds are used systematically. During his 1969 reelection campaign, running against Senator Osmena, he stopped the "scattered gunshots" style of fund distribution because it was wasteful, and insisted that there should be a limit to the funds to be spent. He believes in setting a budget and sticking to it; without a budget the voters and leaders would assume that the sky is the limit; to refuse to "come across" is to court disaster.

During his 1969 campaign, Marcos was criticized for spending too much. But according to him he would have spent more if Osmena as opposition standard-bearer had shown signs of fiscal power.

He believes in pacing expenditures systematically. For instance, a candidate, according to Marcos, must project expenditure in such a way that by the last three weeks of the campaign he would still have 50% of his funds available to enable him to keep his organization intact during the last crucial month. With the money the candidate could hire poll watchers and pay the leaders who would herd voters into the precincts, and take charge of last-minute expenses.

The last lap of a campaign, in the view of Marcos, is most crucial for it is the period of *conversion*, the conversion of popularity and sympathy into votes.

Failure to appreciate this necessity, according to him, proved fatal to Osmena's bid to oust Marcos. In fact Osmena and the big

Liberal leaders did not provide funds for the last lap — they poured too much money too soon on the people and on propaganda. Informed that Osmena was refusing to spend on his organization during that critical period, Marcos knew his challenger was in trouble, deep trouble.

"I don't know whether he ran out of money," Marcos recalls. "One thing is sure: he did not finance the organization during the last two weeks of the campaign."

As a result the Liberals could not even afford to pay for the identification cards of their poll watchers, let alone the regulation P4 a day allowance. And when the Osmena watchers were refused admission inside the precincts for lack of IDs, the Nacionalista leaders helped them and offered them IDs and funds, thus converting them into Marcos partisans.

Marcos as a political strategist believes in and was among the first Filipino politicians to utilize modern technology in his campaigns: the helicopter to enable him to cover the entire archipelago in a relatively brief period; the computer to provide him with systematized records keeping; and professional poll surveys to provide him with clues on where he was strong or weak.

As a political fighter he does not believe in the siege but prefers the swift, lightning attack or *blitz*, the "confident campaign of the veteran intelligence officer who, having coldly and analytically anticipated all possible consequences, chooses the time and place for his encounter, and thus through surprise controls the initiative."[6]

Marcos still uses that element of surprise to his advantage, as he did when he called the February 7 snap polls, though it meant shortening his unserved term of office by one year.

In addition the veteran political tactician believes there is no substitute for personal campaigning, for person-to-person contact with the voters, for what American politicians call "pressing the flesh." As he puts it, the personal appearance is important even if the candidate just stands at the platform repeating the same old platitudes and saying nothing new. One's popularity rises with a single round of handshaking — there is no substitute for it.

Thus, although admittedly poor in health, he kept on physically campaigning in the provinces as much as he could for the snap elections — to the chagrin of the opposition and the consternation of his physicians, family members and close political lieutenants.

And Marcos, a modern politician, is an inveterate user of mass media. He knows the power and peculiarities of television, radio, print, outdoor, direct mail even, and uses them accordingly: projection of a leader aura on TV, discussions of ideas in print, and so on. He knows that a candidate is like a product that must be expertly and attractively packaged, advertised and promoted, as evidenced by the fact that he utilizes the professional services of tested public relations and advertising experts, Filipinos as well as foreigners, and the services of journalists, artists, poets and writers.

THE sophistication of Ferdinand E. Marcos as a political strategist and fighter clearly demonstrated itself again in that 1969 reelection campaign. He wrote history by winning a second term, the first Filipino President to be so reelected. He defeated Osmena Jr., with a total vote of 5,017,343 as against Osmena's 3,043,122 — a commanding winning margin of almost 2,000,000 votes.[7]

The success of Ferdinand E. Marcos in politics stems from his own personal genius, daring and initiative. His skill in capturing power — and keeping it — is unmatched and has not been excelled. He has learned well from the early masters of the art and science of war who maintain with concrete reasons that to be victorious the leader (1) must know when he can fight and when he cannot, (2) understand when and how to use both large and small forces, (3) ensure that his ranks are united in purpose, (4) be prudent and lie in wait for the enemy who is not prudent, and (5) have generals who are able and loyal.[8]

Marcos brought all this — and more — into the arena, the February 7, 1986 snap elections, which was most likely to be the last defense of his championship title. Behind him, aside from the powerful KBL machine, was a broad and formidable base consisting notably of the Ilocano Bloc, his wife Imelda's southern legionnaires, and large blocs of non-Catholic and non-Christian tribes.

The task of wresting the crown — and the throne — from such a man of power who had reigned continuously since 1965 could never be an easy one.

Cory Aquino, the contender, therefore had a big job to perform.

But Marcos, in February 1986, was far from invulnerable.

To be sure, aside from a relatively advanced age (68) based on Filipino longevity standards, and a deteriorating health, Marcos was saddled with the disadvantage of being President for nearly two decades — far longer than any other President had served. That time had been more than long enough to allow the development and growth of a new breed of presidential kin and friends or cronies who took the place of the old oligarchy which he had dismantled. Some of the big issues against him like massive official graft and corruption, crony capitalism and monopolism, hidden wealth and military abuses partly derived from them, but Marcos himself was taking all the blame. In fact one of the President's spokesmen had written about the arrogance of the strutters and promenaders in the corridors of power who had in their time alienated former friends and supporters, the consequences of whose behavior could not be accurately estimated.[9]

The excesses of people close to President Marcos and other real issues such as poverty and unemployment, human rights violations including "salvaging" of citizens had been compressed within the 20-year Marcos regime and given the oppositionists fodder for their propaganda mill. As a result they came up with such a catchy, pithy campaign battlecry reminiscent of Marcos's own famous *"Alis d'yan!"* addressed to Macapagal. This time Marcos was to be the target of the opposition's cry: *"Sobra na! Tama na! Palitan na!"* (Too much! Enough of it! Change him now!)

BECAUSE of the magic of the name she bears and the fact that the murder of her husband, Ninoy Aquino, had left her apparently pitiful and helpless, people were — and are — naturally attracted to Cory Aquino. During that snap election campaign many shared with her the shock of her husband's assassination and sympathized with her plight. Her rallies and meetings were larger and more spontaneous than those of the KBL.

Judging from press accounts and television coverage of her campaign, people from all walks of life, in great numbers, voluntarily and enthusiastically joined her rallies, or waited for her to pass by a street just to get a glimpse of her, or tried to come close enough to touch and kiss her, shower her with yellow flowers, or listen to her adoringly. Some shed a few tears and wept silently as Cory, in her plain, clear woman's voice, related for the nth time the ordeal her late husband underwent while locked up in prison, an ordeal that culminated in his murder at the airport. Ninoy, she told them, died without finishing the task of helping his people enjoy the fruits of justice, peace and freedom, and she, Cory, would take up from where he had left to continue the task Ninoy had begun but left unfinished, knowing, like Ninoy, that she could never forgive herself for failing to do what she knew had to be done for her people.

Judging from overall audience appeal during the campaign, Cory Aquino definitely had the edge over President Marcos. This point need not be argued. If she was equipped with a machine, resources and forces comparable to those which were under the command of Marcos, it was apparent that Cory could easily outvote the President. For among other factors that could spell victory for a candidate, popular sentiment was definitely in her favor, considering the number attending her rallies and their attitudes toward her, the spontaneous outpouring of emotion that characterized their reception of her, the near-delirious, unashamed adulation the masses, uncoached and unencouraged, demonstrated for her, the same high level of naked adoration fanatics display for their favorite movie superstars. Cory Aquino was, in fact, soon to be known lightly as the "Nora Aunor of Philippine politics" because of the way she magnetized big crowds whether in the rural areas or the cities.

Indeed, if Ninoy Aquino's death had inspired the emergence of a phenomenon Mauricio calls "Aquinomania" his equally phenomenal, enigmatic widow gave rise during the campaign to "Corymania."

An election, it has been pointed out by thinkers and analysts, is not won by sheer sentiment or emotion but by the number of votes actually cast by the voter, tallied and reported. There was therefore a real need for an organization, a machine, that could help turn sentiments into actual votes.

The protagonists in the 1986 battle of giants — Ferdinand E. Marcos and Corazon C. Aquino — seemed to be evenly matched. Cory Aquino, the challenger, had many things going for her, and her audience appeal was tremendous. Her main problem, it was obvious then, seemed to be the lack of a well-oiled, disciplined organization of her own or of her party. The Unido, whose banner she was carrying, was the personal organization of her running mate, Salvador Laurel, and could not be expected to go all-out for her. Her party, the PDP-Laban, was too young and too disorganized to be nationally potent and effective enough to convert popular sentiment and belief favorable to her into actual votes. She needed an abundance of funds and a corps of executives to administer the funds in support of the operation of the organization.

At that stage of the campaign, Cory was wanting in what the incumbent Marcos had. If their voting strengths were indeed equal, Marcos would have the edge.

But there is an antidote to an efficient, well-provided organization. To an experienced hand like Teodoro F. Valencia this antidote is a glamorous, overpowering personality like the late President Magsaysay.[10] Such a commanding personality could overcome the built-in advantages of an incumbent President and produce an overwhelming majority to clinch victory. At the rate the crowds were turning out for her, Cory Aquino was such a personality.

IT should be of interest to the reader that one month before the February 7 snap elections, a group of political scientists — lawyers and political science professors — came out with their objective and professional analysis of the electoral contest, using the discipline of political science. The participating scientists, according to the *Philippine Daily Inquirer*,[11] came from such schools as Adamson University, Ateneo de Manila, De La Salle, Philippine Christian University, Philippine Women's University and Trinity College.

In their special report it is claimed that if the snap presidential elections would be decided along the *traditional* pattern of electoral behavior, Marcos would have the overwhelming advantage. From that standpoint traditional Philippine elections are won on the basis of what they called "the four Ms" — Money, Machinery, Media and Man.

On this basis, the political scientists say, Marcos had the advantage because of the following:

(1) *Money*. A campaign must have adequate logistical support: "A well-funded campaign will not ensure election, but it will make it possible. Vote buying and pampering of voters are traditional in Philippine elections and candidates usually reserve approximately one-half of their campaign funds for election day activities."

(2) *Machinery*. The candidate should be supported by a cadre of organized workers who would serve as the primary link to the voters. A well-oiled organization will deliver the votes on election day and make sure they are counted.

(3) *Media*. "Retail" campaign methods —house-to-house campaign, public speeches, etc. — have natural limitations in terms of reach and effects duration. To ensure that the campaign message reaches the majority of the voters, "wholesale" campaign opportunities offered by mass media become absolutely necessary.

(4) *Man*, the candidate himself/herself. All the campaign efforts are geared towards making the electorate accept and support the candidate. He must be perceived by the public as the better candidate vis-a-vis his political rivals. The Filipino electors mainly choose their candidates on the basis of *personalities* rather than issues.

The unnamed participants believed that the February 7 polls could be a non-traditional election, a contest between a veteran supported by a well-oiled and well-entrenched machine and a political tyro riding high on a groundswell of public sympathy. The outcome, therefore, would be rather difficult to predict. Nevertheless they noted the following strengths and weaknesses of the protagonists:

Marcos's Strengths

1.   Grassroots level political machinery with tested vote-getting potential.
2.   Barangay and local government officials, including government agencies and corporations.
3.   Almost total control of traditional media, giving him and the KBL unparalleled audience reach and coverage.
4.   Maturity in running the government and experience in foreign relations.
5.   Proven abilities as campaign strategist and organizer.
6.   Charisma and crowd-pleasing touch.
7.   Old, reliable political base.
8.   Built-in advantage of his equity as the incumbent.

Marcos's Weaknesses

1.   Doubts regarding his health. While the voters might want to give him a fresh mandate, some of them felt he was too sick to effectively discharge the duties of President.
2.   Charges of graft and corruption, and alleged enrichment in office of Marcos and his cronies.
3.   Imelda Marcos and General Fabian Ver as both weakness and strength of Marcos: Imelda because of her reported excesses and extravagance, and Ver for the assassination of Ninoy Aquino.
4.   Human rights violations record, including repression of political dissenters, rampant military abuses, and subjugation of the legislature and the judiciary.
5.   Negative economic conditions: high prices, unemployment, business dislocation.
6.   Lack of credibility "not only within the Philippines but among the foreign audience."

On the other hand, the participating political scientists had these to say about the challenger, Cory C. Aquino:

Aquino's Strengths

Aquino, according to the participants, drew her strengths primarily from the weaknesses of Marcos.
1.   Public sympathy generated by the August 21, 1983

assassination of Ninoy Aquino.

2.   Cory Aquino's perceptible — and believable — sincerity.

3.   Perception of Cory as a symbol of change. "This sector may not necessarily approve of Mrs. Aquino personally but are tired and sick of the present order" that they would be willing to replace it with just anything or anybody.

4.   Possible translation of vast reservoir of public sympathy for Cory into a bandwagon effect that would influence the decision of undecided voters.

5.   Apparent support of the Catholic Church hierarchy, bolstering her sincerity stance and providing her with organized support.

Aquino's Weaknesses

1.   Lack of efficient vote-delivery machinery. At best, her machinery was fragmented and disorganized.

2.   Fragmentation and disunity of the opposition, with the Unido and the PDP-Laban looking at each other with mutual suspicion.

3.   Lack of experience and unpreparedness for the Presidency. "People have qualms on what would happen if she wins."

4.   Ambivalent stand on such election issues as Communism, U.S. relations and bases, Mindanao problem. "A sizeable segment of the electorate is not willing to gamble on the inexperienced leadership of Cory Aquino."

5.   Reliance on her "advisers" which aggravated her weakness of being politically inexperienced and unprepared for the Presidency.

6.   Apparent lack of adequate campaign logistics.

7.   Non-existent or "ad hoc" program of government.

In their summary of the comparative strengths and weaknesses of President Marcos and Challenger Aquino, the participants report:

"A look at the comparative strengths and weaknesses of the two presidential candidates gives Marcos a strong edge in terms of actual vote-getting strengths. However, the actualization of the potential strengths of Cory to get the votes on the basis of sympathy and a clamor for change would decide the elections for her if the non-traditional character of the snap elections holds true on February 7 when the votes are cast and counted."[12]

In a contest where the protagonists are equal or nearly so in voting potential, the evidence indicates that the decisive factor is the efficiency of a candidate's machine or organization. It's what makes victory possible in the end.

The February 7 contest between Marcos and Aquino would be won by the challenger if it proved to be a case of the non-traditional prevailing over the old, traditional pattern of electoral behavior, to use the language of the political scientists cited here. If the potential strengths of Cory Aquino on the basis of sympathy and a clamor for change would be actualized, the strengths of President Marcos based on the customary factors of traditional elections would be overturned.

Those conditions would have to be met if this battle of two political giants would be won by the woman candidate.

TEN

Race for the Top

All we have to worry about now is to make sure that the administration's design to subvert the people's will through fraud and terrorism is thwarted.

— Cory Aquino, in Laguna

IT was proof of Cory Aquino's toughness, strength of character and determination that when she wanted something she would not settle for less. Thus, when she agreed to run for office she would not settle for No. 2, for the Vice Presidency. Neither would she allow anyone in the opposition, even Salvador Laurel himself who was the high priest of the Unido, to run as his party's presidential candidate since the two of them, running for President separately, would risk defeat of the opposition in the hands of Ferdinand E. Marcos, She and Laurel had to run as a team with Laurel as her running mate, even if the latter had already filed his certificate of candidacy for President. and, as proof of her newly evident political sophistication even if she had to run under the banner of the Unido rather than the Laban ng Bayan or People's Fight party which had persuaded and drafted her.

Although Cory Aquino was surrounded by a number (she initially said 50) of advisers it was said that this political decision was purely her own, though she doubtless arrived at it after consulting with them. Mrs. Aquino once told reporters that she had no shadow cabinet: "And even if I did have, I would never disclose the members. What I do is consult some very close advisers, but I prefer to keep their names secret."[1] Of her group of advisers, also known as "Cory's Mafia," the identity of Jaime Ongpin, younger brother of Roberto Ongpin in the Ferdinand Marcos Cabinet, was the first to be publicly known.[2]

The rest of the advisers cited by Teodoro Benigno of the *Agence France Presse* include Ricardo Lopa, brother-in-law of Cory who is married to her sister Tessie and had been known to work very closely with Mrs. Aquino in the campaign and was a close friend and associate of the assassinated Ninoy; Jesuit Fr. Joaquin Bernas, president of the Ateneo de Manila University and a known political commentator and constitutional expert; Ramon del Rosario Jr., businessman-son of Ambassador Ramon V. del Rosario, Emanuel Soriano, former president of the University of the Philippines and a management consultant; Alfredo Bengzon, physician; and business-man, Antonio Gonzalez, propaganda and marketing expert.[3]

Outside of these seven but also known to be close to Cory were Batasang Pambansa members Cecilia Munoz Palma, a retired justice of the Supreme Court, and Neptali Gonzales, and Bernardo Villegas of the Center for Research and Communications.[4] Nevertheless, "Mrs. Aquino is widely known to be her own woman, who makes her own decisions, and the so-called Harvard Mafia reportedly gives her plenty of leeway."[5]

Which might as well be since decisiveness is one virtue of a good, effective President. Arriving at hard and quick decisions is hardly possible, however, if a President relies too much on advisers and counsellors. The tendency in such a case is for the President to hesitate, to bide time and thus delay decision making. In a recent essay on the Presidency, Napoleon G. Rama, a political analyst, warns against presidential vacillation or indecision and contends that the best time for Presidents to make the hard and brave decisions is during the first six months from assumption of office.

"Never is a President," he writes, "stronger and better-loved than during his first six months, if he won the election fair and square. People would ignore and forgive his mistakes. And if the new President committed and corrected his mistakes, people would call it an act of statesmanship." He adds that the most successful Presidents, here and abroad, took advantage of the honeymoon period by making the brave, highstakes decisions having to do with major reforms, reordering society, narrowing the gap between the poor and the rich, overhauling the system, and dismantling powerful apparatuses of the old regime.

Cory Aquino is right when she said presidential decisions are made by her alone after consulting some of her close advisers. For however competent and intelligent a President's key advisers are, there are times when, because of a difference in standpoint and perspective, they may fail to detect dangers the President can readily perceive because they affect him or her. A case of this nature occurred during the February 7 snap elections campaign when Cory Aquino was reported in the media as saying in Davao City on January 17 that she was going to "use Amendment 6 to reorganize and reform the government." This was reported by a newspaper columnist as a turn-around if she did say it, for the truth is that she had been attacking President Marcos for using Amendment 6 to legislate even when the Batasang Pambansa was in session, thus reducing that body into an expensive rubber stamp. The columnist tagged it as a "flip-flop" and proof of the "political immaturity" of Mrs. Aquino and her unpreparedness for the Presidency.[7]

President Marcos himself picked up and put the incident into ultra-sharp focus and twitted his rival for wanting to use a power that she had been attacking; she had promised to have that amendment to the 1973 Constitution repealed. It was indeed a faux pas that was widely reported in the media. Disturbed, a former senior executive assistant of Ninoy Aquino decided to conduct some sleuthing to determine if Cory had indeed made the statement, then confirmed it in his column, "Business of Truth," in the *Malaya* newspaper, saying that: "the statement was part of a speech Cory was to read, written by Fr. Joaquin Bernas, SJ, one of her so-called '50 advisers,' but when Cory saw it, she pencilled it out; unhappily, in the copies of the speech released to the press, it was not cancelled."[8]

BOTH Cory Aquino and the Filipino voters were a revelation during that campaign. Mrs. Aquino, as has been shown earlier, proved to be far from the jelly-willed, sentimental girl she had hitherto been pictured but a tough, politically astute woman with a mind and will of her own. When on December 2, 1985 the Sandiganbayan promulgated its decision acquitting all the 26 accused in the assassination of her husband headed by the Chief of Staff, Maj. Gen. Fabian Ver, Cory merely said she was not surprised at the trial's conclusion. Then on December 4, before a largely emotional, cheering audience at the Mondragon Ballroom in Makati, Metro Manila, she announced she was entering the presidential ring, thus joining the world she had tried to shun while she was the housewife of the wonder boy of Philippine politics.

For the opposition factions the week that followed kept them on tenterhooks: the Aquino-Laurel marriage for political convenience was imperilled. The macho streak and fierce Batangueno pride in Laurel seemed to rule out the possibility of his agreeing to run as Cory's Vice President. It was only on December 11 that the "marriage" was finally performed, with Cory Aquino as the candidate for President and Doy Laurel as her running mate — but under the Unido banner. At it turned out much later, Jaime Cardinal Sin, Archbishop of Manila, admitted that he played the role of political cupid in forming the Cory-Doy tandem.

According to the Cardinal, during the closing rites of the Marian Year at the Luneta in December 1985, Cory Aquino who had been having her retreat at the Hemady monastery of the Pink Sisters, informed him, "I am going to run." As the jocose Cardinal relates it:

"I asked her, 'Are you going to run around the Luneta?'

"And she said, 'No, I will run. I am inspired by my husband.'

"I told her, 'If you are united, you are going to win. But if you are not, then you will lose and you are crazy to run.

" 'Number two, I think you are going to win. First of all, you are a woman, and it is humiliating for Marcos to lose. But that is the way God works — to confound the strong. You are the Joan of Arc.'

"Then with misty eyes she knelt down and I blessed her. I said, 'Cory, you are going to win, in the name of the Father, Son and the Holy Spirit.'

"The following day, Laurel came. He said, 'I want also to run.'

"I said to him, Well, you are not very attractive. Cory is more attractive than you are, and if you run, you will lose. First of all, you should unite.'

" 'All right, Cardinal,' he said, and a drop of tear came down, a sign that there was an internal struggle, 'that is what you like, I'll run as a second.'

"I blessed him, and told him, 'You will win.' "

"I had that premonition that they were going to win. I was the only one who had that premonition. They were all saying that they may get all the votes, but Marcos had already planned the cheating.' "[9]

The cardinal's mediation role had also been underscored in other accounts of the Aquino-Laurel decision to run together.

But within her own party, the Laban ng Bayan coalition, Cory had to do some important mending of dissensions among the various groups and individuals that made up her supporters. For her decision to run under the Unido banner as a concession to Laurel was made unilaterally by Cory. She did not consult the Laban leaders, the political parties and cause-oriented organizations which had backed her presidential bid from the very beginning.

As the Liberal party's Jovito Salonga, president of the Laban coalition, puts it:

"We have always supported Cory, but we were not informed beforehand nor was our consent asked."[10]

The reason the majority in Laban did not agree with Cory's choice of Laurel was that his running as her Vice President would diminish the appeal of her candidacy as a moral crusade. They considered him tarnished by his former association with the KBL and his family's long friendship with the Marcoses. Furthermore they saw Laurel as cast in the mold of the traditional politician who would compromise many of the principles which the coalition had laid down in its declaration of unity.

But Cory Aquino, in a display of independence of mind and political savvy, merely explained her decision thus:

"Many who cared could not understand why the interest of political parties and organizations should constitute a serious impediment to the formation of a truly united and potent force against the Marcos regime . . . I came to the conclusion that while the interests of partisan political groups are obviously important, the interests of the Filipino people are far more crucial particularly at this time of grave national crisis."[11]

Despite the voices of dissent and opposition to the Aquino-Laurel team, some important opposition leaders welcomed the development. Marcelo Fernan of the Unido, to cite one, said: "With the two now forming a common slate, I can smell victory in the air. The nightmares of Malacanang begin." From the Mindanao Alliance, Homobono Adaza, another member of the Batasan, jumped with joy, saying: "Now we have an unbeatable team. The rules of the game are at this point insignificant. Even if they cheat, the Cory-Doy tandem will just snow them under."[12]

Nevertheless the problems of forging unity were real and the coalition of forces was a very fragile one. Bodies had been formed to thresh out differences but the distrust would not disappear overnight. The difference dividing the various groups in the coalition would be aggravated if their candidate should win for then there would be a scramble, a struggle for the spoils of victory: Cabinet and other key government positions, for one. In fact, long before the elections, discussions on the expected spoils of electoral victory had already driven deeper rifts within the coalesced groups.

However, for the meantime the opposition had succeeded in presenting a united front and put up a formidable team — a combination between a crusader with high moral authority born of deep personal suffering and sacrifice, and a veteran politician and pillar of a famous political family. To the oppositionists this was consoling enough; they could look forward to a brief but brawling campaign that could mean the final fall of Ferdinand E. Marcos from power and the ascendancy of the opposition.

CORY Aquino proved to be a revelation in the campaign, too. Like a butterfly just out of its cocoon she evidently savored her new-found freedom, emancipated as she was after so many years from the restricted role of a housewife and mother of five grownup children. Evidently, too, she was beginning to enjoy her new life as *the* candidate *and* politician in the family, the center of everyone's attention and concern with a tremendous attraction and magnetism of her own.

She found that her new life as the united opposition's candidate for President, the first woman to seek that highest office within the gift of her people to give, was the exact opposite of her past life whereby, pursuant to an agreement with Ninoy her husband, she would forever, as long as Ninoy was performing his part, stay in the shadows, in the background, living in discreet anonymity and silence, and preparing and serving coffee and refreshments to Ninoy's friends. The death of Ninoy and the series of subsequent events changed all that: circumstances had pushed her on center stage to perform the role Ninoy had begun but left unfinished.

More significantly, she now found herself, a recently grief-stricken widow, facing in a do-or-die, no-holds-barred combat Ferdinand E. Marcos no less, the shrewdest, most accomplished man of power this country had ever known, the man who was her No. 1 suspect in the assassination of her husband and who had thereby denied Ninoy the Presidency of the Republic. To Cory Aquino this realization must have been humbling, even intimidating, but ennobling; she had joined the biggest league of them all, the contest for the Presidency.

And so she had to campaign harder than she had ever done before, more than she could ever imagine. She was prepared for it, too, prepared to scour and comb every town and city across the country that the brief 45-day campaign period would allow, in search of votes for herself and for her running mate.

JUST after their unity had been forged, Cory Aquino and Doy Laurel fired their opening campaign salvo in Laurel country — Batangas — Cory garbed in her yellow dress and Doy in green. The people received them with great enthusiasm matched by curiosity, wondering perhaps what this frail, once sheltered wealthy widow had to offer to solve the nation's pressing problems which a man, President Marcos, had failed to resolve through two decades of rule. She herself had defined, when she accepted the people's draft to run for the Presidency, the extent, range and magnitude of the nation's problems — but did she have, as a woman, the capabilities to solve them? Cory had told Filipino and foreign trimedia reporters in a press conference on December 4, 1985:

"I look around me and I see a nation that is sinking deeper and deeper into despair," words reminiscent of the emotional rhetoric of Robert Kennedy and Martin Luther King Jr. "I look around me and I see a people who continue smiling bravely even if they are unsure about their next meal and, indeed, are growing increasingly angry and desperate. I sense a growing feeling of helplessness and a creeping belief that no matter what abuse may be thrown at our faces, we are powerless to do anything." Yet, the nation's first woman candidate for President added:

"Yet I remain firm in my conviction that while our nation's problems may be extremely serious, they are by no means insurmountable. I believe that this nation can overcome its present difficulties and eventually find its rightful place among the great nations of the world but only if every single Filipino is prepared to do his or her part in bringing about the meaningful change that we all seek."[13]

What Cory Aquino did in that news conference was to expound on the sordid state of the national situation and at the same time try to raise the people's expectation and exhort them into both sacrifice and action.

Aside from Cory and Doy, those present in the December 4, 1985 press conference, at the presidential table, were opposition luminaries Jovito R. Salonga, president of the Laban ng Bayan coalition: former Senator Lorenzo Tanada, chairman of the original Laban ng Bayan under which Ninoy Aquino ran for the Interim Batasang Pambansa in 1978: *Manila Times* Publisher Joaquin "Chino" P. Roces, chairman of the Cory Aquino for President Movement; and former Justice and Batasang Pambansa member Cecilia Munoz Palma, co-chairperson of the Laban ng Bayan.

Also present, on the floor, were Assemblyman Neptali A. Gonzales, executive vice president of the Unido; Aquilino Pimentel Jr., president of the PDP-Laban; Assemblyman Rogaciano Mercado, president of the National Union for Liberation; Assemblyman Antonio Cuenco and Marcelo Fernan of Pinaghiusa; Homobono Adaza of Mindanao Alliance; Nenita "Inday" Daluz of Cebu; Jose "Lito" Atienza, Enrique Belo, Jaime Ferrer, Ramon V. Mitra.

Victor Ziga; Alberto Romulo, Antonio Martinez and Emigdio Tanjuatco, all MPs; and former Assemblyman Francisco S. Tatad, Con-
con Delegate Bren Z. Guiao and former Secretary of Education
Alejandro "Anding" R. Roces.

MEANWHILE, each using a private plane, Cory in a KingAir
reportedly owned by Jaime Ongpin of Benguet Consolidated Corporation, and Doy in a QueenAir, the opposition candidates hopped
from one island to another without necessarily going back to Manila.
They were drawing large crowds. In the province of Leyte, for
instance, known as "Imelda Country," the *Associated Press* reported
that more than 10,000 persons filled a public park named after
Imelda Marcos's mother, Remedios Trinidad Romualdez, in Tacloban
City, and thousands more heard her in five other rallies across the
island 300 miles southeast of Manila. Thousands of other villagers,
said the AP, many of them barefoot, lined streets leading to rally
sites which included town plazas and public markets, chanting her
name "Cory!" and shouting *Long Live!* in the vernacular, forcing
Cory Aquino to exclaim: "It's fantastic, it's unbelievable. I think
victory is certain."[14]

In nearby Maasin town, where she later addressed a rally
of about 7,000 people outside the Catholic church, screaming
crowds welcomed her, blocking the van she was riding in just to
shake or touch her hands. Earlier she opened the day in Leyte
with a rally attended by some 10,000 in Ormoc town. Then she
flew to Hilongos town, where 4,000 people who packed the square
gave a thumbs-down sign against Marcos on cue from Doy Laurel.
Then at the market in Matalom town she told a big crowd in Tagalog: "We are very happy to be here. I did not know that so many
people love Doy and me in Imelda's country."[15]

There was mass hysteria wherever Cory Aquino — and Doy —
went, whipped up largely by Cory's enigmatic presence or the magic
of her phenomenon that preceded her coming. The *Agence France
Presse* news agency reported during the first week of January 1986,
nearly midway in the campaign, that at the grassroots level Mrs.
Aquino's blitzkrieg campaign continued to outdraw Marcos, "pulling
in an estimated 355,000 people to public plaza rallies and whistle-
stop appearances in 24 provinces and cities."[16]

A veteran political writer, Teodoro Benigno reports that in contrast, Marcos who candidly admitted he was tired and burdened, had
only drawn an estimated 88,500 in eight provinces and cities. Writes
the AFP Manila bureau chief:

"Analysts are quick to point out that the 'Cory crowds' pour out a spontaneous, jubilant and even 'reverential' flood causing Mrs. Aquino's supporters to claim 'the Cory tidal wave' would simply overwhelm the Marcos candidacy."[17]

The same analysts considered an alarming development the President's warning that the 250,000-strong military might mutiny against an Aquino triumph since this could pave the way for Communist rule. Some observers, it is said, interpreted this to mean that to avert possible defeat the President and his frontline generals headed by Gen. Ver could stage a coup before, during or after the elections.

A companion development, however, was an announcement earlier by leaders of the military's Reform Movement, who claimed to have the support of 70% of the officers corps, that they would support Mrs. Aquino if she won the elections — the first time in the country's history that military officers had taken such a forthright stand. But the real dilemma facing Marcos was that he could lose a presidential election considering the widespread popularity of Cory Aquino. It would of course, be a catastrophe, an extreme embarrassment and humiliation for the President who throughout his long political career had never known an election defeat.

BUT more impressive and morale-boosting than the Leyte crowds were the surging throngs of Bicolanos from all walks of life and of all ages who trooped to various towns and cities in the vast Bicol region to listen to Cory Aquino and running mate Salvador Laurel. Buoyed up by the people's eagerness and boundless enthusiasm, and more sure than ever before of what to say and how to say it to send them into spasms of joy and explosions of hope, Cory Aquino skillfully used sarcasm and humor to draw desired audience reactions. In Naga City she appealed to thousands of Bicolanos to take pity on Mr. Marcos who had said he was "already tired."

"Maawa na tayo kay Marcos," she implored her breathless, adoring audience with mock pity. *"Nakikiusap sa atin na gusto na niyang magpahinga. Sa darating na halalan, iboto natin si Cory at si Doy!"* ((Let's take pity on Marcos. He is requesting us to let him rest. This coming election, vote Cory and Doy!) And the audience, thousands of them filling the town plaza and spilling into adjacent areas, burst into wild and spontaneous applause.

But by then Cory and Doy were no longer simply casting a spell on the voters. More devastating to Marcos and his KBL, the oppositionists, backed by local opposition officials, were eating away at the

ruling party's strength with mass defections of KBL or administration officials and leaders into the opposition camp. In that January 11 invasion of the Bicol region, for instance, no less than 74
important political leaders belonging to the KBL and its affiliate,
the Nacionalista party (Roy Wing) joined the Unido and took their
oaths during that opposition show of force. Among them was former
Vice Governor Renato Unico of Camarines Norte who earlier in the
day took his oath before MP Luis Villafuerte, a Bicolano, and scores
of former mayors, vice mayors, members of the provincial boards,
councilors and other politicians with their respective following.[18]

So enthusiastic and receptive were the Bicolanos that night that
they gave the visiting candidates the biggest reception accorded to
any candidate or visiting personality. In Iriga City, for example,
hometown of TV personality Eddie Ilarde and superstar Nora Aunor,
about 10,000 people filled Plaza Rizal to listen to Cory and Doy, and
local officials said not even the fabulously popular *la* Aunor was able
to draw such a crowd on one occasion. An equal number of people,
Malaya reported, attended the opposition rally in Tigaon town,
where a power failure occurred and as the candidate's motorcade
entered the town of Baao, churchbells pealed and rang continuously.

Cory noted to Doy while they were drawing record crowds
in Pili, Ocampo, Tagaon, Baao and Iriga City, that they also drew
huge crowds in the region, specifically in Albay and Sorsogon, when
they campaigned there the month before. But this time they were
heartened not only by the size of the crowds but by the impressive
number of defectors. The fact that veteran politicians formerly
associated with the administration were jumping into the opposition
bandwagon indicated the fast-growing strength of Cory and Doy and
a deepening demoralization in the ranks of the KBL.

But if the voters impressed the tandem in Bicol, they over-
whelmed them in Cebu province and Cebu City, a known cradle of
the opposition. A newspaper correspondent from Cebu City reported that when Cory and Doy flew to Cebu from the Bicol region,
they were deluged by a tide of Cebuanos estimated by most as at
least half a million as they spilled out of houses and offices into the
streets along a 10-kilometer motorcade route from the Mactan International Airport. Arriving in separate planes the bets rode an open-
topped jeep accompanied by some 2,000 other vehicles which proceeded to Cebu City by way of Mandaue City and Lapu-Lapu
City.[19]

The tumultuous reception eclipsed the largest rally crowd for
the opposition of some 150,000 in Naga City the day before and was

coordinated by the Pinaghiusa, opposition umbrella group in Cebu headed by former Senator John Osmena. Even Cory Aquino admitted that the Cebu reception greatly exceeded that of Naga City.

At the rally, Mrs. Aquino reiterated her stand against Communism and said she would never have Communists in her Cabinet in case she won the election.

Reporting on the Cebu opposition assault, the *Associated Press* estimated the "surging crowds" at more than 200,000, calling it the "biggest welcome in the month-old campaign, dwarfing any rally held by Marcos so far."[20]

So thick were the crowds, said the AP, that it took Mrs. Aquino's motorcade four hours to crawl through the swarming masses — the route from the airport to downtown can be normally negotiated in 30 minutes or less — and quoted her as saying: "I continue to be amazed." Then reiterating opposition fears that President Marcos might cancel the election, she said: "I think maybe Marcos is running scared and he will create an artificial emergency where insurgency is again going to be a problem."

In the streets people waved small yellow paper flags, blankets, curtains, flowers and leaves as they crowded the route. "Some brought along roosters," a news agency reported, "dogs, and goats with yellow ribbons around their necks. Yellow is the opposition color of protest."

Cory Aquino, obviously savoring every moment of the rousing occasion as she rode with Laurel in an open jeep, leaned over, ever smiling, to shake hands with people. But midway into the route the jeep ran out of gas and the candidates transferred to an open truck being used by news photographers. The crowds filling the streets roared non-stop with shouts of *"Laban! Laban!"* and "Down with Marcos!" as the motorcade inched its way through the city, finally stopping at the Roman Catholic churchyard where the candidates pushed their way through a jostling crowd of 10,000 and proceeded to the altar. When Cory and Doy emerged from the church, a reporter noted that "their faces were smeared with lipstick marks," doubtless an expression of the crowd's intense admiration for the candidates.

Asked what she would do if Marcos lost but refused to step down and protested her victory, the now completely politicized Cory Aquino replied: "I will ask the Filipino people to stage demonstrations every day in the streets."[21]

IF CORY Aquino could bring the great masses of Filipinos to heights of ecstasy by her mere presence and straightforward speeches, so could she bring even the most jaded and blase captains of business and industry into uncommon fits of adulation and rapture. This was demonstrated one day in the second half of January 1985 when she addressed the biggest crowd of Rotarians ever assembled in one place — 2,000 members and guests of 25 Rotary Club organizations inside the Manila Hotel's Fiesta Pavilion.

When Cory made her appearance at 12:35 p.m., the leaders of the country's big business and industry danced and swayed until she reached the presidential table. Eagle-eyed reporters noted that a bank chairman and president (Victor Barrios of PISO bank) was detected with tears rolling down his cheeks.[22]

Cory delivered a 45-minute speech; it was interrupted by 43 ovations, with the crowd not only clapping but roaring and screaming their hearts out as Cory delivered telling blows against President Marcos. During the ensuing open forum she received 12 additional rounds of applause. The speech was drafted by seven persons, it was reported, assisted by a corps of resource people. Cory herself went over the draft several times and made her own suggestions on substantive issues. A report said the hands of two of the advisers — Emanuel Soriano and Joaquin Bernas, S.J. — could be detected in some parts of the speech. As the reporters noted:

"Obviously it was the men in the jampacked hall that enjoyed her fighting speech most. For many of them, who knew Cory only as the soft-spoken widow of Ninoy with the sob story about him, the fighting candidate they heard was a revelation, and they loved it. One male fan even brought a whistle. Many men had tears in their eyes. Apparently she also proved to be a revelation to the foreign media, who also were more familiar with the sob story of the campaign trail."[23]

In a show of interest akin to that of typical political rally audiences, many Rotarians and guests arrived at the Fiesta Pavilion as early as 10 a.m. to get a good seat. Betty Go-Belmonte, board co-chairman of the *Philippine Daily Inquirer*, and Josie Lichauco, both short girls, were craning their necks as Cory inched her way to the stage and someone told them to take off their shoes and stand on the chairs so they could see Cory. "When they did that, they were pleasantly surprised to see that Jaime Zobel de Ayala, towering as he already is, was also standing on a chair and applauding wildly."

After Cory's speech, many people, wanting to see her, simply forgot all decorum and stood on tables to get one more glimpse of the candidate. As she made her way to her coaster outside, a Manila

Hotel guard, wearing a Marcos button on his lapel, shooed people away, saying, "Make way for the new President!"

THE phenomenal crowds that greeted Cory Aquino and Doy Laurel and attended their rallies in Bicol, the Visayas, and in the great southern island of Mindanao, were replicated in other Southern Luzon provinces. In the province of Laguna, for instance, four members of the politically powerful and prominent Yulo family of Canlubang defected to the opposition when Cory and Doy visited them, almost evenly dividing the clan between Marcos and Aquino.

The opposition team barnstormed vote-rich Laguna (with nearly 700,000 votes), and the province responded by showing its true color as an opposition bulwark by presenting huge yellow crowds in most towns they visited despite intermittent drizzles. Most vehicles displayed Cory-Doy stickers while houses were dressed up on their facades with yellow ribbons and home-made Cory-Doy posters. Leading the reception was Governor Felicisimo San Luis, a former KBL starwart who had defected to the opposition. The governor who had ruled Laguna for 26 years revealed that never in his 38 years in politics had he seen such warmth and fervor as his province was according the opposition presidential ticket, proof that the people were tired of the Marcos administration.

Cory Aquino informed the crowds which warmly greeted them everywhere that the opposition team would sweep the country to victory, judging from the record crowds they had drawn in all the 61 provinces they had so far visited. Claiming that the people overwhelmingly wanted change, the lady presidential candidate said: "All we have to worry about now is to make sure that the administration's design to subvert the people's will through fraud and terrorism is thwarted."[24]

From Laguna, the next target was Cavite, fiefdom of such political figures as Prime Minister Cesar Virata, Governor Johnny Remulla, and MPs Helena Benitez and Rene Dragon, all pillars of the Marcos-controlled KBL. The city of Cavite surprised the team when an estimated 100,000 Cavitenos and people from neighboring towns jammed the few kilometers of the city's main thoroughfares, resulting in a two-hour traffic snarl. For those two hours people who had waited as early as noon stood packed like sardines, but the atmosphere, was, as Cory herself put it, like New Year's eve. Four brass bands kept playing while people lit up torches and firecrackers and danced from fences, while crowds kept chanting "Cory-Doy! Cory-

Doy!" and rained confetti on the candidates' vehicles.

Groups of female admirers shrieked upon recognizing the candidates while the men told Cory protectively, "*Ipaglalaban ka namin!* (We'll fight for you!), and old women wept at her sight. Many foreign correspondents, finding themselves engulfed in the sea of people, looked dazed amid the bewildering pandemonium. Ecstatic, Cory Aquino blurted out: "This tops the entire campaign! This is definitely the most rousing reception we ever got!" She could not help flashing the Laban sign with her hand as she wondered at the spectacle.[25]

CAVITE province was yet to prove to be the biggest surprise for the presidential team. The crowds that waited for and greeted them were huge, notwithstanding Virata, Benitez, Remulla and Dragon. At the main rally at Imus town, some 10,000 people waited up to 10:30 p.m. Seeing their interest and enthusiasm, Cory Aquino said: "I can only conclude that it is people power at work here in Cavite. I must confess that I was apprehensive about coming to Cavite because I thought this is KBL country." And the cheering people of Imus thundered, "No, no!" to Cory's extreme satisfaction.

The Cory phenomenon continued to be at work. In the last three towns of Kawit, Bacoor and Imus, people lined up the street till late at night just to get a glimpse of Cory and Doy. Touched by all this display of admiration, if not sympathy, Cory was moved to say: "What hardships the people are taking just to let Marcos know they are fed up with him."

In Kawit, reports Mrs. Cunanan, an elderly woman banged on the door of the coaster and angrily demanded why the people were being deprived of a chance to see the candidate. Cory stuck her head out to say a few words and her critic melted. In Imus, Bishop Felix Perez waited for the candidates for four hours at his residence, and told Cory that while he had supported the boycott movement in the 1984 Batasan elections he was now all-out for participation because he felt if was the will of the people. Every once in a while along the way someone would thrust a bunch of sunflowers, chrysanthemums or orchids into Cory's hand from the window. Her aide, Fritzie Aragon, would stick them up in a receptacle in a side of the van. At one point Cory, tired of waving, started giving the flowers away to the shrieking women.[26]

She was handed gifts along the way — of biscuits "so you don't get hungry" or some beribboned hats "to protect you from the sun." Someone even gave her an *anting-anting* or amulet "to protect you from harm." A nun thrust a little note into her hand reading, "Our people are afraid to openly welcome you. They will be harassed by their barangay leaders, but be assured we are all for you." If the people were euphoric, so was Cory over the people's genuinely thoughtful gestures.

Then Cory told reporter Phil Bronstein of the *San Francisco Examiner* that she felt her recent seven-day sortie in Mindanao proved to be the turning point of her campaign. She said: "They had told me that Mindanao would not go for me. But after the wild receptions everywhere that I got on the island, I felt I could lick my opponent." In fact, she added, she had no doubt at all that she would win against Marcos, and she said so with confidence.

She reacted to the pandemonium in Cavite City and other Cavite towns with her now typical serenity, looking totally unfazed by the commotion she had caused. She was indeed an absolutely pleased, thoroughly confident presidential candidate and accomplished campaigner. The jitters and uncertainties that used to bother her in the past had gone and in their place had risen the quiet faith and conviction of a winner. When the coaster's lights were turned off so she could rest and get some sleep, Cory saw that many people were still waiting in the streets of Cavite. She reportedly asked that the lights be turned on again so she could wave to them and thus acknowledge their presence — and hardships — with sincere gratefulness.[27]

"Ninoy would have loved all this," Cory said with a sigh. For indeed it was so unlike the 1978 Laban campaign when they were all so scared even just to pass around their campaign handbills. "Ninoy would have loved all this," she repeated.

As the van reached the highway enroute to Manila, the crowds finally disappeared. Cory's courtship of Cavite's nearly 500,000 voters was over at last and she was able to lean back against the comfort of her seat in the van. Then Cory the confident campaigner quipped:

"This is really what I call slave labor — all work and no play."

Her tired, sleepy companions who had missed a nonexistent dinner on the Cavite campaign trail merely smiled and quietly closed their eyes as Cory tried to find some rest in the course of her race for the top.

ELEVEN

Final Show of Force

> *In the course of my campaign, I have traveled the length of our nation and I have seen the sufferings and the hopes. I have learned what must be done. I stand ready to begin the long process of creating a Philippines for all our beloved people where there is liberty, justice and welfare for all.*
>
> — Cory Aquino, on Election Eve

AS the February 7 snap presidential elections neared it was becoming obvious that Cory Aquino, the erstwhile reluctant presidential bet, was emerging as the candidate to beat. Her ceaseless island-hopping all over the archipelago, during which she would ride triumphantly from the airport to a town or city in an open car, truck or jeep inching its way down thoroughfares lined on both sides with people who had been waiting for her for hours had been doing her good. The people would trip over one another to get a glimpse of her, touch or kiss her in unconcealed admiration, while others waved yellow ribbons, pieces of old yellow cloth, yellow leaves and flowers, with still others offering her food, beribboned hats and even amulets to protect her from hunger, from the harsh sun and from physical harm. Some would even shed a tear upon seeing her, in delight and gratitude. All this seemed to give Cory, the murdered Ninoy's widow, a certain aura and mystique that, radiating like a magnetic field from her person, kindled in the hearts and souls of the people stirrings of hope and a revolution of rising expectations.

In sharp contrast, it was becoming more evident that the people's rejection of President Marcos's government was growing wider and deeper. Where Cory Aquino projected change and with it hope for improvement in the life of the people, the President projected in the public mind a perpetuation of the status quo and, worse, an escalation of the rapacity and excesses associated with him, his cronies and members of his official family. The people from whom the truth had been withheld before had come to discover

that the regime had been committing massive official graft and corruption and inconceivable violations of human rights and that the
promised social and economic reformation that the people had met
with hope during the first year or two of martial law had become
impossible to achieve.

The candidates themselves were a study in contrasts. Where the
53-year-old widow evidently relished going to the people whether in
the urban areas or the hinterlands, the 68-year-old President, troubled by poor health, saddled with problems of a highly centralized
Presidency and pestered by the problems of his own political organization, the KBL, was kept mostly in isolation in his office. There was
no way in which he could match the verve and dynamism of Cory
and her running mate, Salvador Laurel.

The younger team, as we have seen in a preceding chapter,
was infinitely more attractive and popular than the two aging candidates — Marcos and the older Arturo M. Tolentino, 75. Aquino and
Laurel drew bigger and more spontaneous crowds everywhere they
went; they did not have to use local officials to herd and "bus"
people to rally points, nor encourage them to attend meetings by
plugging them with cash and material goods like T-shirts, free use
of vehicles and sandwiches. The much younger duo were proving
to be more acceptable than the two grizzled politicos, causing
apprehension in the ranks of administration strategists.

During the first days of the campaign, the Unido and the PDP-
Laban which were backing up Cory Aquino were hampered by lack
of unity and direction, logistics and a single party machinery —
weaknesses that were the strengths of the ruling KBL of President
Marcos. But these problems were soon overcome by the opposition
despite their essential lack of unity and differences in outlook and
philosophy. In place of one efficient fighting machine, for instance,
the opposition had numerous citizens organizations and groups
assisting in the campaign. Instead of paid campaign workers, the
opposition had scores of volunteers, among them the so-called
"Cory's Crusaders," who came mostly from the middle and upper-
classes and offered their time, services and, at times, even resources without obligation on the opposition candidates' part. The
opposition had, in brief, people's power in place of an efficient,
well-oiled political organization like the KBL.

Moreover, aside from their glowing youth and health, which
Marcos and Tolentino no longer had, the opposition candidates
enjoyed the great advantage of credibility at a time when no one
but the Marcos diehards and fanatics could take the President's —

and the government's — words at face value. This credibility, reinforced by tremendous public sympathy for the widow, were an advantage the Marcos administration could not hope to match. The masses, particularly, believed Cory Aquino's words unconditionally and were willing to go with her all the way. This element of belief gave Cory's statements and election promises a ring of truth which the people found easy to accept. Consequently charges hurled by Marcos against her — that she was Communistic and would name Communists to her Cabinet if elected, that she was a landgrabber, and that she would proclaim martial law once given power by the people — were largely rejected by the electorate after Cory had merely denied them. All she had to do was hurl the charges back at Marcos — that Marcos was the No. 1 recruiter of Communists, that Marcos was the landgrabber, and that she would never resort to the use of martial law once elected but, on the contrary, order a restudy of the Constitution — and the people agreed with her.

The much-vaunted strength of the President's political machine, the KBL, eventually showed signs of weakness. For as the campaign progressed and neared the homestretch, the KBL was wracked by dissensions and enervated by a series of defections. In most instances in the past, people switched from a weak to a stronger party, in most cases the majority party. In the case of the KBL, however, a number of important leaders of the ruling or majority party were transferring to the minority or opposition party. Psychologically this was devastating to the KBL: it could only mean that it was weakening and people were deserting or abandoning the ship before it was too late. It could also mean lack of faith in the leadership of the party and disenchantment with its policies.

Among the more important defectees — and the corresponding dates of their defections — were: Laguna Governor Felicisimo San Luis who transferred to the Unido or the opposition on December 23, 1985; Bukidnon Governor Carlos O. Fortich, December 26; former Ilocos Sur provincial administrator Benjamin Baterina (brother of MP Salacnib Baterina, a high KBL official), and Narvacan, Ilocos Sur Vice Mayor Sally Villanueva, January 3, 1986; Leticia Ramos Shahani, sister of AFP Vice Chief of Staff Fidel V. Ramos, and United Nations Assistant Secretary General, January 6; Mayor Apolonio Reyes of Tuguegarao, Cagayan, January 7; Governor Enrique A. Zaldivar of Antique, January 10; former Lanao del Sur Governor Hadji Alawi Dimakuta, father-in-law of incumbent Governor Ali Dimaporo, a KBL stalwart, January 11; no less than 74 big leaders in the Bicol region; Norberto Romualdez II, nephew of Mrs.

Imelda Romualdez Marcos and son of former Leyte Governor Norberto Romualdez Jr., and who was the commercial counsellor of the Philippine Embassy in Brussels, Belgium and special Philippine trade representative in Belgium, January 17; four military officers including Col. Mariano Santiago, former chief of the Land Transportation Commission, January 22; Col Alexander I. Bacalla, AFP Deputy Chief of Staff on Civil Military Relationship, October 26, 1985; Lt. Col. Jaime Gopilan, Philippine Army Intelligence Officer, November 21; and former Cabinet Minister Estefania Aldaba Lim, who joined Cory Aquino's campaign on February 3, three days before the election.

ENCOURAGED, if not fully backed, by the Catholic Church, notably by Jaime Cardinal Sin and the Catholic Bishops Conference of the Phlippines and supported by new and resurrected newspapers, including *The Manila Times* and the *Philippines Daily Inquirer*, Cory Aquino became bolder and more biting in her speeches. She began to taunt and challenge her much older opponent to "get out of Malacanang" and show that he was not afraid of the Filipino people by campaigning among them as she had been doing. She harped on his poor state of health and dared him to prove he was healthy and strong enough to campaign in the provinces rather than in the comfort of the Palace where party leaders were instructed to gather and assemble to listen to his campaign speeches. She wanted the people to know, said Mrs. Aquino, that their President, Marcos, was still healthy enough to continue performing the duties of President should he be given a fresh mandate.

This tactic proved effective in arousing the machismo of President Marcos. It compelled him to leave the Palace every once in a while so he could campaign in the provinces, particularly in the places Cory and Doy had visited. He knew it was unwise of him to shirk Cory's dare; it could only mean he was really too sick and weak to campaign or too afraid for himself to face the people. The President knew it would be politically fatal and suicidal for him to keep himself in the Palace while Cory — and Doy — were having their rendezvous with the people all over the land.

But campaigning in the provinces proved disastrous to the President. In Urdaneta, Pangasinan, for example, he was reported to have "collapsed" due to exhaustion or some other causes while enroute to Dagupan, where newsman were waiting for him. They waited for one and a half hours, but the President had not arrived and no one could tell where he was or what had happened to him.

When he reappeared, the newsmen noted a square plaster at the back of his left palm and another around his left ring finger. He spoke and completed the delivery of his speech   but his voice quivered a little.

Other mediamen who covered the Dagupan rally, according to the newspaper *Malaya*, said the President had to be carried flat on his back up the stage and that before he began his speech he was taken to the rear of the stage. "As he spoke he could not raise his right hand, as he usually does, to emphasize certain points, and could hardly raise his left."[1]

The whole incident did not help any in neutralizing the problem of the President's health but kindled more speculation on the true state of his health and raised questions on his ability to continue discharging his presidential duties.

The President's Information Minister, Gregorio Cendaña, immediately denied news reports that Marcos was stricken ill in Pangasinan although he admitted there was a "slight bleeding" on the President's hand that might have been caused by KBL supporters who had touched him. Cendaña said the bleeding was caused by a woman and other supporters who in their enthusiasm to touch the President scratched his hand as he was being guided to the platform. The opposition Unido would not accept this explanation, however, and announced it was preparing a letter requesting the Palace for a medical bulletin on the President following reports of his illness.

The following day, January 18, in Calapan, Mindoro Oriental, the President spoke at a rally with his left hand thickly bandaged and his right partially covered, but said he was in good health although he admitted he had stumbled during his Pangasinan sortie. "I stumbled, and they laughed," Marcos said.[2]

NEITHER was President Marcos helped by the series of exposes questioning the authenticity of his heroism during the Second World War, questions that greatly destroyed whatever remained of his badly eroded credibility. It was presidential credibility that was at issue when, despite official denial from Malacañang, the electorate expressed fears that Marcos would reimpose martial law, as charged by Cory Aquino, to avert his defeat in the snap elections or that, as charged by former Senator Salonga, massive electoral cheating and terrorism to subvert the people's will on February 7 might give Marcos a reason to reimpose a post-election martial law.[3]

The picture was further compounded when an American lawmaker, Senator Barry Goldwater, was quoted by the *Associated*

Press as saying in Singapore that Marcos would remain in power even if he lost the February 7 special elections. The Arizona Republican reportedly said:

"My honest feeling is that Marcos will win, but if he doesn't win he'll still run the country . . . Marcos is a very strong man. I think thére might be trouble. I think you might see incidents over there in certain parts of the Philippines that don't agree with him and don't agree with him rather violently. I wouldn't want to be living there right now."[4] Goldwater's remarks were made after a speech on U.S. and world affairs.

But what really hit President Marcos hardest was the expose in *The New York Times* on January 22, 1986 in which the U.S. Army branded as "absurd" and "fraudulent" his claim that he was "a heroic guerrilla leader" during the Japanese invasion of the Philippines. Reported from New York by the *Associated Press*, the story, carried in banner headlines in the Philippines by the newspapers *Malaya* and the *Philippine Daily Inquirer* on January 24, 1986 exposed Marcos as "a fake hero" whose claims for official recognition of his unit, *Maharlika*, after the war, saying it had engaged in numerous armed clashes with the Japanese and had been the pre-eminent guerrilla force in Luzon, were "distorted, exaggerated and contradictory." The Army records reportedly contained 400 pages on his military career during the war.

Then on January 26 the *Malaya* banner-headlined another expose, this time from the *Washington Post*, by John Sharkey: "FM link with Japanese war collaborators bared." Datelined Washington, the story says Marcos had claimed for decades that he led a band of anti-Japanese guerrillas during World War II "but the U.S. Army rejected his claim right after the war, according to documents in U.S. archives." The *Post* adds a more damaging note:

"Documents in the archives suggest that Marcos actually worked on behalf of Philippine politicians who collaborated with the Japanese occupation of the islands from 1942 to 1944.

"The documents on file in this country and abroad — some written by Marcos himself during the war — suggest that Marcos' principal objective during the years of the Japanese occupation of the Philippines was to promote the cause of Jose P. Laurel, who served as president of the Japanese-sponsored Republic of the Philippines from October 1943 until the end of the war."[5]

This was followed by the publication in the *Malaya* of an *Agence France Presse* story from New York saying that President Marcos was arrested by U.S. authorities during World War II for "collecting money under false pretense" as reported by the American weekly magazine *Newsweek*, and that he had been ordered arrested at one point by the U.S. leader of guerrilla activities in Pangasinan, Ray Hunt, for "soliciting funds and guerrilla help to construct a landing field . . . supposedly for Gen. Manuel Roxas," a Philippine wartime leader.[6]

The Malacañang information office immediately branded the reports "malicious" and "the most vicious black propaganda" designed to discredit the President and thus influence the results of the February 7 elections.

Then on February 1, 1986, the same local newspaper carried a story from the *Wall Street Journal* saying that Dewey Dee, a business tycoon who fled the country in January 1981 after running up debts worth over P600 million from the country's leading commercial banks and lending institutions, told Canadian officials that he and others acted as "front men for President Ferdinand Marcos in multi-million-dollar deals." Dee, who said Marcos was a "secret partner" in two banks, testified to the dealings as part of his effort to gain asylum in Canada.[7]

In the same issue of the paper, a war veteran, one retired Capt. Cirilo Belen, said to be the commanding officer of the 15th Infantry Division which defended Bessang Pass in 1945, was reported as saying that Marcos's claim of belonging to that division was not in the documents, and that Marcos was not in the roster of officers.[8]

MEANWHILE, President Marcos stood firm on his decision to conduct free, clean and honest elections on February 7 and reiterated his appeal to KBL leaders to help keep the peace and avoid violence. He asked the leaders not to be carried away by the "undisguised agitations of the opposition leaders who virtually ask the people to take the law into their hands." Marcos added:

"The eyes of the world are focused upon us. In fact, there are already meddlers and interventionists in our midst. To preserve our sovereign integrity, we must prove to them nobody need tell us how to hold a clean and democratic election."[9]

Marcos was doubtless referring to the hundreds of international news representatives who had been coming to the Philippines, at his invitation, to report on the election as well as to the U.S. and other international observer teams that had come to the country to serve the polls, also upon his invitation. His invitations indicated to the world that he meant to keep his promise that the elections would be free and clean. Senator Richard G. Lugar, chairman of the U.S.

Senate Committee on Foreign Relations who headed a 20-member American team consisting of Congress members and representatives of the private sector, announced upon arrival that his team came "to watch and not to pass judgment on the elections." He appealed to the officials of the National Citizens Movement for Free Elections (Namfrel) to ensure that voting results were turned in as rapidly as possible so Commission on Elections officials could sign and report them swiftly. The Lugar delegates, breaking up into teams, were allowed to travel freely in the country without restraints on the selection of locations or length of time spent at any location.

The Namfrel itself, headed by Jose Concepcion Jr.,[10] had made extensive preparations to ensure that the elections would be free and orderly. In coordination with other civic and religious groups, it had set up a nationwide network of watchers and poll vigilantes to help police the process and detect and prevent frauds. At the same time it had established a national tabulating center at the La Salle High School in Greenhills, Metro Manila, which would conduct its own tabulation and reporting of election results. Earlier an agreement was reached whereby Namfrel and the Comelec would conduct a joint tabulation but for some reasons the agreement was scuttled and the two bodies decided to conduct their own tabulations. In addition other tabulation groups were allowed by the Comelec, such as those by an organization of broadcasters, an organization of the print media, and the National Press Club represented by NPC president Antonio Nieva. The latter, however, yielded to pressure and withdrew the club's participation.

The Comelec also decided to conduct its own quick count by acquiring and installing a P42-million computer system but this was unanimously junked later on by the Commission because of intense public objections and time constraints.

Three days before the election, however, the Comelec and Namfrel, after abandoning a joint Operation Quick Count operation, reached a compromise by using the same election returns in their separate tabulations. The Comelec tally would be based at the Philippine International Convention Center (PICC) along Roxas Boulevard, managed by Col. Pedro Baraoidan, managing director of the National Computer Center in Camp Aguinaldo whose appointment to the OQC was opposed by Namfrel. Namfrel, on the other hand, would tabulate poll results at its computer center in La Salle Greenhills. University of the Philippines president Edgardo Angara, spokesman for both groups, said the separate tabulations would project the same voting trends because they would be based on the same poll results.[11]

The Comelec also decided, by a majority vote of 6 out of 9 commissioners, to deputize the three main branches of the Armed Forces of the Philippines — army, navy and air force — for the February 7 election, thereby exempting them from the firearms ban. Not included in the deputization were the special forces, home defense forces, barangay self-defense units and other paramilitary groups. As deputies the AFP members were directed to provide security to any polling place and members of the board of election inspectors whenever the need arose; and prevent any armed group from committing acts of terrorism or influence people not to vote or to vote for or against any candidate.[12]

Meanwhile, violence in the presidential snap election, according to Lt. Gen. Fidel V. Ramos, in charge of election security, had claimed 47 deaths as of Wednesday, February 5. The figure, Ramos told the *Associated Press*, was far smaller than in recent past elections. The military had also listed 2,544 villages and neighborhoods where trouble might erupt during the contest between Marcos and Aquino.[13]

Then Ramos made a significant statement. As commanding general of the Philippine Constabulary-Integrated National Police and Deputy Chief of Staff of the AFP, he told a news conference on February 4 that the PC-INP would support presidential candidate Corazon C. Aquino "if she wins the Feb. 7 polls." Evidently it was his way of replying to an earlier threat by President Marcos that the government would not allow Cory Aquino to sit as President in the event that she was elected. Ramos sounded defiant. Was his statement a foreshadowing of things to come? Ramos also warned that Communist rebels were indirectly supporting Marcos's rivals but that his organization, the PC-INP, "will not allow a Communist takeover" in the event of an Aquino victory.[14] In effect, Ramos was saying the PC-INP, of which he was the overall commander, would ensure the sanctity of the ballot and would not allow the legitimate winner to be cheated of victory, not even by President Marcos himself and the military under Gen. Ver. This position would be greatly significant in just a matter of two days.

SOON it was time for the final show of force, the final grand rallies or *miting de avance* of the two protagonists.

In a magnificent display of strength, opposition candidates Cory Aquino and Doy Laurel led a massive final rally at the Rizal Park complex in Manila. One newspaper, the *Daily Inquirer*, estimated that at least 2,000,000 cheering and flag-waving Aquino supporters from all walks of life converged on the historic Luneta on February 4 to listen to Mrs. Aquino's final message. Said the newspaper in its banner story headlined "Cory landslide":

"The park exploded in yellow, Cory's campaign color, as the people who converged on the park from north, west and south wore or carried something yellow.

"It was a sight that has not been seen in many years. The yellow mass of humanity spilled over down Roxas Boulevard.

"Groups waving flags of the boycott movement were seen marching towards the Luneta, causing people to speculate the boy-cotters have had a change of heart and rallied behind Mrs. Aquino."[15]

Shouts and cheers for Cory and Doy were punctuated by exploding fireworks and the tooting of car horns and the entire Luneta itself was closed to traffic. Pigeons were released, yellow rib-bons tied to their legs, symbolizing, the paper said, hope for the cause of freedom. A "snap" stage was constructed just 500 meters across the Quirino grandstand because the opposition rallyists were denied a permit by the Rizal Park management. Reporters were one in their estimate that the crowd was the biggest ever in the 1986 presidential campaign.

The *Malaya*, on the other hand, reported that more than 1,000,000 people showed up for Cory Aquino's penultimate campaign appearance, a crowd that almost rivalled the massive out-pouring three years ago during Ninoy's burial said to be attended by over 2,000,000 people. When Cory Aquino finally delivered her speech at 10:10 p.m., she invoked God's help and asked the crowd to sing with her the Lord's Prayer. She said she had never spoken before a rally as big as that night's. She was repeatedly interrupted in her brief speech by chants of "Cory! Cory! Cory!" as she repeated her campaign slogan that victory was drawing near.[16]

Both Cory Aquino and Doy Laurel summed up the issues in the campaign against the Marcos regime and wrapped up the campaign for the country's first snap presidential elections. As Mrs. Aquino put it, Marcos's 20-year-old regime "mismanaged the national economy, revamped the political structure by entrenching itself, violated the people's human rights, stashed away unexplained wealth abroad, enmeshed itself in graft and corruption and failed to provide moral leadership for the nation."[17]

THE following day, February 5, it was the turn of President Marcos and his running mate, Arturo M. Tolentino, to wrap up the campaign in their own *miting de avance* at the same venue. Some reports claimed the KBL crowd equalled the number at the opposition's penultimate rally. In his speech, in which he alternately used English and Tagalog, Marcos accused his political opponents of sowing anger and the seeds of revolution even as he asked for reconciliation and unity as the avenue to progress. He stressed that he was getting impatient with reports of increasing violence perpetrated by his opponents and warned that if they continued hurting his companions and supporters, he would have them arrested. He warned trouble-makers, particularly those who allegedly hurled stones that afternoon in front of the U.S. Embassy which hurt some of his supporters: "You will reap the strong winds, the typhoons and the whirlwind if you insist on hurting the KBL." He added that "if there is no problem or cause for opposing the proclamation of my opponent, I shall perform my duty as President for a peaceful transition."[18]

That same day both the Commission on Elections and the Namfrel announced they were ready for the elections. Chairman Victorino A. Savellano of Comelec said 26,181,829 registered voters were expected to vote on Friday, February 7. The figure was 1.5 million more than in the 1984 parliamentary elections. He also announced that all voting paraphernalia — official ballots, election returns, indelible ink — had already been shipped to all the 85,938 voting centers throughout the country.

Reporting that all systems, equipment and personnel were in place, Namfrel's Concepcion Jr. said the Namfrel center at the La Salle in Greenhills, San Juan, Metro Manila, was all set to receive the reports of its volunteers throughout the country beginning Friday evening.[19]

For her part, on the eve of the election, Cory Aquino ended her campaign with a vow, stated with the ringing confidence of a sure winner, for a new beginning. In an election eve statement she said:

> Today we are near the end of the first stage of our journey. A journey that began on the tarmac of the Manila airport in 1983. From that dark moment we have arrived at the dawn of a new Philippines. The people have spoken as never before. . .
>
> We have won. We have won the people. We have won the argument. And as the old dictator lurks in his palace with his dwindling band of cronies and his false medals for comfort, I warn him: do not cheat the people on Friday. After twenty years at last find it in yourself, Mr. Marcos, to respect the people's judgment. Already there are reports

of the old tricks of intimidation and fraud that have
protected you for so long in the corrupt luxury of your
palace. Don't, Mr. Marcos. Because this time you will not
get away with it.

You will bring shame on yourself and your country if
you try. This nation has seen its standard of living fall.
Who is better off now than they were five years ago except
the cronies? Too many of our children go unfed. Our
infrastructure has fallen into ruin; our wealth has been
stolen by our leaders and put in their American bank accounts; our military has been demoralized; our once-proud
nation has been divided against itself; our citizens have
been terrorized by a brutal regime.

Now the Filipino people have risen and said, enough
is enough. It would take a braver, stronger man than the
ailing Mr. Marcos successfully to deny the people victory
now. No slick trick with the ballot boxes or intimidation
can rescue you, Mr. Marcos.

To all my fellow Filipinos, I appeal to you: Guard
your ballots. Victory is ours. Make sure there is a free and
fair election and that the new Philippines is born in an
atmosphere of peace and reconciliation.

In the course of our campaign I have travelled the
length of our nation and as I have seen the suffering and
the hopes, I have learned what must be done. I stand ready
with Doy Laurel to begin the long process of rebuilding our
beloved country, of creating a Philippines for all our
people where there is work, justice, liberty and welfare
for all.

On Friday, out of the ashes of twenty years of
misrule, there will be a new beginning. I shall treat your
votes as a sacred trust. You have put your faith in me. I
will prove worthy of it.[20]

With that statement, Corazon Cojuangco Aquino ended a
45-day campaign for the Presidency which actually began on December 11, 1985. She had hopped through the provinces, attracting
record crowds every stop of the way, stunning her rival and his
supporters, and bewildering even her own leaders and followers with
her phenomenal mass appeal, boundless vigor and enthusiasm, and
unmatched drawing power.

TWELVE

Moment of Truth

I'm not asking for violent revolution. This is not the time for that. I always indicated that now is the way of nonviolent struggle for justice. This means active resistance of evil by peaceful means.

— Cory Aquino

ON Friday, February 7, 1986, a total of 26 million voters were expected to go to more than 85,000 polling places throughout the country to elect a President and a Vice President with a term of six years each. It would be the 10th presidential election and the first special polls since September 17, 1935 and the first election for Vice President since November 1969. The voting centers were spread in 60 cities and 1,532 towns or municipalities in 74 provinces throughout the archipelago's more than 7,000 islands. As of election day the Philippines had a total population estimated at from 54 million to 55 million.

Based on certificates of candidacies filed with the Commission on Elections, the list of candidates is as follows:

For President
1. Ferdinand E. Marcos, Kilusang Bagong Lipunan (KBL).
2. Corazon C. Aquino, United Nationalist Democratic Organization (Unido).
3. Reuben R. Canoy, Social Democratic Party (SDP).
4. Narciso S. Padilla, Movement for Truth, Order and Righteousness (Motor).

For Vice President
1. Arturo M. Tolentino, Kilusang Bagong Lipunan (KBL).
2. Salvador H. Laurel, United Nationalist Democratic Organization (Unido).
3. Eva Estrada Kalaw, Liberal Party (LP).
4. Maria Victoria Osmeña-Stewart, United Nationalist Demo-

cratic Organization (Unido).

    5.   Rodolfo T. Ganzon, LP-Timawa Party.

    6.   Roger V. Arienda, Movement for Truth, Order and Righteousness (Motor).[1]

Voting started at 7 a.m. and ended at 3 p.m. except when there were voters present within 30 meters of the polling place who had not yet voted beyond 3 p.m. In such a case voting was allowed to continue but only to enable the voters to vote without interruption.

The Philippine Atmospheric, Geophysical, Astronomical Services Administration (Pagasa), also known as the Weather Bureau, had predicted that weather would be fine throughout the country the whole day of the election, notwithstanding the tropical storm, codenamed "Akang," the first to enter the Philippine "area of responsibility" in 1986, which was still far from Philippine shores. Meanwhile, the efforts of the Comelec and the National Movement for Free Elections (Namfrel) at a quick count of election results were expected to achieve within 24 hours a national profile of how the people voted.

Reaffirming the restriction imposed by law as a police power designed to ensure free, honest and orderly elections and to safeguard the secrecy of the ballot, the Comelec barred members of media, whether local or foreign, from entering the polling places during the voting. It denied a petition of the Foreign Correspondents Association of the Philippines seeking access to the voting centers. Comelec Chairman Victorino Savellano, urging the public to go out and vote, then reminded them of their duties and responsibilities to assure the free expression of the people's will.[2]

The Comelec, however, assured the official U.S. government observer group headed by U.S. Senator Richard G. Lugar that it would be allowed inside polling precincts to observe voting at close range. The team would be escorted by Comelec officials inside the polling places and given access to whatever information they would need. The group, which arrived Wednesday night, February 5, came to observe the electoral process "objectively" and not to pass judgment on the elections.[3]

With all systems set in place, the nation proceeded to vote for their President and Vice President after a fierce and brawling campaign between two giants of Philippine politics: incumbent President Ferdinand E. Marcos and, in effect, former Senator Benigno "Ninoy" S. Aquino Jr., who was assassinated on August 21, 1983 and was represented in this much-awaited electoral contest by his widow, Corazon Cojuangco Aquino.

AT exactly 11:30 a.m. that Friday, President Ferdinand E. Marcos, as has been his custom ever since he became a national politician, voted in his native Batac, Ilocos Norte at the school named after his father, Mariano Marcos Memorial Elementary School. There was a big crowd of followers, townmates and relatives who had gathered to greet and wish him good luck. For the first time in the long political life of their celebrated Ferdinand, he was running in an election against a woman! And, it had been reported, he was "running scared".

The President was in high spirits, according to the *Philippine News Agency*, the government news gathering organization, as he filled his ballot. Wearing the now-familiar red jacket over a red and white striped shirt, he was the 75th voter in Precinct 10, with ballot No. 5777, the last three digits being the lucky presidential numbers.

Accompanying him were his children, Imee Marcos Manotoc, Ilocos Norte Governor Ferdinand Marcos Jr. and Irene Marcos Araneta. Also with him was Gen. Fabian C. Ver.

The large crowd kept chanting *"Marcos pa rin! Mabuhay si Marcos!"* (It's still Marcos! Long live Marcos!) As the President handed his accomplished ballot to Mrs. Felisa Pasetes, poll chairman, a band played a medley of Ilocano songs. The entire brief proceedings were covered by local and foreign newsmen.

After voting, Marcos immediately motored back to the Laoag International Airport and flew back to Manila at noon.

In Manila, meanwhile, Mrs. Imelda R. Marcos cast her vote at the V. Mapa High School in Sta. Mesa. She was the first voter at Precinct 893-A, having arrived there before 7 a.m. The First Lady described the elections as "very significant for the country" and expressed the hope that it would bring peace and fulfillment to the people. *"Vox populi, vox Dei,"* she intoned, adding: "With God's help the Marcos-Tolentino team will win even in Metro Manila."

IN Tarlac province, presidential candidate Corazon C. Aquino arrived early in the morning at the family's Hacienda Luisita compound in the town of San Miguel, accompanied by members of the Aquino family and hundreds of local and foreign media representatives who had motored to the province to "cover" her as she cast her ballot. It was 7:45 a.m. when she voted in Precinct 44 at the Lourdes Elementary School. After voting she thanked the people for supporting her and added:

"Today is my day. I have never been more confident in all my life. I want to thank the Filipino people and the local and foreign media for the coverage of my campaign."

After casting her vote, the lady candidate for President left for Manila.

Salvador Laurel, on the other hand, cast his vote at a precinct in Barangay Natatas, Tanauan, Batangas, at 8:25 a.m. He was accompanied by members of his family. After voting he said the election was so far the most important in local history "because we are in the bridge of a turning point." The *PNA* did not elaborate on what he meant.

For his part, the KBL's vice presidential candidate, Arturo M. Tolentino, cast his vote at 10:15 a.m. at Precinct 336, Juan Luna Elementary School, Cataluña street, Sampaloc, Manila. He was accompanied by his daughter, Emelita, who also voted in the same precinct.

FRIDAY'S voting gave an inkling of how bitterly contested the showdown was and indicated in advance that all would not be smooth and well as far as reporting the results was concerned.

On February 8, for instance, a discrepancy or conflict between the Comelec and Namfrel returns was reported by *Bulletin Today*. The newspaper said initial unofficial returns showed Marcos and Tolentino ahead of Aquino and Laurel. Comelec "certified partial returns" indicated a 54.4—45.3 percent ratio in favor of the President's reelection.

It was a close race in Metro Manila, said the paper, where Mrs. Aquino was expected to win by a big margin. Comelec partial returns showed Marcos getting 2,758 against Aquino's 2,269. But Namfrel figures, much larger than the Comelec's, showed Aquino ahead of Marcos 180,083 against 128,391 for the President in Metro Manila at the same time. As of 12:45 a.m., February 8, according to another newspaper, *Malaya*, Marcos was ahead of Aquino in the Comelec count, 11,593 against Aquino's 6,575. But in the Namfrel count, Aquino was ahead, 883,220 against 614,432 for Marcos.

In the vice presidential race as of that time, Comelec gave Tolentino 9,651 to Laurel's 7,086. But in the Namfrel count Laurel led Tolentino 836,632 against 586,746.

It was obvious, at this point, that Namfrel had a faster count than the Comelec and that where Aquino was leading Marcos in the Namfrel count, the reverse was true in the slower Comelec count.

Meanwhile, President Marcos said in the ABC "Today" television program broadcast live to America the night of the elections that the exercise seemed to be generally clean and that if the trend continued, he and Tolentino would win in all of the country's 73 provinces. Mrs. Aquino, on the other hand, claimed victory over Marcos early Saturday morning, saying that "no power can pry from our hands the freedom we have won this day."[4] At the same time Senator Lugar, chairman of the U.S. Senate Committee on Foreign Relations and head of a 20-member observation team, expressed deep disturbance over the delay of the counting of ballots.

(From Washington, the *United Press International* reported that a U.S. Air Force plane flew Haitian President-for-life Jean-Claude Duvalier out of his island country to an undisclosed destination in exile, according to the State Department. The U.S. government said between 50 and 60 people had died since November 28 in widespread protests against Duvalier's 15-year-rule. Duvalier's family had ruled the Caribbean country for 28 years.[5])

Namfrel, at the same time, denounced on election day alleged massive attempts to harass and intimidate its volunteer workers throughout the country, claiming that "cheating, frauds, intimidation, and harassment were ten times more than those which attended the 1984 Batasan elections."[6]

BY 10:30 p.m., February 8, Marcos maintained his lead in the Comelec count over Aquino, 1,112,275 against 1,079,228. But Mrs. Aquino had a substantial lead over Marcos in the Namfrel count, 4,306,684 for Aquino and 3,455,548 for Marcos. In 'the vice presidential race, Laurel led Tolentino in both the Comelec and Namfrel counts: 1,061,108 for Laurel as against 1,042,359 for Tolentino (Comelec) and 4,028,800 against 3,305,814 for Tolentino (Namfrel).

Exuding confidence, President Marcos told a press conference Saturday, February 8, that "the worst possible scenario" would put him ahead of Mrs. Aquino by only 1.2 million votes, though a better possibility, according to him, would be a margin of 2.2 million. But at the same time Mrs. Aquino told another press conference that "it is to the best interest of our nation that President Marcos concede as circumstances warrant." She said that of the six million votes so far counted by Namfrel and opposition poll watchers, she was leading with 3,469,714 votes, or some 900,000 votes over the President, who had 2,569,498 votes. (In Haiti, meanwhile, a military-civilian council took power after President Duvalier had fled to France.[7])

By February 9, Sunday, Marcos retained his lead over Aquino, 3,056,236 as against 2,903,348 in the Comelec count. But in the Namfrel count, Aquino was ahead, 5,576,319 as against 4,806,166 for Marcos. Tolentino led Laurel in the Comelec count, 2,877,058 against 2,776,596; but in the Namfrel count, Laurel was ahead, 5,035,040 compared to Tolentino's 4,533,300.

The Batasang Pambansa, as the national canvassing board under the Constitution, was scheduled to meet Monday afternoon to start the official canvass of election returns from 74 provinces, 59 cities and seven districts of Metro Manila. Under the law the winners would be proclaimed within 15 session days from the day the Batasan started the canvass unless there was justifiable delay. Deputy Prime Minister Jose A. Roño said the Batasan could finish the official canvass in 48 hours if all the certificates of canvass were submitted.

Meanwhile President Marcos appealed to the people for calm and sobriety in the wake of "provocative acts by the political opposition" to stir up post-election violence. He made the appeal in response to reports that the Unido had started mass actions in support of its claim of victory in the February 7 special elections. Marcos said it was obvious the only purpose the opposition can have in prematurely proclaiming the victory of Mrs. Aquino was to stir up the passions of its partisans so that they could incite a confrontation with the government forces.

In the meantime the opposition expressed fear that the KBL would try to tamper with the results of the elections through forged certificates of canvass to be transmitted to the Batasang Pambansa, which would count the final returns and proclaim the winners.[8] Likewise, a *Malaya* editorial report, "Anomalies may stop Cory's Win," expressed fear that electoral fraud on a massive scale never before seen in the country's political history might overturn what pollsters had forecast as a national landslide for Corazon Aquino into a crushing defeat through vote-buying, intimidation, snatching of ballot boxes and tampering with election returns.[9]

In the Comelec tabulating center, meanwhile, 30 tabulators posted at the Comelec machines at the PICC walked out of their assignments at 10:30 p.m. Sunday, February 9, in protest over the alleged "deliberate changing of the election results directly coming from the precincts into the terminal they were manning." The walkout was initially staged by 16 programmers who were joined by 14 others as they filed out of their posts.[10]

ON February 10, Monday, the Batasang Pambansa constituted itself into a national board of canvassers and created a board of tellers. The Board of Tellers was composed of four KBL members and four opposition members. The KBL members were Assemblymen Rodolfo Albano (Isabela), Salvador Britanico (Iloilo), Concordio Diel (Misamis Oriental), and Manolito Asok (Siquijor). The opposition was represented by Assemblymen Edmundo Cea (Camarines Sur), Ramon Mitra Jr. (Palawan), Aquilino Pimentel Jr. (Cagayan de Oro City), Homobono Adaza (Misamis Oriental), alternates; Marcelo Fernan (Cebu), Antonio Cuenco (Cebu City), alternates; and Emigdio Tanjuatco (Rizal) and Lito Atienza (Manila), alternates. The President named Joaquin Venus Jr., deputy presidential executive assistant, as his official representative in the canvass. Mrs. Corazon Aquino appointed Joker Arroyo as her representative.

In deference to the President's wish, the Batasan decided to allow the Comelec and the Namfrel to continue with their respective canvassings.

Marcos, meanwhile, continued to lead Aquino in the Comelec count. As of 11 p.m., February 10, he had 4,031,633 against Aquino's 3,781,575. But in the Namfrel count (12 p.m., February 10), Aquino led Marcos 6,658,838 to 5,971,693. Tolentino led Laurel in the Comelec figures with 3,802,804 as against 3,629,147. But in the Namfrel count, Laurel led Tolentino with 6,433,250 as against 5,620,591.

President Marcos said in an interview on NBC TV's "Meet the Press" on Monday, February 10, that he had no intention of nullifying the snap elections though there were reports that he might. He also stressed that he could not replace Gen. Fabian Ver as AFP chief of staff because Lt. Gen. Fidel V. Ramos, who was supposed to take his place, had been involved in a human rights case. The President pointedly asked his interviewer: "Why do you want me to appoint somebody as chief of staff when he (Ver) is the personal choice of the President?"

From the opposition side a call was issued to the KBL to "stop pressuring" members of the city election returns or falsifying the certificate of canvass. The call was issued by Assemblyman Aquilino Pimentel Jr. who told a press briefing that the delays in the canvassing of votes were part of a well-orchestrated move to overhaul the lead of Mrs. Aquino and Laurel. Senator Lugar, meanwhile, said in a pre-departure press conference that serious charges had been made against the tabulation system within the last 24 hours of his five-day stay in the country and that he would submit to President Ronald Reagan a preliminary report on the delegation's observations on election abuses and irregularities. He stressed that he and his group witnessed and heard disturbing reports of efforts to undermine the integrity of the electoral process, both during the voting and vote-counting.[11] The entire election process seemed inevitably headed for trouble.

ON Tuesday night, February 11, the Batasang Pambansa board of tellers began to canvass the votes. A motion by the opposition to declare the canvass illegal if not all the certificates of returns had been received, lost by a vote of 117-43. Speaker Nicanor Yñiguez then ordered the ballot boxes which had been deposited in his office brought down to the session hall. As of 9 p.m., 99 out of 140 certificates of election returns had been received by the Speaker's office.

The same day Marcos announced he would invite opposition candidate Cory Aquino to join the Council of State that he would organize to formulate basic government policies. The President said the council, the highest advisory body in government, would be composed of members of the political groups including majority and opposition parties, former foreign ministers, Presidents and candidates for President. The opposition rejected the offer.

From Washington, the White House indicated that President Reagan expected President Marcos to win reelection and that the U.S. would support the Filipino leader, according to the *Philippine News Agency*. The early evening newscasts of the three major TV networks reported that Reagan had signalled his administration's policy to other leaders of the U.S. government. Angered, Mrs. Aquino immediately appealed to the U.S. "not to make the mistake in the name of short-sighted self-interest, of coming to the support" of President Marcos.

As a foreshadowing, Jaime Cardinal Sin and other Catholic Church leaders stepped into the fray. They expressed strong support for all nonviolent forms of civil disobedience to expose and prevent election frauds. Auxiliary Bishop Ted Bacani said the church would give the people the moral support they needed to denounce election irregularities.

As these developments were taking place, the Comelec and officials of the KBL said they were receiving reports of poll violations allegedly committed by volunteers of Namfrel in various parts of the country. Some Namfrel volunteers, it was alleged, were trying to convince voters near the voting booths to vote for Aquino and Laurel, and an unidentified nun in Lingayen, Pangasinan, was representing Namfrel inside the polling place and taking charge of reading the ballots during the counting.[12]

Meanwhile, the Comelec count as of 12 p.m., February 12, showed Marcos with 6,149,330 against Aquino's 5,603,235, while

Namfrel as of 7 p.m., February 11, had it 6,281,510 for Marcos and 6,933,989 for Aquino. For Vice President, Tolentino led Laurel in the Comelec count, 5,860,607 as against 5,467,277. The Namfrel count showed Laurel leading Tolentino 6,718,989 to 5,906,769.

That same Tuesday, February 11, a major violent incident occurred. At 10:30 a.m., ex-Governor Evelio Javier of Antique province, an opposition stalwart, was gunned down in broad daylight in the capital town of San Jose. Javier, 43, was riddled with M-16 bullets by six hooded men and finished off with a single shot in the head. He became the most prominent casualty of the February 7 presidential elections.[13]

PRESIDENT Marcos continued to maintain his lead in the Comelec tabulation. As of 9 p.m., February 12, he had 7,032,905 votes to Aquino's 6,384,364. Tolentino had 6,707,515, and Laurel, 7,237,496. Namfrel, as of 10 p.m., had Marcos behind, 6,532,362 to Aquino's 7,158,679. Tolentino had 6,140,309, and Laurel, 6,950,489.

At the Batasang Pambansa, procedural defects were noted in many certificates of election returns received from the bailiwicks of both the KBL and the opposition, mostly involving the absence of prescribed seals on the certificates although the envelopes containing them were sealed properly. The certificates appeared to have been properly prepared and signed by the corresponding boards of canvassers. In spite of opposition objections, Speaker Yñiguez said that the Batasan could not go beyond canvassing the returns reported in the certificates in accordance with the Constitution and the Omnibus Election Code, stressing that the proper forum for complaints and grievances was the Electoral Tribunal.

From Washington President Reagan announced he was sending veteran U.S. diplomat Philip Habib to the Philippines to "help nurture the hopes and possibilities of democracy" in a land torn by a bitter presidential election.[14] Mrs. Aquino expressed alarm over Habib's designation to act as intermediary between the ruling party and the opposition camps, saying the ambassador's last assignment for Reagan was as head negotiator for the end of the civil war in Lebanon, where he apparently failed.[15]

IN the official canvass by the Batasang Pambansa, President Marcos posted a commanding lead of 859,784 votes over Cory Aquino as of 11 p.m., February 13. He had 6,274,427 votes to Mrs. Aquino's 5,414,643 "in a random canvass of certificates, one province or city at a time, in each of the country's 13 regions." Tolentino, on the other hand, was leading Laurel by 459,853 votes.

Meanwhile the President issued a statement the same day renewing his commitment to honor without reservation the people's verdict at the polls and to extend his hand in conciliation to those who had contested the elections with him. He said that too much which was "regrettable" had already happened since that voting came to a close. He added that greater tension had riven the country and more divisions had come compared to the period of the campaign. He noted that the tense situation had engendered sporadic instances of violence, including the brutal slaying of former Governor of Antique and opposition leader Evelio Javier.

The Namfrel, on the other hand, also announced that it had completed counting its certificates of votes cast at the precinct level in the snap polls. Collected by Namfrel volunteers all over the country, the certificates were duly certified by the boards of election inspectors.

Namfrel Chairman Concepcion, meanwhile, said the "truth will prevail" in response to what he described as a "systematic attempt to discredit" the Namfrel. Contrary to what some newspapers had reported, many Namfrel volunteers had been the victims, not the perpetrators, of election disorder and violence, he emphasized.

The Namfrel, as of 5 p.m., February 13, had tabulated results from 56,736 precincts, or 66.02 percent of the nationwide total of 85,943 precincts. It showed Mrs. Aquino still leading in the Namfrel tally board with 7,158,679 votes as against 6,532,632 for President Marcos. Laurel had obtained 6,950,489 votes as against Tolentino's 6,140.309.

From Washington, the *Philippine News Agency* reported that Rep. Jerry Lewis (Republican-California) who observed the elections described Namfrel as "another partisan group engaged in political trickery and gimmickry," not as the noble citizens watchdog organization it was reputed to be.[16]

ON February 14, the highly active Catholic Bishops Conference of the Philippines issued a strongly worded post-election statement not usually expected from the religious and ecclesiastics. It condemned the February 7 polls as "unparalleled in the fraudulence of its conduct." Not even the political oppositionists themselves had attempted such a sweeping judgment on a purely political exercise. The statement of the 120-member CBCP, whose president is Ricardo Cardinal Vidal of Cebu, attacked the "irregularities" that characterized the election such as the "systematic disenfranchisement of voters," "widespread and massive vote-buying," "deliberate tampering with election returns," and "intimidation, harassment, terrorism and murder." The statement also warned against a government that "assumes or retains power, through fraud," saying that such administration would have no "moral basis."[17]

From Washington the *Associated Press* reported that U.S. Senator Sam Nunn echoed the same charges raised by the bishops. He said that President Marcos was "making an all-out effort to steal the election" by "massive fraud, intimidation and murder" and that the effort should be repudiated by the United States. He said in a letter to President Reagan that "both direct and circumstantial evidence leads to an inescapable conclusion: the Philippine people want President Marcos out and they have elected Corazon Aquino as President." [18]

Compared to the position of the Catholic bishops and some U.S. lawmakers such as Senator Nunn, that of the local political opposition was civil. Acknowledging the inevitability of a Marcos proclamation by the Batasang Pambansa, the oppositionists were set to conduct daily mass actions which would continue until President Marcos voluntarily stepped down from power. They maintained that the Marcos proclamation, if pushed through, would be illegal because of the "very substantial number" of questioned certificates of canvass.[19]

Meanwhile, according to the Batasan canvass, Marcos had widened his lead over Aquino to 1.5 million votes, with only 1.1 million votes uncanvassed, as of Friday night, February 14. The Batasan official tally showed Marcos with 10,184,710 votes as against Aquino's 8,731,999. Tolentino had 9,554,022 to Laurel's 8,635,375.

In the Namfrel count, however, as of 8:15 p.m., Aquino had 7,318,562 as against 6,657,195 for Marcos. Laurel led Tolentino with 7,101,265 votes, against the KBL bet's 6,263,553.

With that insuperable lead, Marcos had virtually clinched the Batasan's proclamation since the remaining uncanvassed votes would no longer alter the outcome.   However, influential forces in the U.S. government, the local Catholic church hierarchy and other anti-Marcos elements in the country had already set into place a program of action designed to repudiate a government that in the words of the Bishops Conference, "retained power through fraud" and had "no moral basis."

AS scheduled, the Batasang Pambansa proclaimed on Saturday night, February 15, President Ferdinand E. Marcos and Member of Parliament Arturo M. Tolentino as the duly elected President and Vice President, respectively, in the February 7 snap presidential elections. As provided by the Constitution they would each serve a six-year term.

Also as expected, particularly by partisans in and outside the Batasan halls, the proclamation came after a heated debate among parliamentary stalwarts of the KBL and the opposition, and a denial by the majority of an opposition motion to defer the proclamation. The whole proceeding ended in a walkout by all the opposition assemblymen.

The majority assemblymen, many of whom were veteran parliamentarians, acted swiftly. After the walkout, MP Alejandro D. Almendras (KBL, Davao del Sur) asked for a roll call to determine whether there was a quorum. There were 122 KBL assemblymen present, and only 96 were required to constitute a quorum.

Exercising his authority and responsibility under the Constitution, Speaker Yñiguez reported to the assembly that President Marcos obtained 10,807,197 votes as against Mrs. Corazon C. Aquino's 9,291,761 or a lead by the President of 1,515,481 votes. Reuben Canoy and Narciso Padilla obtained 34,041 and 23,652 votes, respectively.

In the Vice Presidency, Yñiguez reported, Tolentino obtained 10,134,130 votes, as against Laurel's 9,173,105, or a difference of 961,025 for Tolentino. Eva Estrada Kalaw garnered 662,185 votes, while Roger Arienda had 35,974. (See comparative figures in both Comelec and Namfrel tabulations, this chapter).

Yñiguez then answered questions raised by the opposition. On the claim that 59 certificates did not contain the seal required by the Comelec, the Speaker stated that he received a certificate from the poll body that only five paper seals had been distributed for the envelopes containing the certificates. Thus, there were no more seals left for the certificates.

The Speaker said that other certificates not having been sealed "is a mere procedural one" and that a mistake or even an intentional wrong should not be permitted to disenfranchise a district. He also explained that the non-participation of a party representative in the proceedings or in signing the certificates of canvass did not and would not affect the validity or the acts of the canvassing board. He noted, furthermore, that there was no instance when figures appearing in the certificate varied with the copies of Unido and KBL and did not tally.

Later that night, in the absence of the opposition members who had all walked out, a resolution proclaiming the President and Tolentino was approved by the Batasan.[21]

**FINAL ELECTION FIGURES FOR PRESIDENT
AND VICE PRESIDENT, FEBRUARY 7, 1986 SPECIAL
OR "SNAP" PRESIDENTIAL ELECTIONS**

	COMELEC (Complete)	NAMFREL (70%)
For President		
Ferdinand E. Marcos	10,807,197	7,053,068
Corazon C. Aquino	9,291,761	7,835,070
For Vice President		
Arturo M. Tolentino	10,134,130	6,613,507
Salvador H. Laurel	9,173,105	7,441,313

NOTE: In full-page ads *(Manila Times,* February 25, 1986), Namfrel published a statement on the presidential elections and released the above figures. Claiming that the results of the national canvassing by the Batasang Pambansa did not reflect the real vote of the Filipino people, it revealed that its tabulation was based only on precinct tally sheets which were duly certified by the Board of Election Inspectors and obtained by Namfrel volunteers on election day. "The tabulation represents 60,211 precincts equivalent to approximately 70% of total voter turnout," the statement said. "Namfrel was unable to organize or was prevented from performing its functions in the balance of the precincts. Namfrel believes, based on statistical and field studies, that this tabulation is a fairer representation of the real vote. It may even be an underestimation of the lead of Mrs. Aquino because it includes precincts with questionable results in favor of Mr. Marcos which were duly certified by the Board of Election Inspectors."

Reprinted from *The Manila Times*,
February 25, 1986

THE proclamation of President Marcos as reelected President and former Senator Arturo M. Tolentino as Vice President by the Batasang Pambansa did not catch Cory Aquino by surprise. Neither did she accept it with acquiescence. On the contrary she immediately issued a statement that rings with vehemence. It goes as follows:

> Mr. Marcos controls his Batasan, so what? We never doubted the votes of his puppet members of the Batasan. But when Mr. Marcos called an election it was not with the intention of having to be rescued from defeat by his own assemblymen.
>
> He is finished. He has had to use one trick after another to try and rescue himself from defeat: fraud, intimidation, violence, cheating in a super slow Comelec vote count to the final panic of rushing the canvass through the Batasan. Yet nobody believes he is still President. Because the one vote he does not have is that of the people.
>
> Even before I am finally declared winner of this election I think we can all agree who is the biggest loser: Mr. Marcos. No tinsel and celebration of the President's make-believe win can hide his loss of moral and political authority.
>
> He is beaten. When is he going to go? [22]

In addition the opposition announced that Cory Aquino and Doy Laurel would lead a mammoth *"Tagumpay ng Bayan"* (Triumph of the People) rally at the Luneta on Sunday afternoon, February 16, during which Mrs. Aquino was expected to unfold her "nonviolent program of protest" against the Marcos regime. The rally was billed as a "celebration of the people's recent victory at the polls." The opposition maintained that Cory and Doy were the winners elected by the people, despite the Batasan's proclamation of President Marcos and former Senator Tolentino.

Evidently, the fight for the Presidency was far from over.

The bitter battle of nerves between President Marcos and Mrs. Cory Aquino intensified further with the lady presidential bet's call for civil disobedience. The call was issued on Sunday at the Luneta where between 1-million and 1.5-million people had converged, rivaling in size the *miting de avance* crowd that joined Aquino's penultimate rally on February 4.

Cory Aquino's civil disobedience cry, a novel action in Philippine political history, was calculated to help bring down Marcos to his knees by the simple expedient of making him realize that he was governing the country without the mandate of the people and there-fore without moral basis. It was a takeoff from the *satyagraha* or "force of truth" doctrine of Mahatma Gandhi, a doctrine of active nonviolence with total sacrifice based on love. Under this doctrine Gandhi's diehard followers allowed themselves to be clubbed in the saltworks of India by the state police in 1930. The resulting mas-sacre, dubbed the "Salt March Massacre," made Gandhi's –and the Indians' — fight for independence from Britain and complete re-forms of Indian society an international event that later led to India's liberation.

In her speech at the Luneta Mrs. Aquino called for massive civil disobedience and nonviolent actions. She urged the people to implement the following crippling program of action:

1.   Boycott the so-called "crony" press which she identified as the Manila *Daily Bulletin, Daily Express, Times Journal, People's Journal* and *Tempo*.

2.   Stop patronizing companies owned by Marcos's cronies such as San Miguel Corporation, Rustan's, Union Bank, Traders Royal Bank, United Coconut Planters Bank, Philippine National Bank, and others.

3.   Delay payment of power and water bills until the day when these services were due for cut-off because of non-payment.

4.   Police forces and the military to follow their conscience and stop being loyal to "a President who does not have the people's mandate."

5.   Government employees and employees of private enter-prises to bombard the Social Security System and the Government Service Insurance System with loan applications.

6.   Work stoppage and boycott of all classes on all levels on the day after Marcos took his oath of office as the reelected Pres-ident. (Marcos was scheduled to take his oath on February 25, 10 days after his official proclamation by the Batasan).

7.   Organize on the neighborhood and community levels for concerted protest actions which are nonviolent in nature.[23]

MEANWHILE, from Santa Barbara, California, the *Agence France Presse* reported that in the midst of the raging conflict in the Philip-pines, President Reagan finally had a change of heart and joined the forces against President Marcos. He was quoted as saying that the credibility of the February 7 elections had been "called into ques-tion" by "fraud and violence perpetrated largely by the ruling party," the KBL of Marcos. This position of the American President

was a full turnabout from his earlier stance supporting President
Marcos, saying he would win reelection, and pledging to extend him
support. Reagan's new statement was obviously issued as a result of
his receipt of a report from his observer delegation, for he said:

"Although our observation delegation has not yet completed
its work, it has already become evident, sadly, that the elections
were marred by widespread fraud and violence perpetrated largely
by the ruling party. It was so extreme that the elections' credibility
has been called into question both within the Philippines and in the
United States."[24]

Though uttered 10,000 miles away, Reagan's words had profound repercussions in the Philippines.

At the Luneta rally, Mrs. Aquino said in launching her program of nonviolent civil disobedience:

"I'm not asking for violent revolution. This is not the time for
that. I always indicated that now is the way of nonviolent struggle
for justice. This means active resistance of evil by peaceful
means."[25]

President Reagan's new critical stance could only mean one
thing: the United States would apply stronger, continuing pressure
on President Marcos to force him to step down. He had been convinced that Marcos, a personal friend of his, had outlived his useful-
ness to the United States whose military bases had become imperilled because of his inability to control leftist insurgency and
because, based on reports given to him by his observers, Marcos had
apparently lost the people's mandate. A news agency report from
Washington, in fact, said that the new Reagan position meant "the
beginning of the end of the Marcos regime." Senator Lugar was
quoted as saying that the Filipinos should hold another election,
noting that while Reagan had been very careful to say that the U.S.
was not suggesting "supplanting of anybody" it was nevertheless
"supporting the development of Philippine democracy."[26]

More sanguine than Lugar was Richard C. Holbrooke, Secretary
of State in the Jimmy Carter administration, who predicted that
Lugar's appraisal, followed by Reagan's charge of election fraud
against Marcos, would lead to the early departure of the Philippine
President. Holbrooke was reported to have said: "What we're looking
at now is not a question of whether Marcos is going to leave, but
how and when." He agreed with Lugar that the longer Marcos stayed
in power, the greater strength the Communists would be getting in
the Philippines.

At the same time the mounting pressure for Marcos to give up the Presidency was joined by three other U.S. Senators who urged Reagan to ask Marcos in unambiguous terms to step down from office. The three — Senators David L. Boren, David Pryor and Carl Levin — claimed they saw concrete evidence of election fraud. They charged that Marcos had lost his popular mandate, that Mrs. Aquino won the election "by all impartial observation" and that Marcos should seek a voluntary transfer of power to those who had truly won the election.[27]

Then on Monday, February 17, Reagan's special envoy, Ambassador Philip Habib, arrived in Manila and held private and separate talks with President Marcos and Mrs. Corazon Aquino. Habib was quoted by Marcos as saying that he came here not to render judgment on the conduct of the last elections or to make any suggestion on the running of Philippine internal affairs.

For her part, Cory Aquino, who met with Habib after the envoy's meeting with President Marcos, reportedly told the ambassador that the electoral crisis "will only be resolved by a swift and orderly transfer of power to the Aquino Presidency that the Filipino people have chosen overwhelmingly at the polls."[28]

In reality Habib had warned President Marcos that he must "make democratic reforms and share power" with the opposition or risk losing U.S. military and economic assistance. Habib also told Marcos during private talks that "fundamental reforms" were needed to head off a growing call of an aid cutoff in the Congress. Meanwhile the U.S. Senate, by a vote of 85-9, passed a resolution condemning the Philippine elections as a fraud, thus further increasing the pressure on Marcos.

In the meantime, at a big rally in Angeles City, Pampanga on February 19, Mrs. Aquino told a cheering crowd of about 20,000 Pampanga residents that the opposition would not budge an inch in its active nonviolent campaign unless "we can bring Mr. Marcos down to his knees." She also said, to the amusement of the crowd, that President Marcos was "another Duvalier in the making," implying that he would do a Duvalier and escape from the Philippines.[29]

On Friday, February 21, Cory met Ambassador Habib for the second time in her office in Makati and he asked her about the direction events would take in connection with the opposition's civil disobedience campaign. But she declined to give him details. The U.S. ambassador was scheduled to return to the United States that same day after another meeting with President Marcos, a day after Marcos, objecting at last to the undeniable American interference in Philippine affairs, lashed out at "modern-day imperialists" and vowed to defend "our country's sovereignty against all outside forces that would demean it."[30]   After the meeting with Marcos, Habib returned to Washington to report to President Reagan on the crisis sparked by the reelection of Ferdinand E. Marcos.

On the other hand, Cory Aquino and Doy Laurel were to fly to Cebu City to push the civil disobedience campaign in the provinces. They were evidently heartened by the change in Reagan's position vis-a-vis the Philippine Presidency.

Then on Saturday, February 22, two Philippine newspapers, the *Daily Inquirer* and the *Malaya*, came out with what initially appeared as an insignificant news item: an unverified report that Defense Minister Juan Ponce Enrile had tendered his irrevocable resignation from the Marcos government. The sources of the news story were two U.S. newspapers, the *Philadelphia Inquirer* and the *San Jose Mercury News*, according to the local *Inquirer*. Like a number of other stories in recent years, this one had to be known first by the American people though the person involved was the most powerful government official at the time — Minister Enrile, civilian chief of the 250,000-strong Armed Forces of the Philippines.

The biggest Manila daily newspaper then, *Bulletin Today*, did not carry the story in its February 22 issue.

THIRTEEN

Revolution and Proclamation

I ask our people not to relax but to be even more vigilant in this one moment of triumph. The Motherland cannot thank them enough. Yet, we all realize that more is required of each and everyone of us to redeem our promises and prove to create a truly just society for our people.

— Cory Aquino

DURING the tumultuous session of the Batasang Pambansa on Saturday, February 15, 1986, President Marcos and Member of Parliament Arturo M. Tolentino were officially proclaimed by the Batasan as the duly reelected President and elected Vice President, respectively. Before the proclamation, however, all the opposition assemblymen had walked out of the session hall protesting the haste with which the majority members were rushing the proclamation and the "cavalier treatment" with which the ruling KBL party treated the opposition motion to defer the proclamation. But the proclamation had been consummated; it had become a *fait accompli*, and the next logical step Marcos had to make was to take his oath of office which had to be done within ten days from his proclamation. As scheduled, therefore, the oath-taking of President Marcos and Vice President-elect Tolentino was set at high noon of February 25 in Malacañang to which, for the first time in the Republic's history, no member of the diplomatic corps had been invited.

Malacañang justified the non-presence of foreign diplomats as having a precedent in France where, it was said, the President of France takes his oath of office in the Elysee Palace without the presence of foreign dignitaries or the diplomatic corps.[1]

On Saturday, February 22, during his second and final talk with U.S. Ambassador Philip Habib, Marcos issued a statement warning the opposition that he would take more forceful measures if they continued with their *welga ng bayan* or general strike the day following his oath-taking as they had announced. He stressed that while he would continue to be tolerant of mass protest actions, he would never allow any provisional government contemplated by Mrs. Cory Aquino and her advisers to be set up in the Philippines or elsewhere.

Marcos admitted that Habib's report to President Reagan would be crucial and asked him to "help us clear this matter and establish the truth." He presented Habib with a copy of the Batasang Pambansa's official canvass of the February 7 elections together with documents creating the Commission on Human Rights of the Philippines, the Council of State and the Constitutional Reform Commission. U.S. Ambassador to the Philippines Stephen Bosworth was among those present at the meeting.

While President Marcos and Habib were meeting, an event or tectonic force was beginning to explode.

That Saturday morning, February 22, Defense Minister Juan Ponce Enrile was having coffee with some newspapermen at the Atrium Coffeeshop in Makati, Metro Manila, when an aide asked him to answer the phone. The coffeeshop was astir with talks that he was resigning from the Cabinet of President Marcos that coming Monday as reported by two American newspapers — the *Philadelphia Inquirer* and the *San Jose Mercury News* — and the journalists were checking the story. Enrile got up to answer the phone: at the other end was Trade and Industry Minister Roberto V. Ongpin. He told Enrile that his security people had been rounded up by the military police. Some of the men, it immediately occurred to Minister Enrile, were identified with his ministry for he had assigned them to augment the security force of Ongpin. Upon verification he found that the men were rounded up because they were conducting night military exercises within a restricted military zone under the control of the Philippine Marines.

The defense chief went home that noon for lunch with his wife, Cristina, when two of his top security officers — Col. Gregorio "Gringo" Honasan and Col. Eduardo "Red" Kapunan — arrived. Both were leaders of the Reform the Armed Forces Movement (RAM or Reformists). They begged leave from Mrs. Enrile and led the Minister to a corner of the house to talk among themselves. Enrile was not in the habit of letting his wife know much about his work — or his problems. Mrs. Enrile herself has said that her husband always wanted her to stay in the background. "And perhaps because he wanted to shield me from the magnitude of his own personal problems in office," she observes, "my husband never really discussed details of government affairs at home."[2] In fact, throughout the ensuing February 22-25 event, Mrs. Enrile, her children and grandchildren separately "sought haven from one home to another, praying nonstop."

Honasan and Kapunan informed their chief that Maj. Gen. Fabian C. Ver, AFP Chief of Staff, had organized teams to round up RAM leaders, among other people. A massive crackdown by government soldiers seemed imminent for Enrile and his men learned that intelligence officers on the Malacañang side claimed to have uncovered a RAM-led plot to assassinate the President and take over the Palace that Saturday night, February 22, or, at the latest, on the eve of the inauguration of Marcos on Tuesday, February 25. They considered it a matter of tactical expediency and decided to beat Malacañang to the draw. "Sir," Honasan was saying, "if they issue arrest orders against me and the others, it may eventually implicate you; they might arrest you also."[3] Enrile knew he was in the same predicament as the Reformist officers as he listened to his men. He asked them what options were available under the circumstances. At first Honasan tried to talk his boss into flying to Cagayan province to hide while the Reformists were figuring their next steps. That was one of the options — dispersal. The other option was to regroup. They agreed that if they dispersed they could be hit one by one since Ver's men would hunt each of them. If, on the other hand, they regrouped, they could take their chances. Finally, Enrile said:

"Well, boys, if we regroup and take a stand, the possibility of encounter is very high. And if we will be assaulted, we will either all perish but some of us will naturally survive, and the other side will also suffer heavy casualties. Or the possibility of a stand-off is not far-fetched."[4]

Thus, it was Minister Enrile's decision to regroup rather than disperse. Accordingly, keenly aware of the urgency of the situation, he instructed his men after announcing his decision to assemble in his office at Camp Aguinaldo, Quezon City. He then dressed up, putting on a red-striped shirtjac, flesh-colored jacket and light pants, and stepped into a pair of rubber shoes. From his closet he took some firearms including his favorite Israeli-made Uzi. Wasting no time he instructed an aide to get Lt. Gen. Fidel V. Ramos on the phone, and when the Vice Chief of Staff, AFP, and Chief of the Philippine Constabulary—Integrated National Police, answered, the Defense Minister told him about the information he had received which he said he believed to be true. Then he asked Ramos if he would support and join them. "I will be with you all the way," the general replied; and Enrile said, "If that is the case, then join me at Camp Aguinaldo. I'm going there now."

Enrile believed the veracity of the information about an im-

pending crackdown because about six days before, after the Catholic
Bishops Conference of the Philippines issued a strongly worded
protest statement denouncing the "fraudulence" of the elections and
saying that a government that retained its power through frauds had
no moral authority to continue, he received confirmed information
that the senior generals of the Armed Forces were called to a meeting
in Malacañang: Gen. Ver, Gen. Ramos, Gen. Josephus Ramas of the
Philippine Army, Gen. Vicente Piccio of the Philippine Air Force,
Commodore Brillante Ochoco of the Philippine Navy, and Maj. Gen.
Prospero Olivas of the Metropolitan Command. Two decisions were
reached in that meeting, according to Enrile: (1) to discipline and
stop the RAM from making press statements and arrest their leaders,
and (2) prepare a contingency plan to arrest certain leaders of the
opposition both within and outside the Batasang Pambansa. Among
the names he remembers were those of Assemblymen Neptali
Gonzales, Ramon Mitra, Homobono Adaza, Luis Villafuerte and
Aquilino Pimentel.

Among those outside the Batasan were the so-called "50 advisers" of Cory Aquino, including Rene Saguisag, Jose Concepcion
Jr., Dante Santos, Vicente Paterno, Jaime Ongpin and Vicente
Jayme. Others were clergymen and people identified with the civilian
sector, and people from cause-oriented groups like BAYAN.

At Camp Aguinaldo, Enrile immediately went into a meeting
with Reformist leaders. The camp bristled with machinegun emplace-
ments and crawled with soldiers in battle fatigues armed with high-
powered firearms including M-16 Armalites and Uzis. Snipers were
posted on rooftops. At around 4 p.m. the officers and soldiers began
barricading the ministry.[5] Enrile himself put on a bullet-proof vest.
His rubber shoes and Uzi were conspicuous. To many, he cut a
striking, swashbuckling figure — a dashing rebel leader.

But up to that time Enrile did not seem a likely rebel. A
Harvard-trained lawyer, he joined his father's prosperous law firm as
a partner and taught law until 1966 when then newly elected President Marcos enlisted his services, along with Rafael M. Salas, in the
new government. He was a prominent lawyer with some of the
biggest business and industrial establishments in the Philippines as
clients. And for many of the Marcos years, especially during the
martial law period, he was known as the second most powerful man
in the country. In the 1980s, however, he realized that his hold over
his ministry and the military was slipping into the hands of Ver,
Marcos's Chief of Staff and right-hand man. He did not take kindly
to this development but bore it with patience.

To a degree Minister Enrile began to distance himself from the inner Marcos circle. Tough, brilliant and politically sophisticated, he said in 1984 that he might run for the Presidency in the event Marcos would retire from politics. It was virtually an open declaration of war against Mrs. Marcos whose presidential ambitions were well-known. Moreover he was known to be the only Cabinet member of the Marcos government ever to have the courage to exchange words with the President's wife, when the First Lady called him a "defeatist" after he painted a grim but realistic picture of a mushrooming Communist insurgency. Through the years he never lost touch with reality but had maintained his loyalty to Marcos.

Enrile emerged unscathed from the 1983 assassination of Ninoy Aquino, Marcos's bitterest political opponent, unlike Ver who was placed on trial, although eventually acquitted by the Sandiganbayan.

From Camp Aguinaldo where he had holed up Enrile phoned U.S. Ambassador Bosworth to inform him of the development so that he could inform his government about it. He did the same with Japanese Ambassador Kiyoshi Somiya. Both ambassadors indicated they would inform their respective governments accordingly. "The reason I did that," says Enrile, "was in order that the world would know what was happening in case we would be annihilated."[6] He also asked his wife to relay the information to other media people, and called another friend to contact and warn some of his acquaintances in the opposition and request them for political assistance.

The latter friend was evidently Assemblyman Rene Cayetano, former Deputy Minister of Trade and Industry and a law partner of Enrile. Cayetano says that on Monday, February 17, Enrile went to their law office and informed him that his life was in danger, that some people were out to assassinate him and some Reformists, and that a number of oppositionists were also going to be picked up. Enrile was definitely agitated. He requested Cayetano to tell the story if ever he would be killed. Then he wrote down the story upon Cayetano's request. He was tearful when he handed to Cayetano a sealed brown envelope on which was written this message:

"Rene, in case of my death through assassination, please open this in the presence of the media so that the world and everybody will know. Thank you so much. Please help my family for old times' sake."[7]

Moreover Enrile asked Cayetano to do the following in case he was arrested: call the foreign press; see the U.S. Ambassador; look for friends in the opposition who could help ("Warn them and ask

for help if I'm still alive and may be holed up somewhere"); call
Cardinal Sin; and take care of his family. Enrile also told his friend
that he was going to resign as Defense Minister. "I will ask the President verbally to let me go," he said. "I have served him for 20 years.
I must now serve my country."

On Friday night, February 21, Cayetano saw Enrile in his house
at Dasmariñas Village, Makati. He said the telephones kept ringing
with the press verifying reports that he was going to resign on
Monday. Enrile denied it. Then he told Cayetano that events were
happening very fast and he might be arrested very soon, based on
intelligence reports. He turned melancholy and embraced his friend.
"I don't know when I will see you again," Enrile said. "But perhaps,
if I survive this, it will be a better Philippines." He did not explain
what he meant. Asked what he was going to do Enrile told Cayetano
he might take up soldiery again.

Then that fateful Saturday, February 22, Cayetano saw Enrile
at the Atrium Coffeeshop at about 11:30 a.m. From there he proceeded to their law office. At 3:30 p.m. Enrile phoned him. "Rene,"
he said, "we will be arrested. I'm at Camp Aguinaldo. We're in grave
danger. Do everything and call me back. Also call your ma'am (Mrs.
Enrile). I've already talked to Eddie (Ramos)."

At 4 p.m. Cayetano and his family checked in at the Manila
Garden Hotel and from there called the foreign press as Enrile had
requested and asked them to go to Camp Aguinaldo because Defense
Minister Enrile's life was in danger. Then he tried to call all the rest
his friend had mentioned.

Considering the urgency of the situation Enrile and his men had
to move fast and decisively. After giving instructions to his wife and
friend, he ordered Honasan, his chief security officer, to establish
their defense. "And he did prepare a plan for defense in the area,"
according to Enrile. "I told them that we would not fire the first
shot even if we would be attacked because I wanted to maintain a
dialogue with whoever would be coming to challenge us." Meanwhile, starting with about 200 soldiers, the Enrile group grew to
about 400 men.

Next he called for Brig. Gen. Pedro Balbanero, commander of
the Military Police brigade at the rear of the camp, and appealed to
him to help or at least stay neutral and protect their rear. If this was
not possible, he said, Balbanero and his men could serve as a buffer
between the contending forces, if there were assaulting forces. The
general promised to help. Then Enrile and his men decided to wait
for the arrival of the journalists and "the people who would

challenge us."

GEN. Ramos arrived at about 6 p.m., accompanied by security men in civilian clothes. The bespectacled general wore a gray bush jacket and smoked a cigar. His adherence to physical fitness showed in his trim, tightly muscled form. Like Minister Enrile, Gen. Ramos was a most unlikely rebel.

A graduate of West Point Ramos was well known for his gentlemanly manners and strict professionalism. Like his father, Ambassador Narciso Ramos, he had a penchant for writing, a gift not common among soldiers. He had been a faithful officer through the many years of Marcos's rule. He was also reputed to be a Marcos blood relative. For the past two years he had been hinting that he would resign his commission but had never gone to doing it. He had long been a critic of what he called the "crony chain" of command in the military that evolved under Ver's leadership. And like Enrile he had quietly supported the Reformist Movement although he insisted he was not a party to their protest plans.

Gen. Ramos had been disillusioned with the way the President had been treating the Armed Forces which, he said, had ceased to be the real Armed Forces that was supposed to be the defender of the people. He deplored the development of an elite group within the military establishment and said so in concrete terms.[8]

Ramos said he informed Marcos about the feelings of the small people in the AFP and the PC-INP and his perceptions of the worsening situation in the country, but the President simply ignored them. Meanwhile he was deeply disappointed because the President kept using his name as "a cosmetic, a deodorant, to help prop up his regime." Furthermore, the general said, Marcos allowed the issuance of firearms to unauthorized persons who used them to terrorize people and perpetuate themselves in power.

Local and foreign journalists had rushed to Camp Aguinaldo after being tipped that something unusual was taking place. They gathered at the ceremonial hall of the ministry building which was filled with heavily armed soldiers positioned on all floors, including the rooftop. Enrile and Ramos proceeded to the hall for a press conference during which they would make a public announcement of their decision and of what had been happening. Up to that moment none of the reporters knew what was really happening. They all knew something was brewing but no one could definitely say what it was.

The Defense Minister and the Vice Chief of Staff took their

places at a table before a battery of microphones and against a background of military colors. Young, able-bodied soldiers provided them with security. The entire hall teemed with reporters, press photographers, TV cameramen and crews shoving, pushing one another as they positioned themselves for advantage, their electronic guns flashing intermittently. Then the conference began.

In a subsequent retrospective interview, Enrile said that at that moment they announced over the radio and informed the other media that they — he and Ramos — would never surrender, and that if the government would assault them, they and their men would go down together and die together. He added that they explained the reason why they could no longer support their former Commander-in-Chief, and that reason was in their honest belief Marcos was not the recipient of a mandate from the people in the February 7 elections.[9]

Reporters covering that event which shook the nation to its roots like a giant quake were more generous with their recollections, their memories aided by hastily scribbled notes and tape-recorders. They had been expecting to hear an important announcement but they were not prepared for the impact of the revelation made by Enrile and Ramos. For it meant that a military rebellion had erupted that very moment. They had seized Camp Aguinaldo, seat of the ministry, and transformed it into a fortress and command post, manned, and defended by their own rebelling forces known as the Reformists. The rebellion had begun under the leadership of the Defense Minister himself and the Vice Chief of Staff.

"As of now," Minister Enrile said, his voice steady and clear, "I cannot in conscience recognize the President as the Commander-in-Chief of the Armed Forces. I believe that the mandate of the people does not belong to the present regime, and I know for a fact that there had been some anomalies committed during the elections. I searched my conscience and I felt that I could not serve a government that is not expressive of the sovereign will."[10]

"Our loyalty is to the Constitution and to the Filipino people, to our country," he added, "and I'm calling on all decent elements in the Cabinet, decent elements in the government, decent Filipinos, and the decent soldiers and officers of the AFP who are trained to respect the Constitution and to protect the welfare of this nation and its people, to wake up and support the movement."[11]

Then he appealed to his colleagues in the Cabinet to heal the wounds of the people and to heed their will expressed in the last elections, and charged that in his region, Region II, the KBL cheated in the elections to the extent of 350,000 votes. This charge was however quickly denied by six governors and eight assemblymen from the region in a joint statement to the press published in the *Bulletin Today*, February 24, 1986. In their statement the officials said the elections were free, orderly and honest as shown by the fact that Marcos even lost in some provinces in the solid North, his own bailiwick. They claimed that the Minister was never involved in the campaign outside his own province of Cagayan, adding that Enrile himself voted in favor of the proclamation of Marcos and Tolentino.

It is clear from Minister Enrile's declaration that he had ceased to recognize Marcos as President and Commander-in-Chief of the Armed Forces because he believed he no longer had the mandate of the people. Enrile was convinced that the mandate of the people belonged to somebody else, not to Marcos who continued to be in power only because of anomalies committed during the elections. The Marcos government not being expressive of the genuine will of the people had no right to continue and must be replaced by another which carried the people's sovereign mandate.

Enrile and the Reformists had therefore taken the side of the people. The people's will had been wronged and violated during the elections. They were cheated of their real choice. That wrong must be righted in the interest of the Filipino people, not of one person. The people's will must be respected and their mandate must go to its real owner. This was the cause Enrile and the rest were fighting for, the *why* of the military rebellion.

For his part Gen. Ramos told the world, through the reporters, his reasons for joining Enrile in breaking away from the President and taking their drastic action. He declared that the Armed Forces had ceased to be the defender of public safety and enforcer of the law and had become an elite armed forces that no longer represented the rank and file and the officers corps of the military.[12] Then he issued an urgent invitation in these words:

"As Chief of Contabulary and the Integrated National Police as well as Vice Chief of Staff of the Armed Forces, I would like to direct the troops under my command and all other elements of the Armed Forces of the Philippines that are professionally minded, that are dedicated to the military service in the sense of being the protector of the people, the defender of public safety and the enforcers of the law in our country, to be with me and the Minister of National Defense in our effort to bring about a more normal situation where our people once more can live freely and pursue the aspirations they have in life."[13]

It was during the question-and-answer portion of the press conference that the matter of who had the people's mandate was clarified. When a reporter asked whom Enrile and Ramos were supporting, Minister Enrile answered unequivocally:

"We are committed to support Corazon Aquino. I think, deep in my heart, that she is the real President of the Philippines."

He reiterated with emphasis that Marcos "did not win this election" and was proclaimed by the Batasang Pambansa in a "hasty manner." He also repeated his earlier charge that there had been irregularities in the elections. In answer to another question he denied that they were planning a *coup d'etat* as Marcos had charged. He stressed that with the action they had taken, they were all prepared to defend themselves to death from any assault. They could be killed in their enterprise, said Enrile — so be it. But nobody could live forever, he pointed out; not even Mr. Marcos who himself might not live very long.[14]

While this unprecedented development was taking place, Mrs. Corazon Aquino whom Enrile, Ramos and the Reformists had all but officially installed as President, was out in Cebu City in the South trying to whip up support for her civil disobedience campaign. There she announced to the press that she was setting up a government to take over as soon as Marcos stepped down. From Cebu she called Enrile by phone and asked how he and the others were and what she could do for them. Enrile, who had never had any contact with Cory Aquino except that Saturday night, February 22, gallantly replied: "Madam, there's nothing much you can do for us right now except to pray."[15]

After the press conference several people started arriving: former military top brass led by former Chief of Staff Gen. Romeo Espino, Gen. Ramon Farolan who resigned as Commissioner of Customs and joined them, Gen. Manuel Flores, former superintendent of the Philippine Military Academy who was an influential Reformist leader among the retirees, and several others. Soon Col. Rolando Abadilla, chief of the military intelligence service group, arrived. He asked Enrile to call President Marcos who wanted to talk to him. Enrile demurred. "We have burned our bridges," he said, "we have already taken a stand." He knew his old boss very well: he had certain ways of dealing with any situation — always to his advantage. Abadilla left but returned later to relay the same message. Again Enrile refused to talk to the President and agreed to speak with Gen. Ver instead. Ver expressed surprise about the turn of events and said to the Minister he felt so.

"Well," said Enrile, "I was informed that you were trying to have us all arrested."

"That was not true, that is not true," Ver objected. "There were no such plans, there were no such orders."

Enrile was not convinced, considering his long experience of associating with Ver and the President. He did not want to take any chances. The die was cast — there was no turning back — and he just asked Ver not to initiate any attack on them that night so that they could talk about the problem the next morning. In return Ver asked him to promise that they would not attack Malacañang that night. Enrile assured the Chief of Staff that they would never attack the Palace since "we have no aggressive intention against the Palace."

The Defense Minister and the Chief of Staff ended their conversation on that note — neither side would attack or move their troops that night. In the meantime an increasing number of people kept arriving to visit the rebellion leaders — Enrile and Ramos. They were not alone.

AMONG the callers at Camp Aguinaldo that first night of the military revolt was Agapito "Butz" Aquino, brother-in-law of Mrs. Cory Aquino and a well-known oppositionist activist. As a top leader of the parliament of the streets he had led many a protest rally and demonstration ever since the death of his elder brother Ninoy. He had heard the news of the military rebellion led by Enrile and Ramos over the radio and wondered if it was wise for him to get enmeshed in a squabble involving two high Marcos officials, a virtual family affair. Without checking with Cory, who was in Cebu City, he decided to act and do something.

Within an hour he was standing in Enrile's office. He was struck by what he saw and remembered of the Defense Minister. "He was tense," Aquino said, "he was perspiring, he was wearing a bullet-proof vest. That's what convinced me that this thing was for real." Butz remembered Enrile telling him that he needed all the help he could get, and he blurted out, "All we have is people."

At around 9 p.m. Jaime Cardinal Sin, whom Mrs. Enrile had called by phone earlier, went on Radio Veritas and asked listeners to show their solidarity and support to the military rebels. After some time some nuns showed up at the camp but the streets generally remained almost empty; the initial response was slow. At around 10 p.m., Butz Aquino, still at Camp Aguinaldo, grabbed a phone after talking with Enrile and called on Aquino backers to gather at

Isetann, a large department store in Cubao, Quezon City, to respond to an emergency. Only six persons responded in the first five minutes but in another 15 minutes there were several dozens. "Within an hour we had several thousands," said Butz.[16]

The younger Aquino and his street brigade, now in great numbers, started marching toward Camp Aguinaldo at about midnight. They helped provide the vanguard of the people who supported the Enrile-Ramos military rebellion that was trying to topple the 20-year Marcos regime.

Enrile looks back with delight to that Saturday night, when tens of thousands of people took to the streets to protect military rebels from possible assaults of Malacañang-led forces. "And it was funny that we in the defense and military organization who should be protecting the people were being protected by them," said Enrile.[17]

Meanwhile, Gen. Ramos had returned to his own command post, Camp Crame, after the press conference, followed by some of the reporters. The media people noted that security at the camp was not strict; many of the soldiers were not even armed yet. In his office, the Vice Chief of Staff issued orders to his men in the field to stop obeying unlawful orders, meaning those coming from Malacañang or Gen. Ver. Outside, people kept arriving, filling the entire highway portion from Santolan road to Ortigas avenue. They all came: priests, nuns and seminarians; society matrons, young women, business and industrial figures; politicians, laborers, students and experienced street marchers; itinerant vendors, somnambulists and dreamers — people from all walks of life converging at the campsite for reasons of their own. Gen. Balbanero closed the gates at Camp Aguinaldo to restrict the entry of people for security purposes. Later he also organized food brigades to receive donations which were distributed to the soldiers and some of the participants in the vigil.

Before midnight the people milling around the two camps had grown to about 50,000 as estimated by the *Daily Express*. The whole area turned into a giant carnival site as people continuously chanted, sang and danced, and blew their car horns. Ramos, unable to sleep like the Enrile group at Camp Aguinaldo across the highway, decided to address the people gathered at the E. de los Santos avenue gate of Camp Crame amid chants of "Ramos! Ramos! Ramos!" After delivering his brief pep talk the amiable general returned to his headquarters. Along the way he joked one reporter, Dionisio Pelayo of the *Express*, "Hey, Nonnie, we're both jobless now!" He was in high spirits in spite of the tension.

At that moment, a battalion of PC soldiers were busy preparing the camp's defenses. Like Camp Aguinaldo, Camp Crame had been formally seized by the rebels. The two major camps of the Armed Forces were in the full control of the rebelling Minister Enrile and Gen. Ramos.

Everybody in both camps stayed sleepless through the whole night notwithstanding the assurances given by Gen. Ver to Enrile earlier that night that they would not attack. Everyone believed that President Marcos, the *batang matapang* or brave boy of Ilocos Norte, a much decorated war veteran, would take action to wipe out the rebels. Fear of this possibility kept even the most blase journalists awake.

In the vicinity of Malacañang Palace it was also quiet that night, without any unusual troop movements in or out of the Palace grounds. But soldiers and tanks were believed to be massed in the area as though lying in wait for something to occur. Groups of soldiers in full combat gear could be discerned through the dim lights, but outside everything seemed calm.

The three major approaches to the Palace gates were not heavily secured. As in ordinary days, only a few soldiers could be seen standing guard by the barbed-wire barricades on Mendiola, Gen. Solano and J.P. Laurel streets. As of 8 p.m. children were still biking just in front of the Palace gates while pedestrians walked leisurely down the streets. In front of nearby San Beda College about 50 students had pitched camp and were holding a vigil protesting the February 7 elections. One of the placards read: "We're not good neighbors of Malacañang." Another said: "Feb. election: fake victory for Marcos."

In the meantime radio stations sympathetic to the Enrile-Ramos uprising repeatedly called on the people to go to the camps, if possible with food and drinks, for those holding vigil in the deepening Saturday night.

"To everyone's relief, the night passed without a bloody confrontation," reports Isidro M. Roman of the *Bulletin Today*.[18] "The only event that heightened the tension was a report received by Balbanero that the defense ministry would be surrounded by tanks and marines the following day. Balbanero again appealed to Ver not to proceed with the plan in order to avoid bloodshed."

The night turned into day as the number of people assembling and converging at the rebel camps grew into hundreds of thousands. They understood that the military under Enrile and Ramos had taken their cause for them and now they — the people — were supporting their rebellion.

BELEAGUERED President Marcos called a televised press conference in Malacañang at 10:30 that night. A majority of the people who had not been listening to the radio or watching TV earlier were unaware of what was happening. When the President appeared on the TV screen he appealed for calm as he told the people that a *coup d'etat* on the Palace had failed that very night, a drastic action to be undertaken by military officers. He identified the leaders of the conspiracy as Minister Enrile and Gen. Ramos and announced that the two were holding out in the Ministry of Defense building in Camp Aguinaldo after their attack on Malacañang had been aborted. Part of their plan, said the President, was to isolate him and the First Lady. He then called on them to stop their "stupidity" and negotiate with him on what should be done with them and their men.

The President told the audience of Channel 4, the government TV station, that the coup was scheduled to be staged at 12:30 a.m. on Sunday, February 23, but was discovered that Saturday night by Gen. Ver and Ilocos Norte Governor Ferdinand Marcos Jr. It was unravelled with the apprehension of some officers of the Presidential Security Command who had confessed to the conspiracy, said the President. The President's TV presence was reminiscent of that night in September 1972 when he proclaimed martial law — strong, commanding — though this time he looked much older, with his face heavily made up. He emphasized that the situation was under control — there was no cause for the people to be alarmed. While he had not been able to talk to Enrile and Ramos he said they had agreed with Gen. Ver that there would be no troop movements that night.

Then in a dramatic gesture the President presented on television three uniformed officers whom he identified as Capt. Ricardo Morales of the Philippine Army, Col. Marcelo Malajacan, commanding officer of the 10th Infantry Battalion, and Maj. Saulito Aromin, also of the Philippine Army. Looking tense and agitated before the TV cameras, the officers read statements in which they admitted the existence of a plot to capture the President and their respective roles in its implementation. They identified Col. Gregorio Honasan, chief security officer of Enrile, as the leader of the plot.[19]

Subsequently, the officers revealed in their respective statements there was indeed a plot to attack Malacañang Palace and capture the President. This plan, according to Malajacan, was evolved by a group of young officers, mostly members of Class '71 of the Philippine Military Academy, "in our belief that this is the only option left to save the Republic from a bloody confrontation" or civil war. It was better that they themselves died in the endeavor rather than have the people die in the streets. "Our intention is only to capture the President and talk to him, force him to resign or send him to exile and invite some people whom we feel are credible to the Filipino nation to lead the country back to democracy," Malajacan said. Initially they were only after reforms in the AFP, he added, and though he was not an active member of the Reform Movement, he felt he was a part of it.[20]

Malajacan's revelation of a plot was confirmed in another statement by Maj. Aromin, who confessed his participation in "the plan to attack Malacañang Palace and its environs and capture President Marcos after midnight tonight (February 23)." More specifically he said that the leader of the plot was Col. Honasan. "My other co-conspirators," said Aromin, "are LTC Jack Malajacan, LTC Kapunan, Major Noe Wong, aide of MND and Captain Morales of the Presidential Security Command. My participation is to lead a group of soldiers loaded in three (3) trucks to proceed to Malacañang Palace in the guise of augmenting troops."

Aromin narrated in his statement that the planned taking over of Malacañang was hatched sometime in the second week of February when Col. Honasan asked him to report to him. He and Honasan, also known as "Gringo," were closer than brothers; both were very active in sky diving. On February 15 they discussed their planned entry into the Palace, with Maj. Aromin as one of the group leaders who would secure the Malacañang Palace grounds while the team of Col. Honasan would enter the Palace to look for the President. Other teams to be led by Col. Kapunan would take charge of the southern portion of the Pasig river while the team of Malajacan would reinforce the group and would link up with Kapunan's group. He then described the step-by-step operation as follows:

"H-30 — I will arrive in front of Malacañang to be received by Major Doromal in the guise of augmenting the security of the Palace. My men will man all the positions assigned to the sector of Major Doromal.

"H-Hour — A loud blast would be coming from the Malacañang Park which would start as trigger of the whole operation. My duty would be to secure Col. Honasan while they would be conducting their jobs inside the Palace.

"When the operation would have been finished, some members would be bringing in persons/military officers who would run an interim government.

"I know that we would have support from other groups, like:

"The Battalions of Col. Noble would reinforce from Mindanao via C130.

"The Battalion of Major Brillantes would take charge of any army reinforcements that would move to Malacanang.

"SAF under Major Raton would take charge of any air force personnel who would proceed to Malacanang.

"Helicopters would be with us but I don't know their particular role.

"Col. Paredes would prevent any marine reinforcements."[21]

Aromin denied he was a member of the Reform Movement but stressed that he joined Honasan's group because, as he puts it, "I am afraid of a Communist takeover. It might be too late if we don't act now. The enemy might capitalize on the present political situation and we might be another Vietnam." Accordingly they had several meetings with Honasan and his group to discuss what should be done.

Much later than the publication of the three officers' confessions (February 24, *Daily Express*), Capt. Ricardo Morales, one of the three, confirmed the existence of the plot.[22] He told the newspaper *Malaya* that on Friday a "freeze order" was passed around to RAM members, which meant they should not report to their respective units on Saturday, the 22nd. This was intended to reduce the chances of their being rounded up just as preparations for "The Operation" were in full swing, referring to the attack on Malacañang.

RAM officers knew that Gen. Ver was close on their heels and was ready to strike as evidenced by the noticeable troop buildup in Malacañang where several batallions engaged in counter-insurgency in the provinces had been recalled and assigned to the Palace. Numerous tanks and armored vehicles had also been redeployed around Malacañang. RAM intelligence reports indicated they might be rounded up after the presidential inauguration on Tuesday, February 25.

Morales said he was RAM's inside man in the Palace, having been a security officer of the First Lady for the past four years. He had not been reached by the freeze order because he had proceeded to Malacañang from his classes at the Asian Institute of Management where he was a scholar of Mrs. Marcos. Towards noon he was summoned by Col. Irwin Ver, eldest son of Gen. Ver and key officer of the PSC, for questioning. He denied any knowledge of a plan, as did the others who had also been summoned. They were not tortured but pressured to sign and read prepared statements. It was not necessary to torture them because the circumstances made it very clear that they would be shot if they did not follow orders.

Morales revealed that the RAM had planned to attack Malacañang and force President Marcos to resign six months before the February revolt. They had to do it because they wanted to beat Marcos and Ver to the draw; they were bent on a crackdown on the RAM and opposition leaders. By February they were ready for their blitz. Dynamite for blowing up walls, bolt-cutters for wire fences and locks, ropes for scaling fences, and handkerchiefs laced with chloroform were all prepared. The materiel were needed to neutralize soldiers in Malacañang with as little bloodshed as possible. If the attack succeeded they would convince Marcos to step down peacefully to avoid further bloodshed.

Morales said idealism and nobility impelled them to undertake such a risky endeavor. "Even if we failed and died, it would not have been a useless sacrifice," he said. "It would have been a noble and symbolic protest that would finally open the eyes of the dictator that his time to step down had come because even his own army was against him."

But he denied that there was a plan to liquidate the President and his family, as Marcos had claimed in his Saturday night TV conference. However, if the planned attack on the Palace had not been derailed, they would have put up a multi-sectoral council. He revealed that among the names considered for the council were those of Mrs. Cory Aquino, Prime Minister Cesar Virata, Gen. Ramos and Cardinal Sin. He was silent on Minister Enrile who, Marcos had charged earlier, would head the council. The council would govern the country until a new Constitution was drafted and elections would be held six months after the council had been put in place.

When the hour to strike neared, the RAM worked with clockwork precision. They were divided into several groups, each working in different areas. Only a select few knew of the overall plan. When Ver struck on Saturday by arresting a RAM officer assigned to Minister Ongpin, the Reformists drew up their defense posture in Camp Aguinaldo. The revolt began. If it was indeed their plan to stage their Palace blitz at 12:30 a.m. on Sunday, February 23, Ver's preemptive action had disrupted their own timetable and forced them to take defensive action hours ahead of their scheduled attack.

STILL continuing with his press conference on television, President

Marcos said he could not believe that Enrile and Ramos were really involved in the conspiracy. The first evidence collected by the military intelligence did not link them to the plot, said the President, but they gave themselves away with their action. Enrile and Ramos, according to Marcos, had thought they would be arrested, when no warrant of arrest had been issued for either of them. The Chief Executive claimed "sadness" for the conspirators, particularly the Defense Minister and the Vice Chief of Staff (he prefaced their titles with the word "former"). He could not understand how they could reach "this height of rebellion and treason," he stressed. Then, suing for peaceful negotiations, he said violence should be avoided for if there would be any fighting, it would be "a bloody mess" and mean the "liquidation" of all those people in Camp Aguinaldo. He also told the people that the commanders of all major commands remained loyal to him as their Commander-in-Chief and that he had ordered them not to ring the camp.[23]

The President presented on the TV screen the image of a strong but cool, fatherly and forgiving leader who was in complete control of the emergency. His appearance, speech and gestures must have soothed and reassured many of the TV viewers who had known about the rebellion for the first time.

He promised to find out who were backing the conspirators by way of answering a reporter's question, and would determine how guilty they were. The whole plot was planned by Filipinos but he did not rule out the possibility that Americans were involved in it, and it was something he would also find out. He categorically denied any connection between the conspiracy and the presence of the U.S. Seventh Fleet in Subic Naval Base and declared that as far as he knew no civilians were involved in the plot except for those belonging to the opposition who not only encouraged the plot but supported it financially.

ON Sunday, February 23, President Marcos and Minister Enrile talked by phone. Marcos offered the Minister, Gen. Ramos and their men amnesty. Enrile politely rejected the offer and instead reiterated the Reformist group's demand that the President resign. The President would like Enrile to explore the possibility of getting the RAM to accept that nobody would be punished for the coup or the assassination plot and he told him that what the group wanted — his resignation — was not negotiable.[24]

That Sunday could have been the turning point of the rebellion. Tension continued to rise to a high pitch. There seemed to be a slackening of the demonstrators' will and fervor while it appeared the government was about to launch a punitive offensive action to quell the uprising. It was impossible to predict the rebellion's outcome or even the direction it would take. In fact it was not clear what it was all about, what its aims were, and why and how it happened. People had converged at the Camp Aguinaldo-Camp Crame portion of EDSA (Epifanio de los Santos Avenue) for reasons only they could have known. What indeed makes one join an action whose nature and objectives he hardly knows? One can only surmise. It could be curiousity, excitement over the novelty of an event, a desire to take part in an experiment that could change one's life, to express a grievance against one's miserable and wretched condition, or simply an impulse to lose oneself in a crowd, or even simple *pakikisama.*

The more politically aware among them had their own peculiar motives, while others went as representatives of certain groups and organizations determined to lock arms with the rest to form human barricades designed to protect the camp — and the military inside — from expected attacks by government troopers. They had organized schedules and shifts.

It was the graveyard shift, from 10 o'clock that Sunday night to 6 o'clock Monday morning, of a group called the *Tagumpay ng Bayan* led by Feliciano Belmonte Jr., that went through a crisis during that period. The atmosphere was joyous, even carnival-like, and it was an occasion to meet friends and colleagues in a kind of unplanned reunion. The place had been closed to vehicular traffic since the day before and all vehicles were diverted from the main highway to side streets. Some people stayed at their designated areas but more kept walking about endlessly, greeting friends and acquaintances, smiling at strangers, getting introduced to new faces. Some gathered beside parked cars talking, taking snacks, ice cream, soft drinks and smoking cigarettes; some others had pitched pup tents along the wayside as though in a summer outing. Now and then a voice would make an announcement — of a high government official, a Supreme Court Justice, a general or two, a couple of regional military commanders resigning or withdrawing support from President Marcos and defecting to the rebel cause. The multitude would burst into resounding applause upon hearing such announcements, innumerable hands would quickly flash *Laban* signs, and the cool February night air would continue to be rent by impassioned speeches and protest songs beamed from powerful loudspeakers opened full-blast. Occasionally someone would lead the legions in prayer.

But a little past midnight an announcement agitated the crowd. A full battalion of Marines, deployed at Ugong Norte just a kilometer away south of Camp Aquinaldo, was reported about to move. Another announcement said tanks were poised to reinforce the Marines as they attacked. But no one panicked. Developments during the first day seemed to have put iron in their hearts. Nevertheless, tension remained critically high.

Before 2 a.m. the athletic Gen. Ramos came out of Camp Crame jogging. This gesture perked up the people's morale. But the number of those who remained had greatly diminished.

"I would say we were less than seven or eight thousand by then," recalls Diosdado P. Peralta, a *Tagumpay ng Bayan* leader and a former governor of the Integrated Bar of the Philippines, Greater Manila Region, "where earlier there were hundreds of thousands."

Obviously the people were yielding to exhaustion and sleep as a result of their long vigil.

About 3 a.m. radio announcer June Keithley, the lone remaining voice of the rebels using Radio Veritas, announced that she had transferred to a "bandit" station which she called *radyo bandido;* the Veritas transmitter and other equipment had been destroyed. She alternated, in her excited, high-pitched voice, with Enrile and Ramos in appealing for people's support. The rebel leaders continuously appealed to the military commanders, among whom were Generals Felix Brawner and Artemio Tadiar, to avoid bloodshed, not to soil their hands with the blood of their own countrymen and comrades-in-arms from the Philippine Military Academy, and to support the movement. Radio was at its finest hour then as the communication link between the rebel leaders and forces and the people. Apparently their appeals were heeded for no violent confrontation occurred. However both lanes of EDSA had become practically empty by about 3 a.m., save for a tiny group at the Crame main gate. Across the gate of Camp Aguinaldo some 30 Muslims formed an arc and stood guard. Soon it was announced that government troops had been deployed at Santolan road, near Horsehoe Village, just off Crame. The remaining people rushed toward that direction, but as they were turning from EDSA the man on the improvised tower shouted at the top of his voice asking some of them to return to the main gate because there was only a handful left to protect it.

"Yes," recalls Peralta, "we were that few." It meant that if the government forces had attacked there would be no more human barricades to repel them.

At about 4:30 a.m. the loudspeaker blared that a column of four trucks loaded with heavily armed soldiers was approaching. The few holdovers formed a thin barricade hoping to prevent the trucks from reaching the camp's main gate in case they came. It was a piti- ful but valiant gesture of resolute courage. As the Marine battalion started to march towards the Libis side of Camp Aguinaldo, it was announced that a pincer movement of troops would envelop Crame. Keithley told Ramos that some ROTC volunteers were asking to be armed to help defend the camp. The general acknowledged but rejected the offer; the fighting, if any, should be left to professional soldiers. Then news broke out that another contingent was moving towards the White Plains-Camp Aguinaldo entrance. Volunteers were asked to help stop them, and a couple of vehicles were dispatched to the area where they set up a barricade. There was no fighting, but by about 5:30 a.m. a youth came running and shouting that the hastily formed barricade in Libis had fallen and that they had been tear-gassed by the military. There was no other occurrence of vio- lence.

At the Camp Crame main gate the few who had remained ex- changed morning greetings, glad that no fighting broke out through the long night. Then they resumed to lock arms to form the usual barricades. The Muslims in front of the Camp Aquinaldo gate broke ranks to join the barricade at Crame, a quiet, splendid testimonial of unity with their Christian brothers. Suddenly six helicopter gunships appeared from the direction of the University of Life in Pasig and began to dive towards the camp. The group, understand- ably scared, dispersed, some flashing the *Laban* sign. The helicopters stopped their descent and passed overhead, climbing as they circled, then vanished. Then after a short while the aircraft returned, striking terror in the hearts of the crowd, their spotlights trained on the ground as they descended. Some, if not all, of them might have thought it would be the end.

But one by one the helicopters landed inside the camp. People peering over the walls began to shout in jubilation as the arrivals and the rebels embraced one another and exchanged salutes rather than gunfire. It turned out that the Sikorsky helicopters belonged to the Philippine Air Force 15th Fighter Wing commanded by Col. Antonio Sotelo who led his men in flying from Sangley Point in Cavite province to support the rebellion.

At the time this unusual development took place, Peralta remembers, there were not more than 300 people remaining at EDSA lending support to approximately 150 soldiers inside Camp Crame. He considers the event the turning point in the uprising, and judging from what followed, his conclusion is reasonably based.

That same day the combined power of the people supporting the military rebellion had its shining moment and made history in an episode colorfully described by a news agency in these words: "Two huge armored troop transport vehicles, machine guns in the firing position, were marooned in a sea of people a mile or so from the military camps where rebels were holding out against President Marcos. Soldiers garbed in camouflage without saying a word gazed from the turrets at the thousands of people who had encircled them."[25]

Both Enrile and Ramos were heartened by the people's support and felt they had no need for an amnesty. As Ramos said with emphasis, "We have no intention of surrendering inasmuch as it is the people's power protecting us. This certainly is a more powerful weapons system at our disposal. These people are unarmed. However, the power that they hold to support us is much more powerful than the hardware at (Marcos's) command."[26]

Marcos, on the other hand, declared that he would not resign from the Presidency on the "say-so" of his critics in the country and abroad. He was still hoping to solve his problems with the military as soon as possible. He would not resign because it was his duty to continue running the government. "I consider myself as having been legally proclaimed," he said, "and having been proclaimed, I feel it my duty to run the government as effectively as I can."[27]

Meanwhile, Ramos who was in charge of psychological warfare during the rebellion reported that seven regional commanders of the AFP and majority of the PC commanders and of the Integrated National Police had thrown their support behind him and Enrile. But as he was making his status report thousands of troops loyal to Marcos had been pulled out of the countryside and brought to Manila. From all indications a bloody confrontation between the two contending forces seemed inevitable.

For his part, Gen. Ver found it necessary to address the people in order to counter the rebel propaganda. He issued a statement which said there was indeed a plot to attack Malacañang and assassinate the President but it "was aborted tonight by alert security elements who arrested five AFP officers." Believing that he, too, would be arrested, Minister Enrile barricaded himself together with Gen. Ramos at the ministry of defense office in Camp Aguinaldo backed by ministry security forces and two helicopter gunships.

They then called a press conference, Ver said, and announced that they had joined the opposition. They had therefore lost their authority over any member of the military and the police, he added, then directed the major service and field commanders to stay in their respective posts and maintain their vigilance, assuring the people that the Armed Forces was supporting the government of President Marcos.[28]

At about noon of that Sunday Enrile and his men decided to leave Camp Aguinaldo to join Gen. Ramos in Camp Crame in order to consolidate their forces. Besides, it was risky for Enrile to continue staying in Camp Aguinaldo because it was vulnerable to a tank assault. As Enrile and his men crossed E. de los Santos avenue separating the two camps, he was reported to have said, "The die is cast." For his part, Gen. Ramos, elated by the cheering of the multitudes massed around the camp, announced from the top of a military truck, "This is a revolution of the people." Then perhaps impelled by a sense of history, the two rebel leaders said, "If they succeed in killing us, let our blood be part of this land."

The tension in Camp Crame eased somewhat when Enrile arrived accompanied by Col. Honasan and the other RAM leaders —his men bolstered the Ramos forces. But some reporters saw his transfer as the death of any possibility of reconciliation between the rebel forces and those of Gen. Ver and Malacañang. Tension rose again with reports of approaching armored vehicles and troops and the state of readiness of Marcos loyalist troops at the University of Life compound in nearby Pasig to use their heavy artillery to retake the camps from the rebels. The two leaders went up to the viewing deck to check the reports, then signalled to the crowds gathered at the flagpole not to panic.

Fortunately the attacks did not take place.

Some people attributed the prevention of the expected assault to the presence of thousands of people at the camp. Indeed it was very possible that the troopers did not want bloodshed for an assault would not only liquidate the rebels but massacre a great number of innocent civilians. The troop commanders could moreover be heeding the call of their Commander-in-Chief not to fire the first shot, to be patient and not to start hostilities. Whatever the reason was, the fact remains that at that moment of truth the military demonstrated their humanity and their refusal to stain their hands with the blood of their innocent brothers.

Roman of the *Bulletin Today* said he was able to piece together later information central to the development. He said that the night before, Gen. Ver, Gen. Piccio, Col. Irwin Ver and Navy Capt. Eriberto C. Varona met with Rufino Cardinal Vidal and Msgr. Bruno Torpigliani, papal nuncio to the Philippines, at Villamor Air Base. In that meeting the Cardinal and Torpigliani handed Ver a copy of a message from Pope John Paul II appealing to avoid bloodshed in behalf of innocent civilians supporting Enrile and Ramos in Camp Crame. The papal message was actually in the form of a cable addressed to the local Catholic Church, which says:

"We pray that the Lord will inspire everyone in the Philippines to peaceful and just solution, without violence or bloodshed and having concern only for the supreme good of the nation."[29]

It is interesting to note at this point that before that dramatic freezing of the tanks by the people, Enrile made two calls. The first was to U.S. Ambassador Bosworth. He told the American envoy that there was a tank column and two Marine battalions approaching their direction, and if they attacked, several would be killed, including hundreds of media people, among them a number of Americans. His purpose was to make Bosworth inform the Palace about the condition of the target the government intended to attack. He also hoped the envoy would ask the White House to caution Marcos to take a more prudent course. Next he called Gen. Ver and told him that if they attacked they would kill not only several civilians but also former military officers who had served him and the President, together with many foreign correspondents. He said, "If you are going to kill us, you will not only be the one to be condemned by history. You and the President will both go down in history as butchers of your own officers and men, of Filipinos and foreign mediamen." Then he asked the general to restrain the tank commanders and Ver agreed to stop the operation.[30]

CORY Aquino, who was in Cebu City that Sunday, jubilantly asked the nation to give full support to Enrile and Ramos as she reiterated her appeal for President Marcos to step down from office so that a peaceful transition of power could be effected. Before flying back to Manila (she cancelled another appearance in Davao City) she called on other government officials to dissociate themselves from Marcos and follow the examples of Enrile and Ramos. She called the rebellion a "turning point" in the peaceful struggle to unseat Marcos.

She expressed wonder at the new developments. She learned about the revolt on the day it erupted, February 22, after holding a mammoth rally in Cebu City. She immediately went into a huddle with her advisers and issued a statement that Saturday night calling on Marcos to resign in order to avoid bloodshed, resignation being the non-negotiable demand of the rebels. She had always favored a peaceful transition and hoped the problem would be resolved without violence. Asked if she would work with Minister Enrile in the future, she replied. "I can work with anybody, except Mr. Marcos."[31]

That same night, according to Enrile, some opposition leaders visited the camp, including Assemblymen Homobono Adaza and Luis Villafuerte. Enrile suggested to them that it was perhaps already necessary for them to form a civilian government headed by Mrs. Aquino and Doy Laurel. He did it even before President Marcos mentioned it on TV, he said. "I asked those people to form a civilian government in order to show to the people that we must earnestly try to restore a democratic government in the land," said the Defense Minister, "and also to relieve us of doing some political work while attending to the military component of the effort. We wanted a political group to harness the political effort so that we will be free in dealing with the military."[32]

In saying this, Minister Enrile confirmed what the three captured RAM leaders declared in their statements.

MONDAY, February 24, was the third day of the Enrile-Ramos revolt, a "revolution of the people," according to Ramos. Neither side would budge an inch. The issue dividing them was simple but crucial: the resignation of President Marcos as demanded by the rebels.

In a bold and unprecedented act that day, ranking opposition leaders, joined by some KBL men, proclaimed Mrs. Corazon Aquino and former Senator Salvador Laurel as the newly elected President and Vice President, respectively. The proclamation was held during a gathering at the Club Filipino in San Juan, Metro Manila. Except a few, all were Batasan members and they signed a document proclaiming the annulment of the Batasan proclamation of Marcos and Tolentino on February 15. They then agreed to have Aquino and Laurel take their oath of office at 8 a.m. in the same place the following day, Tuesday, February 25, before Supreme Court Senior Justice Claudio Teehankee. President Marcos had earlier announced he would be inaugurated as the reelected President in the February 7 elections on the same day, Tuesday, in Malacañang. [33]

Rene Saguisag, Mrs. Aquino's spokesman, said that the latest statement from Washington called on President Marcos to step down.

The statement added that any attempt to prolong his 20-year administration was futile. Saguisag interpreted this to mean that the U.S. government had extended "functional recognition" to the government of Cory Aquino. He emphasized that the new government "is now in place by sheer mandate of the people."[34]

The signatories said they were convinced that the sovereign will of the people had been violated and substituted by fraudulent election returns and spurious certificates of canvass, which became the basis of the proclamation of Marcos and Tolentino by the Batasan. They described the new government of Aquino as based on the people's mandate and said that as long as it had a mandate and was recognized by many nations, "a legitimate government exists." The existence of such a government could be tested if the people paid their taxes to it, the solons said. With this position firmed up in the minds of the opposition, they made the decision to install Cory Aquino and Laurel the following day unanimous.

The explanation about the existence of a new government was necessary to clear doubts in the public mind regarding its legitimacy, a question that would not lend itself easily to a quick and facile resolution.

The opposition assemblymen and thinkers were joined in their effort by some KBL assemblymen, namely: Jose Zubiri Jr. of Bukidnon, Antonio Carag and Alfonso Reyno of Cagayan, Renato Cayetano of Taguig-Pateros-Muntinglupa, Edno Joson of Nueva Ecija, Fernando Faberes of Batanes, and Camilo Cabili of Iligan City.

That morning, as if to reinforce the opposition's declaration that a new legitimate government was in existence, Enrile announced inside Camp Crame that a "provisional government" had been established with Mrs. Aquino as President and Laurel as Vice President. Before a huge crowd at about 10:20 a.m., he cried with exuberance, "This is people's power, and the Filipino people have spoken."[35]

Zealously being protected by the people, Enrile and Ramos were waiting that Monday for the arrival of Mrs. Aquino. The advance teams that included Assemblyman Adaza and Teopisto Guingona had entered the camp as early as 5:20 a.m. The rebel leaders were as anxious as their men and backers to see Mrs. Aquino and Laurel, especially the former. Inside the Camp while waiting, they said the new government of Mrs. Aquino would be "of, for and by the people," a democratic government, in short, in which civilian authority would be respected. They took that occasion to thank those in the military and the civilian population who supported them in their "darkest hours" before leaving their command post temporarily to join their innumerable supporters gathered in front of the Camp Crame building.

Ramos announced that the rebel forces that day took over the government-owned Maharlika Broadcasting System on Bohol avenue in Quezon City. The takeover came after clashes and sporadic gunbattle between the government and the rebel forces at about 8:45 a.m. At least four persons were injured. A civilian TV technician named Fred Arias, 55, was reported to have died inside MBS-4 after a heart attack during the raid. Amado Lozada, a Marcos trooper, also died when his gun allegedly fired while he and fellow loyalists were regrouping near Panay avenue. One loyalist soldier was hit in the head. The attack came while Channel 4 was airing a press conference of President Marcos in Malacañang. He went off the air all of a sudden while in midsentence.[36]

The radio broadcasts, stopped during the gunbattle, were resumed an hour after the clashes, while telecasts over Channel 4 began at about 1:30 p.m. — with opposition and rebel groups in control of both radio and TV facilities.

The MBS was the major propaganda center of the Marcos government, housing MBS-4, Office of Media Affairs, Philippine News Agency, Bureau of Broadcasts, Bureau of National and Foreign Information, and radio station DWIM.

At the same time another Army group of 30 men swooped down on another TV station, Channel 7, located just a few blocks from MBS-4. Owned by Republic Broadcasting System, the compound housed Channel 7, radio station DWLS-FM and several other radio stations. The government forces decided to seize and secure it to prevent the rebels from using it for their purposes, for the channel had been abandoned earlier by the employees. Later the government troopers were driven away by the rebel forces.

Enrile and Ramos also announced, to the great delight of the camp crowd, that the new Armed Forces of the Philippines which they headed had almost completely taken over the entire AFP after sizeable portions of the Army, Navy and Air Force defected to their side and renounced their loyalty to President Marcos and Gen. Ver.

That same day a military helicopter made a dive toward Malacañang Palace and fired a grenade launcher at a target in the compound. A tank on the Palace grounds fired back. A few minutes after quiet had returned, an ambulance was called into the Palace grounds. Several explosions and bursts of M-16 rifle shots were heard. One soldier on the grounds said he had been hit by shrapnel and showed minor wounds to an *Associated Press* reporter. After the strafing Col. Vicente Tigas told foreign reporters to leave the ground, saying he could not guarantee their safety. Tigas, an officer of the Presidential Security Command, was one of the accused in the Aquino assassination case.[37]

Meanwhile, helicopter-borne soldiers believed to be supporters of Enrile and Ramos strafed Villamor Air Base at 12:30 p.m., destroying five helicopters parked at the base tarmac. The strafing occurred while most soldiers at the base were taking lunch. The attackers were on board three Sikorsky helicopters.

Earlier that morning five Sikorsky helicopters of the Philippine Air Force 15th Fighter Wing under Col. Antonio Sotelo flew from Sangley Point in Cavite province and landed at Camp Crame. But instead of attacking the camp, as many had feared, the Sotelo group alighted from their aircraft and reported to Minister Enrile and Gen. Ramos in a dramatic switch of allegiance and support.

Sources at the Villamor Air Base revealed that the helicopters that attacked the base were under the command of Maj. Charles Hotskiss, a member of the RAM group. Several PAF members were injured during that surprise raid.[38]

In the afternoon Cory Aquino arrived at Camp Crame where Enrile, Ramos, the RAM officers and a mammoth crowd had been waiting. She was met by a sea of humanity gripped by jubilation and hysteria. Cory addressed them briefly then issued the following statement:

> We have recovered our freedoms, our rights, and our dignity with much courage, and, we thank God, with little blood.
>
> I enjoin the people to keep the spirit of peace as we remove the last vestiges of tyranny, to be firm and compassionate. Let us not, now that we have won, descend to the level of the evil forces we have defeated.
>
> I have always said I can be magnanimous in victory, no more hate, nor more fighting.
>
> I appeal to all Filipinos of both sides of the struggle. This is now the time for peace, the time for healing.[39]

AT about 8 p.m. President Marcos reiterated in an interview on Channel 9 that he would not step down from the Presidency. Saying his family was "cowering in terror in Malacañang because of the threat of bombing by helicopter," he declared:

"We are here, we are not going abroad, no intention of resigning. We are here and we will defend the Republic to our last breath, to the last drop of our blood."[40]

As he was being interviewed live by a panel of four, Gen. Ramos was putting his forces in Camp Crame on alert after receiving reports that Marcos and Ver forces led by Gen. Felix Brawner were regrouping in nearby Camp Aguinaldo and Fort Bonifacio for a "last do-or-die attack." Brawner headed the First Scout Ranger Regiment. In addition there were reports that men from the Second Infantry Division, led by Brig. Gen. Roland Pattugalan, were poised to attack Camp Crame.

Using radio and television, Enrile and Ramos appealed to the two generals not to do anything so inhuman as unleashing their troops at massed, defenseless people in Camp Crame. Ramos likewise pleaded to Marcos troopers not to obey illegal orders from the President and Ver who "are leading people to death and destruction while they remain safe in their haven in Malacanang." The newly liberated Channel 4 was serving the rebels a useful purpose.

About two hours before he appeared on TV, President Marcos was asked by President Reagan to step down. White House spokesman Larry Speakes said that a solution to the Philippine crisis could only be found by a peaceful transition to a new government, according to the *Agence France Presse*, reporting from Washington. Marcos vehemently rejected the suggestion.

At about the time that this news from the White House reached the Philippines, Channel 4 disclosed that two U.S. aircraft were "on standby at Clark Air Base, ready to fly Marcos out of the country" to a possible asylum in the United States. The two planes were of the U.S-Al type, a modification of the Boeing 747 capable of flying nonstop to the U.S. mainland.[41]

Rejecting all suggestions of stepping down, Marcos declared a nationwide state of emergency and imposed a 12-hour curfew from 6 p.m. to 6 a.m. effective Sunday night. He insisted he was in effective control of the government and that he would react with all the powers at his disposal, but again left the door open for negotiation with Enrile and Ramos "to prevent any more bloodshed which they have started." He also said his Tuesday inauguration would go on as scheduled, though no foreign dignitary had been invited. Likewise, he declared that the special session of the Batasang Pambansa contemplated to proclaim Mrs. Aquino President was unconstitutional for only he, as President, could call a special session of the Batasan.

During the press conference Gen. Ver requested the President's permission to attack Camp Crame where Enrile and Ramos were holding fort. The President restrained Ver but instructed all military commanders to defend their military installations and personnel with small firearms. He was emphatic in his directive against the use of any heavy weapons, like tanks, mortars, recoiless rifles and others. However, he authorized the use of anti-aircraft weapons against some helicopters captured by some rebel military men.

It was obvious that the people close to the President and who used to cling to him like barnacles had abandoned him. Not one of his senior assistants or even cronies was present at the press conference — at least not one was seen on the screen, unlike in the recent past. With him were only his own family: the First Lady, Mrs. Marcos, their children Imee, Bongbong and Irene, son-in-law Greggy Araneta, their grandchildren, and ward Aimee.

That third day of the revolt was characterized by sporadic strife and incidents of limited violence. It was to be the penultimate day of the rebellion.

TUESDAY, February 25, will go down in the history of the Philippines for its two-fold significance. First, it was the fourth and last day of the military revolt led by Defense Minister Juan Ponce Enrile and Vice Chief of Staff Fidel V. Ramos which succeeded in forcing President Ferdinand E. Marcos, the nation's brilliant strongman, to step down from the Presidency after ruling for 20 uninterrupted years. That revolt, waged by a mere 300-400 officers and men belonging to the Reform the Armed Forces Movement (RAM) began on February 22 when Enrile and some RAM officers took command of the ministry of defense building in Camp Aguinaldo, Quezon City and declared with Gen. Ramos that they had withdrawn their loyalty and support from President Marcos who was not the real winner in the February 7 presidential elections. Both claimed they were convinced that Mrs. Corazon C. Aquino, widow of former Senator Benigno S. Aquino Jr., had the right to assume the Presidency in accordance with the will of the people expressed in the elections. The revolt, unique in its conception and execution in the political history of the Philippines, was waged to force Marcos out of power and transfer that power to the real owner of the people's mandate or will. Because the revolt succeeded, it may now be rightfully called a revolution, the Revolution of 1986.

Second, February 25 was the day of two presidential inaugurals: those of President Marcos at high noon in Malacañang Palace amd Mrs. Aquino at the Club Filipino. The President was proclaimed by the Batasang Pambansa, Mrs. Aquino by opposition members of the same body. The day also marks another historic milestone, the first time a woman became the nation's President. Moreover, it marks the first time a President of the country was forced to flee to another country with his family to escape the wrath of a triumphant rebellion.

On that last day of the four-day rebellion, President Marcos finally began to capitulate. Events were happening at breakneck speed; almost 80 percent of the entire Armed Forces had been won by the revolutionaries and the whole country was reverberating with the ineffable sound of victory. In Metro Manila and many parts of the land radio and TV stations saturated the airlanes with electrifying propaganda announcing continuous military defections to the Enrile-Ramos side, high officials resigning their powerful government offices and casting their lot with the anti-Marcos elements, Marcos friends and allies escaping from the growing upheaval and struggling with one another for the purchase of airline tickets (many airlines had been booked in advance), and millions of Filipinos across the land joining with the victorious revolutionaries in celebrating the imminent fall of President Marcos and the triumph of their daring enterprise. The capture of radio and TV networks and stations owned by the government or by friends of the President had helped hasten the victory of the military uprising.

AT about 9 or 10 a.m. that Tuesday, President Marcos phoned Enrile from Malacañang. The Defense Minister was at the moment preparing to leave to attend the inauguration of Cory Aquino at the Club Filipino in an enclave of the rich and powerful called Greenhills, in Metro Manila, just a few street blocks from Camp Crame. He was understandably elated over the progress of the revolution and confident of its outcome. Enrile recalls that the following exchange, more or less, took place between him and the President:

> PRESIDENT: How can we settle this problem?
> ENRILE: I really do not know, Mr. President.
> PRESIDENT: Why don't we organize a provisional government? I just want a graceful exit. I will cancel the election, I will organize a provisional government, and I shall remain as an honorary President until 1987 because I would like to leave politics in a clean and orderly manner.
> ENRILE: Mr. President, I do not know about that, but we are not really interested in power. Our mission was not to establish a military junta, or a military government. (He

asked me to talk to Mrs. Aquino). And besides, Mr. President, it's too late because we've already committed ourselves to Mrs. Aquino to support her. Our only mission here is to see to it that the will of the people is respected, whoever the winner is, whether it's you or Mrs. Aquino. But the men perceive that the one who won the mantle is Mrs. Aquino.

PRESIDENT: (Asked if it would be safe for him to leave the Philippines).

ENRILE: Why not, Mr. President?   This is your homeland, there is no reason for anyone of us, at least on our side, to harm you. If you want, we would be willing to protect you —you and your family.

PRESIDENT: If I go abroad, do you think I can come back here and feel safe about it?

ENRILE: Of course, this is your homeland, Mr. President — why not?

PRESIDENT: How about General Ver?

ENRILE: Mr. President, that is something I cannot answer.

It was evident at that point that President Marcos would rather leave the Presidency than continue resisting. All he wanted was a graceful exit, not to leave his seat of power in shame and infamy. Like many great leaders he wanted history to be fair and generous to him, to treat him justly, and he was looking for a basis for a just verdict. He had suggested cancelling the elections and forming a provisional government with him as a mere honorary President up to 1987, the year his unspent term would end had he not called the February 7 "snap" elections. But he gave it up after Enrile rejected it and insisted that the mantle of power be given to the one who really won it which he and the other revolutionaries believed was Mrs. Cory Aquino. Marcos quickly switched to another option: leave the country and come back later — safely and peacefully. Enrile went along with that option, saying he could see nothing wrong with it, the Philippines being the homeland of the President.

That same afternoon, between 5 and 6 p.m., President Marcos once more called Minister Enrile who had just come from a press conference. Enrile had transferred back to Camp Aguinaldo from Camp Crame. Among other things he had received so far that day was a report that presidential pilots had deserted the President. Enrile recalls the following conversation he had with the President:

PRESIDENT. Will you kindly tell your security to the vicinity of the Palace to stop these people who are firing at the

Palace towards our direction?

ENRILE: Mr. President, we have no people there, we have no men there, but anyway I will ask Gen. Ramos to send a contingent to look at the situation and enlist the help of the police.

PRESIDENT: Will you please contact Ambassador Bosworth and ask him if he could make Gen. Teddy Allen and his group available to be my security escort. Teddy Allen, because I want to leave the Palace.

ENRILE: Surely, Mr. President.

(Afterwards Enrile called Ambassador Bosworth and relayed the President's message. After a while the Ambassador called him back and said, "Please ask Gen. Ramos to get in touch with me so that we can explain to him the details of the evacuation of the President from the Palace.")[42]

The capitulation or surrender of President Marcos to his former Defense Minister who had become the leader of the revolution was now complete. The final consummation of the fall of the nation's longest-serving and most controversial leader would be his actual physical departure from Malacañang Palace the night of that same Tuesday, February 25.

Marcos was leaving the Presidency in a storm of yet another controversy that will take a long time to resolve. The wily old fox, as consummate a tactician and strategist as any of the best and brightest politicians the Philippines has produced, had taken his oath of office that noon at the ceremonial hall of Malacañang before an outpouring of support from thousands of people who had trekked to the Palace to see him installed for an unprecedented fourth term as President of the Republic. He was sworn in by Supreme Court Chief Justice Ramon Aquino in accordance with a tradition in the Presidency in the presence of a crowd that spilled into the Malacañang grounds and out onto nearby streets. Traditionally the President took his oath of office in the open, at the historic Luneta in Manila where Jose Rizal was executed by the Spaniards in 1896. Marcos took his oath in austere, no-frills ceremonies declaring his resolve to uphold a constitutional government.

"Today," he emphasized, "that faith is under challenge from certain quarters in our society, which believe that they can impose their will upon the nation, regardless of the illegitimacy of their claim to power."

He expressed deep resolve to do all for the welfare of the people and the country in the face of challenges "posed by forces who seek to destroy the nation's democratic processes."

Just hearing President Marcos speak that noon at his inaugural, the people would not know that earlier that morning he had begun to capitulate to Minister Enrile, and that while he was uttering fighting statements in his usual pugnacious style he was rushing the groundwork for his departure, as he informed Minister Enrile between 5 and 6 o'clock that afternoon.

Conspicuous in their absence from the inaugural rites were Vice President-elect Arturo M. Tolentino, Prime Minister Cesar E.A. Virata, and Ministers Roberto Ongpin of Trade and Industry and Geronimo Velasco of Energy. As the ceremony unfolded, minus the customary pomp and pageantry that characterized past Marcos inaugurals, tears welled up in the eyes of the First Lady, Imelda Romualdez Marcos, and Ministers Jose D. Aspiras of Tourism and Conrado Estrella of Agrarian Reform. The enthusiastic crowd, mostly Marcos loyalists, interrupted the President's brief speech with intermittent chants of his campaign slogan, *"Marcos, Marcos, Marcos pa rin!"* (We're still for Marcos!). The chanting which reverberated in the ceremonial hall 12 times was subsequently taken up by the throng below.

Before Ferdinand E. Marcos left the Palace and fled the country, he had taken formally his oath of office as elected President of the Philippines in the February 7 elections.

EARLIER that morning, at approximately 10:45 o'clock, Corazon Cojuangco Aquino, a most unlikely and reluctant candidate just three months ago, took her oath of office as President of the Republic before Senior Justice Claudio Teehankee of the Supreme Court at the Club Filipino. To associate the venue with history the organizers said they chose it because it was closely linked with the Filipinos' struggle for nationhood. Stalwarts of the Propaganda Movement under the leadership of Rizal and Marcelo H. del Pilar were said to have gathered and met in its original site. The Defense Minister had suggested Camp Crame for purposes of security and history but the choice of the organizers prevailed.

Minister Enrile and Gen. Ramos arrived shortly before 10 a.m. aboard separate helicopters. Enrile wore a red striped shirt with short sleeves over dark pants. The hall shook with endless applause in appreciation of the heroic roles Enrile and Ramos had played — and still were playing — in the revolution. A few minutes later, at about 10:10 o'clock, Cory Aquino arrived, radiant and glowing in a yellow dress with embroidered sleeves, smiling and waving at the crowd as she acknowledged their warm greetings. She looked simple but elegant, feminine but strong — presidential. Then after Vice President Salvador Laurel had been sworn in by Supreme Court Justice Vicente Abad Santos, Cory Aquino took her oath, solemnly swearing that "I will faithfully and conscientiously fulfill my duties as the President of the Philippines. . . . so help me God." As she intoned her oath with her right hand raised before Senior Justice Teehankee, her left hand rested on a red-covered Bible which was held in her hands by Mrs. Aurora Aquino, widowed mother of the slain Ninoy Aquino and her own mother-in-law, a simple act symbolic of their closeness and the continuity of their ties. Of such simplicity and subtlety is history written.

For his part Vice President Laurel cited the people's unflagging display of "courage, pugnacity, and determination to liberate themselves from a wicked regime." Then the man who gave up a chance to run for President and agreed to be the running mate of Cory Aquino said with characteristic flourish: "There is no people like the Filipino people." He pledged to work with President Aquino as he had never done before. "I pledge to serve the people," said the new Vice President, the first to be elected to that office after its abolition in 1972, "to serve them first, to serve them well and to serve them always." Throughout his political career, in his early 50s, he was a renowned orator and debater.

The Aquino-Laurel inauguration brought together political, business, civic, religious and professional leaders. Although it was scheduled to start at 8 a.m. it was not until 10:10, when Cory Aquino arrived in the white van she had been using since the beginning of the campaign, that it began. Unlike the Marcos inauguration that noon, Cory Aquino's installation as President was fully covered on radio and recorded on video tape and then viewed by millions nationwide when it was telecast on a delayed basis on Channel 4, then replayed several times afterwards. In the noontime Marcos ceremonies at the Malacañang ceremonial hall, TV viewers had only a five-minute glimpse of the proceedings because President Marcos and the First Lady had just walked into the hall, both smiling and waving to their well-wishers, when Channel 9 blinked out as a result of the seizure of its station facilities by the Reformist soldiers. It took several days before Channel 9 could go back on the air. The Malacañang rites were instead rebroadcast in four radio stations.

PRESIDENT Corazon C. Aquino removed her eyeglasses and began to read her inaugural address. (*Cf.* Chapter 1 and Appendix A for full text of address). She thanked the people for shattering the "dictatorship" and protecting "the honorable military" and described the new government as one dedicated to the "protection and meaningful fulfillment of the people's rights and liberties." Then she called for national reconciliation "which is what Ninoy came back home for" while emphasizing that "I am very magnanimous in victory."

She ended her brief speech by asking the public to sing the "Lord's prayer" with her, thus underlying her deeply religious character. In addition the first lady President of the Philippines led the crowd in singing the nationalistic song *Bayan Ko* (My Native Land) while everybody raised their "L" (for *Laban* or Fight) sign and ended with a touching mass singing of the national anthem, *Bayang Magiliw* (Adorable Land).

Assemblyman Orlando Mercado, Quezon City, was the master of ceremonies. Bishop Federico Escaler delivered the invocation.

After her address, President Aquino issued Proclamation No. 1 (see Appendix B) mandating her to reorganize the government and simultaneously appointed key Cabinet ministers and task forces to help her run the government.

Among the appointees that morning were Vice President Laurel as Prime Minister and Minister of Foreign Affairs, Minister of National Defense Juan Ponce Enrile as the new Minister of National Defense in her government, and Lt. Gen. Fidel V. Ramos, former Vice Chief of Staff of the AFP, as General and Chief of Staff of the New Armed Forces of the Philippines.

The following day, February 26, barely 19 hours after the departure of former President Ferdinand E. Marcos from Malacañang, Cory Aquino announced the following major appointments to her Cabinet:

Vice President Salvador H. Laurel, Minister of Foreign Affairs. Earlier designated as Prime Minister.

Juan Ponce Enrile, Minister of National Defense.

Neptali Gonzales, Minister of Justice.

Jaime Ongpin, Minister of Finance.

Aquilino Pimentel Jr., Minister of Local Governments.

Lourdes R. Quisumbing, Minister of Education, Culture and Sports.

Rogaciano Mercado, Minister of Public Works and Highways.

Ramon Mitra Jr., Minister of Agriculture.

Jovito R. Salonga, Chairman, Presidential Commission on Good

Government.

    Jose Concepcion Jr., Minister of Trade and Industry.

    Joker P. Arroyo, Executive Secretary.

    Rene Saguisag, Spokesman of the President.

    Luis F. Villafuerte, Chairman, Presidential Commission on Government Reorganization.

    Jose Antonio Gonzalez, Minister of Tourism.

    Ernesto Maceda, Minister of Natural Resources.

    Teodoro Locsin Jr., Minister of Public Information.

    Alberto Romulo, Minister of the Budget.

    Fidel V. Ramos, Chief of Staff of the new AFP, was not included in the announcement, being the head of the military organization.

    Jose B. Fernandez, Governor of the Central Bank.

With the first key appointments made, President Aquino had set up the machinery of her government.

FORMER President Marcos stepped out of Malacañang Palace, the seat of power from which he had presided over the life of the Philippines since 1966, at approximately 9:30 o'clock that Tuesday night, February 25. He was accompanied by what Filipinos had been used to call the "First Family" with the President as the "Sir" to whom everyone deferred: former First Lady Imelda, their children Imee, Bongbong and Irene, their grandchildren and a son-in-law, and their little ward, Aimee. With them was a considerably large group of assistants and help headed by former AFP Chief of Staff Fabian C. Ver. At the Palace grounds two U.S. Sikorsky helicopters were waiting for their passengers led by this 68-year-old ruler who in his rise to power had had to vanquish an army of reigning political and business giants and once installed in power had to liquidate the remaining forces of resistance to his supremacy and leadership.

    Now the aging autocrat was leaving the very nation of 54 million he had ruled for two decades, the longest Presidency in Philippine history. He was leaving every conceivable thing behind: the monuments to his achievements and of his wife's — long ribbons of concrete highways, towering public buildings, scores of giant bridges spanning bodies of water and connecting islands, an intensified land program for tenants and farmers, electrification of the once-unlit countryside, bodies of land reclaimed from the sea and transformed into modern mini-cities, magnificent gleaming buildings of stone and steel which were built as havens of art and culture and sanctuaries of the human spirit. He was saying goodbye to all this

— and more. Yet he was also bidding farewell to a myriad other things — problems: a bankrupt economy, unabated Communist insurgency, unemployment and rising criminality, unending notoriety and graft and corruption in all levels of government, rapidly declining morality nationwide. He was leaving all this, too.

The President of the Philippines for the past twenty years must have taken a last lingering look at the Palace, its surroundings, its majesty and sedate splendor, for after all their separation would in most likelihood be final. He could only have experienced a heaviness of the heart for it must have dawned upon him at last that the days of power and glory were over.

The American crew and pilots of the American helicopters now led the former strongman and his party into the waiting wombs of the great aircraft. Could they have recognized him as he boarded one of the machines? Did he go up the helicopter alone, unaided, walking upright or flat on his back on a stretcher? He had not been feeling well during the past few days of continuous tension; once or twice he was said to be addressing the people on TV but his image could not be seen on the screen, only his voice could be heard. Once, a TV caller asked on the phone if it was the voice of the former that he could hear on the interview program and not that of a well-known voice mimic, Willie Nepomuceno. Marcos, evidently unable to make an appearance, denied the caller's suggestion and tried to prove it was his own voice by answering specific questions — including what day, time and date it was at the moment — asked by an interviewer, reporter Ruther Batuigas.

When all members of the party had boarded the helicopters, the aircraft flew them immediately to the vast American military reservation in Pampanga, Central Luzon — Clark Air Base.[43] This base, together with the giant American naval base in Subic, Zambales, was one of the principal reasons why the U.S. government pressured Marcos to call an election before his term expired in 1987. The U.S. was afraid that the Communists in the Philippines would soon grow strong enough to overrun them.

The flight of Marcos from Malacañang was first confirmed by the U.S. Air Force television station FEN shortly after 10 p.m. The people outside Malacañang Palace had no way of confirming it because the operation was kept in secrecy. The international news agencies followed immediately with their own bulletins. At 10:20 p.m. *The Manila Times* received further confirmation from people whom the former President had left behind in Malacañang, soldiers among them. Then before midnight U.S. Secretary of State George

Schultz gave his confirmation. He was reported by the Voice of America as saying that the U.S. government was recognizing the government of Mrs. Corazon Aquino, and that Marcos and his family had flown off from Clark Air Base to an unannounced destination.[44] As it turned out he was flown to Guam, in the Marianas islands, thence to Hawaii where he was given temporary asylum.

An hour after Washington confirmed that former President Marcos and his family and party had left the country (giving truth to Cory Aquino's statement in Tarlac that she was expecting Marcos to do a Duvalier soon), thousands of people surged like a mighty tide into the Palace and began to ransack and pillage it. Shouting the new President's nickname, the jubilant masses smashed their way into the white-walled, historic building, official residence of all Philippine Presidents beginning with the great and justly famous President Manuel L. Quezon. Once inside the regal Palace, the hysterical, maddened mob began to explode firecrackers, burn books, destroy furniture, hurl appliances, framed pictures, telephone sets, small cabinets and almost everything they could lay their hands on out of the windows. Decent people who were merely curious and anxious to have a glimpse of the presidential Palace were elbowed, thrashed and trampled by the rampaging flood of "emancipated humanity," a considerable number represented by thieves, kleptomaniacs and the frustrated seeking to wreak vengeance on a despised leader by stealing or destroying some discarded tokens and symbols of his regime.

It was a long night of unreined pandemonium and mob insanity as passions long seething and pent-up continued to burst into explosions of joy and hatred reminiscent of what happened as an immediate aftermath of glorious Roman conquests.

Alarmed at the massive looting of the Palace, Gen. Ramos went on television to appeal for calm and restraint and requested the people to stop their rape and pillage of Malacañang. He sent a contingent of soldiers ahead of him to keep peace in the Palace and prepared to join them later so that he could personally take command of the situation. He urged the people to stop stealing and destroying the nation's treasures kept in the Palace. Then, remembering to use his knowledge of psychology, he resorted to argumentum ad hominem in appealing to them. "My beloved fellowmen," Ramos said on television, "please listen to our appeal. If you really love our new President, Mrs. Cory Aquino, please do not destroy or take away anything from the Palace. She will be the one to use that place beginning tomorrow when she begins her work as President.

Show her that you love her by not removing or destroying any article in the Palace before she is able to see them herself. "

But the bedlam and the hysteria continued to rage through the night.

FOURTEEN

Aquino Era Begins

*Now we stand on the edge of a new country, the
frontier of tyranny behind us. A long and arduous journey
lies ahead to the peace, progress and justice for which we
longed and sacrificed.*

— Cory Aquino

WITH the flight of fallen President Ferdinand E. Marcos from the
Philippines on February 25, 1986, the Marcos era, the longest in
Philippine political history, came to an end and the Aquino era was
ushered in. The Marcos era ended not with a bang but with a whim-
per; the Aquino era began plagued by uncertainties and controversies.

The fall of Marcos did not begin with the military revolt on
February 22. It began on August 21, 1983 when former Senator
Benigno Aquino Jr., was assassinated at the Manila International
Airport while returning to the Philippines from a three-year stay in
the United States. Aquino's death triggered explosions of massive
hatred expressed in a series of unprecedented protest actions —
rallies and demonstrations — centering first in the rich town of
Makati then spreading throughout the islands. The nation's economy
suffered setbacks with foreign investors hesitating to renew or to
negotiate new ventures in the Philippines. Labor unrest escalated
and scores of new vigilant, militant groups emerged, engaging the
will, passions and numbers of various sectors of society — students,
teachers, slum and urban dwellers, peasants and farmers, cause-
oriented groups.

Criminality rose to new peaks, and more and more people
became jobless as factories, suffering from a sick economy, closed
shop while many were paralyzed by strikes. Meanwhile, official
graft and corruption of unprecedented scale continued to throttle
the economy with scores of high public men close to the Palace
conniving and conspiring with the President's — and the First Lady's
— favored friends or notorious "cronies" to empty the public

coffers and plunder the country's resources. Promises of reform and change by the Marcos government fell on deaf ears and were rejected by the people because the government had almost totally lost its credibility.

The erosion of government credibility was aggravated by the manner in which Marcos and his men were handling the investigation and eventually the prosecution and trial of the 26 military men accused in the Aquino assassination headed by Maj. Gen. Fabian C. Ver, the President's acknowledged military strongman and Armed Forces Chief of Staff.

As a consequence of all this the Communist and other left-wing elements took advantage of the deepening social and economic crisis and intensified their insurgency campaign. Having considerably grown in number, from a mere handful in 1965 to allegedly more than 15,000 armed guerrillas, the New People's Army, military arm of the new Communist Party of the Philippines, redoubled its attacks on moving troops and military installations by ambushes particularly in the provinces. Many of their sympathizers — and some of the rebel leaders — came not only from the masses and the peasantry but also from the academic and religious communities. A few artists and intellectuals were among them. From the ranks of the rebels sprang some names around which were woven an aura of romanticism, as in the name of the rebel guerrilla priest, Fr. Conrado Balweg of Northern Philippines, who has become a Filipino version of Fidel Castro of Cuba: *Conrado de la Montana.*

All the while disgruntled Muslim Filipinos in Mindanao continued to make noise and emphasize their presence by staging periodic ambuscades and guerrilla blitzes on military camps and installations.

In the regular Batasang Pambansa whose members were elected in May, 1984, the opposition members representing such diverse groups as the Unido, the PDP-Laban, the Pinaghiusa of Cebu, Mindanao Alliance, the Nacionalista party (Roy wing) and Kilusan ng Bagong Lipunan representatives styling themselves as the "Caucus of Independents," industriously performed their role as fiscalizers of the government. Always outvoted, they were hardly outtalked by the ruling party because they were not lacking in articulate and competent lights in politics, law and government. This is not surprising for a number of the 60-odd oppositionists were veterans of the old Congress: former Speaker Jose B. Laurel Jr. Edmundo Cea, Neptali Gonzales, Francisco Sumulong, Eva Estrada Kalaw, Antonio Cuenco, Ramon Mitra, Fermin Caram and others. There were outstanding neophytes, too, like Metro Manila's Alberto Romulo, Gemiliano Lopez, Jose Atienza, Orlando Mercado, and some rising political stars from the North, the Visayas and Mindanao.

The collective voices of this political opposition reverberated beyond the halls of the Batasan, resounded through the streets and, through media, were projected to the hinterlands, thus contributing to the rise of public discontent with the Marcos government.

It was in the halls of the Batasan where reports of the supposed "hidden wealth" in untold millions, even billions, of dollars of the Marcoses were exposed. The opposition filed motions to impeach the President but the attempt was quickly squelched by the KBL. But the damage to Marcos had already been inflicted. Assemblyman Orlando Mercado, Quezon City, a television personality, was deputized by the opposition to take video tapes of the mansions, condominiums and other real properties in many parts of the United States supposedly owned by the Marcoses and their favored friends, and the tapes were subsequently used as part of the propaganda ammunition of the opposition during the campaign for the 1986 presidential elections.

The growing insurgency and the deepening economic crisis in the Philippines continued to cause alarm to Washington. Some newspapers reported that alternative sites for the American bases — Clark Air Base and Subic Naval Base — were being considered by the American government as possible relocation sites for the bases in case the situation in the Philippines worsened further but that no substitute sites were available in the region. The American dilemma lay in the fact that they had no choice but to keep their bases in the Philippines, on one hand, but must contend with the risks posed by the growing Communist menace and the increasingly sordid state of the economy. Reports on these problems continued to flood Washington. Some influential members of the U.S. Congress kept presenting to President Ronald Reagan alarming reports on the situation, notwithstanding the fact that he himself had publicly declared his confidence in President Marcos whom he had called the "alternative to Communism" in the country and in spite of Vice President George Bush's proclamation that he was happy with the manner in which Marcos, in his view, was adhering to democratic principles. "We stand with you, sir," Bush said in June 1981 during his visit to Manila to attend Marcos's inauguration following his reelection victory over Alejo Santos. "We love your adherence to democratic principles and to the democratic processes. . . . We will not leave you in isolation."

Some U.S. Congressmen, particularly Rep. Stephen Solarz, continued to make noise and increased their attacks on President Marcos, claiming among other things that he had lost popular support and therefore could no longer institute political and economic reforms needed to curb the insurgency and slow down the descent of the economy. Marcos was being compelled into decisively acting to resolve the nation's twin problems on pain of losing American and military support which Marcos in turn needed to stay in power. Not-so-subtle hints were also telegraphed to him implying that the U.S. government was not happy with the way the Aquino assassination case was being handled by Marcos and his refusal to appoint Lt. Gen. Fidel V. Ramos as Maj. Gen. Ver's replacement as AFP Chief of Staff. Both matters were claimed to be among the underlying reasons for his loss of the people's support.

In October 1985 Reagan dispatched his close personal friend and confidante, Senator Paul Laxalt, to see and confer with Marcos. The lawmaker was armed with a "demand," not a request, for Marcos to make reforms to deal with the economic crisis and the Communist insurgency.[1] The specific subjects discussed by Marcos and Laxalt were not disclosed to the public but not long after his departure Marcos stunned the nation with an unexpected announcement that elections for President would be held not later than January 1986 with he himself as the issue. This dramatic announcement fell like a bomb but was met with skepticism by the people as reflected in the media; they found it hard to believe that Marcos, the shrewd, foxy politician that he had always been would be so altruistic as to make so great a sacrifice as having his term cut by at least one year without anything in return. Besides some voices from the opposition felt that the announcement was a gambit or one of the Machiavellian tactics employed by the autocratic ruler to divert critical public attention as a result of the bitter and spirited assaults of the opposition in the Batasan. It was easy to believe that the decision to hold elections was reached by the President during his talks with Laxalt but in exchange for what was anybody's guess.

At the time of the announcement the political opposition groups, eagerly spoiling for an opportunity to challenge Marcos and his party, were preoccupied with positioning themselves for the local elections scheduled in May 1986. They had reasons for their optimism. For one, the President's health was progressively deteriorating, a fact that had been causing demoralization among members of his giant but monolithic KBL party organization and which some opposition spokesmen had been amplifying at every opportunity by questioning his ability to continue governing the country. He was indeed the issue and had been so long before he made that announcement about the"snap" elections. His political enemies had been relentlessly hitting at this theme and telling the people that "as soon as Marcos goes, so will the KBL go too," a message implying that it was futile for the KBL partymen and the people to continue depending on and trusting him. For another they were still in a state of well-being because of the victory of approximately one-third of the entire Batasang Pambansa membership in the May 1984 elections. Moreover the Aquino murder case could still give them countless votes, especially in the cities and towns.

If Marcos was bothered by all this he did not show any sign that he was. And in all likelihood there was no reason for him to be alarmed. Compared to his solid personal base and perfectly performing political machine, the opposition were hopelessly divided and were tearing at each other's throats in the heat of their own intramurals and struggle for supremacy. The surfeit of opposition organizations and groupings particularly in the Visayas and Mindanao made unity or even mere coordination an impossibility; it would require a fantastically great miracle to expect the opposition to have only one presidential candidate. Even before Marcos made the announcement, opposition figures such as Aquilino Pimentel Jr. and Homobono Adaza of Mindanao, Ramon Mitra of Palawan, Luis Villafuerte of the Bicol region, and Unido's Salvador H. Laurel were widely bruited about as impatiently waiting to challenge Marcos — Cory Aquino's name had not yet surfaced then.

At first Marcos announced that only the Presidency was at stake. However, he amended this by including a Vice President to be elected with the President, the first time that position would be revived and filled after its abolition in 1972 when Marcos proclaimed martial law — the office was abolished together with the bicameral Congress. This change in Marcos's mind was seen by many observers and political analysts as an imposition by the United States, through the U.S. embassy in Manila, as part of the "return to democracy" process. Then he announced another change: the date of the elections was moved from January to February 7, 1986.

Marcos and his advisers had thought it would be easy for him to win a reelection, that it would be a breeze. He had all the built-in advantages of an incumbent President: unlimited funds, the sprawling bureaucracy staffed by people who owed their positions to him, the Commission on Elections, the military and other government and semi-government institutions, plus his own fully expanded power base. Because he had been in the Presidency, from which all powers flow, for almost 20 years, he had been the benefactor of countless thousands of men and women to whom he had directly or indirectly extended favors.

President Marcos did not have sufficient basis for his confidence. He had lost the armor of invincibility that had enabled him to withstand all the assaults of his enemies who instead became easy prey for his conquests. For the truth was that his unusually long reign had become an obstacle to his dream of further staying in power.

The great national problems which he made the reasons for imposing martial law — oligarchic rule by a few political and economic royalists, poverty, insurgency, graft and corruption, among others — did not only recur but bounced back with more devastating force and extent. The "sick society" he had promised to cure and restore to normalcy had become more debilitated, almost *in extremis.* As a result the people who had given him their trust as evidenced by their passive acquiescence since 1972 became disillusioned and discontented. Unknown to the President and his key Palace advisers they were eagerly awaiting an opportunity to express their pent-up feelings — the election exercise was such an opportunity.

Marcos could hardly be expected to know the real sentiments of the people because of his long isolation from them. For one reason or another, he allowed himself to be a prisoner in the presidential Palace, insulated from the people by an ever-deepening phalanx of assistants, cronies, military subalterns and relatives from his own side but mostly from his wife's. Most of the information he received was funnelled to him by fawning sycophants impelled to dilute and slant details and facts to advance their own selfish interests, the rule rather than the exception in any court of power. Even the results of opinion surveys needed as an adequately reliable basis for presidential decisions are engineered to please the decision-maker. All of these naturally misled him and resulted in erroneous and often disastrous decisions. Why Marcos allowed himself to be virtually detained as a willing prisoner in his Palace is not easy to fathom but lack of access to full information doubtless prevented him from making certain vital decisions with soundness. Access to all available information and its utilization was according to some historians a basis of the success of Franklin D. Roosevelt as America's longest serving President (four terms); lack of it certainly contributed to Marcos's eventual downfall.

A newspaper article expresses this same view, observing that:
"Marcos, after being almost absolute ruler for years and surrounded by men with vested interests, apparently lost touch with his own people and in his calculations left out the people factor."[2]

In retrospect, one will recall that the killing of Ninoy Aquino at the Manila International Airport was the event that started the downfall of Ferdinand E. Marcos. He was never to recover from that catastrophe. His downfall was sealed by the February 7 presidential snap elections. Whatever may be his real motives for calling such elections and whoever pressured him into doing so is not exactly material. The crucial thing is that the election exercise proved suicidal for Marcos.

The irony is that he lost the Presidency *after* he had been officially proclaimed by the Batasang Pambansa and finally fell from power a few hours after his inauguration as the reelected President of the Philippines. He was a victim of post-election actions and events.

TO begin with, Cory Aquino did not—concede the election to Marcos but insisted that he concede himself because it was she who had won. Claiming massive election frauds, she brought her cause to the people and called for civil disobedience, a nonviolent means of forcing Marcos to give up his position. It was obvious that the people, first in Metro Manila and then the provinces, were obediently heeding her call as shown by their reported positive response of boycotting "crony" media, banks and consumer products. There was the Catholic Church, too, largely through the two cardinals — Jaime Sin and Ricardo Vidal — and the Catholic Bishops Conference of the Philippines who acted in unison to support Cory Aquino and Salvador Laurel and openly accused Marcos of immoral possession of power because he allegedly stole it from the people. Likewise, the foreign governments through their embassies decided not to felicitate Marcos on his reelection, a routine function in international relations. Moreover, the United States withdrew support from Marcos, with President Reagan himself charging extraordinary fraudulence, vote-buying and violence in the elections, and asked him to resign and transfer power peacefully to the "real winner" of the people's mandate.

Furthermore, two of his most able men, Minister of Defense Juan Ponce Enrile and Lt. Gen. Fidel V. Ramos, AFP Vice Chief of Staff and Chief of the PC-INP (and a blood relative of Marcos) led a military revolt which was eventually joined by the people. The two leaders of the rebellion withdrew their support from their

Commander-in-Chief and extended it to Cory Aquino. In addition, foreign governments, particularly the 15-nation European Economic Community and the 5-nation European Free Trade Area, led the move to isolate Marcos and his government on a worldwide basis. Finally the Soviet Union withdrew its earlier congratulations, the only one made by another country, after the United States had asked him to step down and effect a peaceful transition of power. This American action made the isolation of Marcos and his government from the family of nations complete.

That sense of isolation stayed with Ferdinand E. Marcos up to his February 25 inauguration in Malacanang. He was a lonely and pathetic figure that noontime, an old man abandoned practically by all who had been in his inner circle for twenty years except his immediate family. That inaugural was his last hurrah as the nation's most powerful citizen, and while it added a somewhat dramatic touch to the historic episode, the ceremony itself was anticlimactic for the entire drama of Marcos as politician ended that morning with Cory's own inauguration as President and Laurel's installation as Vice President under a new government that was decidedly transitory and provisional and which was eventually to be formally enshrined in its own Freedom Constitution as a revolutionary government.

On the eve of the inauguration of Marcos as reelected President opposition members of Parliament together with non-Batasan opposition leaders and a handful of former Marcos men proclaimed Cory Aquino and Salvador Laurel as the duly elected President and Vice President in the February 7 elections.[3] The proclamation was legally based on the doctrine of sovereign will of the people. It was the opposition's own way of setting the stage for the peaceful transition of power from Marcos to Aquino. It meant that they had rejected and repudiated the existence of the Marcos government and replaced it with a provisional government headed by Cory Aquino, the government supported by the military rebellion of Enrile and Ramos.

The proclamation was done through a resolution which directly annulled the February 15 proclamation of President Marcos and Arturo M. Tolentino by the Batasan. A total of 150 persons signed the document called "A People's Resolution." It was read before the body gathered at the Club Filipino by Assemblyman Neptali Gonzales, a legal luminary and dean of the institute of law of the Far Eastern University, and proclaims Aquino and Laurel the real winners in the elections for President and Vice President. The proclamation was signed by all opposition members of the

Batasan and some ruling party (KBL) members, namely: Jose Zubiri of Bukidnon, Antonio Carag and Alfonso Reyno Jr., of Cagayan, Renato Cayetano of Taguig-Pateros-Muntinlupa in Metro Manila, Edno Joson of Nueva Ecija, Fernando Faberes of Batanes, and Camilo Cabili of Iligan City.

Among the non-members of the Batasan who likewise signed the People's Resolution were several prominent political figures led by former Vice President Fernando Lopez. Others were Jose W. Diokno, Ambrosio Padilla, Ernesto Maceda, Domocao Alonto, John Osmena, Jovito R. Salonga, Lorenzo M. Tanada, Emmanuel Pelaez, Rene Espina, Tecla San Andres Ziga, Francisco "Soc" Rodrigo, Mamintal Tamano, Cornelio T. Villareal, Manuel Cases, Benjamin Ligot, Herminio Teves, Fidel V. Ramos, Dakila Castro, Mariano Santiago, Leticia Ramos-Shahani, Precious Javier, Salvador P. Lopez, Felicisimo T. San Luis, Marcelo Balatbat, Bren Z. Guiao, Ernesto Amatong, Cirilo Boy Montejo, Emil Ong, Troadio Quiason, Jaime Zobel, Bea Zobel, Jose Cojuangco, Margarita "Ting-ting" Cojuangco, Enrique Zaldivar, Francisco S. Tatad, Nini Quezon Avanceña, Ricardo Romulo, Dante Santos, Vicente Paterno, Leandro Verceles, Jose Ingles, Fernando Campos, Linda Garcia-Campos, Marcial Pimentel, Rodolfo Palma, Joaquin "Chino" Roces, Ching Escaler, Jaime Ongpin, and Pablito Sanidad.

The now historic document was typewritten on simple bond paper which was badly crumpled since it was passed around from hand to hand for over a hundred signatures.[4] As Gonzales read the names of the signatories, more names were added, passed on to him by others on pieces of paper and the unprinted parts of newspapers, an indication that the resolution had not been prepared in advance and that in all likelihood it was a spur-of-the-moment decision.

The signatories were unanimously convinced that the sovereign will of the people had been violated and substituted by fraudulent election returns and spurious certificates of canvass, which became the basis of the proclamation of Marcos and Tolentino. They described the new provisional government as based on the people's mandate and as long as it had that mandate and was recognized by many foreign nations it was an existing legitimate government. The best test of that government's existence would be the people's willingness to pay their taxes to it.

After completing the proclamation the oppositionists voted as one to proceed with the inauguration of Cory Aquino and Laurel the following day, after which the new President would make her first official acts.

An explanation about the existence and legitimacy of the new government was necessary to clear any doubt in the public mind. How, indeed, could such a provisional government exist legally when the government under the leadership of Marcos was still in existence? Marcos himself was in power in spite of the military rebellion; in fact he had been proclaimed winner by the Batasang Pambansa and would therefore continue to govern without interruption after his inauguration. Before another government could exist, the one in existence must be overthrown or destroyed as a prior condition as in the case of a revolutionary government being established after a revolution had triumphed. In the present case, however, the military revolt had not yet won and Marcos had not been overthrown. How then could the two different governments legally exist?

The answer to this question is provided by the proclamation itself of Aquino and Laurel, in the opposition's view. The People's Resolution which proclaimed Mrs. Aquino and Laurel and which declared null and void the February 15 Batasan proclamation of Marcos and Tolentino was the legal mechanism which bestowed official legitimacy to the new government. Such legitimacy was already established by the belief among the people — and by the international community — that Mrs. Aquino won the elections. Her proclamation had expunged the existence of the Marcos government, and, in its place, a new government was set up. This provisional government had given her a base to claim the allegiance of the rest of the military, the bureaucracy, the local governments and the people themselves. Moreover, it had set the stage for the recognition of her government by foreign countries.

At the time that the work on the Aquino-Laurel proclamation was in progress, the official spokesman of Cory Aquino, Rene Saguisag, revealed that they had received the latest statement from Washington calling on Marcos to step down since any attempt to prolong his 20-year administration was futile. Such official position of the United States definitely meant that the U.S. government had extended "functional recognition" to the provisional government of Cory Aquino and that the new government "is now in place by sheer mandate of the people," said Saguisag,[5] then described that government as "constitutional, de jure and permanent."

On the other hand, Assemblyman Gonzales said the new government was from its inception provisional or temporary, though revolutionary in character, contrary to Saguisag's declaration. That Gonzales was correct in his interpretation was borne out by the fact that the Aquino government found it necessary to frame a new Constitution to be submitted to the people for ratification. That new Constitution or fundamental law would be the bedrock of the government's stability and mother source of its authority.

This need was met by the Aquino government when it issued on March 25, 1986 Proclamation No. 3 entitled "Declaring a national policy to implement the reforms mandated by the people, protecting their basic rights, adopting a provisional Constitution, and providing for an early transition to a new government under a new Constitution."[6] (See Appendix "C" for full text of Proclamation No. 3). Pursuant to this proclamation, a provisional revolutionary government was set up under a "Freedom Constitution." One of the first official acts of the new revolutionary government was the abolition of the Batasang Pambansa, and the consequent concentration of legislative and executive powers in the President.

THE concentration of executive and legislative powers in the President during the transition period as provided under the "Freedom Constitution" is not without precedent in Philippine history. During the period of transition from General Emilio Aguinaldo's dictatorial government to the proclamation of the first Philippine Republic on June 12, 1898 Aguinaldo exercised maximum executive and legislative powers upon the advice of his top braintrusts, notably the great Filipino political thinker Apolinario Mabini. The Aquino advisers and think tank members could only have derived immediate inspiration from the Aguinaldo model — which, in turn, was inspired by foreign models — which found it imperative to invest the leader with optimum and near-absolute powers during the passage of the state from a dictatorship or revolutionary government to a democratic republic. Earlier than Cory Aquino, such concentration of powers was assumed by Ferdinand E. Marcos while waging his so-called "democratic revolution" which he resorted to in order to build "a new society." This explains the inclusion of the controversial "Transitory Provisions," Article XVII, in the 1973 Constitution. Indeed the leader at the helm must be invested with adequate powers to enable him to guide the nation safely through an emergency period fraught with dangers. In the words of Mabini, addressed to Aguinaldo:

"The ship of state is threatened by great dangers and terrible tempests, and this circumstance, in my opinion, renders it advisable that the three powers [executive, legislative and judicial] be to a certain extent combined for the present in a single hand, so that she may be guided with the force necessary in order to avoid all reefs."[7]

Aguinaldo agreed with Mabini, his most trusted political adviser against whom the more highly educated, moneyed members of his Cabinet endlessly intrigued and schemed. He appealed to Congress to understand why the need for more powers.

"You also know that I am charged with the most difficult task of steering the ship of state in these moments fraught with danger," said Aguinaldo, "hence I hope that you will understand that I need such ample powers that I shall be safe above the ebb and flow of public opinion and that you will give me strength and energy to avoid all shoals and to prevent, by adoption of swift and opportune measures, the absolute predominance of brute force."[8]

The same "ample powers" are needed by any leader, including Cory Aquino, during a similar period of transition. Whether the period from her proclamation of a revolutionary government to the establishment of a democratic, constitutional one will be long or short, she needs maximum powers to enable her to lead with decisiveness and dispatch during that crucial, emergency period. She will need those extraordinary powers to utilize the services of the government agencies, the bureaucracy and the military for immediate and urgent projects, like quelling counteractions and reactions to her government's policies by those who had been disenfranchised of their political, economic and social privileges and are naturally attempting, with desperation, to reclaim what they had lost. She needs abundant powers to distribute the nation's scant resources and opportunities in a more equitable and judicious manner rather than allowing them to be misused and abused by numerous vested-interest persons and groups. The successful military revolt which elevated her to the Presidency was characterized by minimum bloodshed for it was largely nonviolent. Yet it resulted in the dismissal of hundreds of thousands, even millions, of people from their positions in both government and private offices. Several thousands more of politicians and their followers were stripped of their privileges, and social prerogatives. To expect them to merely accept their fate with resignation and acquiescence is to betray one's ignorance of human nature and the Filipino character. A President will need all available powers at his or her command to overcome the active resistance and counteraction of all those who had been sidelined or temporarily relegated to the background by the Aquino government.

Concentrating power in the hands of a leader, however, can be very dangerous. That old Actonian adage that power tends to corrupt and absolute power corrupts absolutely is truer than ever. "The greater the powers, the more dangerous the abuse," according to Edmund Burke.[9] Furthermore, as Burke also observes, those who have once been intoxicated with power and have derived any kind of emolument from it such as glory and high social status, no matter how briefly, can never willingly abandon it. Indeed the Hobbesian statement is correct that the desire for power ceases only in death.[10]

To the credit of Cory Aquino she approached the matter of her assuming more power than she already had with studied caution. She did not make a frenetic dash for it though some influential media people, notably Maximo V. Soliven and Luis D. Beltran, publisher and editor-in-chief, respectively, of the newly born *Philippine Daily Inquirer*, were prodding her to declare a revolutionary government to enable her to act more decisively and firmly on vital national problems and to dismantle what they perceived as the remaining structures of the Marcos regime. They were joined in that chorus by such well-known personalities, too, as Edgardo Angara, of the Integrated Bar of the Philippines, and Luis R. Mauricio. Among the remaining structures of the Marcos regime which they wanted abolished was the Batasang Pambansa.

She dilly-dallied with her decision, too, in spite of the pressure applied on her by some of her closest advisers, particularly Minister Neptali Gonzales, Executive Secretary Joker P. Arroyo, Fr. Joaquin Bernas, president of the Ateneo de Manila University and reputedly the most influential presidential adviser, and Finance Minister Jaime Ongpin. She was obviously deferring her decision on the problem because it would entail not only formalizing the revolutionary character of her government but abolishing the Batasang Pambansa which would mean her assuming the power to legislate aside from the already awesome and vast powers of the Presidency. Moreover she knew it would mean dismissing several hundred Batasan employees and casual or emergency workers. But its most drastic effect would be the disenfranchisement and throwing into the streets of all the 60-odd opposition Batasan members who staked their lives and fortunes for her during the campaign for the February 7 elections and made a valiant, if losing, stand for her during the night of February 15 when the KBL-dominated Batasan proclaimed Marcos and Tolentino as the duly elected President and Vice President. As for the KBL Batasan members, from the Speaker down to the least-known member, she knew her decision would alienate them forever, unless of course she would attempt to win them over with some attractive offers as is usually done in politics. Among the members who would be adversely affected by the abolition of the Batasan was MP Cecilia Muñoz Palma, a retired former Justice of the Supreme Court who exerted considerable influence in Cory Aquino's final decision to run for President. Mrs. Palma and many other close associates of the President had urged her to retain the Batasan after majority of the members had assured her of cooperation.

But a decision must be made, one way or the other. Thus, after thoroughly studying the problem and praying hard to God for guidance, she decided to sign Proclamation No. 3 on March 25, 1986. Also known as the "Freedom Charter" or "Freedom Constitution," it abolished the Batasang Pambansa, as noted earlier, and thus concentrated both executive and legislative powers on the President during an indefinite period of transition from a revolutionary to a constitutional government. Mrs. Aquino, however, was said to have found the word "revolutionary" distasteful and had it removed from the proclamation. One salient feature of the transitional constitution is its retention of the Bill of Rights.

Commenting negatively on the subject in his column in the *Daily Express*, Neal H. Cruz quoted former Senator Tolentino as saying, "a revolutionary government is worse than martial law. It is the worst kind of dictatorship!" He could hardly believe that Justice Minister Neptali Gonzales, a very amiable man otherwise, said "that we have a revolutionary government not bound by any Constitution or any law. He said that the Aquino government can do whatever it wants and follow only the laws that it feels like following."[11]

Without realizing it, people's power toppled one dictatorial regime only to be replaced by another, and worse, dictatorship, Cruz said with bitterness. He added: "For under Minister Gonzales's theory, the government can clamp people in jail even without filing charges or issuing warrants of arrest, seize private property, anything. No law, not even the Constitution, can protect us."[12]

Former Supreme Court Justice Muñoz-Palma agrees and told *Panorama* magazine:

"I'd say that this decision to call a provisional government and abolish the legislative branch has multiplied the fronts of dissent and dissatisfaction with the new government. What we should do really is take every step necessary to effect reconciliation, as the President has been saying . . . Now, in the light of this decision that the President has taken, the KBL people are forced into a situation where they're now uniting. Had we opted to reconcile with them, in the sense of accepting their pledge of cooperation in the Batasan, we'd have less trouble."[13]

Identifying the people around Cory Aquino who were inclined to a strong, almost dictatorial government as Executive Secretary Joker P. Arroyo, Justice Minister Neptali Gonzales and Fr. Joaquin Bernas, she emphasized that it would have been more acceptable to the people if a legislative body had been organized under Proclamation No. 3.

"My point is that the President should not exercise both executive and legislative powers," said Justice Palma. "That's precisely what we've been carping against Mr. Marcos and his Amendment No. 6. We'd been shouting ourselves hoarse against Amendment 6 in the Batasan. Now that we've been in power, we're even worse than Amendment 6."[14]

A foreign journalist, Gregory A. Fossedal of the *Copley News Service*, meanwhile, perceived something taking place in the Philippines while U.S. officials were preoccupied with poring over Marcos's financial records and his wife Imelda's shoes and paintings — an emerging one-party rule similar to the Marcos dictatorship. This development began to take place when President Aquino suspended the Constitution and abolished the National Assembly. A new Constitution would be drawn up not by elected delegates but by a committee or commission of "several dozen handpicked Aquino loyalists." Mrs. Aquino was also quoted by *The New York Times*, March 1, 1986, as considering a revolutionary government and tested the waters, first, by cancelling local elections scheduled in May 1986 — "enabling her to replace incumbent mayors who might oppose her party." Then she announced, several days later, the formation of a body to report on the idea of creating a revolutionary government, "overriding the country's legislature and courts for an unspecified period."

All these "chilling steps" where given scant attention by American officials and media. An exhaustive analysis of U.S. press coverage of the Philippines reprinted in the March 7 issue of *The Washington Times* concluded that news of the "emerging threat to democracy in Manila has been shoved to the back pages." Few observers thought the religious and upright Aquino planned "to establish a brutal, Marcos-style dictatorship," said Fossedal. Yet managing a *de facto* martial-law regime may be too much for her, "leading to a *coup* by the very military leaders who helped her gain power."

The *Copley News Service* observer pointed out:

"The politics of retribution, now being played out in Manila and Washington in their obsession with Mrs. Marcos's wardrobe, are at best a silly melodrama. At worst, they are a diversion from real threats; in the case of the Philippines, a clear and present danger to fragile democracy. Friends of freedom and Aquino must speak up now, while there is time."[15]

This reminder is well-taken. Concentration of powers in one person is dangerous. One-man rule by any leader, however well-intentioned, is fraught with perils. For power, according to Will and Ariel Durant, dements more than it corrupts. Likewise, those in power want only to perpetuate it. As Justice Louis D. Brandeis once put it, "No one with absolute power can be trusted to give it up even in part."[16]

OF all past Presidents of the Philippines — Manuel L. Quezon, Sergio Osmeña Sr., Jose P. Laurel, Manuel A. Roxas, Elpidio Quirino, Ramon Magsaysay, Carlos P. Garcia, Diosdado Macapagal and Ferdinand E. Marcos — Corazon C. Aquino is a unique class by herself. She is different from other Presidents by virtue of the following factors:

1.   She is the first woman ever to become President of the Philippines.

2.   She is the first President of the Philippines without any actual political experience, say, as a governor, mayor, Representative or Senator.

3.   She is the only President of the Philippines who became a candidate by a "direct draft" or endorsement by the people, not through a political revolution, with approximately 1,200,000 people signing a resolution requesting her to run for President.

4.   She won the election not on the basis of the actual number of votes counted in her favor but on the basis of a proclamation by military revolutionists and opposition members of the Batasang Pambansa or National Assembly.

5. She was installed after a "snap" or sudden election for President held on February 7, 1986, not in a regular presidential election.

Cory Aquino became the President of the nation through a combination and congruence of historical forces and events. She did not deliberately or consciously plan for it. On the contrary, she was merely pushed into it by a tragic event, the killing of her husband Ninoy Aquino. With the former Senator gone, she was prevailed upon by the people and the leaders of the political groups opposed to President Marcos to run as their grand coalition candidate, a matter which she accepted with reluctance because of her lack of political experience. Nevertheless, she did run and challenge Marcos for the Presidency. She lost in the counting to Marcos, who, together with his vice presidential candidate, Arturo M. Tolentino, was proclaimed elected by the Batasan. However, she insisted that Marcos had cheated her and Salvador Laurel, her running-mate, so instead of conceding she waged a civil disobedience campaign — boycott of products and services, work stoppages, and similar non-violent actions — in order to "bring Marcos down to his knees." While she was waging her campaign, a military revolt erupted under the leadership of Defense Minister Juan Ponce Enrile and Armed Forces Vice Chief of Staff Fidel V. Ramos whose aim was to force the President to resign from the Presidency. The military revolt, which gained the support of the people, gave its loyalty and support to Mrs Aquino. It was thus that she became the President.

As President, Cory Aquino invites comparison with other women national leaders, the most prominent among them being Indira Gandhi of India, Golda Meir of Israel, and the current Prime Minister of England, Margaret Thatcher. Mrs. Aquino's position is, however, different from theirs. For as the President of the Philippines, she is the Head of State and Chief Executive of her country. All other women leaders mentioned here were former Prime Ministers, with only Mrs. Thatcher still in power, but not Heads of State, that position being held by a President or a King or Queen as ceremonial head, as noted in the Foreword.

Of her initial reluctance to run for President, Mrs. Aquino calls to mind Mrs. Meir when she was faced with the prospect of becoming Prime Minister. "I honestly didn't want the responsibility, the stress and strain of being Prime Minister," she said. And when she was nominated — and elected — as the Chief Executive of her beloved Israel, Golda Meir revealed in her autobiography, Golda:

"I know that tears rolled down my cheeks and that I had my head in my hands when the voting was over . . . I had never planned to be Prime Minister; I had never planned any position, in fact."[17]

The Israeli lady Prime Minister knew that in that lofty office, she would have to make decisions every day that would affect the lives of millions of people, and "I think perhaps that's why I cried."

As Prime Minister she realized that governmental power is not as limitless as it seems to be, that she could only do so much. Knowing this she was unsympathetic to the idea of strikes in essential services like hospitals, for example, resulting from the impatience of workers.

"The government cannot do everything all at once," she said, pre-echoing what Cory Aquino as President must be realizing. "It can't wave a magic wand and meet everyone's demands simultaneously: eradicate poverty without imposing taxes, win wars, go on absorbing immigration, develop the economy and still give everyone their due. No government can do all this at one and the same time."[18]

Likewise, as a woman leader without actual experience in politics and public administration, Cory Aquino can be underrated. When Margaret Thatcher won as Prime Minister of England, the men of ex-Premier Edward "Ted" Heath whom she had defeated took a long time to take her seriously. "She appeared naive, badly advised, inexperienced and unlikely to appeal to enough voters to win elections," note the authors of her biography, *Thatcher*. They thought that it was only a matter of time when her impulses would derail her and they had only to wait to resume their control of their party.

The Heath people proved wrong, however, for instead of growing weak, the Prime Minister became stronger largely because of the following developments: (1) the Thatcher image was cultivated with a calculation which assessed the mood of the electorate more shrewdly than the men did; (2) the issues which caused the greatest strains at the top of the party changed in her favor, and (3) the Party hierarchy was subtly moulded to reduce the influence of the old guard.[19]

Still, Thatcher was insecure and her insecurity showed in her aggression; she appeared at the same time contemptuous and slightly afraid of most of her Shadow Cabinet colleagues; some of them were also afraid of her. She talked a great deal, too, at the Wednesday Cabinet meetings, although the stream of words abated later on. Her inexperience was painfully obvious to her senior colleagues and also clear to former Prime Minister Harold Wilson who once said, "Some of us are rather old hands at these matters." But she has prevailed and continues to remain in power since her victory in 1974. She has proved strong, decisive and capable, confirming what she had said, "Iron entered my soul."

The examples of Mesdames Meir and Thatcher are more than sufficient arguments to offset any built-in prejudice against women wielding power. It can prove absolutely embarrassing to underrate them or to belittle their capabilities.

AS President, Cory Aquino appointed, as one of her first official acts, her Cabinet, the body of ministers who would assist her in administering the government. The choice of the President's ministers is crucial for they exert influence in the formulation of government policies and programs. They help the President chart the direction of the government, the kind of foreign policy, economic development emphasis, educational content, and so on, it will pursue.

One noticeable feature of the Aquino government is that while Cory Aquino should of necessity be a populist President since she rose to power through unprecedented popular support, the people seem remote from immediate consideration. This was patently obvious during her inauguration at the Club Filipino on February 25, when not a single representative of the "people" was to be found within the ceremonial hall, much less at the presidential table. The hall was packed full of representatives and extensions of the old power elite in Philippine society — business and industrial tycoons, powerful clergymen, old political figures, professionals, relations of the old rich. Yet the leader to be installed rose to that position not because of them but because of the people, who supported the military rebellion of Minister Enrile and Gen. Ramos; it was people power that supported the uprising — but no people's representatives were present at the ceremony. They were still outside providing "the muscle and the numbers" to protect the revolution from any rear-guard guerrilla action by the forces of Marcos and Ver. Regrettably the masses had remained the fodders of the revolution. As Amando Doronila aptly writes:

"New forces in society crying out for recognition are invisible within the Club Filipino power elite. The proclamation crowd was so stuffingly middle class and upper class. The representation in the power structure is clearly imbalanced. People's power is not only for the streets. It has to be shown that it is adequately represented in the councils of decision."[20]

This elitist composition of the new emerging power structure is not new. It is the same old bourgeois mechanism that has characterized Philippine politics since the turn of the century when wealthy families with considerable political clout influenced policy decisions of government, beginning with President Emilio Aguinaldo. It is to be remembered that when Aguinaldo formed his Cabinet it was dominated by representatives and members of the old power elite, people of wealth, education and political power, some of whom contributed to the failure of his government. About the only outsider in the President's elite circle then was Apolinario Mabini, unexcelled political thinker who served as Aguinaldo's top adviser whom the moneyed power wielders endlessly intrigued against, fought relentlessly, and marked down as the "black Cabinet of the President." He differed with the powerful men around Aguinaldo, such as Pedro Paterno, Benito Legarda, Gregorio Araneta, Felipe Calderon, Felipe Buencamino and T.H. Pardo de Tavera — largely because of their dissimilar economic origins and difference in economic ideas, for though Mabini was an educated person or *ilustrado* like them, he had a humble class origin.

President Corazon Aquino's ministers are in the main wealthy and with deep political background, starting with Vice President Laurel who is concurrently Minister of Foreign Affairs. Not one among them is a representative of the people or the masses, as there is none among her known advisers. Judging from their declared assets and liabilities, most of them are millionaires and multi-millionaires as shown in the accompanying chart, with the exception of Presidential Spokesman Rene Saguisag.

Comparative Net Worth of Some Aquino Government Top Officials

Name	Position	Net Worth
Corazon C. Aquino	President	P17,720,603.55
Salvador H. Laurel	Vice President	19,404,383.00
Jose Antonio Gonzalez	Minister of Tourism	81,490,568.45
Jose Concepcion Jr.	Minister of Trade & Industry	31,400,436.00
Jaime Ongpin	Minister of Finance	28,775,155.00
Juan Ponce Enrile	Minister of National Defense	23,534,447.35
Ramon Mitra	Minister of Agriculture	17,257,200.00
Victor Ziga	Minister of General Services	9,713,552.21
Wigberto Tanada	Customs Commissioner	8,743,130.37
Alfredo Bengzon	Minister of Health	8,461,406.00
Carlos Fernandez	Dep. Min. of Transportation	8,406,900.00
Emil Ong	NFA Administrator	7,177,460.00
Mita Pardo de Tavera	Minister of Social Services	6,290,000.00
Teodoro Locsin Jr.	Minister of Information	5,527,974.47
Jovito Salonga	Chairman, PCGG	4,289,000.00
Ramon Diaz	Commissioner, PCGG	4,215,718.05
Ernesto Maceda	Minister of Natural Resources	3,820,000.00
M. Concepcion Bautista	Commissioner, PCGG	2,265,000.00
Alberto Romulo	Minister of Budget	1,936,654.00
Lourdes Quisumbing	Minister of Education	1,863,782.50
Rene Saguisag	Presidential Spokesman	450,000.00

Sources: *Malaya,* April 18, 1986, page 1 and
Daily Express, April 20, 1986, page 1.

IT IS interesting to take a look at the composition of the Aquino Cabinet. The most potent group within the administration is one that Ninoy Aquino never knew existed for, as noted by Hilarion M. Henares Jr., former chairman of the National Economic Council, its members surfaced only after that tragic day in August 1983. Ironically they are "the most powerful group" within the Cory Aquino administration and they stand against what Ninoy and the opposition stand for: nationalism, economic independence, industrialization and self-reliance.

"In the platforms of Unido and Salonga's Liberal party, in the underlying principles of the Convenor's group, even in the Declaration of Common Principles of the United Opposition submitted by Ninoy to the [Stephen] Solarz Committee two months before he was killed, one promise stood out: independence from the impositions of the IMF and multinational corporations," writes Henares. "And that is what this new group is precisely against."[21]

He identifies this new power group in Cory Aquino's government as the "Jesuit Mafia" which without fanfare had taken over 12 of the most important positions in the administration: Jaime Ongpin for Finance; Jose Concepcion Jr., for Trade and Industry; Lourdes Quisumbing for Education; Jose Antonio Gonzalez for Tourism; Alfredo Bengzon for Health; Teodoro Locsin Jr., for Public Information; Solita Monsod for the National Economic Development Authority; Jose Fernandez Jr., for Central Bank governor; Vicente Jayme for Philippine National Bank president; Cesar Zalamea for Development Bank of the Philippines chairman (has since resigned and been replaced by another Ongpin man, Jesus Estanislao); Bienvenido Tan for Internal Revenue Commissioner; and Jose Cuisia for the Social Security System. Henares claims that the leaders of this group are Ateneo University President Joaquin Bernas and Jaime Ongpin, and adds that the 13th member of the "Jesuit Cosa Nostra" is Aquilino Pimentel Jr., Minister of Local Governments and chairman of the now-powerful PDP-Laban party, who is said to be earmarked for the Presidency after Cory Aquino.

Of the rest of the Cory Aquino originals, PDP-Laban and its political allies have six positions: Pimentel; Neptali Gonzales for Justice; Ramon Mitra for Agriculture; Jovito Salonga for Good Government; Jose W. Diokno for Human Rights; and Teopisto Guingona for Audit.

The human rights group headed by Joker P. Arroyo has, aside from Arroyo as Executive Secretary, Rene Saguisag as Presidential Spokesman; Augusto Sanchez as Minister of Labor; and Antonio

Carpio for the National Bureau of Investigation.

Laurel's Unido also has four: Laurel himself as Minister of Foreign Affairs; Ernesto Maceda for Natural Resources; Luis Villafuerte for Government Reorganization; and Alberto Romulo for Budget.

From the nationalists group are two: Jose W. Diokno of Human Rights, and Wigberto Tañada of Customs. [22]

Knowing the composition — the complexion — of the machinery President Cory Aquino has put together to help her run the government, it becomes more clear that the majority of the people are not fully represented in the administration, the people who helped bring about the collapse of the Marcos dictatorship. As Renato Constantino, the historian and political analyst, puts it:

"The different middle and upper class sectors who predominated in the civilian support for the military revolt now have representation in the government. Despite the populist rhetoric of the administration, apart from some initial moves, there is as yet no clear sign that the long-term interests of the majority are the central preoccupation of the Aquino administration."[23]

The escalating intramurals within the Aquino government arising from the absence of definite, clear-cut policies breed anxiety and apprehension in many quarters and disunity within the coalition that supported her rise to power. Pro-people policies are not being adopted precisely because of the socio-economic pigmentation of the policymakers themselves and because of the pervasive role of external forces. Constantino contends that what is needed is a decisive break from the parameters those external forces impose while Cory Aquino still has both popularity and credibility since if these are eroded, it will be too late.

"Only policies based on the needs and aspirations of the deprived majority and not merely elitist sectors can bring about the unity that eludes us now," Constantino writes. "Only a concrete, unambiguous program based on the long-term interests of these broad masses can bring about that real and lasting national unity that will transcend in significance the joyous February revolution."[24]

THE new President moved fast. She required all presidential appointees to tender their resignations in order to facilitate the reorganization of government. The most important office affected by this decision was the judiciary, notably the Supreme Court, where she reinstated Senior Justice Claudio Teehankee and Justice Vicente

Abad Santos. As expected by many, she gave Teehankee, who administered her oath of office as President, a taste of justice by appointing him Chief Justice of the Supreme Court. The new chief of the high court had been bypassed at least twice for the position because his independent posture was irreconcilable with the demands of the Marcos government.

As reorganized by President Aquino the Supreme Court is constituted as follows: Claudio Teehankee, Chief Justice; Associate Justices: Vicente Abad Santos, Jose V. Feria, Pedro L. Yap, Marcelo B. Fernan, Andres R. Narvasa, Ameurfina Melencio-Herrera; Nestor B. Alampay, Hugo Gutierrez Jr., Isagani A. Cruz, and Edgardo Paras.

At the same time local elective officials were required to resign and were replaced by appointive officers-in-charge chosen largely by Minister of Local Government Aquilino Pimentel. This action naturally raised a storm of controversy with many incumbent officials — governors and mayors — refusing to vacate their offices on the ground that their terms had not yet expired and that they had the people's mandate. Another source of controversy was the claim of the Unido party of Vice President Laurel that Pimentel was packing the local positions with PDP-Laban people, some of whom were found to be of questionable backgrounds and qualifications, in preparation for future elections when the two groupings would most likely challenge each other for supremacy in the local offices.

So controversial has been Pimentel's power to pick and appoint OICs that the question was brought to the Supreme Court for resolution. On April 10 the high court issued a resolution upholding his power as Minister to appoint officers-in-charge as replacements for incumbent governors and mayors in accordance with the March 25 Freedom Constitution of the Aquino provisional or revolutionary government. It ruled that in making the appointments, Pimentel was merely acting as the alter ego of the President. The incumbent mayors and governors were elected under the 1973 Constitution and may continue in office if no replacement is made, but "they should vacate their positions upon the appointment of an officer-in-charge," the court ruled.[25]

On March 25, when she promulgated a Freedom Constitution which clothed her with broad and sweeping but temporary powers for the duration of the transition from a provisional to a constitutional government, a period which she tentatively set as "within a year," she abolished the Batasang Pambansa and dismantled every remaining political apparatus of the Marcos regime. She would call, as provided by the Freedom Constitution, a Constitutional Convention to begin drafting a new Constitution within 60 days, with the time frame of the Convention's work being one year.

Significantly these bold actions of the lady President are supported by the people, at least in Metro Manila. In an opinion survey undertaken by the newspaper *Malaya* in coordination with the Philippine Survey and Research Center, Inc., in mid-March 1986 in Metro Manila, 55% (against 35%) of the total respondents approved of the resignation of the members of the judiciary; 60% (against 20%) approved of the resignation of all local officials and appointment of new ones; 52% (against 28%) favored the dissolution of the Batasang Pambansa, and 64% (against 32%) approved of the calling of a Constitutional Convention within the next six months. The respondents, numbering 300, are aged 15 upwards and cut across all economic classes (ABCDE).[26]

It is also interesting to note that after almost two months in office, Cory Aquino continued to enjoy wide popularity. A survey conducted by the same group in April shows that 4 out of 10 adult Metro Manilans thought her performance "good/very good." A slightly higher percentage, 48%, rated her overall performance as "fair" which could mean that a considerably large segment of the population "is holding a wait-and-see attitude towards her administration." Less than 5% rated her overall performance as "poor/very poor." On the manner Cory Aquino is handling her presidential tasks, roughly 60% of Metro Manilans think she is doing "well."[27]

Another survey by the same organization gives a barometer as to what the people give top priority to among the Aquino government's programs. With respondents coming from all segments of the population, the survey results indicate that a stunning 74% of the people give top priority to economic recovery (attracting investments, generating employment, holding down prices, etc.). A total of 51% favor the investigation and prosecution of human rights violations, and 50% approve of the recovery of hidden or ill-gotten wealth. Next follow reorganization of local governments, 38%, and peace/reconciliation talks with the NPAs/MNLFs, 36%, with 33% considering drafting a new Constitution a top priority.[28]

The high esteem the people have for the President most probably results from her sincerity. Cory Aquino has so far been true to her pre-election promises, proof that she possesses *palabra de honor*, a word of honor. As she had promised she ordered the release of political detainees on February 27, barely on her third day in the Presidency. The first batch consisted of 39 prisoners. Then she announced her government would release a total of 441 detainees, including Horacio "Boy" Morales, Fr. Edicio de la Torre and renegade Lt. Victor Corpuz. Then on March 2, while addressing a thanksgiving rally of around 1 million people at the Luneta, she announced the restoration of the writ of *habeas corpus*, which resulted in the cancellation of all presidential arrest orders (ASSO, PCO and PDA) and would henceforth prevent the arbitrary arrest and detention of citizens.

On March 4 she retired 22 overstaying generals of the Armed Forces headed by former Chief of Staff Maj. Gen. Fabian C. Ver. The following day, March 5, she ordered the release of Jose Ma. Sison, founding chairman of the new Communist Party of the Philippines, and Bernabe Buscayno, alias "Commander Dante," supremo of the CPP military arm, the New People's Army, bringing to 517 the total number of detainees released by her government. She opened Malacañang to the public as she had promised, then created on March 18 the Presidential Commission on Human Rights and appointed former Senator Jose Diokno as its Chairman. On March 19 she attended her first military ceremony as the nation's first woman Commander-in-Chief at the Philippine Military Academy. She proclaimed, as noted earlier, a provisional or revolutionary government on March 25.

On Wednesday, April 23, President Aquino signed Proclamation No. 9 calling for the convening of the Constitutional Commission, which eventually elected former Supreme Court Justice Cecilia Muñoz Palma as President. Later on, April 30, she decided to abandon the controversy-wracked $2.3 billion Bataan nuclear power plant.

She ordered a rollback in fuel prices on May 21, the second in two months, with the reductions averaging .50 centavos per liter, bringing oil price cuts since March to a total of ₱1.70 per liter.

In her effort to demonstrate that her government operates by consultation with the people, she flew to Davao City on Friday, May 23, and presided at a people's meeting, her first out-of-town engagement since assuming the Presidency. She listened to the suggestions presented by multi-sectoral groups, then met with 168 Communist guerrillas whom she amnestied. She ordered Defense Minister Enrile and Chief of Staff Ramos to disarm warlords in the countryside and to go after criminal syndicates. She also assured that local elections would be held after the ratification of the new Constitution.[29]

On Sunday, May 25, her 100th day in office, she attended the 3-month "Reunion of EDSA Heroes" at Camp Aguinaldo, where she dramatically announced the names of 44 appointees to the Constitutional Commission. Then on June 2, performing another historic role, President Corazon C. Aquino addressed the opening ceremonies of the 1986 Constitutional Commission meeting at the session hall of the abolished Batasang Pambansa. She promised not to interfere with the Commission's work but urged the members to expedite the writing of the new Constitution by not wasting their time talking and behaving like politicians. As promised, various sectors are represented in the Commission, a historic body headed by another woman.

THE first three months of Cory Aquino as President indicates that sincerity is among her strongest traits. This is evident in her determination to comply with her campaign promises, particularly with regard to the release of political detainees Jose Ma. Sison and Bernabe Buscayno over the objections, it is said, of the highest leaders of the military organization. She can be firm in her decisions, as when she resisted objections to her personally appointing members of the Constitutional Commission instead of having them elected by the people, and her insistence on going to strife-torn Mindanao for a consultative meeting with multi-sectoral groups in Davao as she had also promised before the election. At the same time she has the marked inclination to support her trusted lieutenants once she has given them her confidence as shown by her refusal to touch members of her official family who had been revealed as having close connections with either former President Marcos, his cronies or his brother-in-law Benjamin "Kokoy" Romualdez, namely former Benguet Consolidated's Jaime Ongpin, and Internal Revenue Commissioner Bienvenido Tan Jr., or has not exactly been in good terms with media people in spite of his position (Information Minister Teodoro Locsin Jr.), or has proved to be both controversial and intractable (Labor Minister Augusto Sanchez). In fact she has been defending them from their critics, saying they are quite new in their jobs and are just learning the ropes, and other justifications for occasional lapses.

Still the more perceptive among her constituency are beginning to ask, even as the euphoria and jubilation of her February ascendancy begin to wear off, what her goal for the nation is. The catchword is "a truly just society" for the people as expressed in Proclamation No. 1 yet one must ask what its features are and how her government hopes to attain it. These two questions have not been clearly answered so far, perhaps because of, as suggested by some people sympathetic to her, the newness of her government whose parts are just beginning to be pieced together. For another thing, Cory Aquino was swept into power after only an incredibly brief period of campaigning, because of which she simply had no time or opportunity to formulate a comprehensive program of government. When she assumed power, therefore, she had to start literally from scratch. Thus, during her first 100 days in office, nothing much was accomplished. Certain institutions identified with Marcos were dissolved snd new appointments made, and she continued to inspire the country and enjoy the goodwill of other countries. But, as a banker associated with the Aquino political side, Tony Gatmaitan, has succinctly expressed, she has not really taken charge of the "cannibalized engine rooms of her government."

"The bottom line is — for the 100 days — President Corazon Aquino truly reigns but has not quite begun to rule," Gatmaitan writes. She is an "indisputed queen but not quite the unchallenged Chief Executive."[30]

Yet there is a real urgent need to make such a clear definition of means to achieve the goal of establishing a *just* society if the President wants the continued support of the people behind her and to see that the people she has selected to help her run the government perform their respective functions with ability and dedication. Without the support of the people her government can never hope to succeed — no government can.

Moreoever, there is a need for the Aquino government to resolve once and for all the nation's identity crisis. What are we and where we are headed for? are the questions foremost in the minds of thinking Filipinos. Filipinos have not really been independent of the United States and the latter has never given up — nor will it ever do — the role of master. This was made extra-evident again during the February 7 elections. Aside from reportedly applying pressure on former President Marcos to call the snap elections, the United States sent delegation after delegation to the Philippines to "observe" the elections. Finding the electoral exercise marked by "fraudulence," including vote-buying and violence, the delegate-observers of both the U.S. Congress and the White House called for the resignation of Marcos then finally convinced President Reagan to ask the Philippine President to step down and effect a peaceful transition of power.

"The American will must prevail," writes Teodoro F. Valencia in his *Daily Express* column. "To the strong belong the right to dictate. Once again, that's what happened   here. Filipinos performed. They sacrificed but the direction and the script were US-made . . . I have been saying that the United States is out to protect American interests here against ours . . . " And of the then unresolved question of who won the elections, Valencia again exposed the U.S. hand when he said that the U.S. had cautioned Marcos against shooting people as implied in his answers to questions in a Channel 9 interview. Marcos said, however, that he would not be able to obey such admonition if he must defend himself and the country. "That's a clear example of what role the United States is playing behind the scenes in this drama," says Valencia, adding, "Whatever you may surmise, the fact remains that the United States is dictating from behind center stage."[31]

And the U.S. was interested in the Philippines case not because, as Hector R.R. Villanueva puts it, Washington loved Mrs. Aquino more and Ferdinand Marcos less but because, by late 1985, the Marcos regime was already a terminal case. "The main concern of the Americans," says Villanueva, "was how to unseat Marcos without the latter going berserk and endangering the stability of the military bases." Thus, American recognition of the Aquino government came in slowly and reluctantly. It was only when indicators showed that the Aquino government received an overwhelming mandate from the people and international recognition that they joined the chorus with promises of economic and military aid.[32]

Indeed it was rather unsettling to see the leaders of an independent, sovereign country like the Philippines openly courting the approval and congratulations of foreign governments and waiting for them to decide who among the Filipino leaders won their own elections. As another Filipino journalist, Nestor Mata, observes with obvious contempt:

"Are we so in awe of foreigners that we cannot trust ourselves to arrive at a consensus and make a decision of our own, but must instead play out our little revolution in front of the international audience in order to find out which player gets the most applause? . . . We see our leaders meeting the same set of foreign ambassadors, negotiating with the same American special presidential envoy ranting against supposedly the same foreign intervention." In reality these leaders are waiting to give either their claim to victory the stamp of authenticity. Indeed one finds it hard to understand why foreign governments, and especially American congressional leaders, should be the ones to vest victory and authority to Filipino leaders. It is a humiliating scenario fit only for a people who had become what

Mata calls "vassals to international opinion."[33]

ALL this notwithstanding, President Cory Aquino is in an enviable
position to make the most of the Presidency. To be sure she
enjoys unprecedented popular support and goodwill. A good number
of the people trust her and believe unconditionally in her sincerity
and determination to do her best for them. Her government, through
her ministers, can manifest signs of disunity, lack of direction and
utter inexperience as well as vindictiveness, but the people would
rather blame *them* than the President — they want her to do no
wrong. They would rather, at this stage at least, close their eyes
to any blunder she may commit in order that her image would
remain pure and unsullied.

But this romance will not last forever. History shows that after
a certain period of time the euphoria that follows a victory begins
to fade and give way to reality. In the case of Presidents this period
of bliss extends to the first few months, at least through the first
half-year, during which the people hold their leader in highest esteem
and consider him or her incapable of committing an error. This is
the reason why Presidents make their big and daring decisions during
the first six months in office. It is the period when those opposed to
a President, including the media, size him up to find if they could
tackle him or if the people have elected a good or a mediocre President. The first impression during the first half-year sometimes stays
longer, says another writer in a recent study, than the whole term
itself, and the initial presidential virtues people find most impressive
are acts of concern for the people, particularly the less fortunate,
decisiveness, coolness under fire and honesty. Those who vote for the
President, on the other hand, would like him or her to "produce"
within six months, too eager to prove they had made the right
choice.[34]

If the above is true, then President Aquino does not have all the
time in the world to continue reigning but not governing. She must
demonstrate, during her first few months in office, that she can make
hard and brave decisions — major reforms, narrowing the gap between the rich and the poor, overhauling the existing system, steering
the nation toward an independent, nationalistic course — and pursue
them with decisiveness. For the nation's 54 million people can enjoy
the novelty of having a woman as President, but that enjoyment
will not last. More than pomp and pageantry, more than   novelty
and romance, the majority are more urgently concerned with the real
problem of how to make a living, the gut problems of food, clothing,

shelter and education.

Her battlecry is reconciliation and this means harmonizing all conflicting elements of Philippine society into one whole national community. But this goal is easier stated than done for the manner in which a number of her men are using their new-found power — drastic, unforgiving and vengeful — makes it impossible of attainment; they have not learned to exercise power without being overbearing. Sometime in May 1986 President Aquino once again called for national reconciliation, for her co-workers in government to let bygones be bygones, to forgive and forget and start anew. But apparently her call was not heeded for the removal from their government positions of people suspected by her people of having worked for the former President continues to this day.

In the same manner President Aquino's administration, elevated to power by the Filipino people who supported the February military revolt, must stop preoccupying itself with pleasing the foreigners, particularly the Americans, as though the people themselves do not count. Descendants of those who died fighting for their independence and sovereignty have all the reason to wonder why their officials, the national leadership, seem to take that sovereignty too lightly. It is as if the government's first consideration in formulating a national policy on, say, economic development, foreign relations and education is how it will be received by a foreign country and not really how it will advance the nation's interests.

However, the Aquino government's official stand on the issue of nationalism was more or less defined — though not yet fully discussed — by the President herself in a talk with reporters in Cebu City on May 24, 1986 in the course of her two-day consultations in central and southern Philippines. "I do not want it to be pro-American and I don't want it to be Communist leaning," the lady President said, referring to the nation's political affairs. "I just want it to be pro-Filipino." Nevertheless, contrary to the original official position of her party, the PDP-Laban, favoring the removal of U.S. bases in the Philippines, she continues to maintain her stand that she is "keeping my options open" on the subject until Manila's bases treaty with Washington expires in 1991.

She finally announced her position, too, on the issue of separation of church and state, a matter that has raised questions because of her apparent closeness with the Catholic hierarchy starting from Cardinal Sin. In fact some people had raised the sensitive question of whether the Catholic church was interfering with state affairs or influencing government policy. Mrs. Aquino's statement on the subject is categorical, thus:

"While I am a religious person, I have also made it clear that the Church cannot interfere in purely government affairs. I have my friends among the religious, but religion is one thing and government is another."[35]

THE task President Corazon Aquino has assumed is gigantic, the Presidency being the toughest, most demanding job in any country whose highest official is a President.   From it come all government decisions that affect the lives of millions of people. Even such questions as whether a person condemned by the courts to die should continue to live is within the President's pardoning power to decide. If the government happens to be revolutionary, as is the case of the provisional or transitory government of the Philippines, the tasks of the President become even more difficult for she is both the formulator and executor of the laws of the land. Even the judiciary is, under the circumstances, not vested with full judicial authority for questions considered "political" in nature are not for the high court to adjudicate — they are beyond judicial jurisdiction. In essence, therefore, all those major powers of government which are ordinarily spread among the executive, legislative and judicial departments are concentrated in one office — the Presidency — the decisions of which are not appealable considering the revolutionary status of the government.

Even under normal circumstances the Presidency is the hardest job on earth. Perhaps its chief attraction to many a presidential dreamer is the power the office wields. "I've got the most awful responsibility a man ever had," President Harry S. Truman told the *New York Times Magazine* on January 13, 1957. When John F. Kennedy was asked why he wanted to be President, he replied, "Because that's where the power is." Of the Presidency, Kennedy said: "This job is interesting ... I find the work rewarding ... There are a lot of satisfactions to the Presidency ... You have an opportunity to do something about all the problems ... This is a damned good job."[36] Indeed all the power a man can ask for is in the Presidency even if in reality and under ordinary circumstances much of that power is merely the power to persuade. Aside from power, there is, of course, the pride and the glory of the Presidency which has been described as "half royalty and half democracy that nobody knows whether to genuflect or spit." "The President is at liberty," Woodrow Wilson once said, "both in law and in conscience, to be as big a man as he can."[37] The latter statement is perhaps inspired by the fact that aside from the powers *expressly* provided in the Constitution, a President can also resort to the powers *implied* in that fundamental law.

Because of the difficulty of the office, not many Presidents have been successful. Success in an election is, after all, one thing, and success in the office is quite another. Even in the United States, only five past Presidents out of a total of 35 as of 1962, are considered "great" as shown in a 1962 poll of 75 experts taken by Harvard Professor   Arthur Schlesinger.   The five "giants" are listed as Abraham Lincoln, George Washington, Franklin D. Roosevelt, Woodrow Wilson and Thomas Jefferson, in the order of the experts' preference.[38]

Great events often determine the powers to be implied in the Constitution and, as a result, have much to do with fixing a President's place in history. And one common denominator among the so-called great Presidents is that "they never hesitated, in the face of emergencies, to use the vast 'implied' powers for the first time."[39] In other words the traits of boldness and innovativeness or creativity are common among them, qualities that helped them realize great achievements.

At this stage in the nation's history, however, any talk about presidential greatness may, at first blush, seem irrelevant. And yet it is not so. For the nation is faced not with routine, day-to-day problems but problems of such magnitude and delicateness as would threaten its very existence. To be sure, the problem, alone, of leftist insurgency has worsened and continues to do so. Its end is neither near nor foreseeable. It may be true that a good number of young people become insurgents not for ideological reasons but as a protest against official abuses and repressions. But it is equally true that many are lured by an exodus to the tranquil hills and serene forests because they have lost all hopes of improving the quality of their lives — many, as a matter of fact, turn to the mountains in search of a solution to their problem of how to make a living rather than how to live life. Insurgency is not a problem in isolation but a result of a collapsed and ever-sinking economy which makes the maintenance of life a critical problem by itself, and of an inequitable and often ruthless socio-political setup which gives the nation's poor hardly any hope for peace, justice and progress. The problem of insurgency is a great one that demands a great leader to resolve; its solution must start with an earnest, well thought out offensive on the economic frontier which may necessitate a presidential review of appointments of key officials invested with the vital function of formulating and administering the government's economic and financial policies. As the President's men in charge of policy decisions, they will determine in large measure the direction and thrust of the nation's economic development.

In addition it has become necessary to invite the President's attention to the worsening relationship between the people and the government, particularly with regard to the bureaucracy. While a victorious new regime has to dismantle the apparatuses and structures of the old in order to ensure its own stability, care must be observed that those institutions and persons innocent of any offenses of the past regime are spared and protected. After all, even in military warfare, where all is fair, it is not wise to destroy everything and annihilate everyone in a conquered city. Sun Tzu's words are apropos, that generally in war the best policy is to take a state intact, and to ruin it is inferior to this. "To capture the enemy's (state) is better than to destroy it . . . those skilled in war subdue the enemy's army without battle. They capture his cities without assaulting them and overthrow his state without protracted operations . . . This is the art of offensive strategy."[40] In like manner, removing or dismissing even Civil Service employees and officials on mere suspicion of serving the past regime — only to replace them with new ones of the present dispensation's choice — or capriciously or in a spirit of vengeance replacing even deserving elected officials with temporary officers of dubious qualifications, is not contributing to national reconciliation which is necessary before any meaningful economic progress could be realized. The February military revolt which succeeded with the support of the people was not intended to remove an abusive regime and to replace it with a new, equally abusive one. Official abuses and repressive action breed resentment — and insurgency.

AT the risk of inviting presidential displeasure, knowing that President Corazon Aquino herself was once quoted in the press as saying she resents unsolicited advice, the writer of these lines feels obligated to state that, as have been observed by some other writers recently, the President needs all the help she can have in administering the affairs of this country of 54 million, not a small country by any reckoning.

Accordingly, as a vital part of her job as President she must have access to all the information she needs. It is not general information per se that helps a President see personal stakes — nor what Richard

Neustadt calls bland amalgams, summaries or surveys. Rather, it is odds and ends of tangible detail that pieced together in his mind illuminate the underside of issues put before him. "To help himself he must reach out as widely as he can for every scrap of fact, opinion, gossip bearing on his interests and relationships as President," says Neustadt. "He must become his own director of his own central intelligence."[41] The President can never assure that anyone or any system will supply the bits and pieces he needs most; he must assure that much of what he needs will not be volunteered by his official advisers.

Presidents are always told (by their official advisers) that because they are busy and too burdened by "big things," they should leave details to others. This advice is dubious and must be considered with suspicion. For exposure to details of operation and of policy provides the frame of reference for details of information. This is the help that starts a man along the road to power. The information in his mind, rightly understood, alerts him to his personal stakes when choices come before him. One of the great American Presidents, Franklin D. Roosevelt, excelled in getting — and using — the right information. According to historian Arthur Schlesinger Jr.:

"The first task of an executive, as he evidently saw it, was to guarantee himself an effective flow of information and ideas . . . Roosevelt's persistent effort therefore was to check and balance information acquired through a myriad of private, informal, and unorthodox channels and espionage networks. At times he seemed almost to pit his personal sources against his public sources."[42]

Roosevelt's personal sources were his "enormous acquaintance" in various phases of national life and at various levels of government. Furthermore, he could depend on his gregarious wife Eleanor and her own variety of contacts. He was said to extend his acquaintanceships abroad, and in the war years Winston Churchill was among his personal sources. He deliberately exploited these relationships to widen his own range of information. He changed his sources as his interests changed, but no one who had ever interested him, according to Neustadt, was quite forgotten or immune to sudden use. His search for information was an "extraordinary, virtuoso" performance; besides, it was effective.[43]

All Presidents need assistants or aides, though great care must be exercised in choosing them. Former Presidents came to learn — to their grief — that their best appointments were still those they had known for years whose integrity had been tested rather than "the bright, swashbuckling, young crusading John-come-latelies who worked very hard during the campaign and hence were rewarded for their industry without much heed to their record of honesty or resistance to temptation.''[44]   To this one may add lack of ability or experience in the job or in dealing with the public. It is also smarter to prefer the old friends or followers with their known vices to new ones with their unknown virtues and vices.

Even in Malacañang Palace the President does not monopolize effective power. What a former aide of Franklin D. Roosevelt wrote once of Cabinet officers could be true of Cory Aquino's Cabinet:

"Half of a President's suggestions, which theoretically carry the weight of orders, can be safely forgotten by a Cabinet member. And if the President asks about a suggestion a second time, he can be told that it is being investigated. It he asks a third time, a wise Cabinet officer will give him at least part of what he suggests. But only occasionally, except about the most important matters, do Presidents ever get around to asking three times."[45]

This proclivity of concealing matters intended for presidential decision is true not only of Cabinet officers but also of a President's staff assistants. Moreover, some aides tend to have more vantage points than a selective memory. In the case of Sherman Adams, President Dwight Eisenhower's assistant, he became so powerful that he was no more dependent on the President than Eisenhower on him. The U.S. President was said to have declared "I need him," when Adams got involved in a gift-taking irregularity and delegated to the Assistant even the decision on his own departure. Was this not the case, too, with Ferdinand E. Marcos and his right-hand man Gen. Fabian C. Ver as pointed out by observers in media? Professor Neustadt says the Adams case is extreme but the tendency it illustrates is common enough. As he further observes, "Any aide who demonstrates to others that he has the President's consistent confidence and a consistent part in presidential business will acquire so much business on his own account that he becomes in some sense independent of his chief. Nothing in the Constitution keeps a well-placed aide from converting status into power of his own usable in some degree even against the President . . . The more an office-holder's status and his 'powers' stem from sources independent of the President, the stronger will be his potential pressure on the President."[46]

The lesson to be derived from this is that it is dangerous for the President to allow any of his assistants to have too much power for he can use that power against the President, his chief, himself. Pathetic indeed is a President who later becomes a victim of his own

Cabinet Minister or Assistant whom he has permitted to acquire excessive influence and power by entrusting him with too much confidence and status. Such a President is reduced to a pitiful figurehead, a ceremonial but powerless President who cannot accomplish anything worthy of the support and faith of the people.

These are not, however, the only dangers to the Presidency of Cory Aquino. One other danger is the possibility that one group of men or another to whom she feels beholden for her candidacy and eventual victory may take advantage of her sense of obligation and dependence and subtly influence presidential decisions. So-called intellectuals, successful business leaders, educators and representatives of motley groups who helped in her campaign and installation as President cannot be beyond having their interests to protect and advance by capitalizing on the lady President's avowed characteristics of trustfulness and compassion. Some may even make her feel so dependent on them — as Adams did President Eisenhower — that eventually she may no longer have the courage to say no to requests they may present to her. Dependence kills resistance.

It is a fact, not a fantasy, that groups, individuals and organizations exist with nothing paramount in their minds but their own vested interests. This is particularly true in public affairs, in politics. "Politicians," says Abraham Lincoln, himself a politician *and* statesman, "are a set of men who have interests aside from the interests of the people and who, to say the most of them, are, taken as a mass, at least one step removed from honest men."[47] Machiavelli earlier put it differently thus: "Politics have no relation to morals." In the hands therefore of a powerful political group, or even of a group of men temporarily bound together by a community of interests, an attractive personality is considered merely as an instrument for the attainment of selfish ends. Likewise, such lofty, idealistic terms and premises as justice, freedom, nationalism and democracy may be utilized by them as empty shibboleths and come-on gimmicks to lure the people. They then "retouch" or "remodel" the subject if necessary, and invest any amount and effort to make it a sensation in the market, using in the process the honed up skills of selected engineers of consent. In the United States, such groups are epitomized by the Tammany Hall, a powerful Democratic party political organization that for many years controlled New York City politics — a kind of American-style Mafia — and the Richard Daley Democratic Machine in Chicago. It is interesting to pose the question of whether a similar organization exists in Manila.

Aside from the purely political organizations, there are as is known far and wide other groups with their own peculiar interests to promote and protect — religious, economic, professional or even civic. It is to be naive to refuse to accept the existence of such interest- and pressure — groups. It is to be doubly naive to expect them not to collect returns from their investment.

The greater danger then to the Cory Aquino Presidency, as in all Presidencies before hers, is the possibility of certain groups whose interests may be opposed to the people's applying irresistible pressure on the President to influence her into making decisions that will aggravate the dichotomy and polarization of the nation.

PRESIDENT Aquino can be expected to resist the importunings of the selfish, whether individuals or groups. She has the keenness of mind and the clarity and range of vision demanded by the Presidency. And as we have seen earlier in this book she is gifted with the necessary determination, strength of will and stamina to pursue her vision for the nation. She is further fortified by her unfaltering faith in God. Furthermore she knows that as President she has the unconditional support of the majority of the people.

At this point it will be greatly instructive to note what four years experience in the Presidency of the Philippines had revealed to former President Diosdado Macapagal as the pitfalls, the dangers, that must be avoided by Presidents, in this case President Aquino. Mr. Macapagal enumerates them as follows:

1.   Isolation of a President from the people and from reality by a cordon of persons who will continually seek to please him and influence his decisions in the guise of promoting his success but in many cases are promoting their own interests. A President needs his best judgment in choosing his advisers, assistants and intimates on the basis of an efficient administration and what is best for the people.

2.   Tremendous temptation of graft and corruption. A President should steel himself against participating in graft and tolerating it, particularly by any member of his family.

3.   Difficult choice between the decisions of a statesman and a politician. A President should decide primarily on (the basis of) what is good for the people, irrespective of political consequences and secondarily only on considerations of his political position.

4.   Necessity for an awareness of the preponderant power of powerful and entrenched interests in our society which has created social injustice and prevented the equali-

zation of opportunities for the attainment of a better life by the greatest number and the consequent obstructive effect on national progress. A President must not be resigned before this awesome power.

5.   Need to possess a genuine recognition that the basic national problem being the age-long poverty of the masses, the alleviation of the plight of the common people must be given authentic emphasis. A President must be guided by an adequate social orientation towards justice to the underprivileged.

6.   An impulse to readily use presidential power without proper regard for the rule of law. Power is never to be used for its own sake. The virtue of power lies in its being used merely as a means for service. A President who is moved not by a consciousness of power but by a sense of duty is a blessing to the people.

7.   A choice of attitude towards criticism — whether to be tolerant about it or, out of a sense of power, to cow, suppress or corrupt it by one means or another.

8.   Possession of an attitude to accept fully the giving up of power at the end of the presidential term as adjudged by the people and to resist the opiate effect of power or its vanity for its perpetuation. Every President must bear in mind that in a democracy the exercise of power under a Constitution is inevitably for a limited period. Therefore, no thought should ever be entertained by a President to keep himself in power over the will of the people through the use of a segment of the physical forces of the state.[48]

It is interesting to note that President Macapagal enumerated these presidential pitfalls in his valedictory on December 29, 1965 at the end of his term on a nationwide radio-TV hookup. He had just lost the Presidency to Ferdinand E. Marcos then. In the morning of December 31, it might be added as another footnote to history, it was the young Ninoy Aquino who fetched Marcos from his residence in San Juan, Rizal (now Metro Manila) and escorted him to Malacañang to pick up President Macapagal for the inaugural ceremonies at the Luneta at noon of that day. After dropping off the incoming President at the Independence Grandstand, Macapagal proceeded to a friend's house where, with his personal and official family, he watched Marcos on television promise to "make this nation great again." It was the last time the nation witnessed any orderly transfer of power in the Presidency.

THE problems of the nation are too numerous and too great for any single President to solve satisfactorily. As Rome was not built in a day, so can no single individual expect to complete the task of building the nation within a single term in the Presidency, or even an entire lifetime; each President can merely add a stone to the edifice — and put it where it is most needed. In the case of President Cory Aquino there is no debating the point that the most pressing problem is economic recovery. This is not possible to achieve as long as the nation is being battered by insurgency, and insurgency will not abate unless its causes are removed. There can be no unified national effort without national reconciliation, but reconciliation is not possible as long as those who are in power are moved and motivated by hate rather than love, vengeance rather than forgiveness and compassion. Those who have suddenly found themselves invested with power, derived from the rise to power of Cory Aquino, must exercise great care and integrity in the use of that power. They must remind themselves that they sorely need humility and caution, and live by President Aquino's oft-repeated declaration that "I am very magnanimous in victory."

The American newspaper, *The Washington Post*, a self-confessed member in good standing of the "Marcos-must-go" school, nonetheless called for a little restraint on the part of people with similar sentiments who had been attacking those who had stayed more or less behind Marcos. In an editorial entitled "Who 'Won' the Philippines?" the newspaper observes:

"What happened in the Philippines was momentous and in many respects thrilling, and inspiring. It may remain momentous, but not be so thrilling and inspiring in the months ahead. Much is yet unsettled. The hold of the new leader is fragile. The possibility of further turmoil is very much alive."[49]

The *Post* adds that no matter how badly things under the new government could turn out, it would not retroactively justify the continuance of the Marcos regime in power. For there was no chance of things getting better, only worse, under his rule. "But this does not mean that Mrs. Aquino is guaranteed success or that her presidency is not in its own way very chancey . . .

"Our point is that, although much that is good and inspiring has happened, there has as yet been no outcome. And what if ultimately there is a bad one? What if Mrs. Aquino's effort comes to grief? Will that, in turn, be taken as proof that those who supported her are *in all similar arguments* wrong? Those who insist on reading a general doctrinal victory into Mrs. Aquino's particular pragmatic triumph are asking for trouble — and also, we think, denying the Philippines' new president the distinctiveness of her achievement."[50]

When Cory Aquino was campaigning for election she was presented to the people as the candidate who was the exact opposite of Ferdinand Marcos. A great number of Filipinos agreed and voted for her as the alternative to Marcos. She would be the President that Marcos was not: honest, God-fearing and loving, independent of cronies and strong pressure groups, just, nationalistic, moral. She would lead by example, and so would her chosen ministers, Palace assistants, leaders of the bureaucracy — her government, in a word.

As the new President she is trying her best to fulfill that promise, to prove that she is indeed the exact opposite of her predecessor. But alone she cannot do it; she needs the help of others, most particularly those whom she has gifted with authority, perquisites and power.

During the brief period since her installation as President, Mrs. Cory Aquino has seen her government shaken to its roots by certain acts of some of the men with whom she has chosen to share the power the people have invested upon her. The ambiguous labor policies of the Ministry of Labor and Employment, the controversial appointments of officers-in-charge of local government offices, the explosive issue of continuous sequestration and freezing of assets or accounts of firms suspected of having been controlled by the former President and his associates, and the endless factionalism of the extremely diverse forces right in her Cabinet seem never to cease rocking the still-fragile foundations of her regime. Moreover, perhaps largely as a result of the absence of a clear and united vision in the leadership, those forces outside of the government are emboldened to directly challenge its power, as evidenced by the increased insurgent activities and the July 6 aborted installation of a new government by former Senator Arturo M. Tolentino.

Similar actions in the future can be averted and controlled by President Aquino as soon as she stops reigning and begins to rule; as soon as she begins to show that she is the Head of State and the nation's Chief Executive at the same time. She still enjoys tremendous, even unprecedented, public support and faith. She must use both now since public goodwill and popular faith are not hoardable assets but depreciate over time when not utilized. Now is the time to remind her assistants, torn they may be by a wide diversity of interests and acute appetite for power, that she is *the* President, their leader, and that she alone controls the levers of command.

Appendix "A"

INAUGURAL ADDRESS OF PRESIDENT CORAZON C. AQUINO
DELIVERED ON FEBRUARY 25, 1986

BELOVED brothers and sisters:

I want to thank you for the power that you've bestowed on me today and I promise that I will offer all that I can to serve you.

It is fitting and proper that if the rights and liberty of our people were taken away at midnight 14 years ago, the people should formally recover those lost rights and liberties in the full light of day.

Ninoy believed that only the united friends of a people would suffice to overthrow a tyranny so inborn and so well-organized. It took the brutal murder of Ninoy to bring about that unity so strong and the phenomenon of people power.

That power, that strength of the people, has ended the dictatorship, protected the honorable military who have chosen freedom, and today has established a government dedicated to the protection and meaningful fulfillment of the people's rights and liberty.

We became exiles in our own land — we, Filipinos who are at home only in freedom — when Marcos destroyed the republic 14 years ago. Through courage and unity, through power of the people, we are home again. And now, I would like to appeal to everybody to work for national reconciliation, which is what Ninoy came home for.

I would like to repeat that I am very magnanimous in victory, so I call on all of those countrymen of ours who are not yet with us to join us at the earliest possible time so that we can rebuild our beautiful country.

Like in the campaign, I would like to end with a plea to you to continue to pray. Pray to the Lord to help us, especially during these difficult days.

Appendix "B"

PROCLAMATION NO. 1

SOVEREIGNTY resides in the people and all government authority emanates from them.

On the basis of the people's mandate clearly manifested last February 7, I and Salvador H. Laurel are taking power in the name and by the will of the Filipino people as President and Vice President, respectively.

By the powers vested in me by the people, I ask all those in the civil service to stay in place. Those who have not done anything against the interests of the people have nothing to fear. I ask that they preserve all records with scrupulous care.

The people expect a reorganization of government. Merit will be rewarded. As a first step to restore confidence in public administration, I expect all appointive public officials to submit their courtesy resignations beginning with the members of the Supreme Court.

I pledge to do justice to the numerous victims of human rights violations.

Consistent with the demands of the sovereign people, we pledge a government dedicated to uphold truth and justice, and morality in government, freedom and democracy.

To help me run the government, I have issued Executive Order No. 1 dated February 25, 1986 appointing key Cabinet ministers and creating certain task forces.

I ask our people not to relax but to be even more vigilant in this one moment of triumph. The Motherland cannot thank them enough. Yet, we all realize that more is required of each and everyone of us to redeem our promises and prove to create a truly *just society* for our people.

This is just the beginning. The same spirit which animated our campaigns, and has led to our triumph, will once more prevail, by the power of the people and by the grace of God.

Done in the City of Manila, this 25th day of February in the Year of our Lord, nineteen hundred and eighty six.

Appendix "C"

MALACANANG
Manila
BY THE PRESIDENT OF THE
PHILIPPINES

Proclamation No. 2

Proclaiming the Lifting of the Suspension of the Privilege of the Writ of Habeas Corpus Throughout the Philippines.

WHEREAS, the then President Ferdinand E. Marcos, issuing Proclamation No. 2045 dated 17 January 1981 and Proclamation No. 2045-A dated 23 July 1983, suspended the privilege of the writ of habeas corpus in the two autonomous regions of Mindanao and in all other places with respect to the persons detained "for all cases involving the crimes of insurrection, rebellion, subversion, conspiracy or proposal to commit such crimes, sedition, conspiracy to commit sedition, inciting to sedition, and for all other crimes or offenses committed by them in furtherance or on the occasion thereof, or incident thereto, or in connection therewith, such as but not limited to offenses involving economic sabotage, illegal assemblies, illegal associations, tumults and other disturbances of public orders, unlawful use of means of publication and unlawful utterances, and alarms and scandals, or with respect to any person whose arrest or detention was, in the judgment of the President, required by public safety as a means to repel or quell the rebellion in the country;"

WHEREAS, the proclamations and decrees mentioned and all the related decrees, instructions, orders and rules were not warranted by the requirements of public safety since the existing rebellion could have been contained by government sincerity at reforms, by peaceful negotiations and reconciliation, and by steadfast devotion to the rule of law;

WHEREAS, instead of serving its purpose of suppressing the rebellion and other threats to national security, the suspension of the privilege of the writ of habeas corpus drove many to the hills and fanned the conspiracy to overthrow the government by violence and force; and

WHEREAS, the Filipino people have established a new government bound to the ideals of genuine liberty and freedom for all;

NOW, THEREFORE, I, CORAZON C. AQUINO, President of the Philippines, by virtue of the powers vested in me by the Constitution and the Filipino people, do hereby revoke Proclamation Nos. 2045 and 2045-A, and do hereby lift the suspension of the privilege of the writ of habeas corpus so that this guardian of liberty and freedom may be available to all.

IN WITNESS WHEREOF, I have hereunto set my hand and caused the seal of the Republic of the Philippines to be affixed to this proclamation.

Done in the City of Manila, this 2nd day of March in the year of Our Lord, nineteen hundred and eighty-six.

By the President:

(Sgd.) CORAZON C. AQUINO

(Sgd.) JOKER P. ARROYO
Executive Secretary

Appendix "D"

MALACANANG
Manila
BY THE PRESIDENT OF THE
PHILIPPINES

Proclamation No. 3

Declaring a national policy to implement the reforms mandated by the people, protecting their basic rights, adopting a provisional Constitution and providing for an orderly transition to a government under a new Constitution.

WHEREAS, the new government was installed through a direct exercise of the power of the Filipino people assisted by units of the New Armed Forces of the Philippines;

WHEREAS, the heroic action of the people was done in defiance of the provisions of the 1973 Constitution, as amended;

WHEREAS, the direct mandate of the people as manifested by their extraordinary action demands the complete reorganization of the government, restoration of democracy, protection of basic rights, rebuilding of confidence in the entire governmental system, eradication of graft and corruption, restoration of peace and order, maintenance of the supremacy of civilian authority over the military and the transition to a government under a New Constitution in the shortest time possible;

WHEREAS, during the period of transition to a New Constitution it must be guaranteed that the government will respect basic human rights and fundamental freedoms;

WHEREFORE, I, CORAZON C. AQUINO, President of the Philippines, by virtue of the powers vested in me by the sovereign mandate of the people, do hereby promulgate the following Provisional Constitution:

PROVISIONAL CONSTITUTION
OF
THE REPUBLIC OF THE PHILIPPINES

ARTICLE I
ADOPTION OF CERTAIN PROVISIONS
OF THE 1973 CONSTITUTION,
AS AMENDED

SECTION 1. The provisions of ARTICLE I (National Territory), ARTICLE III (Citizenship), ARTICLE IV (Bill of Rights), ARTICLE V (Duties and Obligations of Citizens), and ARTICLE VI (Suffrage) of the 1973 Constitution, as amended, remain in force and effect and are hereby adopted in toto as part of this Provisional Constitution.

SECTION 2. The provisions of ARTICLE II (Declaration of Principles and State Policies), ARTICLE VII (The President), ARTICLE X (The Judiciary), ARTICLE XI (Local Government), ARTICLE XII (The Constitutional Commissions), ARTICLE XIII (Accountability of Public Officers), ARTICLE XIV (The National Economy and Patrimony of the Nation), ARTICLE XV (General Provisions) of the 1973 Constitution, as amended, are hereby adopted as part of this Provisional Constitution, insofar as they are not inconsistent with the provisions of this Proclamation.

SECTION 3. ARTICLE VIII (The Batasang Pambansa), ARTICLE IX (The Prime Minister and the Cabinet), ARTICLE XVI (Amendments), ARTICLE XVII (Transitory Provisions) and all amendments thereto are deemed superseded by this Proclamation.

ARTICLE II

THE PRESIDENT,
THE VICE PRESIDENT, AND THE CABINET

SECTION 1. Until a legislature is elected and convened under a new Constitution, the President shall continue to exercise legislative power.

The President shall give priority to measures to achieve the mandate of the people to:

    a)   Completely reorganize the government and eradicate unjust and oppressive structures, and all iniquitous vestiges of the previous regime;

    b)   Make effective the guarantees of civil, political, human, social, economic and cultural rights and freedoms of the Filipino people, and provide remedies against violations thereof;

    c)   Rehabilitate the economy and promote the nationalist aspirations of the people;

    d)   Recover ill-gotten properties amassed by the leaders and supporters of the previous regime and protect the interest of the people through orders of sequestration or freezing of assets of accounts;

    e)   Eradicate graft and corruption in government and punish those guilty thereof; and,

    f)   Restore peace and order, settle the problem of insurgency, and pursue national reconciliation based on justice.

SECTION 2. The President shall be assisted by a Cabinet which shall be composed of Ministers with or without portfolio who shall be appointed by the President. They shall be accountable to and hold office at the pleasure of the President.

SECTION 3. The President shall have control of and exercise general supervision over all local governments.

SECTION 4. In case of permanent vacancy arising from death, incapacity or resignation of the President, the Vice President shall become President. In case of death, permanent incapacity, or resignation of the Vice President, the Cabinet shall choose from among themselves the Minister with portfolio who shall act as President.

SECTION 5. The Vice President may be appointed Member of the Cabinet and may perform such other functions as may be assigned to him by the President.

SECTION 6. The President, the Vice President, and the Members of the Cabinet shall be subject to the disabilities provided for in Section 8, Article VII, and in Sections 6 and 7, Article IX, respectively, of the 1973 Constitution, as amended.

ARTICLE III
GOVERNMENT REORGANIZATION

SECTION 1. In the reorganization of the government, priority shall be given to measures to promote economy, efficiency, and the eradication of graft and corruption.

SECTION 2. All elective and appointive officials and employees under the 1973 Constitution shall continue in office until otherwise provided by proclamation or executive order or upon the designation or appointment and qualification of their successors, if such is made within a period of one year from February 25, 1986.

PROCLAMATION

SECTION 3. Any public office or employee separated from the service as a result of the reorganization effected under this Proclamation shall, if entitled under the laws then in force, receive the retirement and other benefits accruing thereunder.

SECTION 4. The records, equipment, buildings, facilities and other properties of all government offices shall be carefully preserved. In case any office or body is abolished or reorganized pursuant to this Proclamation, its funds and properties shall be transferred to the office or body to which its powers, functions, and responsibilities substantially pertain.

ARTICLE IV
EXISTING LAWS

SECTION 1. All existing laws, decrees, executive orders, proclamations, letters of instruction, implementing rules and regulations, and other executive issuances not inconsistent with this Proclamation shall remain operative until amended, modified, or repealed by the President or the regular legislative body to be established under a New Constitution.

SECTION 2. The President may review all contracts, concessions, permits, or other forms of privileges for the exploration, development, exploitation, or utilization of natural resources entered into, granted, issued, or acquired before the date of this Proclamation and when the national interest requires, amend, modify, or revoke them.

ARTICLE V
ADOPTION OF A NEW CONSTITUTION

SECTION 1. Within sixty (60) days from date of this Proclamation, a Commission shall be appointed by the President to draft
a New Constitution. The Commission shall be composed of not less
than thirty (30) nor more than fifty (50) natural-born citizens of
the Philippines, of recognized probity, known for their independence, nationalism and patriotism. They shall be chosen by the
President after consultation with various sectors of society.

SECTION 2. The Commission shall complete its work within
as short a period as may be consistent with the need both to hasten
the return of normal constitutional government and to draft a document truly reflective of the ideals and aspirations of the Filipino
people.

SECTION 3. The Commision shall conduct public hearings
to insure that the people will have adequate participation in the
formulation of the New Constitution.

SECTION 4. The plenary sessions of the Commission shall be
public and fully recorded.

SECTION 5. The New Constitution shall be presented by the
Commission to the President who shall fix the date for the holding
of a plebiscite. It shall become valid and effective upon ratification
by a majority of the votes cast in such plebiscite which shall be held
within a period of sixty (60) days following its submission to the
President.

ARTICLE VI
HOLDING OF ELECTIONS

SECTION 1. National elections shall be held as may be
provided by the New Constitution.

SECTION 2. Local elections shall be held on a date to be
determined by the President which shall not be earlier than the
date of the plebiscite for the ratification of the New Constitution.

ARTICLE VII
EFFECTIVE DATE

SECTION 1. This Proclamation shall take effect upon its promulgation by the President.

SECTION 2. Pursuant to the letter and spirit of this Proclamation, a consolidated official text of the Provisional Constitution shall be promulgated by the President and published in English and Pilipino in the Official Gazette and in newspapers of general circulation to insure widespread dissemination.

DONE in the City of Manila, this 25th day of March, in the year of Our Lord, Nineteen Hundred and Eighty-Six.

By the President:
(Sgd.) CORAZON C. AQUINO

(Sgd.) JOKER P. ARROYO
          Executive Secretary

Footnotes

ONE

1.   Max Buan, "Parting Shot," *People's Journal*, April 4, 1986. According to this account, members of the "World Kho-Co Family Association" called on President Aquino in Malacanang in April 1986 during their Third Biennial International Convention held in Manila, the first world conference held in the city since February 1986, with member-delegates coming from Hongkong, Taiwan, Thailand, Singapore, Malaysia, Indonesia, the United States and Canada. They traced blood kinship with Mrs. Aquino and donated P500,000 as a gesture of support for her fledgling administration with a pledge to donate more.

2.   Manuel L. Quezon, *The Good Fight*, autobiography; Filipiniana Reprint Series, Renato Constantino, Series Director; Cacho Hermanos, Inc., Mandaluyong, Metro Manila, 1985.

3.   *Philconsa Journal*, Manila, June-July 1975, page 41.

4.   *Philconsa, 1974 Annual*, Manila, page 221.

5.   "Talk of the Town," *Bulletin Today*, Manila, March 8, 1986.

6.   Cristina P. del Carmen Pastor, "Jose Cojuangco Jr.: King-Maker of the Opposition? ", *Malaya Sunday Magazine*, Manila, January 20, 1985, page 12.

7.   Lorna Kalaw-Tirol, "On Ninoy's Birthday, Cory Talks About Her Husband and Best Friend," Philippine *Panorama*, Manila, November 25, 1984, page 5.

8.   Del Carmen-Pastor, *ibid.*

9.   Arnold Atadero, "Cory relative the power behind the presidency? "*Midday*, March 24, 1986, page 1. The story claims that "a close relative of President Corazon Aquino was tagged today the 'power behind the throne' in the new government," quoting "highly placed sources" that the "President's relative is dictating on which officials to replace governors or mayors." The brother is not identified by name in the story but is identified in the column of Jose J. Burgos Sr., "Then and Now," *Malaya*, March 28, 1986 as Jose Cojuangco Jr.

10.   Marcia E. Sandoval, "You've Come a Long Way, Cory," *Sunday Inquirer Magazine*, March 9, 1986, pages 4-5.

11.   *Ibid.*, page 5. The following names appear in a partial list of Cory Aquino's graduating class from St. Scholastica's College: Doris Sapinoso, Fe Palo, Julieta Ramirez, Angela Perez, Carina Tancinco, Leticia Tan, Gloria Lucas, Lilia Lacson, Elvira and Mercy Arrastia, Angelita Trinidad, Norma Labrador, Angelita Kairuz, Betty Nassr, Teresa Torraya, Carmen Bouffard, Teresita Dalupan, Emma Tordesillas, Pilar Cinco, Gloria Lacson, Teresita Borronco, Eliza Toda, Lourdes and Concepcion Delgado, Solita Romans, Eumelia Concepcion, Alice Garcia, Amelita Adriano, Maria Clara Badillo, Celina Olaguer, Celia Elizalde, Lourdes Pilares, Carmen Reinares, Amelia and Magdalena Vitug.

12.   *Associated Press*, New York, "US schoolmates of Aquino jubilant," *Malaya*, February 28, 1986, page 6.

TWO

1.   Lorna Kalaw-Tirol, *op. cit.*, page 12.

2.   Francis X. Clines, "Aquino: Putting it together," *Philippines Daily Express*, May 19, 1986, pages 2, 11.

3.   Tirol, *ibid.*

4.   See this author's *Imelda Romualdez Marcos: Heart of the Revolution*, J. Kriz Publishing, Quezon City, 1980.

5.   *Ibid.*
6.   Tirol, *ibid.*
7.   See President Aquino's inaugural speech, Appendix "A".
8.   Clines, *ibid.*
9.   *Ibid.*
10.   Lupita Aquino Kashiwahara, "Filipino women have climbed the Mt. Everest of local politics," *Sunday Magazine,* Manila, June 15, 1986, pages 8-9.
11.   *Ibid.*
12.   *Ibid.*

THREE

1.   "The Remarkable Rise of a Widow in Yellow," *Newsweek Magazine,* March 10, 1986, page 17.
2.   Tirol, *op. cit.*
3.   Quoted in the *Manila Bulletin* (formerly *Bulletin Today),* April 10, 1986, pages 1, 8.
4.   Margie T. Logarta, "Living with power," *The Manila Times,* March 21, 1986, page 13.
5.   Nick Joaquin. "The Year of Mourning Ends for Cory Aquino," *Mr. & Ms. Magazine,* Manila, August 17, 1984.
6.   Luis R. Mauricio, "The Man Behind the Myth, and Why the Myth Was Born," *Veritas,* Manila, August 19, 1984, page 14.
7.   Nick Joaquin, *ibid.,* pages 5-9.
8.   *Ibid.*
9.   *Ibid.*

FOUR

1.   Graham Lovell, *Reuter,* "Cory Aquino's rise to power," *The Manila Times,* February 27, 1986.
2.   Napoleon G. Rama, "Go! Go! Go!", *Philippines Free Press,* March 30, 1968, page 2.
3.   *Veritas,* Manila, "Promise and Fulfillment," August 19, 1984, page 4.
4.   Luis R. Mauricio, *op. cit.*
5.   Rama, *ibid.*
6.   *Ibid.*
7.   *Ibid.*
8.   "Politics and Justice," *Philippines Free Press,* August 10, 1968.
9.   "Outstanding Senators," *Philippines Free Press,* July 27, 1968, pages 7, 170.
10.   *Ibid.*
11.   *Ibid.*
12.   For a narration of the events from January 26-31, 1970, see this author's *Marcos the Revolutionary,* J. Kriz Publishing, Quezon City, 1973.
13.   Teodoro L. Locsin Jr., "Man of the Year," *Philippines Free Press,* January 8, 1972, pages 2, 47.
14.   *Ibid.*
15.   Quijano de Manila, "Ninoy on the Bad Scene that's Central Luzon," *Free Press,* August 15, 1970, pages 2, 68-69.
16.   *Free Press,* "Man of the Year," *ibid.*

FIVE

1.   Statement of the President on the Proclamation of Martial Law in the Philippines, September 21, 1972. Reprinted in *Marcos the Revolutionary, op. cit.,* Appendix A.
2.   Jovito R. Salonga, "I Remember Ninoy," *Veritas,* Manila, December 1, 1985, page 12.
3.   *Ibid.*
4.   Primitivo Mijares, *Conjugal Dictatorship,* as serialized in *Malaya,* Manila in early 1986.
5.   Lorna Kalaw-Tirol, "Ninoy's Widow Comes into Her Own," Philippine *Panorama,* December 2, 1984.
6.   "The Remarkable Rise of a Widow in Yellow," *Newsweek Magazine,* March 10, 1986, page 17.
7.   Ambeth R. Ocampo, "Cory-Mania," *Weekend Magazine,* Manila, March 23, 1986, p. 12.
8.   Mijares, *ibid.,* in *Malaya,* April 18, 1986, page 10.
9.   Salonga, *ibid.,* page 12.
10.   Mijares, *ibid.,*
11.   *Heart of the Revolution,* "Epilogue as Prologue," pages i-vii.
12.   *Ibid.*
13.   Joaquin, op.cit., "The Year of Mourning . . ."
14.   Associated Press, "Aquino Estate for Sale," *Malaya,* April 5, 1986, page 1. Also, "The Remarkable Rise of a Widow in Yellow," *Newsweek Magazine,* March 10, 1986, page 17, *ibid.*
15.   *Newsweek, ibid.*
16.   Aurora Magdalena, "Boston: A Camelot for Ninoy and Cory," *Veritas,* August 19, 1984, page 12.
17.   *Ibid.*
18.   Tirol, "On Ninoy's Birthday . . .", *op. cit.*
19.   *Ibid.*
20.   *Ibid.*
21.   Jesselyn C. dela Cruz, "August Thoughts from the Aquinos," *Veritas,* August 19, 1984.
22.   *Ibid.*
23.   Aurora Magdalena, *ibid.*
24.   Aurora Magdalena, "How Ninoy's U.S. Friends Remember Him," *Veritas,* December 2, 1984.
25.   *Ibid.*
26.   *Ibid.*

SIX

1.   See Gerald N. Hill and Kathleen Thompson Hill, *Aquino Assassination,* Hilltop Publishing Company, Sonoma, California, 1983, with the cooperation of Steve Psinakis.
2.   *Ibid.,* page 15.
3.   *Ibid.,* page 18.
4.   Nick Joaquin, "The Year of Mourning . . .", *op. cit.*
5.   *Ibid.*
6.   *Ibid.*
7.   Hill and Hill, *ibid.,* page 26.
8.   *Ibid.*

9.   *Ibid.*
10.   *Joaquin,* ibid.
11.   *Ibid.*

SEVEN

1.   "The Conscience of the Filipino," *Philippines Free Press,* February 7, 1986, pages 9, 20. Like all other major publications, the *Free Press* was shut down by the government upon the declaration of martial law in 1972.

2.   Prepared — but unread — arrival statement of Ninoy Aquino at the Manila International Airport on August 21, 1983. *Cf.* Chapter 5.

3.   *Ibid.*

4.   *Ibid.*

5.   Luis R. Mauricio, "The Man Behind . . .", *op. cit.*

6.   Salvador P. Lopez, "In the Light of Truth," *Veritas,* January 19, 1984, page 21.

7.   Among the numerous important appointments made by President Corazon C. Aquino were those of Bienvenido Tan Jr., as Commissioner of Internal Revenue, Andres Narvasa as a Justice of the Supreme Court, and Dante Santos as President of the Philippine Air Lines.

8.   President Aquino named Aquilino Pimentel Jr. as Minister of Local Governments as soon as she assumed office. Pimentel immediately became a highly controversial figure when he started designating officers-in-charge for towns, cities and provinces, replacing those who had been elected to the positions but whose terms of office, he said, had expired.

9.   Alice C. Villadolid, "The Tarmac Tale: How the Conspiracy Was Unmasked," *Mr. & Ms. Special Edition,* October 4, 1984.

10.   *Ibid.*

11.   According to some accounts in the press, what former President Marcos told the Agrava Board members upon receiving their majority report different from their Chairman's was, "I hope you will be able to live with your conscience, with what you have done."

12.   Reprinted from *Mr. & Ms. Special Edition, ibid.,* page 8.

EIGHT

1.   J.R. Alibutud, "No need for Midas: Cory has her millions," *Mr. & Ms. Special Edition,* November 29–December 5, 1985, page 11.

2.   See also Jimmy Vicente, "Of Myths and (wo) men in the Opposition," *Veritas,* December 15, 1985, pages 12-13.

3.   Marlen Ronquillo, "Cory-Doy Compromise Seen, But Backers Still Bickering," *Malaya,* December 1, 1985, page. 1.

4.   Belinda Olivares Cunanan, "Opposition Bets: To Each His Own," *Mr. & Ms. Special Edition,* November 29-December 5, 1985, pages 9-10.

5.   *Ibid.*

6.   Belinda Olivares Cunanan, "Believe It or Not: Cory, Doy Unite," *Mr. & Ms. Special Edition,* December 13-19, 1985, pages 6-7.

7.   *Ibid.*

8.   Sheila S. Coronel, "Politics: "Twas a Year of Cliffhangers," Philippine *Panorama,* January 5, 1986, pages 24-27.

9.   Alex Dacanay, " 'Trial of the Century' Ends in Acquittal," *Panorama,* January 5, 1986, pages 28-29.

NINE

1.   These and all other national election figures in this chapter are taken from the Commission on Elections.

2.   Richard M. Nixon, *Six Crises,* quoted in Len O.'Connor, *Clout: Mayor Daley and His City.* Avon Books, New York, 1975, page 50.

3.   Comelec, *ibid.*

4.   Sun Tzu, *The Art of War,* excerpted in Sir Basil Liddell Hart, *The Sword and the Pen,* Thomas Y. Crowell Co., New York, 1976, pages 27-30.

5.   Much of the background materials for this chapter appeared in a series of three articles by this author entitled "Battle of Giants: Marcos V. Aquino," in the *Times Journal* daily newspaper, Manila, on February 3, 4 and 5, 1986. Also, *cf., Marcos the Revolutionary, op. cit.*

6.   As quoted in *ibid.*

7.   Comelec.

8.   Sun Tzu, *ibid.*

9.   Adrian Cristobal, Spokesman of former President Marcos, as quoted in "Battle of Giants," *ibid.*

10   *Valencia: Thirty Years in Philippine Journalism,* D. H. Soriano, ed., Front Page Newsmakers, Inc., 1976.

11.   *Philippine Daily Inquirer,* Manila, January 2, 1986.

12.   *Ibid.*

TEN

1.   Teodoro Benigno, "The Men Behind Cory Aquino," *Agence France Presse, Bulletin Today, February* 10, 1986, page 5.

2.   One of the first appointees in the Cabinet of President Corazon Aquino was Jaime Ongpin as Minister of Finance. He was reported to have influenced Mrs. Aquino in appointing Jose B. Fernandez as Central Bank Governor although he had served previously as CB Governor under President Marcos, Bienvenido Tan Jr., as Commissioner of Internal Revenue, and Jesus Estanislao as Governor of the Development Bank of the Philippines, as well as others with something to do wihh the nation's economy.

3.   President Aquino appointed Aflredo Bengzon as Minister of Health and Jose Antonio Gonzalez as Minister of Tourism. She later appointed Joaquin Bernas, S.J., president of the Ateneo de Manila University, as a delegate to the Constitutional Commission.

4.   Former Supreme Court Justice Cecilia Munoz-Palma gave up her role as a close adviser to Cory Aquino after the latter abolished the Batasang Pambansa over her objection but was appointed in May 1986 as a delegate to the Constitutional Commission, of which she was eventually elected unanimously as president. Neptali Gonzales was among the first Cabinet appointees – as Minister of Justice.

5.   T. Benigno, *ibid.*

6.   Napoleon G. Rama, "Dangers, opportunities of governing a nation," *Philippine Daily Inquirer,* March 29, 1986, page 14.

7.   Filosopo Tasio, "Media Monitor," *Daily Express,* February 3, 1985, page 5.

8.   Alfonso P. Policarpio, "Business of Truth, " *Malaya,* January 25, 1986, page 4.

9.   Doreen G. Yu, "The Cardinal of the Revolution," an interview with Cardinal Sin, *Sunday Inquirer Magazine,* April 13, 1986, pages 8-10.

10.   Sheila S. Coronel, "The snap Elections: Unpredictability is the name of the Game," Philippine *Panorama,* December 22, 1985, pages 12, 14-21.
11.   *Ibid.*
12.   *Ibid.* Marcelo Fernan was appointed by President Aquino as an Associate Justice of the Supreme Court.
13.   Quoted in Alfonso P. Policarpio, "A Business of Truth," *Malaya,* December 17, 1985, page 4.
14.   Ellen Tordesillas and Benjie Guevara, "Beyond the Crowds and Cheers, Campaigning is a Lot of Hassle," *Malaya,* January 6, 1986, page 12.
15.   *Associated Press,* "Leyteños Agog Over Cory, Give 'Thumbs Down' to FM," *Malaya,* January 5, 1986, page 8.
16.   Teodoro Benigno, *Agence France Presse,* "Halfway through campaign, FM faces foe's groundswell," *Malaya,* January 9, 1986, page 1.
17.   *Ibid.*
18.   Ellen Tordesillas, "Unido bets swear in 74 defectors in Naga," *Malaya,* January 12, 1986, pages 1, 8.
19.   Elias Baquero, ".5-M greet Cory, Doy in Cebu City," *Malaya,* January 12, 1986, pages 1, 8.
20.   *Associated Press* in *Malaya, ibid.*
21.   *Ibid.*
22.   Arturo A. Borjal & Belinda Olivares-Cunanan. "How Rotarians went for Cory," *Philippine Daily Inquirer,* January 27, 1986, page 5.
23.   *Ibid.*
24.   Belinda Olivares-Cunanan, "Cory to FM: 'Isang balota ka lang! '", *Daily Inquirer,* January 27, 1986, page 2.
25.   Belinda Olivares-Cunanan, "A Day with Cory in Cavite," *Daily Inquirer,* January 30, 1986, page 5.
26.   *Ibid.*
27.   *Ibid.*

ELEVEN

1.   Butch Fernandez, "Did Marcos Collapse? " *Malaya,* January 17, 1986, page 1.
2.   Ellen Tordesillas, "Marcos says he stumbled in Dagupan," *Malaya,* January 19, 1986, page 1.
3.   Ben Evardone and Butch Fernandez, "KBL allays fears on martial law," *Malaya,* January 10, 1986; and Jimmy Montejo, "Post-election martial rule? " *Malaya, ibid.*
4.   "Marcos will cling to power," *Associated Press, Malaya, ibid.,* page 1.
5.   John Sharkey, "FM link with Japanese war collaborators bared," *Malaya,* January 26, 1986, page 1.
6.   *Agence France Presse,* "FM's WW II arrest by US bared," *Malaya,* January 28, 1986.
7.   "Dewey Dee bares all," 'I was FM's front man,' ", *Malaya,* February 1, 1986, page 1.
8.   Joey Salgado, "Marcos not at Bessang – RP War vet," *Malaya, ibid.,* page 1.
9.   Quoted in *Bulletin Today,* January 27, 1986, page 1.
10.   Jose Concepcion Jr., head of the Namfrel which actively participated in the February 7, 1986 presidential elections as the citizens' arm of the Comelec, was appointed by President Aquino to her Cabinet as Minister of Trade and Industry. The appointment – and Concepcion's acceptance – was widely criticized as contrary to the "independent posture" of Concepcion and the Namfrel. Concepcion's position in the Namfrel was

later assumed by his deputy, Christian Monsod.

11.   "Separate OQC for Comelec, Namfrel," *Malaya*, February 2, 1986, page 8.

12.   "Ver, AFP men get election duties," *Malaya*, February 4, 1986, page 1.

13.   "Snap poll: 47 killed," *Daily Inquirer*, February 5, 1986, page 1.

14.   "PC-INP to support Cory if she wins snap," *Daily Inquirer*, February 5, 1986. page 1.

15.   "Cory landslide," *Daily Inquirer*, February 5, 1986, page 1.

16.   "Metro Manilans vow support to UNIDO bets," *Malaya*, February 5, 1986, pages 1, 8.

17.   Vicente B. Foz, "Aquino, Laurel sum up issues," *Bulletin Today*, February 5, 1986, page 1.

18.   Willie Ng, "FM Calls for talks on US bases, urges reconciliation at rally," *Bulletin Today*, February 6, 1986, page 1.

19.   From reports of C. Valmoria Jr., and Deedee M. Siytangco, *Bulletin Today*, February 6, 1986, page 1.

20.   As reported by Larry Sipin, "Aquino winds up campaign for Palace," *Malaya*, February 6, 1986, page 8. Text of Cory Aquino's election eve statement is found in the *Daily Inquirer*, February 6, 1986, page 2, "We have won — Cory."

TWELVE

1.   As reported in *Bulletin Today*, February 7, 1986, page 1.

2.   C. Valmoria Jr., "Nation goes to polls today,'" *Bulletin Today*, February 7, 1986, pages 1, 10.

3.   *Bulletin Today, ibid.*

4.   From individual reports of Vicente B. Foz, Marcia C. Rodriguez and Willie Ng, *Bulletin Today*, February 8, 1986, starting from page 1.

5.   "Duvalier of Haiti flees," *Bulletin Today*, February 8, 1986. This case struck a parallel with that of Ferdinand E. Marcos and was mentioned by Cory Aquino in a campaign speech in Tarlac.

6.   *Bulletin Today, ibid.*

7.   From individual reports by C. Valmoria Jr., Willie Ng and Vicente B. Foz, and the *Associated Press*, in *Bulletin Today*, February 9, 1986, page 1.

8.   From *Bulletin Today*, February 10, 1986, using reports by Vicente B. Foz and C. Valmoria, Jr.

9.   "Anomalies may stop Cory's win," *Malaya*, February 10, 1986.

10.   *Malaya, ibid.*

11.   From individual reports of C. Valmoria Jr., Vicente B. Foz and Olaf S. Giron, *Bulletin Today*, February 11, 1986.

12.   See reports of Willie Ng, C. Valmoria Jr., and Rey P. Naval of the *Philippine News Agency*, *Bulletin Today*, February 12, 1986.

13.   Larry Sipin, "'Top Laban leader slain," *Malaya*, February 12, 1986.

14.   *Associated Press* report from Washington, *Bulletin Today*, February 13, 1986.

15.   See *Malaya*, February 13, 1986.

16.   See reports by C. Valmoria Jr. and Willie Ng, *Bulletin Today*, February 14, 1986.

17.   Deedee M. Siytangco, "Bishops assail poll frauds," *Bulletin Today*, February 15, 1986, page 1.

18.   *Malaya*, February 15, 1986, page 1.

19.   Larry Sipin and Carlos Hidalgo, "Daily protests readied," *Malaya*, Feb. 15,

1986, page 1.

20.   Figures from *Malaya's* scoreboard, February 15, 1986.

21.   C. Valmoria Jr., "FM, Tolentino proclaimed by Batasan," *Bulletin Today*, February 16, 1986, page 1.

22.   Philippine *Daily Inquirer*, February 16, 1986.

23.   From reports of the *Malaya* and the *Daily Express*, February 17, 1986.

24.   "Reagan statement on polls," *Malaya*, February 17, 1986, page 3.

25.   *Agence France Presse* report, *Malaya, ibid.*, page 2.

26.   *Agence France Presse*, "Lugar urges new election," *Malaya*, February 18, 1986.

27.   *Ibid.*

28.   From individual reports of *Bulletin Today* reporters, February 18, 1986.

29.   See *Philippine Daily Inquirer*, February 20, 1986; *cf.* Note No. 5, *supra.*

30.   *United Press International* report from Manila, *Bulletin Today*, February 23, 1986, page 1.

THIRTEEN

1.   Willie Ng, "FM warns of more 'forceful measures,'" *Bulletin Today*, February 23, 1986, page 1.

2.   Millet M. Mananquil, *Daily Express*, March 2, 1986, page 2, "The nightmare is over."

3.   Monica Feria, "The Desperate 77 hours: How it all started," *Mr. & Ms. Magazine*, February 28-March 6, 1986, pages 3-5.

4.   "Defense Minister Enrile Tells His Story," a two-part interview, *Sunday Inquirer Magazine*, March 9-16, 1986.

5.   "Military Rebellion," *The Manila Times*, February 23, 1986, pages 1, 10.

6.   Enrile interview, *ibid.*

7.   Marites Danguilan-Vitug, "How much help did US give? ", *Business Day*, March 6, 1986, pages 5, 12.

8.   Daniel T. Florida, "Ramos: The man who got a hot potato," *The Manila Times*, March 11, 1986, page 4.

9.   Enrile interview, *ibid.*

10.   Quoted in Isidro M. Roman, "Special Report: Enrile, Ramos sever ties," *Manila Bulletin*, March 17, 1986, 2nd part of series, pages 1, 5.

11.   "Enrile, Ramos lead revolt against FM," *Philippine Daily Inquirer*, February 23, 1986, page 2.

12.   *Bulletin, ibid.*

13.   *Daily Inquirer, ibid.*

14.   *Ibid.*

15.   Enrile interview, *ibid.*

16.   Joseph Albright, "4 days in February: The final chapter," serialized in *Midday*, Manila, March 10, 1986, page 1.

17.   Enrile interview, *ibid.*

18.   Roman, *ibid.*

19.   "Confessions of 3 coup conspirators," *Daily Express*, February 24, 1986, page 1.

20.   *Ibid.*

21.   *Ibid.*

22.   Manny Velasco, "Now it can be told: Aborted February coup no Marcos 'moro-moro' ", *Malaya*, April 17-18, 1986.

23.   "Involved in coup attempt?", *Bulletin Today*, February 23, 1986, pages 1, 10.

24.   "Enrile rejects amnesty, asks Marcos to resign," *Malaya*, February 24, 1986.

25.   *Agence France Presse*, in *Malaya, ibid*.

26.   Dionisio Pelayo, "FM: "I won't resign; Ramos: no surrender," *Daily Express*, February 24, 1986, page 1.

27.   Miguel Genovea and Ros Manlangit, *Daily Express, ibid*.

28.   "Situation under control — Ver," *Daily Express*, February 24, 1986.

29.   "Pope concerned about new turmoil," *Bulletin Today*, February 24, 1986, page 1.

30.   Enrile interview, *ibid*.

31   Ding Marcelo, "Aquino, Laurel hail rebellion," *Bulletin Today*, February 24, 1986, page 1.

32.   Enrile interview, *ibid*.

33.   Vicente B. Foz, "Solons sign proclamation," *Bulletin Today*, February 25, 1986, page 1.

34.   "US asks Marcos: Resign, " *Bulletin Today*, February 25, 1986, page 1.

35.   Roman, *ibid., page 5*.

36.   *The Manila Times*, February 25, 1986, reported that a civilian TV technician, Fred Arias, 55, died inside MBS-4 after a heart attack during the raid. Amado Lozada, a Marcos trooper, also died when his gun allegedly fired while he and fellow loyalists were regrouping near Panay Avenue, Quezon City. One loyalist soldier was hit in the head. Eight others were wounded, one of them a civilian.

37   "Rebels strafe palace," *Malaya*, February 25, 1986, page 3.

38.   Louie Perez, "5 choppers destroyed in PAF raid," *Bulletin Today*, February 25, 1986, page 1.

39.   Roman, *ibid., page 5*.

40.   Sheila S. Coronel, "Marcos' last stand," *The Manila Times*, February 25, 1986, page 1; *Malaya*, February 25, page 1.

41.   From Coronel and Sipin, *ibid*.

42.   Enrile interview, *ibid*.

43.   Isidro M. Roman, "FM leaves RP," *Bulletin Today*, February 26, 1986.

44.   "Marcos flees: Family, Ver off with him," *The Manila Times*, February 26, 1986, pages 1, 10.

FOURTEEN

1.   *Associated Press*, "FM stunned by US response," *Malaya*, February 27, 1986, page 8.

2.   "Snap poll: Marcos' political suicide," *Midday*, February 26, 1986.

3.   Vicente B. Foz, "Solons sign proclamation," *Bulletin Today*, February 25, 1986, page 1.

4.   Belinda Olivares-Cunanan, *Daily Inquirer*, February 28, 1986.

5.   *Agence France Presse*, "US asks Marcos: Resign," *Bulletin Today*, February 25, 1986, page 1.. See also *Daily Inquirer*, February 26, 1986, page 2, on the nature of the Aquino government.

6.   See Appendix "C", Proclamation No. 3.

7.   Quoted in this author's *Marcos the Revolutionary, op. cit*.

8.   *Ibid*.

9.   Edmund Burke, in a 1771 election speech, in *The Great Quotations*, George Seldes, compiler, Pocket Books, New York, 1967.

10.   Thomas Hobbes, in *Leviathan*, 1651, quoted in Seldes, *ibid.*, page 750.

11.   Neal H. Cruz, "As We See It," *Daily Express*, March 5, 1986, page 4.

12.   *Ibid.*

13.   Cecilia Munoz-Palma, "We're even worse than Amendment 6 ," Philippine *Panorama*, April 13, 1986, pages 4-5.

14.   *Ibid.*

15.   Gregory A. Fossedal, "Another Marcos in Manila," *Midday*, April 16, 1986, page 4.

16.   Louis D. Brandeis, quoted in Laurence J. Peter, *Peter's Quotations*, Bantam Books, 1979, page 415.

17.   Golda Meir, *My Life*, her autobiography, Futura Publications Ltd., London, 1975, pages 316-317.

18.   *Ibid.*, page 333.

19.   Nicholas Wapshott and George Brock, *Thatcher*, a biography of Margaret, Thatcher, Futura Macdonald & Co., London & Sydney, 1983, page 143.

20.   Amando Doronila, "Analysis," *The Manila Times*, February 24, 1986, page 1. See also Doronila, February 26, *Times*.

21.   Hilarion M. Henares Jr., "Snow White's seven dwarfs: The Jesuit Mafia," *Philippine Daily Inquirer*, March 22, 1986, page 6.

22.   *Ibid.*

23.   Renato Constantino, "A fragile unity," *Malaya*, June 2, 1986, page 4.

24.   *Ibid.*

25.   "SC upholds Pimentel on OICs," *Daily Express*, April 17, 1986, page 1.

26.   "Gov't enjoys people's support; nation in revolutionary mood," *Malaya*, April 14, 1986, page 1.

27.   "Aquino doing fine job," *Malaya*, April 23, 1986, page 1.

28.   "Eco recovery, human rights top priority," *Malaya*, April 26, 1986, page 1.

29   For a day-to-day outline of presidential activities during the first 100 days of the new Aquino government, see Recah Trinidad, "Highlights of a Hundred Days," *Sunday Inquirer Magazine*, June 8, 1986, pages 12-19.

30.   Tony Gatmaitan, "She reigns but has not begun to rule," *Sunday Inquirer Magazine*, June 8, 1986, pages 6-7.

31.   Teodoro F. Valencia, "Over a Cup of Coffee," *Daily Express*, February 26. 1986, page 4.

32.   H.R.R. Villanueva, "What US wants US gets," *Daily Express*, May 8, 1986, page 4.

33.   Nestor Mata, "The Foreign Scene," *Daily Express*, February 27, 1986, page 4.

34.   Napoleon Rama, "Dangers, opportunities of governing a nation," *Daily Inquirer*, March 29, 1986, page 14.

35.   Joel Paredes, "No to church meddling — Cory," *Malaya*, May 25, 1986, page

36.   Theodore C. Sorensen, *Kennedy*, Harper & Row, Publishers, New York, 1965, page 367.

37.   In *The Great Quotations*, page 762.

38.   Samuel & Dorothy Rosenman, *Presidential Style: Some Giants and a Pygmy in the White House*, Harper & Row, New York, 1976, page 551.

39.   *Ibid.*, pages xv-xvi.

40.   Sun Tzu, *The Art of War, op. cit.*, page 27.

41.   Richard E. Neustadt, *Presidential Power*, Mentor Books, New American Library, New York, 1964, page 147.

42.   *Ibid.*, pages 149-150.

43.   *Ibid.*, page 150.

44. Rama, *op. cit.,* page 14.

45. Quoted in Neustadt, page 40.

46. *Ibid.,* pages 49-50.

47. Both *quotations* in this author's "Whom are the boycotters hurting? ", *Daily Express,* February 21, 1986, page 5.

48. Cited in Raul S. Gonzalez, "The eight pitfalls of the presidency," *Daily Inquirer,* February 13, 1986, page 7.

49. "Who 'Won' the Philippines?", *The Washington Post* National Weekly Edition editorial, March 17, 1986.

50. *Ibid.*

Index

A

ABC "Today" TV Program 184

Abad Santos, Vicente, 4, 115 261

Abadilla, Rolando, 208

Adams, Sherman, 273

Adamson University, 150

Adaza Homobono, 158, 160, 187 202 223, 224, 243

Agence France Presse, 85, 154, 161, 227, 293, 294, 296, 297

Agrava Board/Commission, 109, 110, 111, 112, 113, 114, 132, 133, 134, 292

Agrava, Corazon Juliano, 106, 112, 113

"Agravatars", 107

Aguinaldo, Emilio, 7, 249, 250, 257

"Akang" (Typhoon), 182

Albano, Rodolfo, 186

Albay, 163

Albright, Joseph, 296

Alfafara, Alhambra, 106

Alibasbas, Huk Commander, 67

Alibutud, J.R., 292

Almendras, Alejandro, 192

Alonto, Domocao, 247

Amendment, 6, 156

America, 89, 90

American Broadcasting Corporation, 113

Anderson, Jack, 86

Angara, Edgardo, 251

Angeles City, rally, 197

Angina Pectoris, 78, 102

"Anting-anting", 79, 168

Antipolo, Rizal, 7

Aquino, Agapito "Butz", 47, 120, 209, 210

Aquino Assassination (Book) 97

Aquino, Aurora, 4, 97

Aquino-Cruz, "Ballsy," 83, 99, 120

Aquino, Benigno Sr., 4

Aquino, Benigno S. Jr., ii
  death is his supreme sacrifice, viii
  his legacy is peace, viii
  "greatest patriot of our times," x
  "brilliant, fearless fiscalizer," x
  "60% of success belongs to wife" — Ninoy, xi

And Cory, xi

  she went through great sacrifices for him, xi
  accepted Ninoy's death with rare composure, xii
  worthy custodian of Ninoy's commitment to freedom, xii
  Ninoy is God's gift to people, Cory to Ninoy, xii

B

D